MIND ASSOCIATION OCCASIONAL SERIES

LEVIATHAN AFTER 350 YEARS

MIND ASSOCIATION OCCASIONAL SERIES

This series consists of occasional volumes of original papers on predefined themes. The Mind Association nominates an editor or editors for each collection, and may cooperate with other bodies in promoting conferences or other scholarly activities in connection with the preparation of particular volumes.

Publications Officer: M. A. Stewart
Secretary: B. W. Hooker

Also published in the series:

Perspectives on Thomas Hobbes
Edited by G. A. J. Rogers and A. Ryan

Reality, Representation, and Projection
Edited by J. Haldane and C. Wright

Machines and Thought
The Legacy of Alan Turing
Edited by P. J. R. Millican and A. Clark

Connectionism, Concepts, and Folk Psychology
The Legacy of Alan Turing, Volume II
Edited by A. Clark and P. J. R. Millican

Appearance versus Reality
New Essays on the Philosophy of F. H. Bradley
Edited by Guy Stock

Knowing Our Own Minds
Edited by Crispin Wright, Barry C. Smith,
and Cynthia Macdonald

Transcendental Arguments
Problems and Prospects
Edited by Robert Stern

Reason and Nature
Essays in the Theory of Rationality
Edited by José Luis Bermúdez
and Alan Millar

Leviathan
After 350 Years

Edited by

TOM SORELL and LUC FOISNEAU

CLARENDON PRESS · OXFORD

OXFORD
UNIVERSITY PRESS

Great Clarendon Street, Oxford OX2 6DP

Oxford University Press is a department of the University of Oxford.
It furthers the University's objective of excellence in research, scholarship,
and education by publishing worldwide in

Oxford New York

Auckland Bangkok Buenos Aires Cape Town Chennai
Dar es Salaam Delhi Hong Kong Istanbul Karachi Kolkata
Kuala Lumpur Madrid Melbourne Mexico City Mumbai Nairobi
São Paulo Shanghai Taipei Tokyo Toronto

Oxford is a registered trade mark of Oxford University Press
in the UK and in certain other countries

Published in the United States
by Oxford University Press Inc., New York

British Library Cataloguing in Publication Data
Data available

Library of Congress Cataloging in Publication Data
Data available

ISBN 0-19-926461-9

3 5 7 9 10 8 6 4 2

Typeset by Newgen Imaging Systems (P) Ltd., Chennai, India
Printed in Great Britain
on acid-free paper by
Biddles Ltd, Kings Lynn, Norfolk

PREFACE

This collection brings together some specially commissioned work on Hobbes's *Leviathan*. Earlier versions of some of the papers were presented to a conference in May 2001 to mark the 350th anniversary of the publication of the book. Virtually all of the conference papers have been revised since being presented, and half of those appearing here have been freshly written since.

In addition to the support of the Mind Association, the editors would like to acknowledge with gratitude the British Academy and CNRS in Paris for sponsoring a special Anglo-French collaboration. For over three years, a group of British and French philosophers and political theorists have been meeting to discuss Hobbes and his influence on twentieth-century political philosophy. The anniversary of *Leviathan* fell within the period of this collaboration, and the conference to mark the anniversary brought many participants from previous meetings, with interests beyond Hobbes, into very fruitful contact with many of the Hobbes specialists who contribute to this volume. The Anglo-French group has gone on to exchange papers on the considerable impact of Hobbes's writings on Continental and English political thought in the 1920s and 1930s, and the renewed influence they have had in America and the wider English-speaking world since David Gauthier published *The Logic of Leviathan*.

The editors would like to thank the contributors, as well as Cécile Fabre, Iain Hampsher-Monk, Ian Harris, John Horton, Jean-Christophe Merle, Véronique Munoz-Dardé, Martine Pécharman, Emmanuel Picavet, John Rogers, Jean-Fabien Spitz, and Jo Wolff.

TS, London
LF, Paris

CONTENTS

NOTES ON CONTRIBUTORS

EDWIN CURLEY is Professor of Philosophy at the University of Michigan. He has produced an edition of *Leviathan* (Hackett, 1994) and many articles on Hobbes and other figures in early modern philosophy.

LUC FOISNEAU is a Senior Research Fellow at CNRS (Maison française, Oxford), and teaches at the Institut d'Etudes Politiques (Paris). He has recently published *Hobbes et la toute-puissance de Dieu* (Paris: PUF, 2000).

KINCH HOEKSTRA is Fellow and Tutor in Ancient and Modern Philosophy at Balliol College, and Lecturer in Philosophy at the University of Oxford.

FRANCK LESSAY is Professor of English Literature and Civilization at the Sorbonne (Nouvelle-Paris III). His main publications include: *Souveraineté et légitimité chez Hobbes* (Paris: PUF, 1988); *Le Débat Locke/Filmer* (Paris: PUF, 1998). He has co-edited *Les Fondements philosophiques de la tolérance* (with Y. C. Zarka and J. Rogers, 3 vols. Paris: PUF, 2002).

NOEL MALCOLM is a General Editor of the Clarendon Edition of the works of Hobbes; he has edited Hobbes's correspondence, and is currently preparing the English and Latin texts of *Leviathan*, for that edition. He is a Senior Research Fellow of All Souls College, Oxford, and a Fellow of the British Academy.

A. P. MARTINICH is Roy Allison Vaughan Centennial Professor of Philosophy and Professor of History and Government at the University of Texas at Austin. He is the author of *The Two Gods of Leviathan* (1992), *A Hobbes Dictionary* (1996), and *Hobbes: A Biography* (1999), which won the Robert W. Hamilton Book Award for 2000.

TED H. MILLER is Assistant Professor of Political Philosophy in the Department of Political Science at the University of Alabama. He is author of several articles published in *Inquiry* and *Political Theory* concerning Hobbes's method, mathematics, and humanism.

KARL SCHUHMANN died in March, 2003. He held the Chair of History of Modern Philosophy since the Renaissance in the University of Utrecht. His scholarly publications include: *Hobbes. Une chronique* (Paris: Vrin, 1998); Thomas Hobbes, *De corpore*, édition critique (Paris: Vrin, 1999); Thomas Hobbes, *Leviathan*, a critical edition (with G. A. J. Rogers, Bristol: Thoemmes, forthcoming).

QUENTIN SKINNER is the Regius Professor of Modern History at the University of Cambridge and a Fellow of Christ's College. His most recent writings on Hobbes are contained in his book *Visions of Politics*. This was published in 3 volumes by Cambridge University Press in 2002, and volume 3 is entitled *Hobbes and Civil Science*.

TOM SORELL is Professor of Philosophy at Essex University. He is the author of *Hobbes* (Routledge, 1986), editor of *The Cambidge Companion to Hobbes* (1996) and co-editor (with John Rogers) of *Hobbes and History* (Routledge, 2000).

RICHARD TUCK is Professor of Government at Harvard University. He is author of *Hobbes* (Oxford, 1989), has produced an edition of *Leviathan* (Cambridge, 1991), is a co-translator into English of *De cive* (Cambridge, 1998), and is contributing to the Clarendon *Hobbes*.

YVES CHARLES ZARKA is Director of Research at the CNRS (the French National Centre for Scientific Research), where he directs two research centres: the Centre for the History of Modern Philosophy, and the Thomas Hobbes Centre. He teaches modern and contemporary political philosophy at the University of Paris I–Panthéon-Sorbonne. In 2000, he published *L'autre voie de la subjectivité* (Beauchesne), in 2001, *Figures du pouvoir* (PUF), and in 2002 (in collaboration with Franck Lessay and John Rogers) *Les Fondements philosophiques de la tolérance* (3 vols., PUF).

Introduction

TOM SORELL

———◆———

These essays attest to the enduring importance of Hobbes's *Leviathan* in the history of political thought. The 350th anniversary of the publication of the book fell in 2001, and it has been continuously in print in many languages and in a whole host of editions since it first appeared. Several new editions in English have been published since 1980; at least two more are planned. And this is to say nothing of the vast secondary literature that the book has sustained. This collection brings together contributions from some of the most distinguished Hobbes scholars, and some promising newcomers. There are three sections. The first considers how *Leviathan* stands among Hobbes's political treatises, and whether it deserves its undoubted pre-eminence. This is not just a question about the English *Leviathan*, since an interestingly distinct Latin version of the work appeared in 1668. Most of the contributors agree that *Leviathan* makes various kinds of advance on the earlier *De Cive* (1642, 1647) and *The Elements of Law* (1640). The second section explores various connections in *Leviathan* between the human passions and politics, including the ways in which sovereignty and subjection are responses to problems posed by the passions. And the third section takes up selected questions about the treatment in *Leviathan* of theology and religion. There is a controversy over the correct interpretation of *Leviathan* on covenanting with God, a further essay on the significance for Protestants and Catholics of Hobbes's denial that Moses was the author of the Pentateuch, and a final contribution on the relation between *Leviathan* and Protestantism.

LEVIATHAN AMONG HOBBES'S POLITICAL WRITINGS

Does *Leviathan* mark the high point of Hobbes's development as a political philosopher? If the English *Leviathan* is meant, Karl Schuhmann's answer is a qualified 'No'. He points out that *Leviathan* has much in common with the earlier *De Cive*, and that it recycles material found in the even earlier *Elements of Law*. Schuhmann concedes that *Leviathan* breaks new ground in its theory of authorization (ch. 16), its materialistic theology (chs. 32–45), and its polemic against Bellarmine (chs. 42 and 44), but not to the extent of threatening the continuity between the third of the political treatises and those that preceded it. On the contrary, *Leviathan* probably owes more to the earlier works than it adds to them. Drawing on his unrivalled grasp of the chronology of the whole body of Hobbes's work,[1] and of the similarities between the Latin and English texts of Hobbes's writings, Schuhmann suggests that the English *Leviathan* was an amalgam of translations of pre-existing Latin works by Hobbes. Foremost among these was *De Cive* itself. Chapters 13–31 of *Leviathan* draw extensively on *De Cive*, Schuhmann shows. Most of the later chapters, with the exception of chapter 43, do not. But often important ideas from *De Cive* are present even where traces of its exact text are not.

Kinch Hoekstra, too, has doubts about the distinctiveness of *Leviathan*. He considers the Review and Conclusion of *Leviathan*, a text which is commonly read as a retraction of Hobbes's royalism. In the earlier political writings, and perhaps in the body of *Leviathan* itself, there are signs of a preference for kingship over other forms of sovereignty. But in the Review and Conclusion Hobbes seems to endorse effective sovereignty whatever its form, including the form of the Protectorate that governed the England of 1651. Hoekstra sides with other commentators, including Quentin Skinner, in holding that Hobbes was from the first a supporter of *de facto* sovereignty, so that the supposed novelty of the position at the end of *Leviathan* is illusory. However, Hobbes is no mere run-of-the-mill *de facto* theorist. Hoekstra argues that Hobbes had distinctive views about sovereignty by conquest. This puts Hoekstra at odds with Skinner.

Other contributors are more convinced of the distinctiveness of *Leviathan* than Schuhmann or Hoekstra. Ted Miller joins many others in the relatively recent literature on Hobbes who think that in the work of 1651 there are many rhetorical innovations.[2] Miller connects these innovations in part to the company Hobbes kept while *Leviathan* was being composed. Hobbes was tutor to the future English king, Charles II, and he was in touch by correspondence with the poet William Davenant, author of *Gondibert*. Hobbes wrote an answer to Davenant's preface to *Gondibert*, and Miller suggests that the two men influenced one another. In particular, Davenant was responsible for Hobbes's using poetic techniques in *Leviathan*. According to Miller, *Leviathan* is a medium for the same sort of eloquence as belongs to a court poet. But this kind of eloquence is to be

---

[1] See Schuhmann's *Hobbes. Une Chronique. Cheminement de sa pensée et de sa vie* (Paris: Vrin, 1998).

[2] Two of the more important contributions to this literature are David Johnston, *The Rhetoric of Leviathan* (Princeton, NJ: Princeton University Press, 1986) and Quentin Skinner, *Reason and Rhetoric in the Philosophy of Thomas Hobbes* (Cambridge: Cambridge University Press, 1996).

distinguished from the kind of eloquence Hobbes always opposed: that of an ambitious citizen trying to jockey for political position. Hobbes's own reflections in *Leviathan*'s Review and Conclusion about how eloquence and philosophy can be reconciled are an attempt to identify this distinctive and politically unthreatening kind of eloquence. And Hobbes's preoccupations there are of a piece with his and Davenant's reflections on how a poem like *Gondibert*, or a poet, should impart moral instruction to princes. *Leviathan*, too, has as its primary audience a ruler, or potential ruler, rather than the politically involved citizen or subject, still less 'the people'. Or so Miller claims. The earlier treatises, *De Cive* conspicuously, *were* directed to citizens. In being directed to a prince or ruler, *Leviathan* took over some of the characteristics of the poetic genre of court masque, according to Miller.

Luc Foisneau locates the distinctiveness of *Leviathan* in its theory of justice. In the third of his political treatises, Hobbes jettisons the Aristotelian theory of commutative and distributive justice and puts in its place an account in which the mechanism of the market comes into its own. In particular, the fairness of an exchange is no longer supposed to be a function of the values that things in the exchange have independently of a transaction, or a function of the worth of the parties to the exchange. Instead, the things have the values that the parties to the agreement agree they have, and fairness is determined by the willingness of self-interested parties to abide by the terms of their transactions. Not that absolutely anything goes if the parties to an exchange agree to it. Some things cannot intelligibly be given up by self-interested parties—their lives, for example; and an agreement or contract to give any of these things up must be null and void; but other things, including, controversially, the right to see to one's own protection, *can* be given up and transferred, and indeed ought to be given up, according to Hobbes, for the sake of peace. The fact that the people act out of fear both when they enter into the transfer of right and when they subsequently abide by it does nothing to make the exchange unfair or unjust or unreasonable. On the contrary, the willingness to limit one's freedom of practical judgement is a condition of the original contract—the one that makes all others, including all economic exchanges, possible. The original contract is the simultaneous transfer from the many to one or a few of the right of self-government in return for security. The market orientation of Hobbes's theory of justice in *Leviathan* is a departure from the tort orientation of the theory in *De Cive* and *The Elements of Law*, according to Foisneau. One effect of the market orientation is to recalibrate the scale for measuring the worth of human beings. Worth is economic or political worth, not aristocratic descent, for example. Understood against the background of a 'market' theory, Hobbes's much-discussed answer to the Foole can be seen in a new light. It also has a notably anti-Machiavellian aspect, as Foisneau points out.

PASSIONS AND POLITICS

The second sequence of essays opens with Richard Tuck's 'The Utopianism of *Leviathan*'. Tuck's central claim is that *Leviathan* in particular, and Hobbes's civil philosophy generally, called for nothing less than a transformation of *ancien régime* political structures, and nothing less than the transformation under government of the passionate nature of human beings. As Tuck understands *Leviathan*, and also, up to a point, the earlier political treatises, Hobbes was not trying to come up with an elaborate rationalization of a monarchy such as the one he knew under Charles I, or as might have been seen on the Continent during his lifetime. He was trying to think out the specification for a genuinely new sort of state. Nor, according to Tuck, was the commonwealth of *Leviathan* tailored to an unfortunate human nature that Hobbes thought could not be altered. On the contrary, the ideal commonwealth can only work if passionate human beings can be turned into something like passion*less* citizens. In what sense of 'utopian' is *Leviathan* utopian, on this reading? We can distinguish between capital 'u' and small 'u' claims of 'utopianism'. In the capital letter sense, *Leviathan* is utopian if it is open to a reading that makes it resemble More's *Utopia* in significant ways. Tuck claims that *Leviathan is* open to such a reading. But then there is the other and more familiar sense of 'utopian' with a small 'u'. To call a political theory 'utopian' is usually to criticize it. Utopian theories call for political arrangements not only at variance with actual ones, which they are able to present as better than actual ones. They call for political arrangements that only ideal people could fall in with, or that less than ideal people could possibly fall in with if the external circumstances were ideal. Utopian theories ask more of human beings than they are normally psychologically able to give, or more of the external world than it gives, and politicians who want, in practice, to realize the vision of the state given by these theories often have to implement methods of 'social engineering' to compensate for e.g. limited feelings of solidarity, an unwillingness to work for tiny wages, and other things. Is the theory of the ideal commonwealth given in *Leviathan* 'utopian' in this sense? Tuck does not say. But since on his reading a Hobbesian politics eliminates or at least radically transforms the passions, there is some reason for thinking that he may be committed to as much. How can a theory aim at changing people psychologically to the degree Tuck suggests *Leviathan* does, and not ask a very great deal either of them or of political institutions?

Quentin Skinner's essay on Hobbes's theory of laughter is in part an explanation of Hobbes's concern to control laughter. Laughter is one of a range of human expressions of contempt, and these incite contention and ultimately violent conflict, the worst of avoidable human calamities. It is therefore better for people not to laugh at one another. Laughter is also, according to Hobbes, the expression of an unattractive passion, namely a kind of exhilaration at one's supposed superiority. To laugh at others is to look down upon them from a sort of puffed up altitude. If the others have done something wrong or acted inappropriately because they are incapable of doing otherwise, or if they have some infirmity or deformity, it is simply discourteous or uncivil to laugh at them. It can even be counterproductive to do so, since, as Hobbes sometimes observes, laughter can be a sort of acknowledgement or unwitting expression of a sense of one's own inadequacy. Hobbes's theory of laughter agrees more than other Renaissance theories of laughter with Aristotle, Skinner points out in a very illuminating discussion, for it connects the object of laughter with the defective. Although Hobbes was a strong critic of Aristotle's metaphysics, ethics, and politics, he was always an admirer of Aristotle's rhetoric, and the continuity of Hobbes's theory of laughter with Aristotle's is a sign of that esteem.

Yves Charles Zarka comes at the connection between politics and passions from a different direction. He is concerned with the way in which in *Leviathan* Hobbes is often taken to reduce citizenship to mere subjection. Someone who submits to the sovereign in either a commonwealth by institution or a commonwealth by acquisition agrees to be guided by the sovereign's laws in all the actions that the laws apply to. Admittedly, Hobbes thinks that a sovereign is well advised not to legislate too much: a law is bad if it isn't *necessary* for orderly communal life. But the sovereign is within his rights to lay down laws about practically anything, which a subject is bound to obey. Has the subject, then, no role as a political agent in his own right at all? It may seem that way. But Zarka locates in the right of resistance for subjects a trace of the fuller idea of political agency. Subjects have a right to resist when not to do so seems to them to put their life in danger. For putting one's life in danger cannot be to one's advantage, and a voluntary action is undertaken for one's own good. The political order has got to square with, and not reduce or frustrate, the desire to survive and the aversion to hurt and death. These passions are universal and inescapable in human beings, and therefore have to be accommodated by human political arrangements. So subjects may refuse directly life-threatening or death-inviting commands. They may also refuse to obey the sovereign when to do so would deprive them of the means of life, or put them at risk of self-incrimination or the incrimination or condemnation of their nearest or dearest. Whether the right of resistance can be reconciled with the sovereign's right to punish is perhaps the most pressing question arising from the scope

Hobbes leaves for political agency, and Zarka thinks the question is hard for Hobbes to answer satisfactorily.

The effect of submission is to make the choice of means to one's own survival more dispassionate. The sovereign's laws declare the means of survival. They come into force to constrain action, and they are addressed in the same way to all subjects, as well as having a goal each person can endorse: namely, peace. It is in this way that a government can be understood to give more or less equal weight to the good of each subject; without government the means of survival would be left to private judgement, which is biased: an individual tends to give great weight to his own good, and much less to anyone else's, great weight to the nearer good and much less to the more distant. He pursues as much gratification as possible rather than just enough. This is how burgeoning self-regarding passion turns the right of nature into a vehicle for slaughter in the state of nature. Delegating the choice of means of survival to the public judgement —the sovereign's judgement—is thus the beginning of wisdom. But now sovereignty in turn can reside in a single man or woman who is no less subject to self-regarding passion than any other individual. What is more, it may seem as if there is nothing, or not much, to stop such an individual using the power of the sovereign for unrelenting self-enrichment and gratification. My own essay indicates how the regulation of personal passion is as urgent for sovereigns as for subjects, according to Hobbes's theory. Although a sovereign never agrees to identify with the union of his subjects rather than with his natural person; although he is not strictly answerable to his subjects or other sovereigns for what he does; although, in a word, he is perfectly free; it is in the interest of the natural person that he is not to make enemies, either of his subjects or of other sovereigns. This means giving his subjects scope for prosperity and even enrichment; and it means not launching into foreign war for the sake of personal glory. Treating the resources of the commonwealth as one's personal property is not only wrong but against one's long term self-interest. The sovereign has to rise above his purely personal appetites to see this. So at the level of the sovereign as much as at the level of the subject, politics counters rather than indulges the passions.

BIBLICAL AND POLITICAL AUTHORITY

The third sequence of essays takes up questions about God and about the authorship of parts of Scripture. In *Leviathan* and other writings, Hobbes famously tried to outlaw the possibility of a conflict between obedience to a civil sovereign and obedience to God. He tried to do this, moreover, partly on the basis of biblical interpretation. The Bible speaks of covenants between God and human beings mediated, in the first instance, by prophets like Moses. In Hobbes's theory, obedience to God is mediated by the sovereign, and the obedience is called for by the terms of a covenant that the subjects of a commonwealth enter into with God through their representative: their sovereign. Edwin Curley's contribution runs through difficulties in Hobbes's claims about covenanting with God, difficulties that he claims Hobbes never satisfactorily met. Curley's criticisms agree in part with those of two contemporaries of Hobbes: Clarendon and Filmer. Perhaps Curley's most damaging criticism is that a covenant to obey God, mediated or not, is pointless, given that for Hobbes God's omnipotence by itself creates a divine right to be obeyed by all humanity. Omnipotence is at the basis of God's authority over the Earth in the kingdom of God by Nature (*L*, ch. 31). Why doesn't omnipotence make redundant a right of God to be obeyed by members of a particular commonwealth based on a mediated human promise or covenant to obey? Hobbes's attempt to conjure an answer to this question out of Scripture seems to Curley to fail. But the failure is not entirely Hobbes's fault. The Christian tradition, with which Hobbes tries to make his political theory square, itself exhibits the tension that Hobbes's writing does, and the tension in Hobbes may originate in Christian thought. Curley thinks that Hobbes was aware of this tension, and that this awareness is reflected in his use of the book of Job to explain the kingdom of God by Nature. It is possible that Hobbes was trying to call the attention of his readers to this tension, and to make them sceptical about Christian thought in this connection.

A. P. Martinich takes issue with Curley. He does so against the background of a general theory of textual interpretation, which is supposed to explain why theist interpretations (like his) and nontheist interpretations (such as Curley's) of Hobbes's comments on e.g. revealed religion are unlikely to converge. Martinich's general argument is that the tensions detected by Curley in Hobbes's treatment of covenanting with God are typical of Hobbes's political philosophy as a whole; yet no one thinks that revealing these tensions is Hobbes's aim in the rest of the political philosophy; so why should one credit him with such an aim in the theory of what grounds obedience to God? A preferable explanation is that the tensions are unintended but real, and that they reflect a confusion in Hobbes or an intellectual difficulty in one of Hobbes's topics. If there are tensions in Hobbes's texts, it is hardly surprising that contemporary readers attributed conflicting theses to Hobbes, as in the case of Clarendon and Filmer. In fact, Martinich says, both Clarendon's and Filmer's interpretations of Hobbes are correct up to a point. But this is not because Hobbes was intentionally presenting an internally inconsistent Christian-sounding theory of obedience to God in order to subvert it. It is not even true, Martinich claims against Curley, that when Hobbes spoke of covenants having to be mediated by a sovereign, he was meaning to deny covenants with God full stop. Another interpretation is possible, which

Martinich outlines. This interpretation is supposed to cohere with more of Hobbes's text than Curley's, and is supposed to require less 'reading between the lines'.

Chapter 33 of *Leviathan* concerns the authorship and authority of books of Scripture. Hobbes thinks that the evidence for Moses being the author of the Pentateuch is slight, and he thinks that most of us cannot know even of the books of the Bible whose authorship is certain that they contain the word of God. If the books of the Bible have authority, it is, at bottom, because the sovereign determines as much. The lines of thought in chapter 33 are often taken to start a movement in modern philosophy that culminates in the dismissal of the Scriptures as fiction. Noel Malcolm's contribution presents a far more sophisticated understanding of what is going on, especially in relation to the question of Moses's authorship of the Pentateuch. Both Protestant and Catholic churchmen saw Hobbes's ascription of most of those texts to Ezra as subversive of faith. Protestants took this view, because they believed that the Scriptures deserved to be seen as the word of God, and that Hobbes's claim went against their content being divine. Catholics took this view because, though they thought the text of the Scriptures had become corrupted in transcription and translation up to the seventeenth century, they believed that an accurate interpretation could be supplied by their Church. Hobbes went against the Protestant orthodoxy more thoroughgoingly than the Catholic, for he had a theory that first of all restricted the possible divine content of Scripture to words attributed in Scripture to God, and he thought that words attributed to God by those in a position to know in the Bible could not be transmitted to others with their original authority. It was left to the Church to determine the weight to be placed on texts, but not the Church acting autonomously. It was the Church as authorized by the sovereign. This is not the doctrine of an atheist, for it is compatible not only with the belief that God exists but that God spoke (though unverifiably) to some of the writers of the books of the Bible. Hobbes, then, is probably wrongly lumped together with his far more heterodox successors, such as Voltaire.

Franck Lessay's essay shows that while Hobbes was a Protestant, he was a Protestant of a very unusual kind. There are aspects of his religious and theological thought that align him with the Church of England, and others that show he has views in common with Anabaptists and Socinians. But these convergences are partial, and doctrinally he stands on his own. Over the sacraments, the Trinity, and over the nature of heresy, his views are famously idiosyncratic. What if anything unifies the disparate and quirky elements of his Protestantism? Hobbes's politics to a large extent, Lessay suggests, particularly the cardinal doctrine that sovereignty cannot be divided. But there is also a certain view of history, particularly church history, in which mainstream Protestantism is not seen as all that much of an advance on

Catholicism, and in which the superstitious and power-grabbing tendencies of any church loom larger than the enlightenment of one sect or another. Finally, there is a theological background to Hobbes's Protestantism which, as Lessay admits, is never separable from the politics. Lessay rightly locates the elements of Hobbes's peculiar Protestantism in a wide range of his writings, but *Leviathan* plays its usual role as a place where, intellectually, Hobbes innovated in both his theology and his views about the location of churches in civil states.

PART ONE

Leviathan *among Hobbes's Political Writings*

Leviathan *and* De Cive

KARL SCHUHMANN

---

1. INTRODUCTION

Twentieth-century interest in Hobbes's political philosophy has been focused almost exclusively on *Leviathan*. *The Elements of Law* (1640) has only been reprinted from a nineteenth-century edition[1] and only one, purportedly 'critical', edition of *De Cive* (1642) exists,[2] whereas *Leviathan* (1651) has attracted the efforts of no less than a dozen editors,[3] and some of their editions have gone through countless printings and reprintings. The clear message of this activity is that *Leviathan* far surpasses Hobbes's earlier work in significance.

Now this is generally understood in one of two ways. First, *Leviathan* is sometimes considered to be the culmination of Hobbes's political thought, a high peak, so to speak, in comparison with which the earlier works are mere foothills. According to this account, we can perceive a development leading from those precursors to the full-fledged statement of his political theory in *Leviathan*. This view is illustrated by reference to the relative size of the works in question: *The Elements of Law* is only slightly shorter than *De Cive*, but *Leviathan* is three times the length of the latter. The second way of understanding *Leviathan's* pre-eminence is different. On this reading, *Leviathan* constitutes an authentic new beginning, in the sense that it departs from the framework of those earlier works and attempts something new. Perhaps it establishes 'modernity' (whatever this may be taken to mean), substitutes for a project of pure science a rhetorical enterprise, or puts political theory on a completely new and different basis.

---

[1] *The Elements of Law Natural and Politic by Thomas Hobbes. Edited with a Preface and Critical Notes by Ferdinand Tönnies. Second Edition. With a new Introduction by M. M. Goldsmith* (London, 1969 (reprint of Tönnies's 1889 edition)).

[2] Thomas Hobbes, *De Cive. The Latin Version . . . A Critical Edition by Howard Warrender* (Oxford, 1983).

[3] In the twentieth century *Leviathan* was edited—to mention them in the order of their first publication—by A. R. Waller (1904), W. G. Pogson Smith (1909), A. D. Lindsay (1914; reissued by Kenneth R. Minogue in 1973), Michael Oakeshott, s.d. [1946], C. B. Macpherson (1951), an anonymous editor (Scolar Press Facsimile, 1969), Richard Tuck (1991), Edwin Curley (1994), J. C. A. Gaskin (1996), Richard E. Flathman, and David Johnston (1997).

Against the view that *Leviathan* marks the culmination of Hobbes's political thought, it will probably suffice to remind the reader of what Quentin Skinner has said in a different context: 'this explanation fails to take account of the place in Hobbes's intellectual development of the Latin *Leviathan* of 1668',[4] a work that 'embodies extensive revisions of the English text'.[5] Hobbes wrote four, not three, treatises on politics, and before putting the third above the fourth, one should first be clear about Hobbes's last major work on political theory: is it after all the most mature expression of his thought, or is it a disappointing repetition of earlier positions which had long been superseded? Partisans of this first theory generally fail to address this preliminary question and prefer to ignore the Latin *Leviathan* altogether. But the second view is not without difficulties. The thesis of a *rupture* (as the French like to put it) in Hobbes's development is rendered suspect by two facts. First of all, one cannot deny that 'sich für *fast* jede einzelne inhaltliche Behauptung des *Leviathan* ein Vorbild in *De Cive* oder den *Elements* findet'.[6] Secondly, *De Cive* was the third and last part of Hobbes's grand project, the *Elementa Philosophiae*, and was never revised, let alone replaced, in this role; on the contrary, in 1668 Hobbes republished it *alongside* his Latin *Leviathan*.

In addition to material that is already to be found in *The Elements of Law* and *De Cive*, the English *Leviathan* contains passages that have been grafted onto this old core (and which put that core in a new light). So there may be good reason to assess the novelty of *Leviathan* by discerning those parts that have no equivalent in the earlier treatises. It is well known that there are roughly three elements which are unique to *Leviathan*: the development of the notion of the juridical person as connected with the idea of authorization (ch. XVI); a so-called materialistic theology (chs. XXXII–XLV), which centres on the notion of God's (past and future) kingdom on earth; and the polemics against Bellarmine (chs. XLII and XLIV), almost a book within a book.

In what follows, I shall not consider such innovations, however striking they may be; rather, I shall focus on what all three of Hobbes's political treatises have in common. More precisely, I propose to describe in some detail how *Leviathan* relates to the earlier *De Cive*. I shall first gather the few pieces of evidence we possess about the way the composition of *Leviathan* relates to *De Cive*. This will prepare the ground for a chapter-by-chapter comparison between the later and the earlier work.[7] This will allow me to draw certain conclusions.

---

[4] Quentin Skinner, *Reason and Rhetoric in the Philosophy of Hobbes* (Cambridge, 1996), 427.

[5] Ibid. 3 n. 15.

[6] Bernd Ludwig, *Die Wiederentdeckung des Epikureischen Naturrechts. Zu Thomas Hobbes' philosophischer Entwicklung von* De Cive *zum* Leviathan *im Pariser Exil 1640–1651* (Frankfurt am Main, 1998), 41.

[7] These sections will be based on findings to be presented, often in a fuller version, also in the Introduction to the forthcoming critical edition of *Leviathan* by G. A. J. Rogers and Karl Schuhmann (Bristol: Thoemmes Press).

I will use *De Cive* in the full version first published in January 1647. As to *Leviathan*, I rely, on the one hand, on the Egerton MS 1910, regarding which I concur with Richard Tuck's judgment that this MS (or 'the MS', as I will simply call it) embodies an earlier textual version than any printed edition.[8] Moreover, I shall use the first printed edition of the work, the so-called 'Head' edition.

2. THE GENESIS OF *LEVIATHAN*

There exists no contemporary evidence as to exactly when Hobbes began to write *Leviathan*, how he went about it, and what the different stages (if any) of this undertaking were. We have neither plans nor notes, drafts or letters about the evolution of this project. In the spring of 1646, Hobbes, then living in Paris, prepared the first public edition of *De Cive*; among other things he added to the earlier text a 'Preface to the Reader' and some twenty annotations. He planned to leave Paris that summer for Montauban, the home-town of his friend Thomas de Martel, in order to complete *De Corpore* there. However, nothing came of it. For in July 1646 the young Prince of Wales took up exile in Paris too, and Hobbes was asked to be his teacher of mathematics. Nevertheless, he seems to have worked up to the end of the year and possibly even during the first half of 1647 on *De Corpore*, until in September he fell gravely ill. His hopes to have the work ready by Pentecost 1648 did not materialize either. It was only when the Prince of Wales left Paris in June 1648 that he finally had the opportunity to rearrange his materials for *De Corpore*. Around June 1649 the manuscript which was to go to the printer was almost finished, and Hobbes even had a number of plates printed with the diagrams and figures he needed for his mathematical and optical demonstrations. The last piece of information we possess concerning Hobbes's work on *De Corpore* is a letter from Charles Cavendish written from Antwerp on 5 October 1649, according to which Cavendish had recently received a letter from Hobbes containing a mathematical problem which was to be included in *De Corpore*; moreover, Hobbes had told him that he hoped to have *De Corpore* 'printed the next spring'.[9] But instead of finishing the work and having it actually printed, Hobbes turned to a new major project: *Leviathan*.

One should not lose sight of this development of Hobbes's activities between early 1646, when he prepared the publication of *De Cive*, and

---

[8] Cf. Richard Tuck, 'A Note on the Text', in Thomas Hobbes, *Leviathan*. Revised Student Edition (Cambridge: Cambridge University Press, 1997), pp. liii f.

[9] Letter quoted in K. Schuhmann, *Hobbes. Une chronique. Cheminement de sa pensée et de sa vie* (Paris, 1998), 113.

autumn 1649. After his work on *De Cive*, Hobbes concentrated for several years on the preparation of *De Corpore*. It is not known why he should suddenly conceive the idea of writing another major work on political philosophy, this time in English, after having published two editions of *De Cive* in 1647, the latter of which had come out only in December of that year, i.e. less than two years earlier. If there was a need of a version of Hobbes's political philosophy for an educated non-academic English public that preferred reading English books to Latin ones, the most obvious strategy would have been to translate or have translated *De Cive* into English. As a matter of fact, Hobbes had welcomed such a translation as planned and possibly in part carried out by Edmund Waller already in 1645.

Yet Hobbes's motives for abandoning *De Corpore* and embarking on the new vast project of *Leviathan* are not the only problem surrounding the origin of this work. It is also unclear why later in life, when commenting on his writing *Leviathan*, he made no mention at all of his three years' work on *De Corpore* and presented matters as if already from mid-1646 onward he had been working exclusively on *Leviathan*. Hobbes's prose 'Vita' says that he 'spent the time' which the tutorship of the Prince of Wales from summer 1646 onward left him, 'in writing . . . *Leviathan*' (OL i, xv, and xlvii).[10] And the 'Vita carmine expressa' mentions the summer 1646 plan to complete *De Corpore*, only to go on to say that Hobbes saw himself

forced to delay it . . . I decide to prepare the divine laws [= *Leviathan*] as soon as possible; this I do step by step and in permanent unrest. For when attending to the mathematical studies of the Prince, I could not always attend to my own studies. Then I lie for six months ill . . . In the end I finished the book in my native language.   (OL i, p. xcii)

This way of presenting things, however, is contradicted by one of the last phrases of *Leviathan* itself: 'I return to my *interrupted* Speculation of Bodies Naturall'[11] (EW iii. 714), i.e. to the finishing of *De Corpore*. This seems to reduce *Leviathan* to a mere interlude.

Hobbes's work on *Leviathan* from winter 1649 onwards seems to have made incredibly rapid progress, not only in comparison with his work on *De Corpore* during the three preceding years, but also given the fact that in January 1650 he must have put aside his manuscript of *Leviathan* in order to write his 'Answer to Sir William Davenant's Preface to *Gondibert*'. This text contains the first allusion to *Leviathan* that I am aware of. Hobbes here

---

[10] References to Hobbes's works will, as usual, indicate the volume (in roman numerals) and page number (in arabic ones) of Molesworth's standard edition. The *Opera Latina* will be referred to as OL, the *English Works* as EW.

[11] In the texts quoted all original italics, capitals, etc. will be ignored. Words which are actually of relevance in the texts under consideration for reasons of emphasis or of comparison will be printed in italics.

states that he has used his friend's, the poet Davenant's, judgement 'in many things of mine, which coming to light will thereby appear the better' (EW iv. 465). Also in January 1650, in a letter to his long-standing friend Robert Payne, who at that time lived in Abingdon, Hobbes apparently discussed the role of bishops in the state, defending his view (expressed also in *Leviathan*) that their power is derived from that of the sovereign.[12] The next and first precise piece of evidence is contained in a letter written by Payne on 23 May 1650, according to which he had previously informed Hobbes about an impending translation of *De Cive*, but in reaction to this had been told by his friend that at present 'he hath another trifle on hand, which is Politique in English, (of which he hath finished thirty-seven chapters, intending about fifty in the whole,) which are translated into French by a learned Frenchman of good quality, as fast as he finishes them'.[13] Again a mystery pops up: nothing is known of such a synchronous French translation or of its translator. At all events, this information shows that Hobbes had already progressed far into the Third Part of the work, and that he had a fairly precise idea as to what the whole book would amount to: *Leviathan* as published contains 47 chapters. In summer 1650, we are told, Hobbes wrote to Payne that 'he shall set down and confirm, that the Civil sovereign (whether one or more) is chief pastor, and may settle what kind of Church government he shall think fit for the people's salvation'.[14] This Hobbes in fact did in chapter XXXIX. The next information we have is that *Leviathan* was registered by the Stationer's Company in London on 30 January 1651. So it must have been practically finished at that time. The Epistle Dedicatory of *Leviathan*, which was added only at a very late stage, is signed 25 April 1651. Edward Hyde, who in May of that year visited Hobbes in Paris, later reported that at that time *Leviathan* 'was . . . Printing in England' and that Hobbes 'thought it would be finished within little more then a Month'.[15] And this is indeed what happened. Already on 16 May 1651 Payne could note that he had been 'advertised from Oxford, that Mr. Hobbes' book is printed and come thither'.[16]

It looks as if it took Hobbes no more than one year to write *Leviathan*, namely the period between winter 1649–50 and winter 1650–1. Notwithstanding the fact that, given the length of the book, the period of composition is extremely short, it is nevertheless long enough to make possible a sort of refining of the ideas within it. Hobbes most probably did not write it in one single and uninterrupted flow, handing the manuscript to the printer exactly as it had come from his pen. The fact that at the end he had to append not only a conclusion, but also 'A Review' of the whole book, argues against this. On the other hand, it is most unlikely that Hobbes

---

[12] Cf. Schuhmann, *Hobbes. Une chronique*, 114–16. [13] Letter quoted ibid. 117.
[14] Ibid. 119. [15] Ibid. 122. [16] Ibid. 123.

would have found the time for major revisions or for a number of successive drafts that would represent markedly different stages of its development. The truth lies somewhere in between. A few shreds of evidence, both in the MS and in print, testify to a certain development of the text.

To begin with, there are a few announcements which are left unfulfilled in the work. There is, for example, the title of chapter XIII: 'Of the Naturall Condition of Mankind as concerning *their Felicity* and Misery'. This entire chapter deals with the miserable condition nature has placed us in, without ever mentioning a possible felicity of the human race at all. Elsewhere in the text, Hobbes announces that 'in what cases the Commands of Soveraigns are contrary to Equity, and the Law of Nature, is to be considered *hereafter in another place*' (EW iii. 235) As J. C. A. Gaskin understates it: 'it is not clear where this other place might be in *Leviathan*'.[17] Again, after mentioning the distinction between temporal and spiritual power (EW iii. 575), the MS continues: 'I entend to examine it in another place therefore passing it ouer for the present'. As was pointed out by Richard Tuck, this sentence does not reappear in print, because this intention had not materialized.[18]

Next, there occur two incorrect cross-references in ch. XX to 'the precedent Chapter' on 'the Rights and Consequences' of sovereignty and dominion (EW iii. 186, 190), which, as was noticed first by Edwin Curley,[19] are in fact to ch. XVIII. That these references are remnants of an earlier version is suggested also by the original title of ch. XVIII: in print it is only on 'the Rights of Soveraignes'; but according to the MS, it is 'the *consequences and* Rights of soueraignty'. These two references in XX to XVIII are mirrored by a connected one in ch. XXI, which this time refers to ch. XIX as 'the precedent chapter' (EW iii. 209). Taken together, these cross-references make it clear that Curley is right to suggest: 'Perhaps at one stage the order of chapters xix and xx was reversed'.[20] Indeed, in Hobbes's original conception chapter XIX on the three kinds of commonwealth and monarchical succession had come only *after* the actual ch. XX on paternal and despotical dominion. A trace of this conception can still be found in the work as published, where at the end of ch. XVII, after having distinguished between a commonwealth by institution and a commonwealth by acquisition, Hobbes says that he will first 'speak of a Common-wealth by Institution' (EW iii. 159). This he does in the next ch. XVIII. However, only

---

[17] Thomas Hobbes, *Leviathan*, ed. with an Introduction and Notes by J. C. A. Gaskin (Oxford and New York, 1998), 490.

[18] Richard Tuck, 'A Note on the Text', in Thomas Hobbes, *Leviathan*. Revised Student Edition, p. liii.

[19] Thomas Hobbes, *Leviathan with selected variants from the Latin edition of 1668*. Edited, with Introduction and Notes by Edwin Curley (Indianapolis and Cambridge, 1994), 128 n. 3 and 131, n. 11.   [20] Ibid. 145 n. 27.

the actual ch. XX (i.e. the original ch. XIX) goes on to treat the next topic, namely 'A Common-wealth by Acquisition' (EW iii. 185). So it is these two chapters that link up with ch. XVII, in so far as they specify the two main types of 'generation' of the commonwealth, whereas the actual ch. XIX (i.e. the original ch. XX) interrupts this sequence by discussing the three types of internal organization of the commonwealth, once it has been constituted one way or the other. To sum up, Hobbes's original sequence of chapters is most logical, but the sequence in the published version is not. It remains unclear why Hobbes regrouped these chapters, i.e. why he returned to a sequence observed already in *De Cive*, chs. VI–VIII.

3. THE PARALLELS BETWEEN *DE CIVE* AND *LEVIATHAN*

In considering the relation between *Leviathan* and *De Cive*, it must be underlined that what is meant by 'relation' here is not a comparability or coincidence of ideas or views expressed in the two works, but rather a more tangible connection, in the sense of a manifest similarity, between their wording. Now in order to count as an element of similarity, there should be a close textual correspondence between the comparable phrases of the two works, which makes it highly probable that a given text in *Leviathan* actually *derives* from a parallel one in *De Cive*. Given the fact that the earlier work was written in Latin, and the later one in English, this means that it should be probable that a given phrase in *Leviathan* was developed and, to some degree at least, directly translated out of its counterpart in *De Cive*. This can be authenticated most easily if there exists a close verbal parallelism between the texts in question. Another criterion is provided by the fact that there can be found in the English text certain devices of translation which were customary in the seventeenth century. The most conspicuous device of this kind can be seen in what seem to be double translations of a given single Latin term.[21] One seldom comes across English sentences which contain grammatical errors that are best explained as resulting from an imperfect translation of some Latin textual basis. In one or two cases such an uneven rendering is still present in the MS, but was smoothed out in print.

Before considering *De Cive* as a source, and indeed a major source, of *Leviathan*, it should be mentioned that scrutiny of this work for possible traces of translation makes it clear that there is more to be accounted for

---

[21] On the technique of translating by means of doublets cf. Frederick M. Rener, *Interpretatio. Language and Translation from Cicero to Tytler* (Amsterdam and Atlanta, GA, 1989), 108–12. It should be underlined that Rener's work is fundamental for understanding seventeenth-century techniques of translation in general.

than what a simple appeal to *De Cive* can explain. This will bring to mind
a problem first argued for by Zbigniew Lubienski.[22] This problem was afterwards formulated by François Tricaud in the following terms: was there a
Latin proto-*Leviathan*?[23] Since both Lubienski and Tricaud argue exclusively on content, it should immediately be pointed out that the general—
but, as far as I can tell, unsubstantiated—rejection of their (or, more
precisely, Tricaud's) thesis has no bearing on our problem. Though one
should agree with most scholars that Hobbes did not conceive the project,
or write drafts, of a Latin *Leviathan* first, this is not because it would be a
pseudo-problem or a thesis refutable in a mere aside or footnote, if such an
original draft in Latin were posited. On the contrary, there *is* a genuine
problem here, and there *is* something to be explained. But even the assumption of a Latin proto-*Leviathan* would hardly account for the cases of translation that belong to this category.

For a couple of these cases,[24] it seems sufficient to postulate the existence
of Hobbesian MSS originally written in preparation of the later *De Corpore*
and especially *De Homine*. This mainly concerns items in the first twelve
chapters of *Leviathan*. But it is noteworthy that a certain number of these
traces of translation are concentrated in the Bellarmine chapters XLII and
XLIV;[25] and there are occurrences of Latin biblical name forms especially
in ch. XXXIII.[26] In order to account for this, one might suggest a Hobbesian
plan to write a polemical work against Bellarmine's *Disputationes de controversiis christianae fidei adversus hujus temporis haereticos*. Such a work
had of course to be written in Latin. In view of the composite nature of the
Disputationes, it would have been possible for Hobbes to collect materials
for such a refutation in the spare time left from tutoring the Prince of Wales

---

[22] Cf. Z. Lubienski, *Die Grundlagen des ethisch-politischen Systems von Hobbes* (Munich, 1932), 253–74.

[23] Cf. Thomas Hobbes, *Léviathan. Traité de la matière, de la forme et du pouvoir de la république ecclésiastique et civile. Traduit de l'anglais, annoté et comparé avec le texte latin par François Tricaud* (Paris, 1983), pp. xix–xxii.

[24] Thus the MS has the wrong sentence 'when soeuer any affirmation is false, the two names of wch it is composed put together and made one, is senselesse, and signifyes nothing', where both 'put together and made one' and 'is senselesse, and signifyes nothing' look like double transla-
tions. The Latin sentence underlying this text should have been close to the corresponding one conserved in the Latin *Leviathan*: 'Quandocunque . . . affirmatio aliqua falsa est, ex duobus nominibus quibus constat si fiat nomen unum, illud *erit insignificans*' (OL iii. 30), which explains also the MS's incorrect singular 'is'. In the text as printed, this was corrected to 'whensoever any affirmation is false, the two names of which it is composed, put together and made one, *signifie nothing at all*' (EW iii. 27).

[25] Among possible doublets in these chapters are 'the Canonizing, or making the Scripture Law' (EW iii. 514), 'the Sentences, or Judgments' (EW iii. 515), 'Lieutenant, or Vicar generall' (EW iii. 553), 'the greatest, and main abuse' (EW iii. 605).

[26] To give but one example: the marginal note '*Ezra* and Nehemiah' is appended to a paragraph that opens with the words 'The Books of *Esdras* and Nehemiah' (EW iii. 371).

and from work on *De Corpore*, so that he could work on it 'step by step', as the *Vita* in verse already quoted puts it regarding the bringing about of *Leviathan*. This would also explain why at that time Hobbes must have undertaken a thoroughgoing study of the Bible with the aim of developing a political theology in line with his political philosophy. The very title of the book must have grown out of Hobbes's preoccupations with the Bible at the time. However, these activities were apparently superseded in late 1649 by the new project of an English work, into which the earlier material was, perhaps in some modified form, absorbed. In this way, one can understand all of the following: why Hobbes always dates the beginnings of *Leviathan* to 1646; why this work presents a well-worked-out theology; and why it contains such a long digression on Bellarmine's *Disputationes*, a digression as such lost on the international world of scholars, who in contrast could read Bellarmine's own Latin work.

The one major disadvantage of this hypothesis is that there is no contemporary evidence to support it. But why not assume that, just as the other parts of *Leviathan* do, its second half draws on earlier Latin manuscripts? This would also account for the amazing speed with which the work as a whole was composed.[27] This much is certain: among the factors enabling Hobbes to write it so quickly was undoubtedly *De Cive*. It is the dependence of *Leviathan* on this work that I will now discuss.

The existence of such a dependence is first suggested by the subtitle of *Leviathan* ('The Matter, Forme, & Power of a Common-wealth . . .'). For it corresponds to the programme announced in the 1646 Preface to *De Cive*: 'a *civitatis materia* incipiendum, deinde ad generationem et *formam* ejus . . . progrediendum esse existimavi' (OL ii. 145). Also at *De Cive*, XVII.21 Hobbes speaks of the 'materia civitatis' as opposed to its 'forma' which consists 'in legitima *potestate*' (OL ii. 397); so the 'and' connecting 'form' and 'power' in the subtitle of *Leviathan* is to be understood not as additive, but as explicative. And in both works the course of the argument is the same: it moves from 'matter' to 'form'. Philosophical book titles containing these scholastic technical notions were not uncommon at the time. Thomas White's *De Mundo Dialogi tres, quibus Materia . . ., Forma . . ., Causae . . . et tandem Definitio . . . aperiuntur* had been published in Paris in 1642

---

[27] About the writing down of *Leviathan* John Aubrey reports: 'He walked much and contemplated, and he had in the head of his staffe a pen and inke-horne, carried alwayes a note-book in his pocket, and as soon as a thought darted, he presently entred it into his booke, or otherwise he might perhaps have lost it. He had drawne the designe of the booke into chapters, etc. so he knew whereabout it would come in' (Andrew Clark (ed.), *'Brief Lives,' chiefly of Contemporaries, set down by John Aubrey, between the Years 1669 & 1696* 2 vols. (Oxford, 1898), i. 334 f.). As a matter of fact, this description applies not so much to *Leviathan* (cf. however its chs. VI and X with their strings of definitions), but rather to the three Sections of Hobbes's *Elementa Philosophiae*.

and met with an immediate and extensive refutation by Hobbes (compare White's title also with the title of *Leviathan*, ch. XVII: 'Of the *Causes, Generation, and Definition* of a Common-wealth').

It should also be noted that *Leviathan* refers to itself exclusively in terms such as 'this discourse' (EW iii. 325, 343, 414, 639, 647, 707) and 'this Treatise' (EW iii. 263, 348, 573). The Epistle Dedicatory is somewhat more explicit in speaking of a 'discourse of Common-wealth'. However, the most detailed self-characterization of *Leviathan,* which moreover explicitly alludes to its subtitle ('a Common-wealth Ecclesiasticall and Civill'), occurs in its 'Review and Conclusion', where Hobbes calls it 'my Discourse of Civill and Ecclesiasticall Government' (EW iii. 713). This terminology gives *Leviathan* the air of a more or less sober and scientific treatment of its subject-matter. The only element that does not harmonize with this is its main title which alludes to a biblical monster, and not to some entity or concept of a philosophical nature. And yet it is connected with its purely philosophical, i.e. scientific, subtitle by an explicative 'or'.

Why, then, did Hobbes call the work *Leviathan*? An answer could be looked for in the fact that the subtitle speaks of 'a Common-wealth *Ecclesiasticall* and Civill', mentioning the problem of the Church before that of the State. The momentum of the work does not so much consist in its philosophical views, which had been displayed already in *De Cive* and therefore were not all that new, but rather in its revolutionary doctrine of the Church. Contemporary polemics were apparently right to concentrate on the 'Atheists' Catechism'[28] supposedly contained in the second half of the book.

Leviathan actually follows *De Cive* only from ch. XIII onward. Yet there are a few literal parallels between this chapter and *De Cive*, ch. I. *Leviathan* generally expands the earlier text by adding comments and drawing consequences from it. A phrase from the 1646 Preface to *De Cive* is also taken over.[29] And in *De Cive*, XVII.12 (OL ii. 387 f.) the list of commodities in life runs parallel to the list of those things which would be lost if people reverted from the commonwealth to the state of nature (EW iii. 113).[30] This is noteworthy for the reason that in the same chapter of *De Cive*, namely at XVII. 27, there occurs also the comparison of states to gladiators, regarding which *Leviathan*, ch. XIII (EW iii. 115) could directly depend on *De Cive*.

[28] This term was used by Charles Wolseley against Hobbes in 1666. Cf. Samuel I. Mintz, *The Hunting of Leviathan* (Cambridge, 1962), 39 f.

[29] 'When taking *a journey,* he *armes* himselfe . . .; when *going to sleep,* he locks his dores; when even in his house he *locks his chests*; and this when he knowes *there bee Lawes*' (EW iii. 114)—'Videmus etiam in ipsis civitatibus, ubi *leges sunt* . . ., cives tamen singulares neque *in itinere* esse sine *telo* . . . neque *dormitum ire* nisi *obseratis . . . arcis*' (Praef.; OL ii. 146). *De Cive* repeats this in a 1646 annotation to ch. I.2, which in part is still closer to *Leviathan*: '*Qui dormitum eunt, fores claudunt; qui iter facit, cum telo est*' (OL ii. 161).

[30] This remark will reappear in *De Corpore*, I.7 (OL i. 6 f.)

Ch. XIV: The first half of this chapter makes selective use of some of the sections making up *De Cive*, ii.1–9, but expands them considerably. Into this first half Hobbes inserts (at EW iii. 119) materials corresponding to *De Cive*, III.3 with its comparison of injustice to logical absurdity. The second part of the chapter follows *De Cive*, II.11–22 more closely; towards the end of the text which corresponds to *De Cive*, II.11, Hobbes adds a paragraph mirroring the 1646 annotation to this section (EW iii. 125).

Ch. XV: The first paragraph of ch. XV corresponds in part to *De Cive*, III.1, but is followed by long passages of new material (EW iii. 131–5). When returning (in a rather irregular sequence) to *De Cive*, III.2–7, *Leviathan* again does not so much translate the earlier text as comment more or less freely on the topics that had been treated there. The rest of the chapter, by contrast, relates rather closely to *De Cive*, III.8–23 and 25–33; III.9 in particular is almost literally translated (EW iii. 138 f.). It is characteristic of a text using the vernacular that *De Cive*, III.14 'Vocatur . . . hujus legis . . . violatio . . . πλεονεξία;' (OL ii. 190) is rendered by 'The Greeks call the violation of this law πλεονεξία; that is, a desire of more than their share' (EW iii. 142), thus identifying πλεονεξία as a Greek term and adding an explanation of its meaning in English. The same translation device had been applied already by *The Elements of Law*, II–IV.2: 'The breach of this law is that which *the Greeks call* πλεονεξία which is commonly rendered *covetousness*, but seemeth to be more precisely expressed by the word *encroaching*' (EW iv. 104). Yet, as is made clear by the different translations *breach* vs. *violation*, *covetousness/encroaching* vs. *a desire of more than their share*, the later work does not depend directly on the earlier one, but presupposes a Latin intermediary of the type we find in *De Cive*. It is also interesting to note that at *De Cive*, III.33 the laws of nature had been called 'conclusiones' (OL ii. 198), a term whose meaning has repeatedly been misinterpreted in its logical sense of 'proposition drawn from premisses'. Precisely in order to avoid such a misunderstanding, *Leviathan* translates it by the explanatory doublet 'Conclusions, or Theoremes' (EW iii. 147). This latter term with its obvious geometrical ring makes it clear that 'conclusion' is to be taken here in its general scholastic meaning of 'a provable thesis or proposition'.

Ch. XVII: The title of this chapter ('*Of the Causes, Generation, and Definition of a Common-Wealth*'), which opens Part II of *Leviathan* 'Of Common-wealth', is close to that of *De Cive*, V ('*De Causis* et *Generatione Civitatis*'), the opening chapter of its Second Part on 'Imperium'. But *Leviathan* offers a different and more elaborate introduction. The earlier sections V.2 and V.3 are followed more closely. From V.4 only a few expressions are taken over, whereas V.5, with its refutation of Aristotle's doctrine of political animals, is translated almost literally. After a few reminders of V.6 (cf. EW iii. 157 f.), Hobbes goes on by drawing on *De Cive*, VII.7, instead of the following section V.7. The end of the chapter loosely corresponds to *De Cive*, V.8, 9, and 12. In general, *Leviathan* XVII contains several doublets testifying to its Latin background.[31]

Ch. XVIII: The subject-matter of this chapter—the rights of the sovereign—corresponds to that of *De Cive*, VI. Nevertheless, there is little direct contact between them. A few traces of some other passages in *De Cive* have been integrated into this chapter. Only the sixth, seventh, and tenth rights enumerated in *Leviathan* were to a degree taken over (in this sequence) from *De Cive*, VI.11, 15, 9, and 10. The last paragraph of the chapter was in part developed out of the 1646 annotation to *De Cive*, VI.13. So *Leviathan* once again changes the original order of the old materials it draws upon.

Ch. XIX: The materials used in this chapter come from three different chapters of *De Cive*, in addition, large pieces of new text have been inserted. The chapter opens with the distinction between three kinds of government, rejecting a further distinction between three kinds of misrule, just as in *De Cive*, VII.1–2; already the first marginal note of the chapter ('The different Formes of Common-wealths but three': EW iii. 171) is close to that of *De Cive*, VII.1 ('Civitatis tres esse tantum species': OL ii. 235). From *De Cive*, X.12 and 6 (notice the inverted sequence) are derived the third, fourth, and fifth advantages of monarchy. And the discussion of succession (EW iii. 182 f.) puts to use *De Cive*, IX.11 and 14–16.

Ch. XX: The discussion of dominion by generation derives from *De Cive*, IX.1–5, but that of despotical dominion is only loosely related to *De Cive*, VIII.2–4. The biblical confirmation of the right of monarchs repeats (with some omissions) the corresponding quotations in *De Cive*, XI.2–6. Note that even the erroneously inverted reference to Col. 3:22 and 20 at *De Cive*, XI.5 (OL ii. 280) is repeated verbatim (EW iii. 193).

Ch. XXI: Only *De Cive*, X.8 may be said to have been worked into the text in a more or less palpable manner.[32] For the rest this chapter is new.

Ch. XXV: The opening remark of *De Cive*, XIV.1—the difference between law and counsel derives from the difference between command and counsel—is clearly at the basis of this chapter.[33] But the specific discussions of chapter XXV are independent of it.

---

[31] 'Of so visible and conspicuous moment' (EW iii. 155)—'conspicui momenti' (V.3; OL ii. 211); 'to reforme and innovate' (EW iii. 156)—'novare' (V.5; OL ii. 212); 'their desires, and other affections' (EW iii. 157)—'affectus suos' (V.5; OL ii. 212); 'Power and Strength' (EW iii. 158)—'vires' (V.8; OL ii. 214).

[32] 'There is *written on the Turrets of the city* of Luc<c>a *in great characters* at this day, the word *Libertas*' (EW iii. 201)—'Etsi . . . portis *turribusque civitatis* cujuscunque *characteribus* quantumvis *amplis libertas inscribatur*' (X.8; OL ii. 271). *Leviathan*, one sees, makes the story more concrete by giving the name of the town.

[33] Cf. 'COMMAND *is*, where a man saith, Doe this, or Doe not this, without expecting other *reason* than the *Will* of him that sayes it' (EW iii. 241) with '*MANDATUM* . . . est praeceptum, in

Chs. XXVI and XXVII: The topics of these chapters ('Of Civill Lawes' and 'Of Crimes, Excuses, and Extenuations', respectively) come from a single chapter of *De Cive* (ch. XIV ('De Legibus et Peccatis')). But the definition of civil law in *Leviathan* (EW iii. 251) diverges considerably from the one given in *De Cive*, XIV.2. Yet there do exist also some genuine parallels between chapter XXVI and *De Cive*, XIV. Moreover, the description of the sovereign as being above the laws (EW iii. 252) is taken from *De Cive*, VI.14. The remark on commentaries derives from *De Cive*, XVII.18, where it functions in a different context.[34] Thus Hobbes once again rearranges his earlier materials.

Ch. XXIX: The title of this chapter ('things that . . . tend to the *Dissolution of a Common-wealth*') is close to that of *De Cive*, XII ('De Causis . . . Civitatem Dissolventibus'). But only the six seditious doctrines enumerated in ch. XXIX are more or less literally translated out of *De Cive*, XII.1–7, albeit again in different sequence.

Ch. XXX: The title of this chapter ('Of the Office of the Soveraign Representative') once again has a counterpart in *De Cive*, specifically in the title of its ch. XIII ('De Officio eorum qui Summum Imperium administrant'); here it is the Latin which resorts to circumlocution for an idea more easily expressible in English, since the matter referred to—sovereignty—is an issue of modern times only. In the chapter itself some phrases are directly translated out of *De Cive*, XIII. In addition, a remark from *De Cive*, XII.9 is reproduced here.[35]

Ch. XXXI: Not only does the title of this chapter ('Of the Kingdome of God by Nature') answer to that of *De Cive*, XV ('De Regno Dei per Naturam'), but Chapter XXXI, the whole of the last chapter of Part II of *Leviathan*, translates rather literally, often down to its summaries, *De Cive*, XV, which is the first chapter of the Third and last Part of *De Cive*. This explains also why in ch. XXXI the Psalms are quoted according to their Vulgate numbering: these references have simply been copied out of *De Cive*. It is an interesting fact that there occur almost no double translations

---

quo parendi *ratio* sumitur a *voluntate* praecipientis' (*De Cive*, XIV.1; OL ii. 313). *Leviathan* once again puts things more concretely and lively.

[34] 'When question is of the Meaning of written Lawes, *he is not the Interpreter of them, that writeth a Commentary upon them. For Commentaries . . . need other Commentaries; and so there will be no end of such Interpretation*' (EW iii. 266)—'*Neque interpres* Scripturae canonicus *unusquisque est, qui commentarios in eas scribit . . . commentarii . . . novis commentariis indigebunt sine fine*' (XVII.18; OL ii. 394). What *De Cive* had said about Holy Scripture is in *Leviathan* transferred to civil law. One also sees how the English expands the more concise Latin original.

[35] 'It is not enough, *for a man to labour for* the maintenance of his *life; but <he has> also to fight, . . . for* the securing of his *labour. They must . . . do as the Jewes did . . ., build with one hand*, and *hold the Sword in the other*' (EW iii. 333)—'*laborandum esse iis*, quibus patrimonium non est, *ut vivant, sed etiam pugnandum, ut laborent*. Unusquisque *Judaeorum*, qui . . . muros Hierusalem aedificabant, *una manu faciebat opus, altera tenebat gladium*' (OL ii. 292).

in this chapter; on the contrary, some doublets present in *De Cive* are reduced to one single English term. Thus 'End' (EW iii. 350) renders 'scopus et finis' (XV.13; OL ii. 339) and 'in Publique' (EW iii. 355) translates 'palam et publice' (XV.15; OL ii. 344). Of special interest is the expression 'Proclamation, or Promulgation by the voyce' (EW iii. 345), which translates 'verbo sive voce promulgant' (XV.3; OL ii. 333). For 'by the voyce' reduces 'verbo sive voce' to a single term, whereas 'Proclamation, or Promulgation' is a double translation of 'promulgant', which moreover applies the technique of *mutatio* from verb to substantive.

Ch. XXXII: Most chapters of Parts III and IV of *Leviathan* are only loosely related to *De Cive*. Thus ch. XXXII, the first chapter of Part III, contains little more than two biblical quotations (EW iii. 363 f.), which are given in the same sequence in which they occur *De Cive*, XVI.11.

Ch. XXXIII: This chapter contains only a single phrase (EW iii. 379) from *De Cive* (XVII.21).

Ch. XXXV: Only the discussion of God's reign over Adam and Abraham derives from *De Cive*, XVI.2–3.

Ch. XXXVI: Part of Hobbes's remarks on the 'word of God' (EW iii. 408) is taken from the treatment of this topic in *De Cive*, XVII.15.

Ch. XXXIX: This chapter on the notion of 'church' draws rather freely on *De Cive*, XVII.19 and 21. *Leviathan* and *De Cive* have three biblical quotations in common and equate the senses of the words *ecclesia* and *concio*, *ecclesiastes* and *concionator*.

Ch. XL: Here the same topic is treated as in *De Cive*, XVI—the history of God's kingdom over the Jewish people—but it is done in a strikingly different way. Nevertheless, ch. XL certainly developed from its predecessor. For both chapters have no fewer than seven biblical quotes in common, although chapter XL comments upon them in an entirely different way.

Ch. XLI: This chapter and *De Cive*, XVII both deal with the kingdom of Christ, and some clusters of biblical quotations are the same in both cases. But once more, the text of *De Cive*, XVII is only the occasion for developing chapter XLI, and not so much its direct source.

Ch. XLII: The longest chapter of *Leviathan* takes over a few clusters of biblical quotations present also in *De Cive*, XI.6 and XVII.25–6. Out of these last sections, as well as two others, some phrases have been translated almost literally.[36]

Ch. XLIII: This chapter is the great exception to the general rule that the second half of *Leviathan* is but incidentally connected to *De Cive*. The title of

---

[36] Thus 'a Deacon, whether the *charge* he undertook *were to serve tables*, or *distribute* mainte-nance to the Christians, when they *lived* in each City *on a common stock* . . . as in the first *times*' (EW iii. 530) translates 'Ministrorum *munus erat inservire mensis* . . . , portionesque (quo *tempore* . . . *de communi alebantur*) in singulos *distribuere*' (XVII.23; OL ii. 398). This gives a fair idea of how the translation may rearrange the stock of words of a Latin sentence.

the chapter ('*Of what is Necessary for* a Mans Reception *into the Kingdome of Heaven*') is particularly close to that of *De Cive*, XVIII ('*De Necessariis ad Introitum in Regnum Coelorum*'). As for the rest of the chapter, it follows rather closely *De Cive*, XVIII, though not without some major omissions and additions of its own. An objection which Hobbes raises here against his own doctrine, is based on the 1646 annotation to *De Cive*, XVIII.6.[37]

Ch. XLIV: According to the closing section of *De Cive* (XVIII.14), most religious controversies, including those concerning celibacy and the canonization of saints, are in fact about power; in religion also, philosophical problems such as transubstantiation are discussed, and some ecclesiastical rites are just remnants from gentilism. Out of these few remarks grew Part IV of *Leviathan* on the Kingdom of Darkness. But this Part has no direct precedent in *De Cive* for its detailed discussions.

So far we have identified those bits and pieces in *De Cive* that made their way into *Leviathan*. Before leaving this topic, it is worth noting that in some cases this must have been a process that took place in several stages. The MS has preserved only a few incidental traces of this trajectory, so that it certainly cannot be described in full. But a page bearing two interesting items of this kind is to be found towards the end of ch. XXXI, the last chapter of Part II. Here the printed version has the (correct) marginal note 'Job 38. v. 4.' (EW iii. 347); the MS, on the other hand, gives it (with a wrong verse number) in Latin as 'Job. 38. v. 3 et seqq.'. This reference was directly copied out of *De Cive*, XV.6, where the corresponding note reads 'Iob 38. v. 3. & sequentibus' (OL ii. 335). On the same page the printed version quotes Rom. 5:12 as 'Death entred into *the* world' (EW iii. 347). The MS reads '. . . into *this* world', following the quotation as found in *De Cive*, XV.6: 'Mortem intrasse in *hunc* mundum' (OL ii. 336).

There is one instance where we can even look over Hobbes's shoulder as he is developing his text. In ch. XXIX it is said that by private judgement of good and evil 'the Common-wealth is distracted and Weakened' (EW iii. 311). This consideration derives, as was said above, from *De Cive*, XII.1. Now the MS at this place originally continued with one or two sentences which are almost illegible today, because they were heavily struck through, most probably by Hobbes himself. It is clear that these sentences correspond to the end of *De Cive*, XII.1 which, supported by quotations from Gen. 2 and 3, excludes the legitimacy of such a judgement. Maybe Hobbes deleted this passage because he had used it in a comparable way already towards the end of ch. XX (EW iii. 194). Anyway, in print the sentences in question have disappeared.

---

[37] 'But a man may here aske' (EW iii. 597)—'Assertionem hanc . . . novitate sua theologis plerisque displicere posse video' (XVIII.6; OL ii. 421). The theologians of *De Cive* become just anybody in *Leviathan*.

Still more illuminating are some changes which Hobbes introduced in chs. XIV and XV, the chapters on the laws of nature. In the earliest stage of the preparation of his autograph he simply seems to have followed the pattern of *De Cive*. There, ch. II.2 lays down what in the corresponding marginal note is called 'the fundamental law of nature'. From this Hobbes derives in II.3 (to translate the marginal note of that section) 'the first special law of nature'; in III.1–25 he finally adds the special natural laws 2–20. In the text of the MS as copied by the scribe, this must already have undergone some revision. For the MS still retains the marginal note of *De Cive*, II.2 ('yᵉ Fundamentall Law of nature'; this note is present also in print: cf. EW iii. 117). But the marginal note corresponding to *De Cive*, II.3 now mentions 'the *second* law of nature' (this note is once again identical to the one to be found in print), and this law, which in *De Cive* is called only '*one* of the laws derived from that fundamental one' (OL ii. 170), is correspondingly qualified in the English text of both the MS and the print as 'this *second* Law' (EW iii. 118). Ch. XV then opens, again in the MS as well as in the printed version, with 'the Third' law, which is given this number also in the corresponding marginal note (EW iii. 130); it is equivalent to 'the second law of nature' of *De Cive*, III.1. But then the MS goes on, in harmony with the old *De Cive* numbering of these laws, to call the following laws the *third* to eighteenth law. In the MS these laws were afterwards renumbered by Hobbes himself from four to nineteen, and this is how they subsequently appeared in print (cf. EW iii. 138–44).

4. SOME CONCLUSIONS

A first result of our comparisons is that *De Cive* is a major, if not *the* major, direct source of *Leviathan*, and more specifically of its chapters XIII to XLIII; also, some of the seeds of the fourth and last Part of the work come from *De Cive*. To a degree this close relation between the two works is confirmed by Hobbes himself. For in *The Questions concerning Liberty, Necessity and Chance* published in 1656, he reports that before 1640 he had already pondered the question whether rebellion against the present government 'were conformable or contrary to reason and to the Word of God. And after some time I did put in order and publish my thoughts thereof, first in Latin [= *De Cive*], and then again *the same* in English [= *Leviathan*]' (EW v. 453).[38]

---

[38] It is *Leviathan* (and not, e.g., the anonymous English translation of *De Cive*, the *Rudiments Concerning Government* of 1651, as Luc Foisneau believes in his translation *Les Questions concernant la liberté, la nécessité et le hasard* (Paris, 1999), 417 n. 3) to which Hobbes here refers, as is confirmed by his assertion that in these works he had 'maintained that the office of the clergy, in respect of the supreme civil power, was not magisterial, but ministerial' (EW v. 454). In *De Cive* there is nothing to this effect as regards the present Church (this work only describes the

And Hobbes's friend Robert Payne stated after a short inspection of *Leviathan* that 'much of his De Cive is *translated* into it'.[39]

A question still to be answered is: which edition of *De Cive* did Hobbes use for this purpose? As *Leviathan* draws on the annotations first published in 1647, it cannot have been the 1642 edition. It also cannot have been Hobbes's personal copy of this edition containing the handwritten additions in question, for this copy served for printing the first 1647 edition and was no longer available to Hobbes after April 1646. It is also unlikely that *Leviathan* is based on the 1642 edition plus certain MSS that were used by Hobbes for preparing his personal copy for print. For near the end of ch. XIV (EW iii. 128) Hobbes uses materials corresponding to the 1642 version of *De Cive*, II.19, together with its expansion as printed in 1647 in the same sequence in which these pieces were printed in *De Cive* in 1647. The same applies, as was said, to his use in ch. XIV of the text of *De Cive*, II.11 and the annotation appended to it. But the second public edition of December 1647 cannot be the source either. For among the names rightly to be attributed to God, ch. XXXI of *Leviathan* enumerates 'Superlatives, as *Most High*, most Great' (EW iii. 352). This clearly derives from *De Cive*, XV.14: 'superlativa, ut . . . maximus . . . , *altissimus*' (OL ii. 342). At least, this is the (correct) version of the 1642 edition, as well as of the first public one from January 1647. In the December edition of that year the word 'altissimus' by accident dropped out.[40] Thus it is most likely that when writing *Leviathan*, Hobbes used the January 1647 edition as his basis. This is plausible also in view of the fact that he had received a number of free copies of this edition; among these was a bound one which probably was meant to become his (new) personal copy of the work.[41]

The only chapter of *De Cive* entirely left out of *De Cive* is ch. IV, which consists almost exclusively of biblical quotations that are to underpin the different laws of nature. Chapters VII on the three kinds of state, XIII on the duties of the sovereign, and XVI on God's kingdom over the Jews are used only in part. However, of the central philosophical parts of the work nothing has been put aside, retracted or superseded. But when cross-checking this balance, things look different. Only in a few cases (mainly in chs. XV, XXXI and XLIII) does *Leviathan* translate major sections of the earlier text almost word by word. More often than not, the later work uses

---

Jewish priesthood and that of the early Church in terms of *magisterium* and *ministerium*). In con-tradistinction to this, the terms 'magisterial' and 'ministerial' serve to determine the role of the (present) Church in *Leviathan*: 'Preachers . . . have not Magisteriall, but Ministeriall power' (EW iii. 497); pastors are 'but . . . Ministers' of the sovereign, (EW iii. 539); a king, being head of the Church, will 'commit the Ministeriall Offices to others under him' (EW iii. 541 f.).

[39] Letter to Gilbert Sheldon of 16 May 1651, quoted in Schuhmann, *Hobbes. Une chronique*, 123.   [40] Cf. Warrender's edition, p. 227 n. 3.

[41] Cf. Schuhmann, *Hobbes. Une chronique*, 101.

the wording and phrasing of *De Cive* only as a starting-point of its own exposition or weaves into it large parts of new text. The sequence of the sections is often inverted, and one and the same chapter of *Leviathan* can draw on different, even widely distant, chapters of *De Cive*. Again, sometimes only the ideas expressed in both works can be compared, not their wording, so that in this respect *Leviathan* is independent of *De Cive*. No less than twenty-one chapters of *Leviathan*—certainly half the text—have no full counterpart in *De Cive*.

Leviathan not only applies the techniques of translation which were prevalent at the time, but expands the text by relying on the whole arsenal of rhetorical devices and techniques disposable in the seventeenth century. Thus even if one assumes other Hobbesian manuscript sources for the work, *Leviathan* is in no way reducible to an English version of *De Cive*. But it is not a completely new and free-standing work either. For the influence of *De Cive* spreads over each of its four Parts. The first three chapters belonging to Part I of *De Cive* (on 'Libertas') went into *Leviathan*, Part I ('Of Man'). Chs. V–XIV of *De Cive*, which make up Part II of the work (on 'Imperium'), constitute—together with *De Cive*, XV, which is already the first chapter of the Third Part of the work (on 'Religio')—the core of *Leviathan*, Part II ('Of Commonwealth'). The remaining chs. XVI–XVIII of *De Cive*, Part III are at the base of certain chapters and remarks in *Leviathan*, Part III ('Of a Christian Commonwealth').

So it would therefore be wrong to maintain that *Leviathan* is radically different or a great departure from *De Cive*. The earlier work is the mould out of which the later one is formed. To be sure, *Leviathan* goes beyond *De Cive* in exploring religion. But it does so only by applying the general principles of Bible interpretation laid down already in *De Cive*—only this time to matters such as prophecy, the kingdom of Christ, eternal life, and hell. Now it is exactly the function of the *Elementa Philosophiae*, as their very title indicates, to lay the first principles of philosophizing in all fields of knowledge. The concrete and detailed working out of these fields on the basis of these principles lies by definition beyond their scope. Thus Hobbes apparently never felt the need to absorb at some later stage the mathematics of, say, his *Rosetum Geometricum* (1671) into the mathematical Part III of *De Corpore*, or the results of *The Questions concerning Liberty, Necessity and Chance* into the second half of *De Homine*. For the same reason he never deemed it necessary to incorporate the discussion of religion worked out in great detail in Parts III and IV of *Leviathan* into one of the later editions of *De Cive*. For these discussions are no longer 'elementary' in the sense of being basic and fundamental. Indeed, the *fundamental* tenet of Christian faith is in place already in *De Cive*. *Leviathan* repeats this thesis, but once the fundamental truth, that Jesus is the Christ, has been established, it moves towards the discussion of topics contained only implicitly in this basic statement (cf. EW iii. 597). The fact that there is one genuine philosophical innovation in *Leviathan*, namely the notion of authorization and the fictitious person in ch. XVI, confirms rather than contradicts this view. For the gist of this chapter was—I would suggest, precisely for this reason—later added to *De Homine* as the last chapter of that work.

The de facto *Turn in Hobbes's Political Philosophy*

KINCH HOEKSTRA

———◆———

I looke uppon them as wethercockes w^{c}h will turne about with the winde . . . with them thearfore whear thear is might thear is right, it is dominion if it succeed, but rebellion if it miscarry, a good argument for pyrates upon the sea, & for theeves upon the high way, fitter for hobbs & Athiests then good men and christians.

(William Fiennes, Viscount Saye and Sele to Philip Wharton, Baron Wharton)[1]

I am confident if mens Minds were but truly fixt upon the Center of this Discourse, they would not prove such Weather-cocks, to be turned about with the wind of every false Doctrine, and vain Opinion. We should then be free from those Disorders which threaten distraction to the Soul, and Destruction to the Common Wealth.

(Seth Ward, preface to Thomas Hobbes, *De Corpore Politico*)[2]

It is broadly agreed that one of Hobbes's greatest accomplishments is his theory of the foundations of political obligation and sovereign authority. There is deep disagreement, however, about the nature of that theory.

I owe thanks for support to Balliol College, the Arts and Humanities Research Board, and the UCLA Center for Seventeenth- and Eighteenth-Century Studies. The helpful librarians at the William Andrews Clark Memorial Library met constant demands with exemplary patience. Johann Sommerville, A. P. Martinich, George Wright, Luc Foisneau, Quentin Skinner, and John Watts generously provided thoughtful comments. I am especially grateful to S. A. Lloyd for constructive discussions, and to Tim Hoekstra for detailed suggestions.

[1] Letter of 29 Dec. 1657, subscribed 'ffor the Right Honorable the Lord Wharton' and signed 'W. Say & Seale' (Bodleian MS Carte vol. 80, fo. 749^r).

[2] Sig. A2^v–A3^r. *De Corpore Politico* (London, 1650) was a publication of the last 16 chapters of *The Elements of Law*; the first 13 chapters were published separately in the same year as *Humane Nature*. The letter 'To the Reader' before the former is unsigned. Hobbes reports that he was told that it was Ward who had been 'pleased once to honour' his doctrine of civil policy 'with praises printed before it' (p. 57 of *Six Lessons to the Professors of the Mathematiques . . .* , printed with *Elements of Philosophy, the First Section, Concerning Body* (London, 1656): *The English Works of Thomas Hobbes of Malmesbury*, ed. William Molesworth, 11 vols. (London, 1839–45), vii. 336). Anthony Wood reports that Ward was the true author of the epistle before *Humane*

Hobbes asserts that the king has sovereign authority even while a usurper holds sway, and some scholars characterize him as a royalist. As he maintains that the possession of power gives rise to authority and obligation, others have argued that he is a *de facto* theorist. He claims that obligation and authority depend on the agreement of the ruled, so many hold instead that Hobbes is a consent theorist. These three theories appear to be inconsistent.[3] In the first three sections below, I assess each interpretation of Hobbes according to one or more of its best representatives. I also adumbrate, especially in the final section, a distinct approach to explain how Hobbes could have advanced the preceding, seemingly contradictory, claims.

With great acuity and erudition, such scholars as John Wallace, Quentin Skinner, and Richard Tuck have significantly strengthened our grasp of the contemporary affiliations of Hobbes's principles of political authority and obligation, and of the nature of those principles.[4] At the heart of most attempts to clarify these issues has been the interpretation of the final section of the English *Leviathan*, 'A Review, and Conclusion'.[5] The Review has prompted sharply diverging claims about the continuity of Hobbes's political theory. On the one hand, the Review was written subsequent to all (or very nearly all) of the rest of *Leviathan*, in a rapidly changing political situation, and some scholars discern in it a sharp departure from the political theory to be found in the other works, or even in the body of *Leviathan* itself. On the other hand, the concluding section of *Leviathan* seems a promising place to look for the kernel of Hobbes's work, and others see therein a succinct expression of the theory found throughout Hobbes's major works. I first examine a view according to which the Review veers off in a different direction from Hobbes's earlier royalist theory; then the interpretation that it encapsulates and extends the *de facto* theory found in Hobbes's earlier work; and thereafter

---

Nature (Athenae Oxonienses. . . , ed. Philip Bliss, vol. iii (London, 1817), col. 1209). That epistle to the reader, bound after Hobbes's dedicatory epistle, is signed 'F. B.', presumably for Francis Bowman, for whom it was first printed. Given this signature and Hobbes's report, it is likely that Wood or his source mistook a claim about *De Corpore Politico* to be about its companion, *Humane Nature*.

[3] So, for example, if obedience is only owed to a power to which we consent, then power is not sufficient for authority, obedience is not owed to merely *de facto* power, and the legitimate sovereign need not be royal.

[4] Skinner has published newly revised versions of most of his essays on these topics in *Visions of Politics*, iii: *Hobbes and Civil Science* (Cambridge University Press, 2002) (cited hereafter as *Visions*). I provide some indication of where Skinner still endorses earlier claims (by simply giving the earlier source as an additional reference), or may implicitly distance himself from them (by offering a reference for comparison, or citing only an earlier source). It is because I think he is the contemporary scholar who has brought our understanding of these issues the furthest that I frequently take Skinner's work as my critical starting point.

[5] Hereafter referred to as the Review. Unless otherwise specified, all references to *Leviathan* are to the English version; citations are according to chapter, paragraph, and page number of the 1651 Head edition (1651 pagination is given in most modern editions). Citations of *The Elements of Law* and *De Cive* are to chapter and article number. I follow Ferdinand Tönnies's edition of the *Elements* (variously reprinted), but refer to continuous chapter numbers. (To convert to the

the idea that Hobbes first fully endorses a consent theory in *Leviathan* that is best articulated in the Review. In the seventeenth century, 'review' could mean 'recapitulation' or 'revision'—which is Hobbes's Review?

I. ROYALISM: THE REVIEW AS THE EXCEPTION

It has frequently been claimed that in the Review Hobbes changed his theory of political obligation to conform to the times. For example, Ferdinand Tönnies writes that Hobbes 'made his peace with the new order of things by publishing the *Review and Conclusion* of his *Leviathan*'.[6] In his introduction to *Leviathan*, Richard Tuck observes that 'even people who had formerly admired Hobbes and his philosophical writings were affronted by the book' when it appeared, for 'it seemed to justify submission to the new republic introduced after the king's execution'. Tuck maintains that Hobbes wrote *The Elements of Law* and *De Cive* 'in support of the king and against Parliament', which is why his new work was met by royalists with 'shock at this *volte face*'.[7] While Hobbes's *De Cive* was considered to be 'principally erected to the assertion of Monarchy',[8] and royalists assumed that its translation into English would further their cause,[9] his *Leviathan* was seen to support the opposite side. So Henry Hammond writes in 1651 that 'Mr. Hobbes is the author of the book De Cive, in which he entitles himself *a studiis* to the king; but . . . having now a mind to return hither, hath chosen to make his way by this book.'[10] Robert Payne reports shortly after the appearance of *Leviathan* that although 'much of his *de Cive* is translated into it', Hobbes 'seems to favour the present Government'.[11]

two-part scheme used by Tönnies, it suffices to know that chapters 1–19 equal I.1–19, and 20–29 equal II.1–10.) I follow Howard Warrender's edition of the Latin *De Cive* (Oxford: Clarendon Press, 1983), providing the page number when I cite the preface.

[6] 'The Editor's Preface' (1889), p. xi n. 1 of Tönnies's edn. of *The Elements of Law*.

[7] *Leviathan*, ed. Richard Tuck (Cambridge: Cambridge University Press, 1991), p. ix.

[8] J[ohn] H[all], *The Grounds & Reasons of Monarchy Considered* (n.p., 1650), 50. Cf. Descartes on *De Cive*: 'His whole aim is to write in favor of Monarchy' (letter of 1643(?) to an unidentified Jesuit, in *Œuvres de Descartes*, ed. Charles Adam and Paul Tannery, new edn., vol. iv (Paris: Vrin, 1996), 67: 'Tout son but est d'écrire en faueur de la Monarchie').

[9] The publisher of the 1651 translation was the arch-royalist Richard Royston. Noel Malcolm has shown that the translator was also a committed royalist ('Charles Cotton, Translator of Hobbes's *De Cive*', *Huntington Library Quarterly* 61 2 (1998), esp. p. 278). M. M. Goldsmith calls attention to the royalist iconography of the work in 'Picturing Hobbes's Politics: The Illustrations to *Philosophicall Rudiments of Government and Society* (1651)', *Journal of the Warburg and Courtauld Institutes* 44 (1981), 232–7.

[10] [Henry Hammond] to 'A. Cl'. [Matthew Wren], 21 Oct. 1651, in 'Illustrations of the State of the Church During the Great Rebellion', *The Theologian and Ecclesiastic* 9 (1850), 295. Cf. Edward Hyde, earl of Clarendon, *A Brief View and Survey of the Dangerous and pernicious Errors to Church and State, in Mr. Hobbes's Book, entitled Leviathan* (Oxford, 1676), 7–8.

[11] R[obert] P[ayne] to Gilbert Sheldon, 6 May 1651, in 'Illustrations', *The Theologian and Ecclesiastic* 6 (1848), p. 223.

Walter Pope simply maintains that Hobbes published his *Leviathan* 'to curry favour with the Government',[12] and Gilbert Burnet sees Hobbes shifting during the composition of *Leviathan* itself: 'For he writ his book at first in favour of absolute monarchy, but turned it afterwards to gratify the republican party.'[13]

Tuck leaves no doubt that he agrees with the royalist judgement of such a turn. He writes that although most of *Leviathan* was written while the royalist party was still capable of mustering a strong army, it 'was obviously completed in the political climate following Dunbar', Cromwell's watershed victory in September 1650. 'It was at this time, in particular, that Hobbes penned the Review and Conclusion with its explicit call for submission to the new regime.'[14] In short, while 'much of *Leviathan* was written while Hobbes was still in some sense a royalist . . . the last chapters and the Review and Conclusion illustrate that Hobbes had effectively abandoned . . . royalism by April 1651.'[15]

While Tuck does not explore the details or resolve the interpretative difficulties attending the thesis of a volte-face, Deborah Baumgold has attempted to do so. Like Tuck, she argues that in the body of *Leviathan*, 'the main lines of his thinking were laid down well before the defeat of the Stuarts', and concludes that if Charles I had won the war Hobbes would never have had the occasion to write the Review. The continuity between Hobbes's early political theory and his post-Restoration writings, she says, is broken by the 'Engagement remarks' in the Review, an 'about-face' from his earlier and later reliance on what she calls the 'traditionalist' foundation of authority.[16] In his other works and elsewhere in *Leviathan*, Baumgold

---

[12] Pope, *The Life of the Right Reverend Father in God Seth, Lord Bishop of Salisbury . . .* (London, 1697), 117–18.

[13] *Bishop Burnet's History of His Own Time*, i (London, 1724), 188.

[14] Tuck (ed.), *Leviathan*, p. xi; for similar claims, see Tuck, *Philosophy and Government, 1572–1651* (Cambridge: Cambridge University Press, 1993), 335; and Arihiro Fukuda, *Sovereignty and the Sword: Harrington, Hobbes, and Mixed Government in the English Civil Wars* (Oxford: Oxford University Press, 1997), 61. A 'call for submission to the new regime' is not 'explicit' anywhere in the Review: on such an interpretation, see pp. 43–4, below.

[15] Tuck (ed.), *Leviathan*, p. xxv. Tuck says that the end of *Leviathan* shows that 'Hobbes had effectively abandoned both kinds of royalism'—that of the *Elements* and *De Cive*, and that of the body of *Leviathan* akin to royalist works calling for an alliance between the king and the Independents. Both here and in *Philosophy and Government*, Tuck gives two arguments for his thesis that in the last chapters and the Review Hobbes changed course to support the new government, that he upheld their ecclesiastical policy by shifting to support Independency (a suggestion already made by Clarendon, *A Brief View*, 308–9), and that he upheld political obligation to it by shifting to a *de facto* justification. I restrict myself to the latter claim; the former is called into question by Johann Sommerville, in 'Hobbes and Independency', *Rivista di storia della filosofia* (forthcoming in 2003).

[16] Deborah Baumgold, 'When Hobbes needed History', in G. A. J. Rogers and Tom Sorell (eds.), *Hobbes and History* (London and New York: Routledge, 2000), p. 37. On the 'Engagement' theorists, see section II, below. In February 1649, members of the Council of State

maintains, Hobbes provides a 'historical contractarian argument' which has 'been obscured . . . by the very different account of sovereign right' in the Review, where he provides an 'a-historical defence of *de facto* authority'.[17] In 'the about-face signalled by his rejection of the principle of indefeasible hereditary right', Hobbes puts forth 'the Engagement model', which is not to be found in the works of the 1640s, nor after 1660, nor even in the body of *Leviathan*.[18] In all of these places, Baumgold claims, Hobbes argues that sovereign legitimacy in England is based on traditional hereditary monarchy, rather than the isolated 'principle of Hobbes's Engagement remarks in the conclusion of *Leviathan*: "the mutuall Relation between Protection and Obedience" '.[19]

Clarendon, a leading royalist who had been a friend of Hobbes's, was surprised and outraged by what he saw as the new arguments of *Leviathan*.[20] In his book-length criticism, he objected that Hobbes undermined the sovereign, 'giving his Subjects leave to withdraw their obedience from him when he hath most need of their assistance, for *the obligation of Subjects to the Soveraign is understood (he saies) to last as long, and no longer, then the power lasts to protect them*'.[21] This appears to fit perfectly with the analysis of Tuck and Baumgold. However, Clarendon is here quoting from chapter 21, in the first half of *Leviathan*. Clarendon's charge that Hobbes wrote *Leviathan* in support of the new government is about the work as a whole,[22] which he says countenanced and justified 'woful

---

were required to take an Engagement to the present parliament and the 'future . . . Republique, without a King or House of Peers' (see the *Resolves of Parliament*, printed 20 Feb.); there were suggestions in subsequent months to extend this requirement to officeholders and others. On 11 Oct., parliament passed resolutions requiring most of the literate population to vow allegiance to the Commonwealth by 1 Jan. In the Act of 2 Jan. 1650, 'For Subscribing the Engagement', they required 'That all men whatsoever within the Commonwealth of England, of the age of eighteen years and upwards, shall . . . take and subscribe this Engagement following; viz. I Do declare and promise, That I will be true and faithful to the Commonwealth of England, as it is now Established, without a King or House of Lords' (C. H. Firth and R. S. Rait (eds.), *Acts and Ordinances of the Interregnum, 1642–1660*, ii (London: HMSO, 1911), 325; cf. Blair Worden, *The Rump Parliament, 1648–1653* (Cambridge: Cambridge University Press, 1974), 226–32. Hobbes quotes the Engagement in *Behemoth, or The Long Parliament*, ed. Ferdinand Tönnies (Chicago: The University of Chicago Press, 1990), p. 164.

[17] Baumgold, 'When Hobbes needed History', 32; cf. pp. 35, 37.   [18] Ibid. 36.

[19] Ibid. 39 n. 12, quoting the last paragraph of the Review.

[20] See Clarendon's letter to Barwick of 25 July 1659, where he says that 'Mr. *Hobbs* is my old Friend', but draws a sharp distinction between 'his former Books' and *Leviathan* (*The Life of the Reverend Dr. John Barwick, D.D.* (London, 1724), p. 430; cf. *A Brief View*, 6–8, 197–8; cf. also Clarendon to John Earles, 1 Jan. and 12 Feb. 1647, in *State Papers Collected by Edward, Earl of Clarendon*, ii (Oxford, 1773), 322–3, 341).   [21] Clarendon, *A Brief View*, 90.

[22] Ibid. 317: 'The Review and Conclusion, is only an abridgment and contracting the most contagious poison that runs through the Book, into a less vessel or volume, least they, who will not take the pains to read the Book, or reading it may by inadvertency and incogitancy not be

desertion, and defection':

> *Cromwel* found the submission to those principles produc'd a submission to him, and the imaginary relation between Protection and Allegiance so positively proclam'd by him, prevail'd for many years to extinguish all visible fidelity to the King, whilst he perswaded many to take the Engagement as a thing lawful, and to become Subjects to the Usurper, as to their legitimate Soveraign.[23]

The passage from chapter 21 quoted by Clarendon continues uncompromisingly:

> For the right men have by Nature to protect themselves, when none else can protect them, can by no Covenant be relinquished . . . . The end of Obedience is Protection; which, wheresoever a man seeth it, either in his own, or in anothers sword, Nature applyeth his obedience to it, and his endeavour to maintaine it.[24]

In supposing that this 'appears to have been written in the same period' as the Review, Baumgold is using her theory to establish the likely order of composition, rather than vice-versa, and so risks gerrymandering.[25] But it is hard to see how else she or Tuck or anyone else can read the Review as a call for submission to the new regime on new principles. Moreover, there are several other passages from the body of the work that would have to be set aside as later additions if *Leviathan* is to be carved up to make the principle of the mutual relation between protection and obedience an opportunistic afterthought.

In chapter 27, for example, Hobbes provides an argument that would require many of his readers to obey the new Commonwealth:

> Where a man is captive, or in the power of the enemy . . . the Obligation of the Law ceaseth; because he must obey the enemy, or dye; and consequently such obedience is no Crime: for no man is obliged (when the protection of the Law faileth,) not to protect himself, by the best means he can.[26]

Earlier, Hobbes makes the related point that when one submits, it is for protection; and when 'there is no protection to be had from the Law . . . every one may protect himself by his own power'.[27] In chapter 26, Hobbes asserts that 'it is a Dictate of Naturall Reason, and consequently an evident Law of Nature, that no man ought to weaken that power, the protection whereof he hath himself demanded, or wittingly received against others'.[28] The protecting power of the sovereign is weakened by disobedience, so the law of nature requires obedience whenever one accepts protection.

hurt enough by it, may here in less room, and more nakedly, swallow his choicest Doctrine at one morsel'.

[23] Ibid. p. 92.   [24] *Leviathan* 21.21, p. 114.

[25] Baumgold, 'When Hobbes needed History', 41 n. 36: she is referring here to the immediately following passage, but her thesis apparently commits her to the late composition of the whole paragraph.   [26] *Leviathan* 27.24, p. 156.

[27] Ibid. 19.18, p. 100; 27.3, p. 152.   [28] Ibid. 26.16, p. 142.

Tuck and Skinner both find it significant that it is only in the Review that Hobbes first explicitly invokes the formula, so popular with *de facto* theorists, of the mutual relation between protection and obedience.[29] Hobbes undoubtedly appropriates the exact formulation to make a polemical point, but the principle, as can be seen here, is to be found in the body of the work. Hobbes writes in the final paragraph of the Review that he wrote *Leviathan* 'without other designe, than to set before mens eyes the mutuall Relation between Protection and Obedience'.[30] That may be a simplification, but such a design can be discerned throughout.[31]

What is supposed to be royalist or traditionalist about the bulk of *Leviathan*? Baumgold argues that, outside the Review, Hobbes upholds 'the principle of indefeasible sovereign right', and bases the sovereignty of present government 'on a constitutional compact and hereditary descent'.[32] She makes this claim immediately after quoting from the body of *Leviathan*: 'For he that wants protection, may seek it any where; and when he hath it, is obliged . . . to protect his Protection as long as he is able.'[33] This, however, is the very principle of an 'ahistorical' relation between protection and obedience that Baumgold regards as Hobbes's rejection of traditionalism. Moreover, Hobbes makes clear early in *Leviathan* that sovereignty *is* defeasible by conquest.[34] Chapter 20 is about the case of commonwealth by

---

[29] Tuck, *Philosophy and Government*, 335; Skinner, *Visions*, 305–7 ('Conquest and Consent: Thomas Hobbes and the Engagement Controversy', in G. E. Aylmer (ed.), *The Interregnum: The Quest for Settlement, 1646–1660*, 2nd edn. (London and Basingstoke: Macmillan, 1974), 96–7).

[30] Review, par. 17, pp. 395–6.

[31] The scope is evident even when Hobbes does not employ these words. Protection is 'the very essence of Government' (*Leviathan* 21.17, p. 112), but Hobbes often refers instead to the closely related concepts of 'safety', 'security', or 'peace and security'.

[32] Baumgold, 'When Hobbes needed History', 35.

[33] *Leviathan* 29.23, p. 174. In arguing that *Leviathan* 'manifestly asserts the cause of Usurpers', and that 'No person that hath suckt in Hobs his Principles, can be a loyal Subject', John Dowel mischievously cites this as: 'For he . . . is obliged . . . to protect his Protector as long as he is able' (*The Leviathan Heretical: or The Charge Exhibited in Parliament against M. Hobbs, justified . . .* (Oxford, 1683), 137, 142). Clarendon is even more cavalier: 'he is obliged . . . to protect, and assist the Usurper as long as he is able' (*A Brief View*, 167; for a pointed misquotation equivalent to Dowel's, see p. 193).

[34] In many passages, including those where he describes a lapse into the state of nature, Hobbes indicates how sovereignty can be defeated or nullified. In others, he discusses how sovereignty can pass from one holder to another. Nonetheless, he does sometimes suggest that we can never understand a sovereign to forfeit his right, and such passages (though they often specify that a sovereign can never be understood to forfeit his right *unless he does so explicitly*) may give the impression of indefeasibility. In such passages, Hobbes apparently attempts to undercut claims (rife in the 1640s) that rebellion is justified because the sovereign has forfeited his right to rule by particular actions—and he occasionally does so in a way that is ostensibly in tension with his view that peace requires us to understand that sovereignty can be extinguished or pass from one party to another. Such a tension can be eased, if not eliminated, by distinguishing between a sovereign forfeiting his right and a sovereign's right being forfeit: if he is killed along with all known heirs, say, he does not cede sovereignty, but his sovereignty is nonetheless at an end.

acquisition, 'where the Soveraign Power is acquired by Force', that is, when people 'for fear of death, or bonds, do authorise all the actions of that Man, or Assembly, that hath their lives and liberty in his Power'.[35] Baumgold claims that 'the authorization covenant is transparently a defence of the Stuart monarchy', but whether Hobbes was writing this after the execution of Charles I in 1649, or after Dunbar in the spring of 1651, he would not have thought that his English audience would see in *this* model of fearful authorization of the presently powerful 'Man, or Assembly' an indefeasible obligation of fealty to the Stuart monarchs.[36]

Central to Baumgold's argument that Hobbes supported a 'traditionalist' justification of indefeasible hereditary sovereignty is Hobbes's contention that 'England was an absolute monarchy by virtue of subjects' consent to the Conquest; and the Stuarts had inherited their title to the throne from William.'[37] The case of William the Conqueror, however, shows that sovereignty *is* defeasible, for the sovereign authority of Harold II was extinguished by William's conquest.[38] If the sovereign authority of the Stuarts was founded on assent to that conquest, the sovereignty of parliament would follow from assent to the conquest of the parliamentary army.[39]

---

[35] *Leviathan* 20.1, pp. 101–2.

[36] Baumgold, 'When Hobbes needed History', p. 31. Nor would the authorization model Hobbes employs in his discussion of sovereignty by institution have supported the Stuarts; for their rule, as Hobbes describes it, was instead an instance of sovereignty by acquisition. Baumgold suggests here that there is an unintended 'hole in the argument', for although it 'is framed with a monarchy in view, authorization is a general formulation applying to all forms of government'. Hobbes is well aware of this consequence of the generality of his formulation, repeatedly going out of his way to stipulate that to authorize 'is to conferre all their power and strength upon one Man, or upon one Assembly of men' (*Leviathan* 17.13, p. 87), and discussing the details of the authorization of an assembly of 'many men' (*Leviathan* 16.15–17, pp. 82–3).

[37] Baumgold, 'When Hobbes needed History', p. 32.

[38] Skinner argues against the originality of Hobbes's view that English sovereignty stems from conquest, on the basis that Hobbes does not articulate it until after the restoration, by which time he had been anticipated by others, including the *de facto* theorists (*Visions*, 254–6: 'History and Ideology in the English Revolution', *The Historical Journal* 8/2 (1965), 168–70). In the *Elements* and *De Cive*, however, Hobbes clearly defends the right of sovereignty by conquest, and in *Leviathan* he also specifically traces English sovereignty to William's conquest (*Leviathan* 19.3, p. 95; 24.6, p. 128).

[39] So the officers of the army point out to parliament: 'If therefore our Kings claim by right of Conquest, God hath given you the same against him' (*A Remonstrance of His Excellency Thomas Lord Fairfax* . . . (London, 1648), 48). Cf. Francis Osborne, *A Perswasive to a Mutuall Compliance under the Present Government* . . . (Oxford, 1652), who says that 'the *Norman Conquest*, hitherto the fairest flower in the Crowne of our *Kings*, and this of the *Armie's*, were cut out with the *same Iron*, by the hand and direction of a like *Providence*' (p. 4). Assuming that both are conquests (that is, setting aside the view of many in the army that they were not conquering, but nullifying the conquest of William and returning England to the laws and liberties of Edward the Confessor), important juridical distinctions remain. Unless one of them were taken to have done so by implicit signs of the will, sovereignty was not strictly speaking transferred to parliament from Charles I or Charles II, for neither of them consented to the protection of parliament (when not in arms, Charles I was in captivity (cf. *Leviathan* 21.22, and especially 21.25,

Baumgold thinks, however, that 'on the key point of indefeasible sovereign right', Hobbes 'contradicted himself'. 'As if to telegraph the contrast . . . Hobbes goes on [in the Review] to mock the opinion'—which he had maintained in the body of *Leviathan* and as he was to maintain in works after the Restoration—'that the Norman Conquest has authority over present political arrangements'.[40]

What Hobbes says in the Review (expanding on what he had affirmed in chapter 29) is that one cause of the dissolution of commonwealths is that all civil sovereigns attempt to

justifie the War, by which their Power was at first gotten, and whereon (as they think) their Right dependeth, and not on the Possession. As if, for example, the Right of the Kings of England did depend on the goodnesse of the cause of *William* the Conquerour, and upon their lineall, and directest Descent from him; by which means, there would perhaps be no tie of the Subjects obedience to their Soveraign at this day in all the world.[41]

This does not signal a new view, however, as Hobbes never claims that English regal right depends on the goodness of William's cause or the perfect directness of lineal descent from him.[42] Hobbes does say that Charles I 'had the Soveraignty from a descent of 600 years', but this descent was transparently not direct and lineal.[43] Hobbes did not consider these to be criteria of legitimate succession, and his rejection of them was a cause of royalist indignation.[44] Hobbes instead maintains that 'the disposing of the

p. 114), and Charles II abroad). If either had assented to the authority of parliament, even tacitly by living freely under their dominion, the right of sovereignty would have passed from them to their protectors. As it was, subjects were conquered without the sovereign having been conquered. Protective power is a necessary condition of sovereignty, however; so Stuart sovereignty was extinguished when that power was lost.

It is also important to remember that whereas William was a foreigner, and thus had no precedent obligation to obey any English sovereign, Hobbes thinks that the parliamentary and army leaders violated precedent obligations to obey the king. (Edward Symmons, for example (*Scripture Vindicated, from the Misapprehensions Misinterpretations and Misapplications of M*^r *Stephen Marshall* . . . (Oxford, 1644), 60), depends on the distinction: '*right by Conquest* (unlesse of Rebells) *is no usurpation*'; contrast Osborne, *Perswasive*, 4.) This does not, however, affect their sovereign authority, for the sin and injustice of their rebellion does not invalidate their subsequent right.

[40] Baumgold, 'When Hobbes needed History', 35.   [41] Review, par. 8, p. 391.

[42] Hobbes gives William as an example of someone who came 'into possession of a Land by warre' (*Leviathan* 24.6, p. 128). In contrast to Clarendon, who thinks that William qualified for legitimate sovereignty because of his eventual concessions, limitations, and adherence to previous laws, Hobbes criticizes William for limiting his power (*Leviathan* 29.3, pp. 167–8).

[43] Ibid. 19.3, p. 95.

[44] See Clarendon's denunciation in *A Brief View*, 60–2; on p. 121 he calls this doctrine 'Seditious'. Cf. John Bramhall, *Castigations of Mr. Hobbes his Last Animadversions* . . . (London, 1658), 522. Hobbes would have it that succession depends on the will of the present possessor of sovereignty: absent his contrary indication, the sovereign is understood to endorse the established custom of succession; and where that is wanting or disputed, the default assumption is direct lineal primogeniture. Traditional hereditary principles can always be overruled by sovereign determination, and if they

Successor, is alwaies left to the Judgment and Will of the present Possessor'.[45] Descent from William only means that after he had established his right to sovereignty by possessing the land by conquest, each possessor implicitly or explicitly nominated his or her successor.[46]

If the Review eschews a royalist and traditionalist political theory in favour of the justification of *de facto* authority, then it appears that *Leviathan* as a whole does, too. Nonetheless, Clarendon and fellow royalists

hold it is only because they have his tacit approval until he declares otherwise. The historical and traditional succession may provide a way to *identify* the sovereign to whom one owes obedience, but this is on the assumption that protection is being provided.

[45] *Leviathan* 19.18, p. 100. Hobbes's emphasis on the absolute right of 'the present Possessor' is one of many places in the body of *Leviathan* where Clarendon sees Hobbes to be arguing on behalf of the new regime. 'I must appeal to all dispassion'd men what Mr. *Hobbes* could have in his purpose in the year One thousand six hundred fifty one, when this Book was printed, but by this new Doctrine scarcely heard of till then, to induce *Cromwell* to break all the Laws of his Country, and to perpetuate their slavery under his Progeny' (*A Brief View*, 60–1). Hobbes holds this doctrine, however, both under Charles I and under Charles II. I see no reason to accept Glenn Burgess's claim that Hobbes's last known contribution to political thought (Chatsworth Hobbes MS D5, given in full in Skinner, *Visions*, 34–5) is an attempt 'to show that his theory could be used as the basis for Royalism (in particular that it was not incompatible with ideas of indefeasible hereditary right)' (Burgess, 'Contexts for the writing and publication of Hobbes's *Leviathan*', *History of Political Thought* 11/4 (1990), 701). In reply to a question specifically about the hereditary right of kings, Hobbes argues for the mutual relation between protection and obedience, for the devolution of sovereignty onto whomever the present king designates, and for the view that, if the king dies without any such designation, 'the people is a Multitude of lawlesse men relapsed into a condition of warr of every man against every man'. Although there is no way in which a subject can rightfully nullify it, there is no doubt that sovereignty is defeasible.

[46] This view is a severe simplification of the historical succession, to which there were nearly as many exceptions as to the view that it followed indefeasible primogeniture. The idea that the king could name his successor came to the fore under the Tudors, and was affirmed with vehemence by Henry VIII during disputes about his testamentary provisions and acts of succession. Nonetheless, the successions of 1399, 1461, 1483, and 1485, for example, had been contrary to the apparent will of the previous king. (They also occurred in circumstances that may be considered states of nature, but that would still undermine Hobbes's claim in *Leviathan* 19.3, p. 95, that there had been a descent of 600 years.) A common justification for ignoring the ruler's choice of successor was that he was a usurper or tyrant and so had no such right. Richard III is the most famous such case; others include Henry IV, Henry V, Henry VI, and Edward IV. Hobbes clearly rejects any such justification.

Hobbes could have adjusted his doctrine at no theoretical expense so that Charles I's right of sovereignty depended on succession from, for example, the conquest of Henry VII. This would have been out of step with Stuart doctrine, however, which traced the royal lineage back to William or to pre-Conquest kings. It is worth note that when Hobbes quotes Edward Coke on the 'De Facto Act' that cancelled Henry VII's attaint upon his accession to the throne, he drops all reference to Henry. The remaining impression is that the principle is a questionable piece of Common Law rather than one that has governed the actual succession (*Leviathan* 15.4, p. 72). When Hobbes claims that Charles had held the sovereignty from a descent of 600 years, perhaps this is best understood as either a reflection of what he perceived to be the Stuarts' own justification of their rule, or of the consensus about it: the remaining considerations on this list (that the king 'was alone called Soveraign, had the title of Majesty from every one of his Subjects, and was unquestionably taken by them for their King') are not immediate claims about the legitimacy of the sovereignty of Charles, but about the perception of or signs of that legitimacy.

who thought of the entire work as a betrayal of their cause were wrong. First, they overlooked the principles in Hobbes's work before *Leviathan* that aligned him with their party only so long as they were in power. Second, their reaction to these principles when they did see them blinded them to elements in *Leviathan* that showed Hobbes to be more sympathetic to the royalist party than the parliamentarian.

Many seventeenth-century royalists—to begin with their second error—complained rancorously that Hobbes wrote *Leviathan* to ingratiate himself with the Commonwealth or even with Cromwell. But in *Leviathan* Hobbes clearly declares that monarchy is the best form of government; says that Charles had undisputed sovereign right from a descent of 600 years, of which no subject could lawfully despoil him; dismisses as absurd the nature of the parliamentary claim to sovereignty; denounces the incompetence of any 'great Assembly' unless 'the finall Resolution is in one man'; criticizes the *custodes libertatis* set up by the Commonwealth; and even invokes the comparison (dear to the newborn cult of Charles, king and martyr) of the late king to Christ and the Presbyterians to Judas—implicitly correlating army and parliamentary leaders with the crucifiers.[47] Hobbes could not have thought such views would be welcome to the leaders of the new government in England.[48] Indeed, he clearly condemns their behaviour as unlawful: 'they that are subjects to a Monarch, cannot without his leave cast off Monarchy, and return to the confusion of a disunited Multitude; nor transferre their Person from him that beareth it, to another Man, or other Assembly of men'.[49] Hobbes's statements are carefully crafted to allow the behaviour of royalists who from necessity engaged or compounded,[50] while censuring those royalists who are still refractory, and especially castigating the anti-royalists who pulled down the previous power. When he argues that actions are not criminal if there is no sovereign power, he adds his own variation on an exclusion of certain individuals from amnesty for crimes committed during the war, specifying that 'this is to be understood onely of those, that have not themselves contributed to the taking away of the Power that

---

[47] *Leviathan* 19.4–9, pp. 95–8; 19.3, p. 95; 25.15–16, pp. 135–6; 19.9, pp. 97–8; and 3.3, p. 9. Critics of Hobbes after the restoration frequently ignore or misconstrue such passages (see, e.g., Thomas Tenison, *The Creed of Mr. Hobbes Examined; In a feigned Conference Between Him and a Student in Divinity* (London, 1670), 156).

[48] Skinner maintains that Hobbes correctly assumed that the 'message of *Leviathan* was likely to be warmly received by supporters of the Rump', and that Hobbes 'duly found a warm welcome' on his return (*Visions*, 22, 23). If we set aside the accusations of bitter royalists, however, there is little to support these claims. [49] *Leviathan* 18.3, p. 88.

[50] 'Compounding' (or 'Composition', as Hobbes calls it in the Review, par. 6, p. 390) allowed royalists to return to their estates upon swearing an oath of submission to parliament and paying them a percentage. Both terms are frequent in Hobbes's edition of Thucydides; for example, he uses them both to translate *sumbainō*, the coming to terms of conquered and conqueror (cf., e.g., III. 25 and 27, IV. 54 and 128).

protected them'.[51] Far from currying favour with his *Leviathan*, Hobbes could predict that its doctrine might antagonize all parties except the former royalists who had opted for a quiet life in England.

Tönnies's claim that it is specifically in the Review that Hobbes strives to make peace with the new regime is no more plausible. Hobbes does there stress the relation between protection and obedience, but his interpretation of it serves to excoriate anew the parliamentary and army leaders. The law of nature he adds in the Review requires one '*to protect in Warre, the Authority, by which he is himself protected in time of Peace*'; those who warred against Charles I, therefore, violated the moral and divine law.[52] Hobbes even specifies that one has the liberty to submit to a new sovereign only when 'the means of his life is within the Guards and Garrisons of the Enemy'; and if he is a soldier, he 'hath not the liberty to submit to a new Power, as long as the old one keeps the field, and giveth him means of sub- sistence'.[53] Hobbes condemns anyone who fought against the king before being captured by his enemies (and thus condemns the actions by which the leaders of the new government came to power), while also condemning any- one living under the Commonwealth who disobeys or undermines it. Again, it is difficult to see such a doctrine as ingratiating to anyone in power.

The royal court in Paris certainly did not receive the doctrine gladly, as Hobbes ruefully reports, but that hardly shows that Hobbes himself turned about with the work or in the work.[54] Influential courtiers reacted with hostility, especially after Hobbes presented a fine scribal copy of his book— including the Review—to Charles II. Yet the fact that he made this gesture is significant, for it is unlikely that Hobbes would have presented Charles with what he regarded as an attempt to impress the new rulers in England with principles especially favourable to them.[55]

---

[51] *Leviathan* 27.24, p. 156; he also says that while one may lawfully obey the enemy when under his power, this is only if the enemy has come to that power 'without his own fault' (27.3, p. 152). Note that Hobbes's principle that one owes obedience in exchange for protection appears to prohibit one who fled England and received protection elsewhere to return and compound, unless allowed to do so by the power presently protecting him.

[52] Review, par. 5, p. 390. Hobbes repeatedly equates the law of nature with the moral and divine law, e.g. at *Elements* 29.7, *De Cive* 4.1, and *Leviathan* 33.22, p. 205. Tenison duly saw Hobbes's addition of a law of nature in the Review as an attempt to show himself a supporter of the royal cause (*The Creed of Mr. Hobbes*, 156–7).

[53] Review, par. 6, p. 390. Johann Sommerville suggests that Hobbes did not want to be read as encouraging desertion from the army of Charles II, the remnant of which held the field until 3 Sept. 1651 (*Thomas Hobbes: Political Ideas in Historical Context* (London: Macmillan, 1992), 185 n. 3).

[54] See the sensible remarks in Leslie Stephen, *Hobbes* (London: Macmillan, 1904), 41–2.

[55] A point nicely brought out by George Croom Robertson, *Hobbes* (Edinburgh: William Blackwood, 1886), 70–1; cf. pp. 65, 68. Moreover, Hobbes might have expected that the Review would be one of the parts of the work that Charles would be most likely to read.

Rather than interpreting Hobbes's presentation of his work to Charles II as a miscalculation of the views of the court, it may be seen as unlucky timing, as these views were just about to shift. Hobbes's

The other way in which the royalists are wrong to think of *Leviathan* as a betrayal is that Hobbes had all along held principles according to which he would be aligned with their party only so long as the king had protective power over him. Tuck says that Hobbes fled to Paris 'after writing and publishing works of political theory at the beginning of the English Civil War in support of the king and against Parliament'.[56] There is a sense in which this is true, but not the one normally intended by those who claim that Hobbes's writings are royalist. His principles support the royal party if the royal party has sovereign power, but they are designed to support a new sovereign if and when there is one, of whatever kind. Although this position may provide contingent support for the royal party, it is not a royalist political theory. This is as true of *The Elements of Law* and *De Cive* as of *Leviathan*.[57]

Royalists who were too quick to see Hobbes as their apologist (even an extreme and absolutist one) in the earlier works were therefore too quick to see him as a turncoat in *Leviathan*. He is a royalist in the sense of expressing a preference for monarchy through all of these works; in none of them is he a royalist in the sense of maintaining the king's indefeasible right to rule, or of rejecting the mutual relation between protection and obedience.[58] In 1650, Marchamont Nedham exploited the royalist misreading of Hobbes's early work, quoting sections from *De Corpore Politico* to show that even someone they esteemed as one of their own number and a theorist of Stuart absolutism held principles supporting submission to present powers.[59] Defenders of the idea that Hobbes was a true royalist before *Leviathan*, or before the Review, have not shown why Nedham's appropriation is unjustified.

It is true that, especially before 1651, there were some who would have considered themselves royalists who rejected indefeasibility and accepted the mutual relation between protection and obedience, or at least the idea that conquerors and even usurpers become legitimate rulers once their

---

supporters, Newcastle chief among them, dominated the court so long as their policy to win back the throne by arms prevailed. Hobbes presented Charles II with the manuscript of Leviathan shortly after Charles returned to France at the end of October 1651; that return was the mark of the final failure of the policy of war, and Charles soon replaced his chief advisers with Clarendon and Nicholas, who were more hostile to the views in *Leviathan*, especially those on absolutism, mixed monarchy, succession, and episcopacy. Cf. Johann Sommerville's account at pp. 261–7 of Tom Sorell, (ed.), *The Cambridge Companion to Hobbes* (Cambridge: Cambridge University Press, 1996).

[56] Tuck (ed.), *Leviathan*, p. ix.

[57] Note that Hobbes emphasizes the similarity of *Leviathan* to *De Cive* in the Review (par. 16, p. 395).

[58] For a brief consideration of apparent counterevidence, see pp. 46–7, below. Hobbes is often considered to be a royalist because he associated with or acted like others widely regarded as royalists. In rejecting the suggestion that Hobbes is a royalist, I am instead addressing the question of whether his theory of political obligation and authority is distinctively royalist.

[59] Nedham, *The Case of the Commonwealth of England, Stated*, ed. Philip A. Knachel (Charlottesville: The University Press of Virginia, 1969), 129, 135–9.

dominion is settled. Such a doctrine was born of the need to justify the rule of the English monarchs, many of whom had been conquerors or usurpers. This was soon eclipsed by the need to justify the claim of Charles II to sovereignty, despite his defeat and his father's execution at the hands of what became a settled government. These would-be royalists were confronted by the fact that their principles no longer supported the royal claim to sovereignty, and were forced to abandon the principle of legitimation via dominion. Hobbes, by contrast, holds fast to his double-edged sword, and continues to insist in 1651 on the defeasibility of sovereignty and the mutual relation between protection and obedience. While under the Protectorate, he writes of *Leviathan*: 'I believe it hath framed the minds of a thousand Gentlemen to a consciencious obedience to present Government, which otherwise would have wavered in that Point.'[60] While royalists denounced this as a shift of principles, they had been the ones compelled to shift.

In the Review, Hobbes openly declares that *Leviathan* contains new doctrines, but he suggests that these are ecclesiastical.[61] All of the basic positions of political theory that are taken to be deviant principles invented to support the newly settled government turn out to have been formulated in Hobbes's works from the beginning, before the Commonwealth was even a gleam in the eye of parliamentary and army leaders. In his early works, Hobbes insists that the sovereign must be obeyed absolutely, even if it be an assembly or the body of the people;[62] he argues that succession need not be hereditary or traditional, but follows the will of the present sovereign power;[63] he claims that there is a right of conquest;[64] and he specifies that one who yields to the sword or is otherwise conquered is both discharged of the obligation to his former sovereign and absolutely bound to the conqueror.[65]

The temptation to read the Review as newly or especially endorsing the rights of and duties to conquerors, and the mutual relation between protection and obedience, arises in part from the neglect of Hobbes's account of sovereignty by acquisition in favour of his account of sovereignty by institution.[66] After reading the respective chapters on sovereignty by mastery or

---

[60] *Six Lessons to the Professors of the Mathematiques*, p. 57 (*English Works*, vii. 336).

[61] Review, par. 14, p. 394.

[62] *De Cive* preface (pp. 83–4) and 6.13; cf. *Elements* 20.19. At some stylistic expense, he assiduously reminds us that full sovereign right can reside in a group (for example, by periodically referring to the sovereign as 'he, or they').

[63] *Elements* 23.11; *De Cive* 9.12 ff.   [64] *Elements* 22.9.

[65] Ibid. 21.14, 22.7, *De Cive* 7.18; cf. *Elements* 21.15, 22.6, and *De Cive* 8.9.

[66] It also arises from the idea that Hobbes's view of the relation between protection and obedience may be explained by the influence of the *de facto* theorists' articulation of this view in their works of 1649–51. The doctrine of this mutual relation was already common, however, when Hobbes was writing his earlier works. Edward Coke, for example, treats it as an established principle in discussing Calvin's Case of 1608, as does John March writing in 1642; in 1645 William Ball refers to it as 'an Axiom' (Sommerville, *Thomas Hobbes*, 68–9).

conquest (*The Elements of Law* 22, *De Cive* 8, and *Leviathan* 20), these principles come as no surprise. Even outside these chapters, Hobbes argues that in order to have security, a man 'giveth up, and relinquisheth to another, or others, the right of protecting and defending himself', and thus 'subjecteth his will' to the protectors.[67] 'Subjection of wills', or obedience, 'is necessary for human security'; and if they do not receive security, people are free from such subjection.[68] 'The preservation of peace and lasting defence' requires that they obligate themselves by a '*submission* of the *Wills* of all of them, to *the will of one man*, or *one Assembly*'.[69] Without obedience, there is simply no commonwealth to provide security.[70]

Regardless of the origin of the present government, those who accept its protection must obey it as sovereign. Those who fought against Charles I, having previously received protection from him, are guilty of sin and injustice, as are those living in England who are still active royalists.[71] Hobbes's first political commandment, analogous to God's commandment to have no other gods, is that people 'ought not to be in love with any forme of Government they see in their neighbour Nations, more than with their own, nor . . . to desire change'.[72] Hobbes tells his readers that he writes from the hope that 'You will reckon it better to enjoy the present state, even if it is not the best, than to stir up war.'[73] He later makes clear that it is prohibited to articulate any negative judgement of one's present government, forbidding not only oppositional partisan rhetoric, but even a primary pursuit of traditional political theory:

And of the three sorts [monarchy, aristocracy, and democracy], which is the best, is not to be disputed, where any one of them is already established; but the present ought alwaies to be preferred, maintained, and accounted best; because it is against both the Law of Nature, and the Divine positive Law, to doe any thing tending to the subversion thereof.[74]

---

[67] *Elements* 20.5.

[68] *De Cive* 6.3: 'requiri ad securitatem hominum . . . subiectionem voluntatum'.

[69] *De Cive* 5.6, 5.7: 'conseruationem pacis, & defensionem stabilem'; '*Voluntatum . . . submissio omnium illorum, vnius hominis voluntati, vel vnius Concilij*'.   [70] *De Cive* 6.13.

[71] By contrast, it may seem that Charles II and the royalist exiles legitimately exercise their state-of-nature right if they invade England as enemies. This too is constrained by the law of nature, however, as there is a power in England sufficient to protect them, and they are thus guilty of not seeking peace when it may be had. Finally, it may seem that those excepted from pardon (like Clarendon and Newcastle) would be free to fight; but they would thereby reject the protection they enjoyed on the Continent, so choosing war when they could have peace.

[72] *Leviathan* 30.7, p. 177.

[73] *De Cive*, preface, p. 83: 'Ut statu praesente, etsi non optimo, vos ipsos frui, quàm bello excitato . . . satius duceretis'.

[74] *Leviathan* 42.82, p. 301. Hobbes frequently opposes disputation and obedience: cf., e.g., the preface to *De Cive*, p. 78; *De Corpore* 26.1; and *A Dialogue Between a Phylosopher and a Student, of the Common-Laws of England* (London, 1681), 2.

It has not been noticed that this position raises serious questions about the status of Hobbes's arguments for the superiority of monarchy over aristocracy and democracy. That monarchy was by Hobbes 'accounted best' may merely reflect the fact that he was protected by a monarch, and tell us nothing about what he thought to be, in the abstract, the best form of government.[75]

We can take as programmatic Hobbes's prefatory statement in *De Cive* that he writes as a supporter of peace rather than of any particular party.[76] He argues on behalf of present government, of whatever kind.[77] In the dedicatory epistle of *Leviathan*, he compares his writing to the noise of the geese who saved Rome from the Gauls by alerting the people's representatives, besieged in the Capitol, to a stealth attack.[78]

I speak not of the men, but (in the Abstract) of the Seat of Power, (like to those simple and unpartiall creatures in the Roman Capitol, that with their noyse defended those within it, not because they were they, but there,) offending none, I think, but those without, or such within . . . that favour them.[79]

As it happens, the geese in that instance defended a republic within from a king without. But that is just as it happens.

II. *DE FACTO* THEORY: THE REVIEW AS THE RULE

If defenders of the royalist Hobbes are right about the *de facto* theory in the Review, but wrong to think that its 'Engagement' principles are absent from or incidental to the rest of Hobbes's work, then it seems that they are left with the position from which they were distinguishing themselves. That

---

[75] See pp. 46–7, below, on Hobbes's 'doctrine of doctrines'.

[76] *De Cive* preface, p. 84: 'non partium sed pacis studio'. Hobbes here twists the historical requirement articulated by Tacitus to write 'sine . . . studio', i.e. 'without . . . partialitie' (or without 'affection': the former is the translation and the latter the paraphrase on p. 248 of [William Cavendish?], *Horae Subseciuae* (London, 1620), a work in which Hobbes probably had a hand). In saying that his study concerns peace in general, Hobbes also says that he *is* partial—not to a party, but to peace. In *Leviathan*, he wishes to make it unambiguous that he is not a partisan, comparing himself in the first paragraph of the work to the 'unpartiall' geese, and in the last paragraph submitting that he has written 'without partiality' (sig. A2ᵛ; Review, par. 17, p. 395).

[77] In his verse autobiography, Hobbes writes of *Leviathan*: 'Militat ille Liber nunc Regibus omnibus, & qui / Nomine sub quovis regia Jura tenent'. The specification 'under whatever name' is unlikely to refer to the names of different kings, and suggests that the sense of 'regia Jura' is not 'royal Right' (except as a turn of thought), but 'the Right of rule': 'That Book now defends all Kings, and all who, under whatever Name, hold the Right of rule' (*Thomae Hobbesii Malmesburiensis Vita* (London, 1679), 8).

[78] The story of the Capitoline geese is told by Livy (5.47), and Plutarch in his life of Camillus. The most likely source for Hobbes's analogy may be Florus, whose epitome of Roman history Hobbes evidently knew well. Chatsworth Hobbes MS D1, a dictation book used for lessons with Hobbes, contains passages from the first book of Florus, which includes this and other stories to which Hobbes later refers (pp. 160–54, inverted).   [79] *Leviathan*, sig. A2ᵛ.

position—now associated most prominently with Quentin Skinner, but accepted by many readers of Hobbes since the seventeenth century—is that Hobbes's *de facto* remarks in the Review, while they may be especially pointed there, represent the consistent principles of Hobbes's political theory.[80]

Central to that political theory, on this interpretation, are the ideas that sovereign right follows from the actual possession of power, and that there is a mutual relation between protection and obedience. Also according to this interpretation, Hobbes's theory (at least as it is articulated in the Review) is seen as a variant of similar positions staked out from around 1649. John Wallace put Hobbes in the context of the 'Engagement theorists' or 'loyalists'—theorists like Francis Rous, Anthony Ascham, John Dury, and Marchamont Nedham, who argued for the acceptability of taking the Engagement to the newly proclaimed Commonwealth.[81] In his earliest work on this group of thinkers, Skinner follows Wallace in calling them 'Engagers', or refers to them more generally as 'the writers on Sovereignty'; but he later prefers to characterize them as 'the *de facto* theorists', because people engaged to uphold the Commonwealth for very different reasons.[82] Thus, the label of 'Engager' (or even, more accurately, 'one who argued for the acceptability of subscribing the Engagement') was not sufficiently precise. This seems right.[83] I shall argue, however, that the label '*de facto* theory' is itself insufficiently precise, and even misleading.

---

[80] Skinner himself has endorsed the idea of a shift with *Leviathan* and especially the Review. In his early essays, he subscribes to that part of the royalist theory that says simply that Hobbes becomes more of a *de facto* theorist in *Leviathan*, and especially the Review (see *Visions*, 305–7: 'Conquest and Consent', 96–7; and 'Thomas Hobbes et la défense du pouvoir "de facto" ', *Revue Philosophique* 163 (1973), esp. p. 153 n. 2).

In a later piece, however, Skinner briefly *distinguishes* Hobbes's theory in the Review from *de facto* theory (*Visions*, 232–7: 'Thomas Hobbes on the Proper Signification of Liberty', *Transactions of the Royal Historical Society*, 5th series, 40 (1990), 145–51). 'Royalists' like Tuck and Baumgold have been more convinced by the case for their identification than Skinner himself has turned out to be. Although in the next section I shall briefly address Skinner's later view and *its* version of a turn in Hobbes's thought, I focus in what follows on the impressive corpus of his early articles in favour of the identification. I do so because (1) they have been deservedly influential, and many remain persuaded by the key suggestions; (2) he has recently republished them in revised form; (3) his explanation in 1990 is too cursory to dismantle the earlier case; and (4) it is not clear that Skinner should concede what he does, or that his alternative account is successful (see sections III and IV, below). In several early articles, Skinner marshals evidence to show that Hobbes's contemporaries overwhelmingly interpreted him as a *de facto* theorist: if this demonstration and Skinner's later interpretation that he is not one are both right, this indicates limitations of contemporary interpretation as a guide to correct interpretation.

[81] Wallace, 'The Engagement Controversy 1649–1652: An Annotated List of Pamphlets', *Bulletin of the New York Public Library* 68/6 (1964); *Destiny His Choice: The Loyalism of Andrew Marvell* (Cambridge: Cambridge University Press, 1968), 232–7. On the Engagement, see n. 16, above.

[82] For the earlier usage, see 'History and Ideology'; for the later point, see 'Conquest and Consent', 80.

[83] Not all of the theorists who argue for obedience to the authority of present power do so with the aim of justifying the Engagement. The arguments of Ascham, Rous, Nathaniel Ward,

The most significant drawback of this classification is that it lumps together two importantly distinct theories. I shall call the first theory, the most impressive representative of which is Anthony Ascham, 'the *de facto* theory of obligation'. *De facto* theorists of obligation hold that subjects are obligated to obey the holders of *de facto* power even though their rule is not *de jure*.[84] The other theory, which I shall call 'the *de facto* theory of authority', is most notably represented by Marchamont Nedham.[85] *De facto* theorists of authority maintain that possession of *de facto* power is by itself sufficient for *de jure* authority.[86] I argue that Hobbes is not a *de facto* theorist of obligation, and that he clearly rejects the leading form of the *de facto* theory of authority.[87] And it is in the Review—precisely where even the 'royalist' interpreters agree that Hobbes is a *de facto* theorist—that he takes particular pains to distance himself from contemporary versions of both kinds of *de facto* theory.

A '*de facto* theory' is often taken to mean a defence of the legitimacy of all *de facto* governments. However, several figures labelled *de facto* theorists by Skinner take as their starting point the presumed *illegitimacy* of *de facto* government.[88] Many on both the radical and royalist sides regarded

and others were largely formulated before the Engagement Act of 11 Oct. 1649. Even after that Act, Ascham stands behind the position that usurpers 'would finde it a greater security to put a penalty upon those who should question their rights, then to force their subjects to acknowledge their pretensions by this oath' (*Of the Confusions and Revolutions of Governments* ... (London, 1649), 84).

[84] Although the avowed aim of these theorists is often to show only that subjects *may* obey a merely *de facto* power, they almost invariably go on to support the stronger thesis that subjects *should* obey such a power.

[85] When referring to the protean Nedham in this essay, I restrict myself to *Case of the Commonwealth*. Even as *de facto* works of both kinds attempted (in the words of a related work) 'to further the speedy settlement of the snarl'd, and contortuplicated affairs of the State, and Church', they led to an equally 'snarl'd, and contortuplicated' series of intellectual differences and alliances (*To the High and Honorable Parliament of England now assembled at Westminster. The Humble Petitions, Serious Suggestions, and dutifull Expostulations of ... the Easterne Association* (London, 1648), 30). Without room for a nuanced account of the range of writings relating to this controversy, I must focus on a few salient figures and what I regard as a central distinction.

[86] In a sense, these thinkers are not *de facto* theorists at all, in so far as they hold that there is no such thing as a merely *de facto* power (as any such power entails authority). But the label '*de facto* theory of authority' is, I think, nonetheless clear, and allows us both to recognize the important difference between this group and the *de facto* theorists of obligation, and yet to follow Skinner in referring to both groups together as '*de facto* theorists'. The distinction between Ascham and Nedham is limned by Deborah Baumgold, *Hobbes's Political Theory* (Cambridge: Cambridge University Press, 1988), 130–1, and Franck Lessay, *Souveraineté et légitimité chez Hobbes* (Paris: Presses Universitaires de France, 1988), 161–2.

[87] In section IV, I suggest a specific way in which Hobbes may nonetheless be considered a *de facto* theorist of authority.

[88] So Rous begins *The Lawfulnes of obeying the Present Government* (London, 1649) by promising 'Proofes, that though the change of a Government were beleeved not to be lawfull, yet it may lawfully be obeyed' (p. 1). Cf., e.g., *A Logical Demonstration of the Lawfulness of Subscribing the New Engagement* (London, 1650), 5, and the citations from Ascham, below.

the prevailing power as usurpatory, the work of a conquering or unlawful army. After the regicide early in 1649, the perception of the illegitimacy of the present power spread, and it was chiefly then that Ascham and Rous and their associates argued that their readers owed obedience to it even if illegitimate, that is, even lacking just title to rule. These theorists maintain that one has an obligation to obey a *de facto* power that is not *de jure*; Hobbes holds that the *de facto* power that protects one has legitimate authority, so the power one has an obligation to obey is both *de facto* and *de jure*.[89] Simply calling Hobbes a *de facto* theorist, therefore, conceals as much as it reveals.

Consider Skinner's characterization of Hobbes's position as exemplary of *de facto* theory. 'The possession of power itself established a title to be obeyed: as the aim of subscribing to government was self-preservation, so this presupposed an obligation to obey any power with the capacity to protect.'[90] Skinner writes as if the obligation to obey and the right of ruling were necessarily correlative for those he calls *de facto* theorists, and as if they affirmed that *de jure* authority follows from *de facto* power. To some extent, these positions *are* held by Nedham, Michael Hawke, and others;[91] but this shows how different they are from the likes of Ascham and Rous, who (along with the 'Exercitator', their ablest opponent[92]) make the denial of these positions their cornerstone. As for Hobbes, it does follow from what he says that the right to rule and obligation to obey are not necessarily correlative. For he argues that in the state of nature one may have the right to rule over another while that other has no corresponding obligation to obey (either because one does not have the other in one's power, or because one holds the other in bonds as a slave). However, whereas Hobbes holds that there can be a right to rule with no corresponding obligation to obey, he rejects Ascham's central contention, that there can be an obligation to obey with no corresponding right to rule.

---

[89] In building his characterization of the *de facto* theorists to whom he assimilates Hobbes, Skinner (*Visions*, 253: 'History and Ideology', 168) cites Lewis de Moulin, *The Power of the Magistrate in Sacred Things* . . . (London, 1650), that it is just to yield 'fealty or Homage to him that hath possession *de facto*, though not *de jure*'. Hobbes, by contrast, never claims that we should obey someone who lacks *de jure* authority. In a sense, Hobbes's theory was more strongly in favour of the Commonwealth than that propounded by Ascham et al., for once the Commonwealth was settled Hobbes's principles required him to recognize its authority over its subjects as legitimate. In this, he ends up temporarily aligned with the more radical elements who had maintained parliamentary sovereignty during the war.

[90] Skinner, 'Ideological Context', 307; cf. *Visions*, 276.

[91] For arguments that *de facto* entails *de jure* power, cf., e.g., *A Disingag'd Survey of the Engagement* (London, 1650), 21; [Herle?], *The Exercitation Answered*, 36–8; and N. W., *A Discourse Concerning the Engagement: or, The Northern Subscribers Plea* . . . (London, 1650), 11–12. The entailment is sometimes explained in terms of divine sanction (e.g., by Richard Saunders, *Plenary Possession Makes a Lawful Power* (London, 1651), and Osborne, *A Perswasive*).   [92] [Gee?], *An Exercitation*, 1, 3–4, 8, 10, 12–13, etc.

Skinner calls *de facto* theory 'a theory of political obligation in terms of which the new government could be legitimated'.[93] The obligation to obey a government, however, is in principle independent of its legitimacy.[94] Skinner's conflation is unfortunate, as the theorists who can most appropriately be called '*de facto* theorists' are especially insistent about just this distinction.[95] Ascham, for example, says that 'the very question' is 'Whether obedience be lawfull to Titles visibly unlawfull?'[96] He repeatedly chides critics for shifting the question from the legitimacy of obeying the present power to the legitimacy of that power, claiming that even the present

---

[93] Skinner, *Visions*, 287 ('Conquest and Consent', 79).

[94] The point here is that figures central to Skinner's analysis argue that the obligation of obedience does not necessarily imply the legitimacy of power, not that they are right so to argue. N. W., for example (*Northern Subscribers Plea*, 11–12), criticizes this influential argument from the parliamentary side: 'to our sense, the objectors seem rather nice then wise. We never knew how to divide the hair, or distinguish betwixt a conscientious subjection to any powers over us, and an owning them, as full and lawful powers ordained of God. Conscientious submission consignifies a conscientious owning the powers, and presumes or implies their lawfulness'.

In his later work on these thinkers, Skinner continues to treat *de facto* theorists of obligation as if they were *de facto* theorists of authority. He considers Ascham and Nedham to belong to the same group, which is marked by the belief that the fact that a government is set up by conquest does not impugn 'either its legitimacy or its title to allegiance'. 'The point on which these writers all agree', he says, is that conquest is another means 'by which political authority comes to be lawfully acquired': they can thus all be characterized as defenders of *de facto* powers (*Visions*, 230–2: 'Proper Signification', 144–5). And in his recent revision of this piece, he underlines that 'the defenders of *de facto* sovereignty' include 'such enthusiastic defenders of *de facto* powers as Anthony Ascham, Marchamont Nedham and their ilk' (*Visions*, 232).

[95] Correspondingly, the use of Romans 13 differs in writers like Hobbes and those like Ascham and Rous. For Hobbes, ordination by God means not only that subjects must obey, but also that present sovereigns have the right to command; all princes, Christian and infidel, have 'lawfull Authority' by divine dispensation (cf. *Leviathan* 42.10, p. 270). Again, according to such a theory, one's obligation is always to *de jure* authority. See also Nedham's *Case of the Commonwealth*, 32 (but cf. p. 47). Rous ridicules such a reading on the first page of *Lawfulnes of obeying*; cf. Ascham, *Confusions*, p. 148, and [Ascham], *A Reply to a Paper of Dr Sandersons, Containing a Censure of Mr. A. A. his Booke of the Confusions and Revolutions of Goverment* (London, 1650), sig. A2ʳ and p. 12; there is an interesting ambiguity in [Ascham], *The Bounds & bonds*, 22 (for this work, see next note). For a sermon published by order of Charles II that contrasts an interpretation of Romans 13 with what is apparently Hobbes's 'Philosophical Theory' that 'tells us in effect, that Might is Right', see Seth Ward, *Against Resistance of Lawful Powers: A Sermon Preached at White-Hall, Novemb. Vth 1661* (London, 1661), esp. pp. 35, 38–9.

[96] *The Bounds & bonds of Publique Obedience. Or, a Vindication of our lawfull submission to the present Government, or to a government supposed unlawfull, but commanding lawfull things* (London, 1649), 32; citations are to this edition unless noted. Wallace has provided good reasons for ascribing this to Ascham rather than Rous, as had been usual ('Engagement Controversy', 391–2; he adds a further consideration in *Destiny His Choice*, 47 n. 2). The case is strengthened by further similarities (e.g., in *The Bounds & Bonds*, 61, the author says that states must act *ex bono & aequo* conjunctively, which is repeated exactly on p. 148 of the *Confusions*; and see the similar collapsing of active into passive obedience, and the concluding use of the metaphor of war as a tragedy).

'Lawfull' and 'unlawfull' cannot be understood here by reference to either the laws of the usurped or the usurper; they seem to mean 'legitimate' and 'illegitimate', respectively (perhaps as determined by divine law).

government requires only recognition of the legitimacy of obedience.[97] Ascham argues that 'simple obedience to an establisht Vsurper' does not necessarily 'affirme his right'; what is more, even a royalist can obey, for he does not thereby 'deny anothers' right, 'but affirmes rather the irresistibility of the possessors present power'.[98] By contrast, Hobbes argues that 'in the natural state of men, *sure and irresistible power confers the right of ruling and commanding those who cannot resist*'.[99]

Viewed from this angle, Hobbes roughly agrees with those theorists, including Nedham, who maintain that no features of power other than its plenary possession are necessary to entail the legitimacy of that power and the obligation of obedience to it.[100] On the central questions of sovereign right and the mechanics of obligation, therefore, he does not belong with those theorists who maintain that one must obey illegitimate or unlawful

---

[97] [Ascham], *The Bounds & bonds*, 2–3: 'in all these answers it is evidently granted, That we of the people may lawfully give obedience to an unlawfull power; this onely is denied, That it may not be with an acknowledgement of their authority and right, which is very uncasuistly and unconscientiously inserted here, because that is not the Peoples present case, But the Governours, these onely asserting that, contenting themselves with simple obedience from us'. Apparently, it did not take long for the government to disabuse Ascham of the impression that they would not demand recognition of their legitimacy, for in the second edition (London, 1650), the relevant passage ('which . . . us') is dropped. He continues to insist, however, on the irrelevance of any argument that 'relates more to the Commanders then to the obeyers, (of whom our controversie onely is)' (p. 3). Although Ascham is deeply sceptical about the possibility of knowledge of sovereign right (cf. especially *Confusions*, 32–3), he does not think that the lack of secure knowledge in itself allows us a free hand in determining when and to whom we owe obedience.

[98] [Ascham], *The Bounds & Bonds*, p. 33; cf. *Confusions*, 137. Ascham clearly states the principle that to obey is not to endorse the legitimacy of the authority obeyed in *Confusions*, 141, 148, and 157. Nonetheless, Ascham is more willing to style the present government as unlawful and usurping in the anonymous work. In the *Discourse* and *Confusions*, published under his name, he is somewhat more cautious (though arguably thereby less persuasive to royalists and some Presbyterians), posing the question 'if we would be warranted of a just submission to the orders of one who commands us *perhaps* unjustly' (*Discourse*, p. 24, emphasis added; cf. *Confusions*, 34), and at one point even countenancing the idea that 'possession . . . generally is the strongest title that Princes have' (*Discourse*, p. 23, *Confusions*, 32: but this is 'if the parties rights be but one as good as anothers'—*then* 'his is the best who hath possession'). In general, whereas Ascham argues that we must rely on possession because sovereign right is doubtful and disputable, Hobbes bases right itself on possession.

[99] *De Cive* 1.14: 'in statu hominum naturali, *potentiam certam & irresistibilem, ius conferre regendi, imperandique in eos, qui resistere non possunt*'. Cf. *Elements* 14.10 and 14.13; *De Cive* 1.10, 8.10, 15.5; and *Leviathan* 31.5, p. 187.

[100] The fit is imperfect, since for Hobbes the nature of the submission to the power is arguably essential, whereas Nedham's theory more nearly approaches the simple view that might is right (see section III, below). Also, theorists on both sides of the divide, including Hobbes and Ascham, qualify the extent of obligation according to how power is used. Although they describe obligation as correlating to protection, and often explain this as obligation to whomever has the power to destroy one—'For one who has enough strength to protect everyone, likewise has enough to oppress everyone' (*De Cive* 6.13 n.: 'Nam qui satis habet virium ad omnes protegendos, satis quoque habet ad omnes opprimendos')—they both think that the imminent threat of such destruction dissolves the obligation.

powers. Hobbes disagrees with *de facto* theorists of obligation precisely about the justification of *de facto* power.

Before this conclusion is firmly established, however, there is evidence to consider that would support a closer alliance between Hobbes and *de facto* theorists of obligation like Ascham.[101] There are many passages in which Hobbes apparently endorses their central tenet, that one may rightly obey the government that protects one without recognizing its right to rule. So in the *Considerations*, for example, Hobbes says that while in exile Charles II 'had the Title, Right, and Reverence of a King'; that those who remained in England during the interregnum were not to be blamed if they 'lived quietly under the Protection, first of the Parliament, and then of *Oliver*, (whose Titles and Actions were equally unjust)'; and that it was not to be concluded that they were 'defenders either of *Oliver*'s or of the *Parliaments* Title to the Soveraign Power' simply because 'by their stay here openly they accepted of the *Parliaments* and of *Oliver's* Protection'. Moreover, Hobbes here condemns parliament as usurpatory, and suggests that one may 'save himself from violent death, by a forc'd submission to an Usurper'; he maintains that the question at hand is at what point in time one 'becomes obliged to obey an unjust Conquerour'.[102]

This apparent contradiction of Hobbes's earlier theory may be resolved by an appeal to 'the doctrine of doctrines'. It is imperative that interpreters of Hobbes keep in mind his doctrine that one must not propagate doctrines that contradict those sanctioned by one's sovereign.[103] Hobbes expresses the view of the injustice of Cromwell's rule only under the rule of Charles II. This has been taken as evidence of Hobbes's timidity or self-interestedness, but it is better explained in terms of Hobbes's position that he should only express positions consistent with those of his sovereign. And the official position of his sovereign was very clear. To take just one example, Hobbes's sovereign after 1660 required that his subjects acknowledge his

restauration to the actual possession and exercise of his undoubted, hereditary, sovereign, and real authority over them (after sundry years forced extermination

---

[101] Skinner points out that Filmer considers Hobbes and Ascham to be of the same party (*Visions*, 281: 'Ideological Context', 310 n. 193). Filmer does not group them because of their common endorsement of *de facto* theory, however, but because he thinks they agree (together with Grotius and Selden) that power is originally in the people, and that (along with 'the heathen Philosophers', the civil lawyers, Grotius, and Selden) they hold that there is an original condition of liberty ([Filmer], *Observations upon Aristotles Politiques, Touching Forms of Government, Together with Directions for Obedience to Governours in Dangerous and Doubtfull Times* (London, 1652), p. 45 and sig. A2ᵛ).

[102] *Mr. Hobbes considered in his Loyalty, Religion, Reputation, and Manners* . . . (London, 1662), 8, 12, 25, 22 (*English Works*, iv. 415, 417, 423, 422). Cf., e.g., *Behemoth*, 131, 180.

[103] For another attempt to articulate the doctrine of doctrines and interpret in light of it, see Kinch Hoekstra, 'Tyrannus Rex *vs*. Leviathan', *Pacific Philosophical Quarterly* 82/3, 4 (2001), esp. pp. 432–5, on Hobbes as a principled trimmer.

into foreign parts, by the most traiterous conspiracies, and armed power of usurping tyrants, and execrable perfidious traitors).[104]

According to the political theory of *The Elements of Law*, *De Cive*, and *Leviathan*, Charles II was not the rightful English sovereign during the interregnum. According to that same theory, however, Hobbes was required thereafter to go along with the doctrine that Charles had unbroken authority and right to rule from the moment of his father's execution, and had only been deprived of its possession and exercise; and that the power to which Hobbes had explicitly submitted at the beginning of 1652, and by which he was protected until the Restoration, was not a legitimate sovereign but a usurping tyrant.[105]

If such evidence as there is for Hobbes's acceptance of the basic thesis of the *de facto* theorists of obligation can be explained away as a surface phenomenon and later development, we might expect to find indications that he previously distinguished himself from them, or vice versa. In the central case of Hobbes and Ascham, this is just what we find. While in the *Confusions* Ascham does draw on Hobbes's *De Cive* (twice explicitly), he also sharply censures him. Ascham's central criticism of Hobbes makes clear that he, for one, does not think that Hobbes is a *de facto* theorist of obligation. He argues against Hobbes's requirement of a 'totall resignation of all right and reason' upon entering civil society. 'Mr. *Hobbes* supposes,' Ascham says, 'that because a man cannot be protected . . . unless all his rights be totally and irrevocably given up to another, therefore the people are irrevocably and perpetually' subject to the sovereign.[106] According to the *de facto* theory of obligation, by contrast, the obligations of subjection shift with *de facto* power.

Ascham's criticism is inaccurate, as Hobbes holds that some rights are inalienable, and allows a subject to be released from obedience when sovereignty is extinguished or transferred, or when the subject's safety is immediately threatened. Nonetheless, other criticisms that Ascham levels against Hobbes make clear that their views of political obligation diverge at the root. The most involved of these is an argument that Hobbes is wrong to think that we surrender our right of private judgement upon entering civil society, for God allows citizens to retain this right, as shown by the '*Ius zelotarum*' in the Jewish commonwealth. This was 'a right of judging and

---

[104] 12 Car. II cap. 14, 'An Act for a perpetual anniversary thanksgiving on the nine and twentieth day of May' (i.e. for the restoration). Cf., e.g., *An Act for Confirmation of Judicial Proceedings* (London, 1660), esp. pp. 8–9; and *A Proclamation of Both Houses of Parliament* (London, 1660), a proclamation of 8 May that Charles II became king at his father's death and had only been kept by violence from his rightful throne.

[105] This explains how Hobbes can say, in *Mr. Hobbes Considered* (p. 13: *English Works*, iv. 418), that the imposing of the Engagement was 'a very great Crime'.

[106] Ascham, *Confusions*, 121.

punishing acts notoriously contrary to the light of nature and reason' without going through established civil procedures or authorities.[107] Hobbes would have found this doctrine mistaken in its premises and dangerous in its implications. Moreover, as Ascham's was one of the first published criticisms of Hobbes, advanced in a work with a high public profile—especially after the author's notorious assassination by royalists in mid-1650—it is likely that the arguments would have been brought to Hobbes's attention, and that he would have weighed his reply.

Whether because Hobbes does not name his target, or because scholars have been convinced that Hobbes, at least in the Review, espouses a *de facto* theory, it has not been noticed that Hobbes *did* publish a reply. That reply is in the Review itself. Hobbes there makes clear that his dissatisfaction with 'divers English Books lately printed' has prompted him to add some remarks. A detailed set of observations that Hobbes 'omitted to set down' in the body of *Leviathan*, 'not then thinking it a matter of so necessary consideration, as I find it since', is especially incongruous.[108] For why does Hobbes, at such a critical juncture in political and intellectual history, devote much of the conclusion of his great *Leviathan* to an antiquarian issue he had not so much as mentioned therein, the question of the *ius zelotarum* in the Jewish state?[109] This would be an enigma were it not for Ascham's recent criticism of Hobbes on this very topic.

Hobbes specifies that the 'English Books lately printed' do not adequately explain 'in what point of time it is, that a Subject becomes obliged to the Conquerour; nor what is Conquest; nor how it comes about, that it obliges men to obey his Laws.'[110] In his book, Ascham had set out to explain just these matters. He distinguishes *'betwixt the over-running and the conquering of a Country, and secondly betwixt Conquest and Victory'*.[111] Ascham cites the authority of Hobbes and Grotius at the outset of the first distinction, and launches his criticism of them after the second. Ascham argues that overrunning is seizure without the exercise of dominion, as in the mere looting of a country; victory is when a person or party replaces by war the one that had been governing, while leaving the systems of law and property in place; and conquest occurs when the victor changes these systems as well as replacing the former government.[112] In chapter 20 of *Leviathan*, Hobbes had argued that the right of dominion comes about by the covenant or submission of the vanquished, and not by victory or conquest (which he apparently equates); he opposes one who 'is Conquered; that is to say, beaten, and taken, or put to flight' to one who 'commeth in, and Submitteth to the Victor'.[113] Now he

---

[107] Ascham, *Confusions*, 121.   [108] Review, par. 10, p. 392.

[109] Review, paras. 10–11, pp. 392–3.   [110] Review, par. 6, p. 390.

[111] Ascham, *Confusions*, 119.   [112] Ibid. 119–20.

[113] *Leviathan* 20.11, p. 104. Fukuda notes that Hobbes's vocabulary in this chapter is different from that in the Review (*Sovereignty and the Sword*, 61–6).

appropriates the distinction between victory and conquest to make his point, while defining away the substance of Ascham's distinction.

> He . . . that is slain, is Overcome, but not Conquered: He that is taken, and put into prison, or chaines, is not Conquered, though Overcome . . . But he that upon promise of Obedience, hath his Life and Liberty allowed him, is then Conquered, and a Subject. . . . So that *Conquest* (to define it) is the Acquiring of the Right of Soveraignty by Victory. Which Right, is acquired, in the peoples Submission, by which they contract with the Victor, promising Obedience, for Life and Liberty.[114]

Ascham regards changes of governments as events that befall the people, and concerns himself with showing them that they need not fight to defend shadowy claims of right, but may tender their obedience to the latest arrival and get on with their lives. Hobbes forges a closer link between obedience and right, arguing that government only changes with the will of the people.

It thus emerges that intellectual historians are right to think that in the Review Hobbes engaged in a debate of the day. Such historians must be wary, however, of the occupational temptation to think that seminal political events (such as the execution of Charles I and the settlement of the Commonwealth) or intellectual events (such as the defences of obedience to the new regime, whether on the foundation of *de facto* power or popular consent) must be reflected by a shift in the thought of philosophers.[115] What we find in Hobbes's case is that, for the most part, he briefly enters the fray in order to show that his theory is *un*affected by such events—while cleverly using the vocabulary of contemporary theorists to do so.

Hobbes can no more be grouped with the *de facto* theorists of obligation than he can be grouped with the royalists. Indeed, he rejects their central thesis, that we owe obligation to a power that is *de facto* but not *de jure*, and he pointedly criticizes and is criticized by their pre-eminent theorist, Anthony Ascham. Integral to Hobbes's criticism is an insistence that one becomes obligated to obey a conqueror as one's rightful sovereign if and only if one consents to his protection. This position also serves to distinguish him from the contemporary theorists who derive *de jure* authority immediately from *de facto* power, and their most prominent theorist, Marchamont Nedham. The supposedly *de facto* Review is particularly helpful in measuring Hobbes's distance from this kind of *de facto* theory as well.

---

[114] Review, par. 7, p. 391. The addition of 'overcoming' appears to be Hobbes's adaptation of Ascham's 'over-running', transposed to the individual scale Hobbes prefers to illustrate the distinctions, and again shorn of the content Ascham had attributed to it.

[115] The vice of historians who insist that major political and intellectual upheavals must be reflected by adjustments in philosophy may be considered the excess corresponding to the deficiency of those who naively assume that a philosopher's corpus has an underlying coherence regardless of the changing circumstances in which it was written. The latter is convincingly criticized by Skinner in *Visions of Politics, Volume 1: Regarding Method* (Cambridge: Cambridge University Press, 2002), 67–72.

III. CONSENT THEORY: THE REVIEW AND
THE ACCEPTANCE OF RULE

Of the other 'English Books lately printed', the one that Hobbes is most likely to have in mind is the second edition of Nedham's *The Case of the Commonwealth of England, Stated*, which appeared by late October of 1650. This work, by a Commonwealth propagandist, included an appendix in which extracts from *De Corpore Politico* were used to support the argument for the authority of the new government. Attached to the royal court and writing a book he probably intended to dedicate to Charles II, Hobbes is not likely to have welcomed the attention. Nedham had just addressed the three questions about conquest that Hobbes says have not been adequately answered in the books he has recently read,[116] and had missed the basic point that Hobbes thinks explains what conquest is, and how and when the conquered become obliged. That point, which 'implyeth them all', is the voluntary submission of the conquered.[117]

Like Ascham, Rous had argued that 'those whose Title is held unlawfull, yet . . . may lawfully be obeyed'.[118] Nedham appropriates Rous's evidence and argument,[119] but continues far beyond their original scope: 'Thus by all the premises it is undeniably evident . . . that the present prevailing party in England have a right and just title to be our governors; and that this new government . . . is as valid, *de jure*, as if it had the ratifying consent of the whole body of the people.'[120] Nedham's case, however, is precisely that no such ratifying consent is necessary for the conquest to have taken place or for the new government to rule by right. To the 'objection which insinuates that our present governors have no call or consent of the people', Nedham flatly replies: 'the controversy touching government is decided by the sword. For, *ipso facto*, the sword creates a title for him, or those, that bear it and installs them with a new majesty of empire, abolishing the old.'[121] Nedham

---

[116] As Wallace observes, 'Nedham differs from other Engagers chiefly in being more explicit and uninhibited in his view of the conquest which has taken place' ('Engagement Controversy', 399).

[117] *Review*, par. 7, p. 391.   [118] Rous, *Lawfulnes of obeying*, 6.

[119] On p. 28 of *Case of the Commonwealth*, Nedham quotes without acknowledgement this passage (and more) from Rous. Nedham strikes out on his own from there, adding: 'Nor *may* they only, but they *must*; . . . such as refuse may be punished as seditious and traitorous, the victors being ever allowed, *jure gentium* . . . to exercise a right of dominion over the conquered party.' Nedham only alludes to his debts to Rous at a couple of places, and never by name. The first such point comes in discussing Henry VII: 'This Henry, from whom the late King derived his claim, came in with an army, and, as one hath well observed, by mere power was made king in the army and by the army' (p. 27). Nedham is quoting here from *Lawfulnes of Obeying*, p. 5; Rous's own account of Henry VII is based on John Speed, *The History of Great Britaine under the Conquests of yᵉ Romans, Saxons, Danes and Normans* (London, 1611), 710–52.

[120] Nedham, *Case of the Commonwealth*, 40.

[121] Ibid. 38. Invoking Christoph Besold's 1620 *Synopsis politicae doctrinae*, Nedham maintains that a change of government may occur *either* by force and power, *or* by consent.

declares that 'the Power of the Sword Is, and Ever Hath Been, the Foundation of All Titles to Government', and gives example after example, from Nebuchadnezzar ('being once in possession by conquest, his title became right and good') to William the Conqueror (who 'legitimated his title by the success of several battles') and beyond.[122] Most recently, then, the king, lords, and excluded members of the House of Commons had all lost their titles by right of war, and the remaining victorious parliament bears the sole right of rule.[123]

Nedham's rejection of the requirement of popular consent for the right of rule makes him a good representative of the *de facto* theorists of authority, and a good candidate for someone whom Hobbes is attacking in the Review. This rejection demonstrates the seemingly irreconcilable difference between Nedham and Hobbes on exactly the question of how *de facto* power is justified. Repeating his argument from *The Elements of Law*, *De Cive*, and the body of *Leviathan*, Hobbes argues in the Review that one is only 'Conquered, and a Subject' upon his own 'promise of Obedience', and that 'the Right of Soveraignty by Victory' arises only via 'the peoples Submission, by which they contract with the Victor, promising Obedience'.[124] For Hobbes, political obligation and authority depend on popular consent, the traditional requirement of the revolutionary. Taken on its own, this insistence on founding *de jure* authority on the consent of the people is more like the view of Milton than of Ascham, or Nedham, or a traditional royalist.[125] In reiterating the theory of his earlier works, which depends on both consent and possession, Hobbes employs some premisses dear to Independents and democrats, and others more typical of moderate Presbyterians and *de facto* theorists.

In his classic analyses of Hobbes and his relation to the *de facto* theorists, Skinner repeatedly elides Hobbes's persistent prerequisite of the consent of the conquered. Both those who aligned themselves with Hobbes and those who distanced themselves from him characterized him as one who thinks that power alone gives the right of dominion, and Skinner uses this as evidence for the accuracy of his characterization.[126] He maintains that Hobbes—along with Hawke, Nedham, and Ascham—holds that 'the possession of power itself established a title to be obeyed.'[127] Warrender succinctly points out the incompleteness of this account: 'Hobbes cannot go the whole way with naive

[122] Nedham, *Case of the Commonwealth*, 15, 19, 26.   [123] Ibid. 36–7.

[124] Review, par. 7, p. 391.

[125] See, e.g., Clarendon, *A Brief View*, 59: 'His Majesty is inherent in his office, and neither one or other is conferred upon him by the people.' For Milton's insistence on the consent of the people as a necessary condition for political authority, see especially *The Tenure of Kings and Magistrates* (London, 1649).   [126] Skinner, 'Ideological Context', 301–3; cf. *Visions*, 271–3.

[127] Skinner, 'Ideological Context', p. 307. Here the assimilation is with Hawke; on p. 312, a similar 'Hobbesian defence of *de facto* power' is attributed to Nedham and Ascham. Cf. *Visions*, 276, 278–80.

de facto theory. He is very firm on the position that it is not conquest *per se* that gives the right to dominion, but the covenant of the vanquished.'[128] In a striking reversal, Skinner himself has acknowledged that for Hobbes, 'right and obligation can never be derived simply from conquest or victory.'[129] Skinner concludes that, contrary to his earlier interpretation, Hobbes's view of political obligation cannot be assimilated to that of the *de facto* theorists.[130]

Hobbes's conclusions about the right of dominion and the obligation of obedience are, Skinner argues, 'based not just on a clarification but on a revision of his earlier arguments'.[131] Thus, 'in *The Elements of Law* he still espouses the orthodox position he repudiates in *Leviathan*', where (especially in the Review) 'he unequivocally asserts' that one who submits to a conqueror to avoid death submits voluntarily and as a free man.[132] And Hobbes is hereby able to make 'a novel and dramatic intervention in the arguments about conquest and allegiance'.[133] According to Skinner's account, Hobbes intervenes both against the Levellers' view that the Rump Parliament lacked consent and therefore lacked rightful authority, and against those defenders of the Rump who argued that despite lacking consent they had a right of conquest. To some extent, however, Hobbes's polemical objective in these arguments is to support the paradoxical conclusion that the royalists (if otherwise unprotected) are at liberty to submit to the parliamentary government, while the supporters of parliament were not, having had contrary obligations.[134] The parliamentarians thus find one of their favourite claims inverted: in the context of the English civil wars, only those they regard as *royalists* submit to the government as free men.

In addition, the account Skinner offers may overplay the uniqueness of *Leviathan*. The position he finds there is one that Hobbes also holds in *The Elements of Law* and in *De Cive*. Hobbes states in *The Elements of Law* that the victor obtains a right of dominion over the conquered by a covenant, which is a voluntary act; equates liberty with lack of subjection; distinguishes between the servant or subject who bound himself freely and the slave without obligation; insists that both sovereignty by mutual covenants of the subjects and sovereignty by covenant with a master are based on fear, and that actions done from fear are voluntary; and holds that

---

[128] Warrender, 'Political Theory and Historiography: A Reply to Professor Skinner on Hobbes', *The Historical Journal* 22/4 (1979), 938.

[129] Skinner, *Visions*, 232 ('Proper Signification', 146): Skinner is evidently working from *Leviathan* 20, where conquest and victory are synonyms, rather than the Review.

[130] Skinner, *Visions*, 232 ('Proper Signification', 145 and n. 155); cf. *Visions*, 305 n. 116.

[131] Skinner, *Visions*, 236 ('Proper Signification', 149).

[132] Skinner, *Visions*, 236 ('Proper Signification', 149–50). On the Review, see *Visions*, 233–4, 237 ('Proper signification', 147–8, 151).   [133] *Visions*, 236 ('Proper Signification', 150).

[134] Cf. Review, paras. 5–6, pp. 390–1.

covenants made from fear are obligatory.[135] And he continues to hold these positions in *De Cive*.[136] It is true that there are some apparent inconsistencies with these doctrines in these works. There is no need to appeal to current events or debates, however, to explain why Hobbes eliminated ambiguities or contradictions in subsequent redactions of his theory (as anyone who has worked through several drafts of an argument can attest). And it is worth asking whether what appear to be contradictory claims about the indispensability of consent for obligation and authority—*including* cases thereof from *Leviathan*—are truly contradictory.

Hobbes is concerned with liberty in the Review, as Skinner effectively underlines. Hobbes is also interested in a kind of necessity, which he often calls 'natural necessity'. For Hobbes, liberty and necessity are compatible, and this is certainly true of natural necessity: striving for self-preservation is a natural necessity in which one nonetheless engages freely. One who submits to a conqueror does so voluntarily, but one also does so necessarily.[137] If the sovereign's right and the subject's obligation both flow from the necessity of the subject's nature, the distance between possessing supreme power and bearing *de jure* authority—supposed to be the dimension of consent—shrinks, perhaps to nothing.

Moreover, as Skinner himself compellingly demonstrated in earlier essays, a host of contemporaries read Hobbes as saying that power alone could confer right and require obligation. *De facto* theorists of authority claimed Hobbes as one of their own,[138] and critics regarded him as the leading exponent of such a theory. At the University of Cambridge, Daniel Scargill is required to recant his Hobbesian tenet 'that all right of Dominion is founded onely in power', while at the University of Oxford, members are forbidden to read *De cive* and *Leviathan*, which are burnt for the teaching that 'possession and strength give a right to govern'.[139] John Bramhall thinks that Hobbes's 'greatest errour is ... to make Justice to be the proper result of Power';[140] Samuel Parker thinks that according to the drift of

---

[135] *Elements* 21.15, 22.2, 22.7, 29.2 (covenant with a conqueror is voluntary); 23.9 (liberty is the state of not being a subject, except for one sense); 22.2–3 (servants vs. slaves); 19.11, 12.3 (actions from fear voluntary); 15.13 (validity of covenants extorted by fear).

[136] e.g. *De Cive* 2.16, 5.12, 7.18, 8.1–4, 17.6.

[137] Again, this is 'natural' necessity: Hobbes emphasizes that people do act against the dictates of nature and reason. For an enlightening account of this emphasis, see S. A. Lloyd, *Ideals as Interests in Hobbes's* Leviathan: *The Power of Mind over Matter* (Cambridge: Cambridge University Press, 1992).

[138] e.g., Michael Hawke, *Killing is Murder and No Murder* (London, 1657), 12.

[139] *The Recantation of Daniel Scargill, Publickly made before the University of Cambridge* ... (Cambridge, 1669), 4 (cf. p. 1); *The Judgment and Decree of the University of Oxford Past in their Convocation July 21, 1683* ... (Oxford, 1683), 4.

[140] Bramhall, *Defence of True Liberty from Antecedent and Extrinsecall Necessity* ... (London, 1655), 85 (Hobbes, *English Works*, 136).

Hobbes's teaching, when men 'have Power to shake off Authority, they have Right too; and a prosperous Usurper shall have as fair a Title to his Crown as the most lawful Prince'.[141] Thomas Tenison says that Hobbes 'placeth right in present might', and that he holds that the title of Charles I 'was extinguish'd when his adherents were subdu'd; and that the Parliament had the Right for that very Reason, because it had possession.'[142] Hobbes is read this way even before the wave of tendentious reaction to *Leviathan* distorted public perception; the earliest German reactions to Hobbes, for example, focus on his derivation of the right to rule from power.[143] These are just a few of the scores of such characterizations published during the seventeenth century. If a chorus of his contemporaries is to be believed, Hobbes holds that *de facto* power is sufficient for *de jure* authority. We have seen evidence, however, that Hobbes holds that power does *not* suffice; and it is possible, of course, that all of these contemporaries were wrong.

If to be wrong in this sense is to attribute to Hobbes something he never said, these contemporaries were so far manifestly right. In passage after passage, Hobbes subscribes to some version of the thesis that sufficient power by itself confers the right to rule. In *The Elements of Law* he argues that 'irresistible might in the state of nature is right'; that according to nature '*jus* and *utile*, right and profit, is the same thing', and 'in manifest inequality might is right'; and that 'this right of conquest, as it maketh one man master over another, so also maketh it a man to be master of the irrational creatures.'[144] The sovereign in a despotical or patrimonial state has all the same rights of sovereignty as a sovereign by institution, even though such a body is generated 'out of nothing' by 'natural force'.[145] In *De cive*, he maintains that 'in the state of nature the Measure of *right* is Profit', that 'the victor may by *right* compel the vanquished, or the stronger the weaker', and that 'in the natural state of men, sure and irresistible power confers the right of ruling and commanding those who cannot resist'; and he concludes that 'Those whose power cannot be resisted, and by consequence God *omnipotent*, derive the right of dominion from the *power* itself.'[146]

---

[141] [Parker], *A Discourse of Ecclesiastical Politie* . . . (London, 1670), 141.

[142] Tenison, *The Creed of Mr. Hobbes*, sigg. b2ʳ, A3ᵛ; cf. pp. 144–6, 152, 156–7.

[143] Noel Malcolm, *Aspects of Hobbes* (Oxford University Press, 2002), 474 n. 63. Malcolm refers to criticisms of *De Cive* by Franz-Julius Chopius in *Philosophia juris vera* (Leipzig, 1650), and by Hermann Conring in a letter of 23 Jan. 1651.

[144] *Elements* 14.13, 14.10, heading of 14.13, 22.9. For the last point, see *De cive* 8.10: 'right over animals lacking reason is doubtlessly acquired in the same way as over the *persons* of men, by natural strength and power' ('eodem modo acquiritur ius in animalia ratione carentia, quo in *personas* hominum; nimirum viribus & potentiis naturalibus').

[145] *Elements* 23.10, 20.1 (cf. *De Cive* 9.10). He also distinguishes conquest and voluntary submission, while insisting that they do not entail any different rights of ruling.

[146] *De Cive* 1.10 ('in statu naturae Mensuram *iuris* esse Vtilitatem'), 1.14 (cf. n. 99, above), and 15.5 ('Iis . . . quorum potentiae resisti non potest, & per consequens Deo *omnipotenti*, ius dominandi ab ipsa *potentiâ* deriuatur').

He further claims that 'All right over others is either from *Nature* or from *Agreement*', and 'a *natural commonwealth* . . . may also be called *Acquired*, seeing that it is acquired by power and natural strength.'[147]

In *Leviathan*, too, Hobbes argues that sovereign right may arise from pact *or* from nature, and that 'to shew how that same Right may arise from Nature, requires no more, but to shew in what case it is never taken away. . . . To those therefore whose Power is irresistible, the dominion of all men adhaereth naturally by their excellence of Power.' One way to attain sovereignty is 'by Naturall force', and the rights of this form of sovereignty are the same as those of sovereignty that arises by mutual covenant.[148] Skinner says that in the Review Hobbes treats it 'as an error to suppose that plenary possession makes a lawful power';[149] two sentences after the evidence Skinner quotes for this, however, Hobbes argues that it is an error for civil sovereigns to maintain that their right depends on the justification of how they came to power, rather than on the possession of that power.[150] And he says that over all people outside the Jewish commonwealth, God reigns as sovereign 'not by their consent, but by his own Power'.[151] Not least, Hobbes repeatedly collapses relevant distinctions that earlier theorists had laboured to delineate: in particular, he frequently treats power as interchangeable with authority, rule or command, and dominion.[152]

These passages and others like them are frequent and central enough to preclude setting them aside as passing simplifications or exaggerations. Criticisms of the view that Hobbes holds that power justifies—including Skinner's own later disavowal of that view—have relied solely on pointing out that it does not account for other passages that require consent, without providing any explanation of the kind of passages cited above. Hobbes repeatedly says that the right of the sovereign can arise from mere power;

---

[147] *De Cive* 15.5 ('Ius enim omne in alios vel à *Natura* est, vel à *Pacto*') and 8.1 ('*ciuitate naturali* . . . & *Acquisita* dici potest, quippe quae acquiritur potentiâ & viribus naturalibus': cf. 5.12).

[148] *Leviathan* 31.5, p. 187; 17.15, p. 88. In *Leviathan* 27.10, Hobbes says that men have 'observed how in all places, and in all ages, unjust Actions have been authorised, by the force, and victories of those who have committed them'. Hobbes does not explicitly question this observation, but only the faulty reasoning by which false principles are drawn from it (that justice is but a vain word, that whatever a man can get is his own, etc.). If he does mean to question it implicitly, it is in the sense of Review, par. 8, pp. 391–2: actions that were unjust before one had sovereign power are not themselves retroactively justified by that power (though if the sovereign requires public acknowledgement of their justice, one must obey), while subsequent actions are just so long as power is retained.

[149] Skinner, *Visions*, 235 ('Proper Signification', 149).   [150] Review, par. 8, p. 391.

[151] Review, par. 10, p. 392.

[152] For an excellent discussion of the synonymy of these terms, see Luc Foisneau, 'Le vocabulaire du pouvoir: *potentia/potestas, power*', in Yves Charles Zarka (ed.), *Hobbes et son vocabulaire* (Paris: Vrin, 1992), 83–102. Because he believes that for Hobbes power justifies only in the case of God (cf. n. 160, below), Foisneau is driven to consider it a 'misuse' when Hobbes uses 'potentia' (i.e. mere power or strength) as if it were a further synonym in this chain: 'strictly speaking, the right of sovereignty results from contract, and not at all from power' (p. 95).

he also repeatedly requires consent (or covenant, or assent) to such power as a condition of such right. He even says that the natural sovereignty that arises by force rather than agreement is itself dependent on consent.[153] Again, contemporaries criticize and reflect the apparent equivocation. If the conqueror is in the state of nature, Filmer reminds us,

when he conquers he hath a right without any Covenant made with the conquered: . . . why is it said *the Right is acquired in the Peoples submission, by which they contract with the victor, promising obedience for Life and Liberty?* hath not every one in the state of nature a right to Soveraignty, before conquest, which onely puts him in possession of his Right?[154]

And Anthony Wood mirrors the ostensible ambiguity in his summary of Hobbes's political views: 'As for policy', Hobbes holds 'that might is right', *and* 'that the victor can have no right or dominion over the vanquished, but only by the vanquished's consent'.[155]

The confusion is understandable. By turns, Hobbes seems to be a committed consent theorist and a resolute *de facto* theorist of authority, and he is repeatedly described as one or the other by commentators who regard these two theories as incompatible. Hobbes appears to have endorsed both approaches, and sometimes to have presented them side by side: how might he have regarded them as consistent? The answer to this question takes us to the heart of Hobbes's theory of political obligation.

IV. NATURALISM: DERIVING 'OUGHT' FROM 'IS', AND 'IS' FROM 'OUGHT'

An initial way forward is to pick up the distinction mentioned above between two kinds of right. The first kind is a state-of-nature right, which one has without others having corresponding obligations. Everyone in the state of nature has the right to anything (or anything one judges to be necessary for self-preservation); so two or more people may have a right to a given thing that only one of them will be able to use or possess. The other kind, normally found within a commonwealth, is a right in virtue of which others are obligated to respect one's entitlement. The right to rule can operate in either way. In the state of nature, anyone has the right to rule over anyone else; but if no agreement is made, then the ruled has no obligation of obedience. This distinction helps to explain some of the preceding passages: the right of dominion over animals, for example, is a right one has

---

[153] *De Cive* 8.1.

[154] [Filmer], *Observations Concerning the Originall of Government, Upon Mr. Hobs Leviathan, Mr. Milton against Salmasius, H. Grotius De Jure Belli* (London, 1652), sig. A4ʳ, quoting the Review, par. 7, p. 391.   [155] Wood, *Athenae Oxonienses*, iii, cols. 1210, 1211.

because of the *absence* of any relations of obligation. In such a case, one must 'obey' only because one cannot do otherwise. And in this sense, the power one has over others does not create a right, but (as Filmer notices) puts one in the possession of, or in a position to act on, a precedent right. Therefore, it is not strictly true in such cases that strength *confers* right, or weakness obligation.[156]

This distinction is indispensable, but it does not explain all of the instances where Hobbes evidently countenances the idea of power conferring right. For example, as we have seen, Hobbes explicitly says that power alone *can* confer right: 'those whose power cannot be resisted, and by consequence God *omnipotent*, derive the right of dominion from the *power* itself.'[157] This is not a mere state-of-nature right, for Hobbes makes clear that a corresponding *obligation* follows from lack of power. He holds that if God has the right to reign on the basis of his omnipotence, it is evident that men incur the obligation to obey him because of their weakness. And both the obligation and the right to command 'arise from nature without the occurrence of an agreement'.[158] Yet Hobbes says that 'no one is obliged to render obedience before entering an agreement.'[159] A puzzle remains to be solved.

A simple solution to it has been proposed. A fundamental premiss of important studies by Howard Warrender and Luc Foisneau, and accepted by many others, is that for Hobbes right can be derived from power only in the case of God.[160] If this were accepted, no further consideration of the question of Hobbes's derivation of right from human power would be required. Hobbes, however, endorses just such a derivation. He argues that the victor, by virtue of his greater *force*, may *rightly* compel, and that it is 'in the natural state of *men*' that 'sure and irresistible power confers the

---

[156] Note that Hobbes does say (e.g., at *Elements* 22.2) that even a covenant may merely make an already existing right 'effectual'.

[157] *De Cive* 15.5: cf. n. 146, above. Such a claim also shows the insufficiency of understanding Hobbes's apparent equivocation about whether power justifies as an alternation between two senses of 'power', one of which connotes authority and the other mere power. In statements like this one, Hobbes is clearly restricting himself to the latter: his argument is about 'power *itself*', from which the right of dominion is *derived*. (On contemporary usage, see [Ascham], *A Reply to a Paper of Dr Sandersons*, sig. A2ʳ and p. 12; and Richard Tuck's informative '*Power* and *Authority* in seventeenth-century England', *The Historical Journal* 17/1 (1974), 43–61.)

[158] *De Cive* 15.7: 'nullo intercedente pacto, à naturâ oritur'.

[159] *De Cive* 17.6: 'neque obligatur quisquam ad obedientiam praestandam ante pactum initum'.

[160] This is a basic point of Warrender's *The Political Philosophy of Hobbes: His Theory of Obligation* (Oxford: Clarendon, 1957). See, e.g., p. 317: 'Though there is a sense in which irresistible power obliges and justifies itself, less power does not, and for all the less degrees of power there is always a clear distinction in Hobbes's doctrine between having the power to do something and having the right to do it.' It is also central to Foisneau's *Hobbes et la toute-puissance de Dieu* (Paris: Presses Universitaires de France, 2000): 'the transformation of power into right only holds for God: the right of the stronger remains at the horizon of the human condition, but this horizon is by definition unreachable' (pp. 3–4; cf. pp. 142–4, 148–50, 281–2, 398).

right of ruling and commanding.'[161] The principle that right derives from irresistible power is taken to follow from ('from this may also be understood, as a corollary') what can be granted in human situations: 'And the victor may *by right* compel the vanquished, or the stronger the weaker (as one hardy and healthy may one who is feeble, or an adult an infant).'[162] Elsewhere, Hobbes refers to one who 'hath already subdued his adversary, or gotten into his power any other that either by infancy, or weakness, is unable to resist him': it is 'out of' such *human* examples that Hobbes concludes that 'irresistible might in the state of nature is right.'[163] Hobbes hereafter says that 'no man is of might sufficient to assure himself for any long time, of preserving himself thereby, whilst he remaineth in the state of hostility and war'; this is not to say, however, that there can be no irresistible human power, but only that it cannot be enduringly irresistible.[164] If there is no contrary prevailing power, irresistibility confers right; and *therefore* omnipotence confers right over everything, or absolute right.

In his dispute with Bramhall, Hobbes does say that 'Power irresistible justifieth all actions really and properly in whomsoever it be found. Less power does not. And because such power is in God only, he must needs be just in all his actions.'[165] Hobbes must mean 'irresistible' without limitation here, which is why such power is in God only and it justifies *all* his actions. Bramhall takes Hobbes to be limiting justification by power to God in this passage, but points out that 'the same privilege which *T.H.* appropriates here to power absolutely irresistible, a friend of his in his book *de Cive* . . . ascribes to power respectively irresistible, or to Sovereign Magistrates . . . *T.H.* will have no limits but their strength. Whatsoever they do by power, they do justly.'[166] Hobbes clarifies his position, not by denying that might makes right in the case of the human sovereign, but by affirming that only God has absolute right on this basis: 'I said no more but that the Power which is *absolutely* irresistible makes him that hath it above *all* Law, so that *nothing* he doth can be unjust. But *this* Power can be no other than the Power divine.'[167] Hobbes's point is not that only absolutely irresistible

---

[161] *De Cive* 1.14: 'in statu *hominum* naturali, potentiam certam & irresistibilem, ius conferre regendi, imperandique' (emphasis altered).

[162] *De Cive* 1.14: 'ex quo intelligitur etiam, tanquam corollarium'; 'Potest autem victor victum, vel fortior debiliorem (vt sanus & robustus infirmum, vel maturus infantem) . . . *iure* cogere.'

[163] *Elements* 14.13.

[164] Ibid. 14.14. Hobbes's examples of human irresistibility are typically of one individual wielding irresistible power over another; he recognizes that such irresistibility may be compromised by time (e.g., the infant may grow in strength), and also that it may be negated by number (e.g., the feeble may resist the strong if there are enough of them). In *Leviathan*, for example, Hobbes emphasizes the importance of confederacy or number at 13.1, p. 60; 13.3, p. 61; and 17.3, pp. 85–6.

[165] *The Questions Concerning Liberty, Necessity, and Chance* (London, 1656), 89 (*English Works*, v. 116); cf. *Leviathan* 31.5, p. 187.

[166] *Defence of True Liberty*, 82–3 (*Questions*, 101–2: *English Works*, v. 133).

[167] *Questions*, p. 111, emphases added (*English Works*, v. 146).

power justifies, but that only absolutely irresistible power justifies everything. The puzzle persists, for Hobbes does countenance the justificatory capacity of human power and the potential for human weakness to create obligation. One way to state the predicament would be: how is it that there is plentiful evidence for Skinner's earlier claim that for Hobbes power can suffice for authority and obligation *and* for his later claim that Hobbes requires consent, and therefore power cannot suffice?

Hobbes explicitly holds that consent is a necessary condition for obligation and authority. He also holds that consent can be inferred from certain states of affairs. So it is understandable that Hobbes sometimes states that obligation and authority follow from certain states of affairs. In casting the net of obligation as widely as possible, consent is sometimes stretched vanishingly thin. He allows consent to be tacit, so that one who openly lives under a government and receives protection from it thereby consents, and so authorizes the sovereign and obligates himself.[168] This extension of consent allows us to see how it is that Hobbes sometimes treats the possession of sovereign power as sufficient for sovereign right. If one possesses secure power over a body of people (who are, as can be expected, receiving protection from that power), his power is consented to by them, and therefore he is their legitimate sovereign. If the government were contested by enough of the population, there would be civil war rather than sovereign authority. Thus, the legitimacy of power and the obligation of obedience reliably follow from (and are indicated by) the possession of power.

Hobbes employs a related and even more extended use of consent, giving rise to the temptation to describe authority and obligation as arising without consent. To retain for now the ambiguity about whether this is true consent or a mere ascription of consent, I shall call this 'attributed consent', 'presumed consent', or (following usage of the sixteenth and seventeenth centuries), 'interpretative consent'. Hobbes argues that the covenant of obedience, usually thought to be undertaken through declaration by word or deed, can instead be *attributed* when a given will or intention can be understood or assumed. The argument, very briefly, is this.[169] 'Every man, not onely by Right, but also by necessity of Nature, is *supposed* to endeavour all he can, to obtain that which is necessary for his conservation'; 'every man is *presumed* to do all things in order to his own benefit.'[170] These are conclusions from Hobbes's anthropology, his theory of human nature. To choose that by

---

[168] Review, par. 7, p. 391; cf. *Questions*, pp. 136–7, 347 (*English Works*, v. 180, 453). The 'mutuall Relation between Protection and Obedience' (Review, par. 17, pp. 395–6) makes no mention of consent, as if obedience is due immediately to one's protecting power; the consent must be implied or understood, as Hobbes's discussion of the relation makes clear.

[169] For a more detailed version of the argument, see Part Two of Hoekstra, *Thomas Hobbes and the Creation of Order* (forthcoming from Oxford University Press).

[170] *Leviathan* 15.17 and 31, pp. 76, 78; emphases added.

which one is left in or returns to a state of nature would be to contradict this naturally necessary desire: 'for every man by natural necessity desireth his own good, to which this estate is contrary'.[171] Not to covenant to obey a sovereign able to protect one when there is a realistic option of such a sovereign would be to act contrary to one's own preservation or benefit.[172] Therefore, one may be presumed to covenant. We can see here why contemporaries say that Hobbes holds that the power to rule constitutes the right to rule: might implies consent, and consent confers right, therefore might implies right.

One can choose to emphasize that if consent follows from power, then power *alone* can never entail right. This is to surrender, however, the essential objection against the thesis that might makes right—that there may be a power that has no right. It may be objected that Hobbes, in his most thorough defence of the ineliminability of consent for obligation, makes clear that 'the Conquerour makes no Law over the Conquered by vertue of his power; but by vertue of their assent.'[173] Hobbes says, however, that even 'in receiving . . . protection they have assented',[174] so the mere fact of their being alive counts for assent (whenever there exists a power that can destroy them). The objection could be pressed that Hobbes does not regard this as a *reductio ad absurdum*: 'May not I rather dye, if I think fit?'[175] At this point, however, we may conclude that all of the living have consented to the power over them, if there is one. The only people free of obligation to the present power are the dead (and slaves in shackles). To say that might makes right over the subdued is to say that might makes right.

Hobbes's requirement that all obligation depends on consent ('there being no Obligation on any man, which ariseth not from some Act of his own'[176]) is often cited to show that he is, foundationally, a liberal of some kind, or that, more particularly, he is a consent theorist. However, the very ubiquity of consent, as the foundation of all obligations, has an opposite effect.[177]

---

[171] *Elements* 14.12.

[172] Such a covenant is required by the law of nature, so it will be a dictate of moral duty as well as prudence (cf., e.g., *Leviathan* 14.3, p. 64).

[173] *Questions*, pp. 136–7 (*English Works*, v. 180).

[174] *Questions*, p. 137 (*English Works*, v. 180).

[175] *Questions*, p. 136 (*English Works*, v. 180).

[176] *Leviathan* 21.10, p. 111. Note that the requisite 'Act' need only be a sign of the will, and this can, in turn, be assumed in some circumstances without (or even in spite of) a contrary indication of the will. The will can be signified by silence or inaction in the face of what can be supposed to be a natural priority. Cf. *Elements* 23.11–15, 29.10; *De Cive* 2.18–19, 6.20, 7.17, 9.14–19, 17.27; *Leviathan* 14.8 (p. 66), 14.29–30 (p. 70), 18.17 (p. 93), 19.18–22 (pp. 100–1), 21.20 (p. 113), 22.11 (p. 117), 23.3 (p. 124), 27.28 (p. 157); *Behemoth*, 118.

[177] In *Questions*, even moral requirements such as that not to kill are founded on consent; that consent is, again, the consent that can be presumed to be given to the necessary means for our survival. Hobbes argues that the law of nature itself is a law with our assent, and even that 'the Law of Nature is the Assent it self, that all men give to the means of their own preservation' (*Questions*, 137: *English Works*, v. 180). Elsewhere (e.g., *De Cive* 14.2, 16.10), Hobbes says that

Whereas Hobbes is often understood to use consent as the test of whether or not there is obligation, at times he instead infers consent from a situation in which there must be obligation. In this sense, one *has* consented when one *ought* to have consented.

In a number of passages where Hobbes has been taken to be outlining a contract by which citizens authorize a government, he is, strictly speaking, describing the supposition of a covenant given the necessity of it. So, for example, he says that 'it is *necessary* for the preservation of individuals that there be some one Assembly or one man who has the rights' of sovereignty; 'It is to be *understood*, therefore, that the individual citizens *have transferred* their whole right of war and peace to one man or assembly.'[178] Hobbes argues that obligation to the sovereign 'must either be drawn from the expresse words, *I Authorise all his Actions*, or from the Intention of him that submitteth himselfe to his Power, (which Intention is to be understood by the End for which he so submitteth)', namely, internal peace and external defence.[179] That is, the contours of the subject's obligation may be determined by those of an attributed intention. Hobbes attempts to undermine the Aristotelian bifurcations between tyrant and king and between despotical and political rule; he also strives to disable the distinction between *de facto* and *de jure* rule that underlies these. With the theory of attributed consent, Hobbes argues that 'whatsoever is *necessary* to be by covenant transferred for the attaining thereof [i.e. of security], so much *is* transferred.'[180] In an ordinary case of *de facto* rule, we can justifiably presume consent, and so the rule is *de jure*.

This explains how Hobbes appears to be a consent theorist and a *de facto* theorist of authority. If tacit and attributed consent count as consent, then he may be considered a thoroughgoing consent theorist. If they do not, then he is, after all, a *de facto* theorist of authority of a particular kind.[181] And it is on this issue that there is an especially interesting connection with the major *de facto* theorists, for each one discussed above articulates a theory of attributed or interpretative consent.

---

natural laws do *not* arise from consent; but he nonetheless insists that they are dictates of reason that ensure self-preservation (cf., e.g., *De Cive* 1.15, 2.1, 3.26–9, 3.32). If the laws of nature obligate without our consent, they will provide further bonds of obligation to protecting power: so, for example, the law of nature of gratitude requires those who have received a benefit from another not to cause him to regret having bestowed it (e.g. *Leviathan* 15.16, p. 75).

[178] *De Cive* 6.7, emphasis altered: '*necessarium* est ad singulorum conseruationem, vt sit *Concilium* aliquod *vnum*, vel *homo vnus* qui ius habeat . . . . Intelligendum ergo est singulos ciues in *vnum*, vel *hominem* vel *concilium* totum hoc *Ius belli* & *pacis* transtulisse.'

[179] *Leviathan* 21.10, p. 111. Cf. *De Cive* 3.19: 'The reason that dictates the end also dictates the necessary means' ('Ratio enim, quae iubet finem, iubet etiam media necessaria').

[180] *Elements* 20.5, emphases added.

[181] This is not to say that he is not *also* a consent theorist: he certainly thinks that sovereign right can arise, for example, from explicit consent.

Ascham devotes a section of the *Confusions* to the topic of 'How Contracts may be made with us without our Consents', in which he argues that 'there is an Obligation, yea Contract here, which comes not by consent' but by the great benefit which is received or likely to be received by someone having the power to provide for 'the Peoples Protection'.[182] Drawing on Suárez, Lessius, and Salon, Rous argues that if we are not allowed to obey someone lacking legitimate title, then—because clear titles are so rare, and so difficult to discern—we will end up in a kind of state of nature, with many tyrants instead of just one.

And hence ariseth that which they call an Interpretative consent of the people; because it is understood and supposed that every rational man doth consent, that there should be order, property and right given to every Member of a Common-Wealth under a Tyrant, rather then all to be under confusion, oppression, Robberies, & Murders.[183]

Nedham follows Rous's lead, drawing on Suárez and Grotius to argue that 'none, even of the conquered party, can be so unnatural as to desire' the violent confusion that would ensue without government: 'in this case there is no need of their express positive consent to justify a new government, so a tacit or implied consent is sufficient; which consent, as one saith well, is the very dictate of nature or common reason.'[184]

The convergence on this peculiar conception of consent is intriguing. Hobbes would not have drawn on these theorists for his understanding of

---

[182] Ascham, *Confusions*, 140, 146–7, 148.

[183] Rous, *Lawfulnes of Obeying*, 2nd edn., pp. 16–17; cf. through p. 23, esp. p. 19: 'Thus is the authority of Acting in this case grounded upon a tacite or implyed consent, which consent is the very dictate of nature or common reason, because it is better to have some justice then none at all, some coercive power and Government, then that all shall be left to disorder, violence, and confusion.' Cf. also N. W., *Northern Subscribers Plea*, 5–6; and *The Exercitation Answered*, 50: 'There is therefore a *Tacite*, and *Interpretative* consent of the people . . . when (as reason wills) they consent that the Power which is peaceably possest should Governe *pro tempore*, rather then that confusion and Warre should destroy the Common-Wealth. And such a consent is sufficient to constitute such a Magistrate.' In criticizing Rous, the author of the *Exercitation* (p. 82) agrees with the acceptability of interpretative consent: 'Every rationall man consents indeed that there should be order, property and right', etc.; but he points out that this may lead to stipulative exclusion ('you choose to suppose them that will not consent . . . to be out of the number of rationall men'), and questionable attribution ('it will be difficult to finde out, and agree, when such an interpretative consent is given by the people'). He also makes the point that a *de facto* theorist of obligation has to explain how it is that the people can consent (interpretatively or otherwise) to the rulers over them without those rulers thereby becoming legitimate, against his supposition. In condemning the 'Exercitator', Filmer simply rejects the idea of such 'supposed' consent (*Observations upon Aristotles Politiques*, 40–1; but cf. p. 49, where he reflects the influence of the *de facto* theorists and relies on 'presumed . . . will').

[184] Nedham, *Case of the Commonwealth*, 39–40. (The unnamed authority is again Rous: Nedham quotes the passage from *Lawfulnes of Obeying*, 2nd edn., p. 19, given in the previous note.) Cf. Nedham on Salmasius: 'though such as are subdued by arms lose their power by force, yet, being necessitated to yield submission to the victor, he is supposed to rule over them by their own consent' (*Case of the Commonwealth*, 130).

attributed consent, as it is an important component of his theory from 1640.[185] It is possible that they rely on him in developing the idea, but there is no evidence that they did. A more plausible hypothesis is that Hobbes drew on some of the same or related sources. Nonetheless, the affinity cannot conceal the abiding difference between Hobbes and these theorists.[186] Ascham and Rous use the notion of interpretative or attributed consent to show that plenary possession implies an obligation to obey without in any way implying the legitimate authority to rule; Nedham uses the notion alongside an argument that possession can entail obligation and authority with no consent whatsoever. Hobbes, however, had already argued that the possession of power and consent to it (in which he includes attributed consent) are the necessary and sufficient conditions for both the obligation to obey and the authority to govern.

At points in his writings, Hobbes seems to endorse royalism, a *de facto* theory of obligation, a *de facto* theory of authority, and consent theory. Faced with a brilliant philosopher who subscribes to such evidently contradictory doctrines, philosophers and historians tend to react differently; simplifying greatly, the difference may be crudely characterized as follows. Philosophers, presumably in the name of charity of interpretation, ascribe to Hobbes the view that they take to be strongest, and regard the others as more or less unfortunate utterances. Thus, they tend to focus on Hobbes the consent theorist, setting aside Hobbes's apparent royalist and *de facto* claims. Historians are inclined instead to offer a developmental account, according to which Hobbes changed his mind over time as his circumstances changed. According to Tuck, for example, Hobbes was a royalist until late in *Leviathan*, at which point he abandoned royalism for *de facto* theory; whereas Skinner (in his more recent work on the subject) thinks Hobbes revises his view from something more like *de facto* theory to a clear statement of consent theory in *Leviathan*. Briefly, the problem with the philosophical approach is that it dismisses much of what Hobbes says.[187]

---

[185] For example, in the *Elements* Hobbes says that servants have 'no other bond but a *supposed* covenant, without which the master had no reason to trust them'; and that 'it is to be *presumed*, that he which giveth sustenance to another, whereby to strengthen him, hath received a promise of obedience in consideration thereof' (22.3 and 23.3, emphases added; cf. 20.5, quoted above).

[186] Moreover, the theory of attributed consent is not at this time the exclusive domain of *de facto* defenders of obedience to the Rump, for it is also found in the works of more activist and radical writers. So John Goodwin argues that 'men's consents unto all acts manifestly tending to their relief are sufficiently expressed in their wants and necessities' (*Right and Might Well Met* (1649), in A. S. P. Woodhouse (ed.), *Puritanism and Liberty*, 2nd edn. (London: J. M. Dent, 1974), 216). See also *The Law of Freedom in a Platform: or, True Magistracy Restored* (London, 1652), at p. 538 of George H. Sabine (ed.), *The Works of Gerrard Winstanley* (Ithaca, NY: Cornell University Press, 1941).

[187] If by utterance '*U*' someone may as plausibly have meant *X* as *Y*, and if *X* and *Y* are inconsistent and *X* is a stronger theoretical view, then (other things being equal, and there being no other

The problem with the historical account is that Hobbes upholds a *de facto* theory, a kind of royalism, and consent theory *in the same works*.

The difficulty of how Hobbes can endorse both consent theory and the *de facto* theory of authority cannot be resolved by a developmental explanation, but it can be resolved conceptually, via an understanding of tacit and attributed consent. This conceptual resolution is, nonetheless, supported by contextual and textual evidence. An assimilation of Hobbes to *de facto* theory will be misleading unless it is clear that he is not a *de facto* theorist of obligation, and that he argues that *de facto* powers are *de jure* only via what he calls consent (or in the sense of a state-of-nature right). An assimilation of Hobbes's view to consent theory will be unhelpful unless what he means by consent is understood; and such an understanding precludes a complete disentanglement from the *de facto* theory of authority. The difficulty of how Hobbes can expound royalism and the *de facto* theory of obligation while still holding a kind of *de facto* theory of authority can be resolved by appealing to his presentism and his doctrine of doctrines. This is a developmental account—so Hobbes only publishes the *de facto* theory of obligation after the Restoration, and only proclaims royalist principles while under the protection of a monarch—but this account *follows from* reading Hobbes as writing consistently with his own conceptual analysis of political obligation and authority.

Hobbes's theory of authority and obligation involves two sets of what are taken to be facts—the fact of power and the facts of human nature—and the normative requirements and entitlements that he argues follow from their conjunction. Thus, he is more aptly characterized as a political naturalist than as a *de facto* theorist.[188] It is because of what he previously concludes about the 'nature, need, and designes of men', that he argues that the

---

candidate interpretations) X should be attributed as the meaning of '*U*'. This is what charity of interpretation requires. If, however, someone expresses distinct views, then it should be a move of last resort (all else being equal) to set aside a weaker view as in some way not really that person's view on the sole basis of his support for what is perceived as a stronger view inconsistent with it.

[188] Again, this is not to say that he is only a naturalist: although he apparently thinks that normative commitments and entitlements may follow from sets of facts, it does not follow that he thinks that this can be their only source.

Consideration of Hobbes as a naturalist has focused on the contract as the philosopher's stone that is supposed to transform facts into values. This emphasis, however, has often obscured the nature of Hobbes's naturalism. 'The contractarian is expressly opposed to any theory of the state that would see it as natural rather than as a product of human choice', argues Jean Hampton (*Hobbes and the Social Contract Tradition* (Cambridge University Press, 1986), 272): 'there are no natural masters and no natural slaves; so rulers must be chosen, because they do not arise naturally.' Hobbes is rather a kind of 'compatibilist' between natural sovereignty and sovereignty by consent. Rulers do arise naturally, but nonetheless must be consented to; and their power itself can generally be a sufficient sign of consent. So 'choice' of the naturally predominant is tantamount to artificial predominance, which is tantamount to sovereignty and its attendant authority and obligation. (An argument for inequalities of power and patterns of dominance in Hobbes's state of nature is presented in Part One of Hoekstra, *Thomas Hobbes and the Creation of Order*.)

fact of sovereign power requires them to act in certain ways.[189] Hobbes's naturalism proceeds via the attribution of artifice given human nature in the context of present power.

Hobbes's basic commitment to peace and security precludes a fixed allegiance to any person, family, party, or form of government. The consistency of Hobbes's principles is not compromised by their requiring obedience now to the royal party, now to the parliamentary, for it is the same principle, based on the facts of human nature, that requires obedience to each in turn as the political facts change. Hobbes did not turn his political theory away from its underlying allegiance; rather, that allegiance required a political theory that would turn with the times.

---

[189] *Leviathan* 20.15, p. 105. So James Lowde complains of Hobbes that 'sometimes from the meer Fact he infers the *jus* of a thing' (*A Discourse concerning the Nature of Man, both in his Natural and Political Capacity* . . . (London, 1694), sig. [A6]ᵛ. Cf. Leibniz's criticism of Hobbes's derivation of right from power: 'This is a failure to distinguish between right and fact. For what one can do is one thing, what one should do, another' (Patrick Riley (ed.), *Political Writings*, 2nd edn. (Cambridge: Cambridge University Press, 1988), 47; Riley dates this to 1702–3). Such quick dismissals of naturalism, relying on assumptions that any such theory depends on a simple fallacy or category mistake, continue to be commonplace.

The Uniqueness of Leviathan: Authorizing Poets, Philosophers, and Sovereigns

TED H. MILLER

What, if anything, makes *Leviathan* unique? Most readers will not be troubled to read more than one of Hobbes's books, and *Leviathan*, his signature work, is their most likely choice. Asking the question may seem to be a way of asking what makes Hobbes unique, but for Hobbes scholars the question suggests something more complex. It asserts itself first against the background of a perceived similarity between the three systematic and comprehensive statements of his political philosophy. The two others are *De Cive* and *Elements of Law*.[1] On second blush, *Leviathan* covers numerous facets of Hobbes's philosophy, not merely his political philosophy, and this has meant that points of comparison also suggest themselves with Hobbes's entire corpus.[2] Thus, claims concerning *Leviathan*'s uniqueness have typically demanded that one show that there are real differences between the different versions of his political philosophy. The practice has become so well developed that we are now at the point where some interpreters have argued that differences thought to be appreciable are in fact only skin deep.[3] *Leviathan*'s uniqueness has, however, proven a productive question. Although Hobbes scholars find themselves constrained to approach it in terms of comparisons between works, the conclusions have often included claims that purport to tell us what made Hobbes at least an

---

[1] Howard Warrender's edition of the seventeenth-century translation of *De Cive*, *Philosophical Rudiments Concerning Government and Society*, invites comparisons between *De Cive*, *Elements of Law*, and *Leviathan*, through the inclusion of marginal references to the corresponding, or non-corresponding, passages in the later two. These references and Warrender's remarks on the preparation of the edition exemplify the tensions that the presumptive sameness between editions has created for Hobbes scholars: Thomas Hobbes, *De Cive: The English Version*, ed. Howard Warrender (Oxford: Clarendon Press, 1983), 11, *passim*.

[2] See, e.g. F. S. McNeilly, *The Anatomy of Leviathan* (New York: St. Martin's Press, 1968), especially Part I.

[3] e.g. Johann P. Sommerville, *Thomas Hobbes: Political Ideas in Historical Context* (New York: St. Martin's Press, 1992), 119–27, concerning what he suggests are merely superficial differences on matters of church authority between *De Cive* and *Leviathan*.

original and in some cases a unique scholar. David Gauthier's discussion of the doctrine of authorization in *The Logic of Leviathan* is one of the better known examples, although Gauthier himself has since departed from elements of his well-known 1969 interpretation.[4]

For Gauthier and others who have stressed *Leviathan's* uniqueness, it has been important that this text was the last of the three systematic political statements. *Elements of Law* was published in two parts (*Humane Nature* and *De Corpore Politico*) in 1650 and 1651, but Hobbes wrote and distributed the work a decade earlier during the crisis of the Short Parliament. His dedicatory letter to the Earl of Newcastle is dated May 9, 1640.[5] *De Cive* was first published in a limited printing in Paris in April of 1642; a second, augmented, edition including marginal notes and the work's Preface was published in 1647. *Leviathan* was first published in an English edition in 1650; the Latin edition was published in 1668.

Maturation has been a point of departure for many such claims concerning *Leviathan's* uniqueness. F. S. McNeilly's fundamental concern was with Hobbes's scientific development, and in *Leviathan* he finds a text less muddled in its logic than its earlier political and philosophical counterparts.[6] Gauthier also traces differences between iterations in terms of philosophical problems either solved, or nearly solved.

The maturation theme carries through not only in interpretations that focus on specific philosophical arguments, but also in those that find significance in what is perhaps the most conspicuous difference—the style Hobbes employs in *Leviathan* in making his arguments. David Johnston and Quentin Skinner, among others, have offered arguments that stress the rhetorical character of *Leviathan*. They tell the story of a political philosopher whose intellectual development took him in one direction, but when later confronted with the exigencies of politics was forced to reverse course. For these authors Hobbes's scientific career began with a break with humanism. Rhetoric may have been necessary equipment for humanist political practitioners, but Hobbes is said to have abandoned it for a new and more promising aid in political and intellectual combat: the more perfect reason of the New Science

---

[4] David Gauthier, *The Logic of Leviathan* (Oxford: Oxford University Press, 1969), 99–177. Authorization and the alienation of right which he (later) took it to imply are central to his concerns. See David Gauthier, 'Hobbes's Social Contract', *Nous* 22 (1988), 71–82.

[5] On the timing and likely disappointments associated with the *Elements* see Ted Miller and Tracy Strong, 'Meaning and Contexts: Mr. Skinner's Hobbes and the English Mode of Political Theory', *Inquiry*, 40 (Sept. 1997), 323–56.

[6] McNeilly (1968). Thus, for McNeilly, Hobbes is not merely moving towards a more coherent doctrine in *Leviathan* than in *De Cive* and *Elements of Law*. *Leviathan* also represents an improvement over *De Corpore*, which he stresses was begun before *Leviathan* was composed. Here one might wonder why revisions that reflected an improvement in the philosophy would not be incorporated, especially when we consider some of the other frantic revisions incorporated into the text with regard to his attempt to square the circle.

of his seventeenth- and late sixteenth-century contemporaries. Enthralled with Harvey, Galileo, and geometry, Hobbes was happy to spurn humanist means of suasion for the more compelling force of methodical reason. The shameful, dubious, and in some cases dangerous techniques of rhetoric could be left behind; this new, demonstrative, means of reasoning did not require such assistance. The more perfect reason could compel minds with a civil science that would be capable of putting an end to centuries-old disputation.[7]

By the time Hobbes had written *Leviathan*, we are told, he had learned his lesson the hard way. Reason may have persuaded the few who were ready and willing to hear its voice, but the intransigent flaws in human conduct, seditious political demagoguery, and, for Johnston, the undermining effects of commonly accepted religious doctrines meant that even Hobbes's improved reason unassisted was not sufficient. To persuade his readers, Hobbes did not abandon scientific reason but he understood that he would have to call upon the help of eloquence, as well as a more aggressive theological argument, to defeat reason's potent enemies.[8]

Like Skinner and Johnston, I believe that the rhetoric of *Leviathan* calls for an explanation. Unlike them, I am not convinced that the differences in *Leviathan* can be attributed to the school of hard knocks in the domain of public philosophy. Rather, we need to see the differences in terms of the company Hobbes was keeping and the gesture that *Leviathan* was, or could have been, in light of this company. If I am correct about the uniqueness of *Leviathan*'s style of presentation, we will have grounds to conclude that his approach has at least as much to do with Hobbes's good fortune as ill, with his hopes and ambitions and not merely his frustrations. Political exigencies must still help us to account for *Leviathan*'s uniqueness, but I hope to draw attention to the exigencies brought about by a change in audience rather than a lesson learned concerning rationalist over-confidence. I am also convinced that philosophical maturation can be a misleading notion in exploring the things that make *Leviathan* unique. We should give equal or greater weight to the possibility that the progress Hobbes was making at the time he composed *Leviathan* had more to do with his court and political contexts than with the fine-tuning of philosophic justification.

My goal here, therefore, is not to add or subtract from a detailed list of philosophical or theological arguments that may or may not make

---

[7] Quentin Skinner, *Reason and Rhetoric in the Philosophy of Hobbes* (Cambridge: Cambridge University Press, 1996), chs. 6–8, and esp. 257, 282, 290, 299, 323; David Johnston, *The Rhetoric of* Leviathan (Princeton: Princeton University Press, 1986), chs. 1, 2, and esp. 23, 61, 65. These are by no means the only works that consider Hobbes's use and/or rejection of rhetoric. Skinner's bibliography cites many recent treatments.

[8] Skinner (1996) chs. 9, 10, and Conclusion, esp. 346–56, 431–7; Johnston (1986), chs. 3–7, esp. 66–91, 98–106, 113, 119, 128–33.

Leviathan unique, but to reinterpret the significance we assign to two of the aforementioned elements that most interpreters already agree make *Leviathan* unique: the addition of a doctrine of authorization and the work's rhetorical characteristics. These make their appearance in *Leviathan*, I believe, for a set of reasons different from those thus far suggested in the Hobbes literature. Making this argument will require as much attention to the circumstances of *Leviathan*'s composition as to these features of the text itself.

THE COMPANY HE KEPT

In the 1640s Hobbes became a well-known political philosopher. As noted, *De Cive* was first published in a limited printing in April 1642. Although he was already held in admiration by Mersenne at the time of its first publication, Hobbes's reputation was growing larger still. One admirer, Samuel Sorbière, became his agent for the second and third editions of *De Cive*, as well as the first (and best-known) French translation of this work.[9]

The first printing of the second edition of *De Cive* included something that caused Hobbes great consternation when it was issued in 1647. The first page included a portrait of Hobbes and beneath it an inscription, 'Serenissimo Principi Walliae à studiis praepositus' [Academic Tutor to His Serene Highness the Prince of Wales]. Hobbes wrote to Sorbière in March 1647 in a panicked plea to remove as many copies of this *De Cive* from the shelves as possible. It would give the royal family's enemies an excuse to associate Charles I with 'a political theory which offended the opinion of almost everyone'. Enemies and critics, Hobbes noted, will suggest that it reveals the kind of sovereignty the embattled monarch would expect and demand. Hobbes feared being blamed for granting such a gift to the king's opponents;[10] he also feared that the title would prevent him from returning to England if 'the desire to return ever comes over me'.

---

[9] See Sorbière's letters of 11 July 1645, and Hobbes's letter to Sorbière, 16 May 1646. Printed in *The Correspondence of Thomas Hobbes*, ed. Noel Malcolm (Oxford: Oxford University Press, 1994), i. 121–3; 125–7; see also Malcolm's biographical entry for Sorbière in ibid. ii. 893–9. His translation was entitled *Elemens philosophiques due citoyen Traicté politique, où les fondemens de la société civile sont decouverts*, and was published in Amsterdam in 1649.

[10] It is worth noting that at this point Charles I was in captivity and was negotiating with multiple parties (the Parliament, the Scots, and ultimately the Army). His strategy, however unsuccessful, was to temporize and equivocate in these attempts at settlement. Any text which might pin Charles I to a particular set of expectations of how he would govern, let alone an absolutist doctrine, would indeed have been a disservice. A recent and detailed account of Charles I's strategy and aspirations can be found in Robert Ashton, *Counter-Revolution: The Second Civil War and its Origins, 1646–1648* (New Haven: Yale University Press, 1994), esp. 7–42.

Moreover, he explained, he did not possess the title, and his enemies, 'and they are not a few', will say, 'that I lied out of ambition'.[11]

Hobbes was not given an official title. His patron, the Earl of Newcastle, already held the title as Governor of the Prince of Wales (awarded in March 1638, and lost to parliamentary protest in 1641), but was by this time otherwise occupied first as the leader of Charles I's northern army and then, following defeat, in scrounging money and establishing a home in exile in Antwerp.[12] Under normal circumstances, Newcastle's title would have meant great influence in Britain's political affairs, not least if Charles I expired before his son reached maturity and a normal succession process took place. In exile in Paris the queen, Henrietta Maria, was in control of the Prince of Wales, but it is reasonable to assume that Hobbes's employment was not merely due to his prominence as a philosopher. His connection to Newcastle seems a likely factor; it has been suggested that Hobbes's employment as tutor was arranged through Henry Jermyn, the queen's favorite and the leading royalist in the Paris exile community.[13]

His protests to the contrary, Hobbes's employment at court was by no means a trifling thing. Even in the context of an embattled and exiled absolutist court, permission to occupy the same space with the Prince of Wales (in this case, in the Paris suburb of Saint Germain, but Hobbes also spent time at the Louvre, the home of the exiled court[14]) was an accomplishment. Mere proximity was a measure of privilege in this context.[15] Hobbes, his friends, and no doubt Newcastle, would have understood the importance of having a man at court.

In a prior letter Sorbière congratulates Hobbes, whom he pronounces *Vir Maxime* ('most excellent Sir'), on being 'promoted to the service of the Prince'. It was a well-deserved honor, he suggests, and goes on to note 'How fortunate your country will be when it receives a King full of wisdom and imbued with your teachings!'. He also does nothing unusual in asking if 'in your exalted position at Court' Hobbes could 'do anything' for

---

[11] Letter of 22 Mar. 1647 in *Correspondence*, 155–9. Cf. Thomas Hobbes, *Considerations on the Reputation, Loyalty, Manners, and Religion, of Thomas Hobbes of Malmesbury*, in *English Works*, ed. Molesworth, 11 vols. (London: John Bohn, 1839), iv. 415.

[12] He was reappointed by Charles I as Gentleman to the Robes of the Prince. See Geoffrey Trease, *Portrait of a Cavalier: William Cavendish, First Duke of Newcastle* (New York: Taplinger, 1979), 76–7, 87, 90–104, 159, 167.

[13] Somerville (1992), 21. The Earl of Clarendon's attack upon Hobbes probably ought to be understood in light of the contention between Clarendon and Newcastle. Trease (1979) *passim*.

[14] Letters from Hobbes available from this period are from both Saint Germain and Paris. See *Correspondence*, letters 40–62 (1646–8).

[15] For a discussion of patronage and Charles II's court see Gerald E. Alymer, 'Patronage at the Court of Charles II', in Eveline Cruickshanks (ed.), *The Stuart Courts* (Thrupp: Sutton Publishing, 2000). For a discussion of the importance of proximity in general in court settings see Norbert Elias, *The Court Society* (Oxford: Blackwell, 1983).

a young physician du Prat and to help another mutual friend, de Martel, in finding a place to live in Paris.[16]

Hobbes replied with a letter designed to temper his friend's enthusiasm for his success. Although Sorbière nowhere suggests in the previous letter that the prince's lessons will be in Hobbes's politics, the philosopher goes out of his way to emphasize that they are not:

I acknowledge your goodwill in congratulating me on my present employment; but beware of thinking it more important than it is. For I am only teaching mathematics, not politics. I would not be able to teach him the political doctrines contained in the book which is being printed [De Cive], both because he is too young, and because my doing so will always be forbidden by those whose counsels, justly, govern him. If I earn any favour with him for my daily services, I shall use it all, I assure you, not so much for my own benefit as for that of my friends— and of your friends too, if you recommend any to me. But neither my humility nor his age will allow me to hope for very much.[17]

Leviathan was already a work in the making at the time this letter was composed. I want to suggest that Leviathan, whatever else it may be, was a strenuous attempt to change this state of affairs.[18] Understanding what makes Leviathan unique requires that we appreciate how the text's innovations reflect this effort.

The Prince of Wales arrived in Paris in 1646. Not long afterwards Hobbes was made his mathematics instructor, and from Hobbes's own writings we can surmise that he began to compose Leviathan shortly after the prince's arrival. We also know that the composition of the text was subject to a number of interruptions.[19] The daily instruction of the prince was certainly one. Hobbes also fell ill while performing these services at Saint Germain, and did not begin writing again until early 1648. By this time, the Prince of Wales had left Saint Germain for Holland to make plans for the next war against the Commonwealth. It was also during this period that Hobbes found himself in the position of commentator on Sir William Davenant's Gondibert.

By this point in his career, Davenant was already a great success in operating the patronage system. From his origins as the son of an Oxford

---

[16] Letter 44, late September 1646 in Correspondence, pp. 136–7.

[17] Correspondence, 4 Oct. 1646 reply from Saint Germain, Letter 45, ibid. pp. 138–41.

[18] Aside from Hobbes's own protestations in his Considerations, see Glenn Burgess, 'Contexts for the Writing and Publication of Hobbes's Leviathan', History of Political Thought, 11 (1990), 675–702, for the contextual evidence that Leviathan was a work of royalist persuasion, and not, as its critics such as Clarendon and Wallis charged, a work to justify by de facto power the rule of Cromwell.

[19] In his Latin verse autobiography, Hobbes notes the return of the Prince of Wales and the start of this new book. A contemporaneous translation of the verse biography is reprinted in Curley's edition of Leviathan (Indianapolis: Hackett, 1994). Pertinent passages are in lines 193–204. For the dates, see Skinner (1996) 330, 331, n. 38, who also notes the concordance with Hobbes's Considerations.

tavern owner, he had gone on to become Poet Laureate, and enjoyed the favor of the queen in particular. So much so that she insured that Davenant became the Earl of Newcastle's Ordinance Officer to the Northern Army, an office he appears to have performed with competence. Already annoying his contemporaries in the exiled court by flaunting his close connections to Jermyn, Davenant would go on to receive yet more prestigious appointments: during the second Civil War (contemporaneous with his time with Hobbes while composing *Gondibert*) Davenant would find himself appointed Lieutenant Governor of Maryland. This amounted to a *de facto* governorship as Lord Baltimore had crossed Charles II by appointing high officials with parliamentary sympathies, and Davenant's appointment was intended as a remedy. Davenant never made it to America. His ship was captured in the channel and he was imprisoned by parliament in the tower, but covering this further takes us too far afield.[20]

DAVENANT AND HOBBES: GENRE AND AUDIENCE

Davenant's *Gondibert* is an epic poem written with the aim of advising noblemen in the virtues (Davenant) thought appropriate to political affairs. It is a work of political education in poetic form.[21] Its preface was addressed to Hobbes, and the philosopher reciprocated with an answer. In its preface the poet reports that Hobbes allowed him a 'daylie examination' of the text, and, perhaps anxious to advertise his association with a renowned philosopher, Davenant published 'The Author's Preface to His Much Honor'd Friend, M. Hobbes' along with 'The Answer of Mr. Hobbes to Sir Will. D'Avenant's Preface before Gondibert' in 1650 through a Parisian publisher; he registered *The Preface* on the Stationer's Register in London on February 15 of that year.[22] These early publications did not include the three (of the planned, but incomplete, five) books of *Gondibert*: they were first published in 1651. Scholars interested in *Leviathan*'s rhetorical characteristics have been attracted to Hobbes's *Answer* as it announces an alliance

[20] Arthur H. Nethercot, *Sir William D'avenant: Poet Laureate and Playwright-Manager* (Chicago: University of Chicago Press, 1938), 21–37, 166, 200–65, esp. 257.

[21] Although much more might be said of *Gondibert*, its didacticism is quite evident. Aside from the dramatic action of the epic itself, Davenant employed some of the most straightforward didactic techniques of his day, including 'Charactery'. The first book of *Gondibert* includes admiring portraits of, among others, King Aribert, who is made to exemplify, in what can be described as a Hobbesian way, the virtues of a militarily capable monarchy (William Davenant, *Sir William Davenant's Gondibert*, ed. David Gladish (Oxford: Clarendon Press, 1971), 59).

[22] *The Author's Preface to His Much Honor'd Friend, M. Hobbes* in Davenant (1971), 3, Hereafter referred to as *Preface*. The Parisian publisher was Matthieu Guillemot, who brought out two editions, including what would have been an expensive de luxe octavo. For the publication history of the *Preface* and Hobbes's answer see Nethercot (1938) 255.

between poetry and philosophy. I hope to show that attention to Davenant's *Preface* and Hobbes's reply will reap further rewards, especially as these two essays speak to the question of the relationship of author to audience.

Davenant inspired much derision in his own day, and he seems only recently to be making a recovery.[23] Was Davenant an influence on Hobbes? Hobbes himself seems to suggest so in his reply when he tells Davenant: 'I have used your Judgment no lesse in many thinges of mine, which coming to light will thereby appeare the better.'[24] This pregnant suggestion leads one to think immediately of *Leviathan*, but it is not my purpose to make an argument that hinges on the influence of a particular author or confidant.

What has been most interesting in Davenant's *Preface* and Hobbes's *Answer* is the way they raise the question of the relationship between philosophy and poetry, or, as I shall stress, between philosophers and poets. In his essay, Hobbes strikes a theme he used in other works: philosophy, or at least true philosophy, must be given credit for the progress and comforts that human beings enjoy.[25] Here, however, Hobbes links these accomplishments to the work of fancy—our imaginative capacity and the characteristic skill of poets[26]—when it is guided by philosophical precepts:

[S]o far forth as the Fancy of man, has traced the wayes of true Philosophy, so farre it hath produced very marvellous effects to the benefit of mankind. All that is bewtifull or defensible in building; or mervaylous in Engines and Instruments of motion; Whatsoever commodity men receave from the observation of the Heavens, from the description of the Earth, from the account of Time, from walking on the Seas; and whatsoever distinguisheth the civility of *Europe*, from the Barbarity of the *American* sauvages, is the workmenship of Fancy, but guided by the Precepts of true Philosophy. But where these precepts fayle, as they have hetherto fayled in the doctrine of Morall vertue, there the Architect (*Fancy*) must take the Philosophers part upon himself.[27]

What would it mean for Fancy to take the philosopher's part 'upon himself'? Here one must refer to at least two examples from Hobbes's

---

[23] See the satiric *Certain Verses Written by severall of the Author's Friends to be Re-Printed with the Second Edition of* Gondibert, in Davenant (1971) 272–87. Kevin Sharpe makes a plea for a more serious consideration of Davenant as a politically and socially engaged critic: Kevin Sharpe, *Criticism and Compliment: the Politics of Literature in the England of Charles I* (Cambridge: Cambridge University Press, 1987). Nethercot (1938) is a critical biographer, but see J. P. Feil, 'Davenant Exonerated', *Modern Language Review*, (July 1963), 335–42, and Mary Edmond, *Rare Sir William Davenant* (Manchester: University of Manchester Press, 1987), where some of Nethercot's claims are contradicted.

[24] *The Answer of Mr. Hobbes to Sir Will. D'avenant's preface Before* Gondibert, in Davenant (1971), 54. Hereafter referred to as *Answer*.

[25] Cf. *Elements of Law*, I. 13. 3; *De Cive*, 'Dedicatory'; *De Corpore*, I. 7 (Thomas Hobbes, *English Works*, ed. William Molesworth, i (London: John Bohn, 1839), pp. 7–10.).

[26] 'Fancy begets the ornaments of a Poeme' (Hobbes, *Answer*, in Davenant (1971), 49.

[27] Ibid. 49–50.

contexts where the boundary between philosophy and poetry had become permeable. Poets such as Davenant had reason to associate their work with the refinements of philosophical learning. James I had cultivated an image as a philosopher-king, and did so with the assistance of court poets such as Jonson and Samuel Daniel. Charles I and Henrietta elected to distance their regime from the reputation of Charles's dissolute father, but did not depart from the tradition of searching for philosophically learned celebrations of legitimacy. They bathed their own images in the light of an ideal of Platonic love. As Poet Laureate, Davenant was called upon to put these ideals into words and on stage in court masques (created in collaboration with the architect and king's surveyor, Inigo Jones).[28] Indeed, it has been suggested that Hobbes played a role in one of the last court entertainments written by Jonson for Charles I and performed at his patron's castle at Welbeck.[29] Part of what Hobbes was doing, therefore, was commending the role that Davenant and some of his predecessors and contemporaries had already assumed for themselves.[30]

For our purposes, however, the more immediately interesting boundary-crossing is the one in the opposite direction. Not only were poets turning themselves into philosophers, but Hobbes, the philosopher, appears to have turned himself into something of a poet. In his last work Hobbes nearly became a poet, producing what even he considered a less than stellar rhyming translation of Homer, but this is not our present concern.[31] In what way did Hobbes employ the poet's skills in *Leviathan*?

Skinner's recent study deciphers the above passage in light of Hobbes's observations in *Leviathan*'s 'Review and Conclusions' where Hobbes poses the problem of whether natural faculties held contrary can be reconciled in a single person. The natural faculties in question are 'severity of judgment' and 'celerity of fancy'. Severity of judgment is a necessary characteristic among philosophers. Celerity of fancy is the characteristic associated with poets and eloquence. The poet's faculty may be suspect. It clearly was in Hobbes's earlier works, and the excesses of fancy arguably remain so

---

[28] Much has been published recently on the subject. Here is a partial listing: Stephen Orgel and Roy Strong (eds.), *Inigo Jones and the Theater of the Stuart Court*, 2 vols. (Berkeley: University of California Press, 1973); Stephen Orgel, *The Illusion of Power* (Berkeley: University of California Press, 1975); R. Malcolm Smuts, *Court Culture and the Origins of a Royalist Tradition in Early Stuart England* (Philadelphia: University of Pennsylvania Press, 1987); Kevin Sharpe, *Criticism and Compliment: The Politics of Literature in the England of Charles I* (Cambridge: Cambridge University Press, 1987); Erica Veevers, *Images of Love and Religion: Queen Henrietta Maria and Court Entertainments* (Cambridge: Cambridge University Press, 1989); Hilary Gatti, 'Giordano Bruno and the Stuart Court Masques', *Renaissance Quarterly*, 48 (1995), 809–42.

[29] A. P. Martinich, *Hobbes: A Biography* (Cambridge: Cambridge University Press, 1999), 88.

[30] This is certainly supported by the text following the quotation: 'He therefore that undertakes an Heroique Poeme . . . must not onley be the Poet, to place and connect, but also the Philosopher, to furnish and square his matter' (Hobbes, *Answer*, in Davenant 1971), 50.

[31] Thomas Hobbes, *The English Works*, vol. x.

in *Leviathan*. Important for Skinner, however, Hobbes concedes in this chapter of *Leviathan* that the two may be reconciled, and must be if philosophy is to have a fighting chance: 'if there be not powerful eloquence, which procureth attention and consent, the effect of reason will be little'.[32] Resorting to a classical defense of eloquence,[33] Hobbes acknowledges that fancy may find itself on the side of error, but judgment and fancy can be exercised in turn, and he suggests that an advantage will accrue to truth, and tip the balance in its favor.

Here, then, is a key part of the argument made by Skinner that Hobbes reversed himself on matters of rhetoric, and he goes on to detail the connections between the rhetoric of *Leviathan* and specific rhetorical techniques of Cicero, Quintilian, and more contemporaneous guides by Thomas Wilson, George Puttenham, and Henry Peacham.[34] I wish, however, to pick up on a strand that is begun but I think ultimately lost in Skinner's treatment of Hobbes's eloquence.

For Hobbes and his contemporaries, eloquence was not merely a matter of technique, but a matter of persons. What does one's writing or speech suggest about a person? What kinds of writing or speech are appropriate to a good citizen, courtly servant, client, or subject? Skinner rightly notes that Hobbes's attacks upon eloquence in *De Cive* and *Elements of Law* contain an attack upon the *vir civilis*, the eloquent citizen capable of participating in public deliberations on political questions.[35] Hobbes would have substituted the obedient subject for the talkative citizen. But one is left to wonder if the *vir civilis* is brought back on the scene with Hobbes's about-face on rhetoric. I would suggest (whether or not we could discover a complete rejection of eloquence in Hobbes's earlier works) that the *vir civilis* remains banished. The eloquence Hobbes employs and concerns himself with is that of the *vir maxime*, as Sorbière put it. His eloquence is that of the courtly denizen seeking to secure and maintain favor and honor.[36]

---

[32] Thomas Hobbes, *Leviathan*, ed. Edwin Curley (Indianapolis: Hackett Publishing, 1994), 'Review and Conclusions', sections 1–4 (subsequent references to *Leviathan* will refer to chapter number, or name where appropriate, and Curley's numbered paragraphs—which in most cases track to the Molesworth edition); Skinner (1996), 352–3.

[33] 'wheresoever there is a place for adorning and preferring of error, there is much more place for adorning and preferring truth, if they have it to adorn' (*Leviathan*, Review and Conclusions, 4).

[34] Skinner (1996), 376–425.

[35] Quentin Skinner, *Reason and Rhetoric in the Philosophy of Hobbes* (Cambridge: Cambridge University Press, 1996), 66–110, 284–93.

[36] This strand of the humanist tradition is discussed ibid. 69–72, but Professor Skinner does not return to it. Skinner has, however, argued that *Leviathan* left the world with the legacy of an English style of philosophizing: droll, satiric, and unmercifully logical in its assault upon its opponents (ibid. 436–7). I am not questioning that this was Hobbes's legacy, but I would suggest that Hobbes's rhetorical efforts in *Leviathan* are the reflection of a context where more immediate forms of recognition were available to him.

The question of persons and the eloquence appropriate to persons, moreover, is central to what makes *Leviathan* unique. In Hobbes's (then) courtly contexts favor was sought and granted to learned men who could counsel their betters with exceptional and noteworthy works. One sought to honor and delight, and to show oneself worthy of a patron's favor. The learned sought to create some work, a gift or tribute to the patron. One's gift should be something superb, something that would yield recognition and distinction and yet remain within the bounds of opprobrium given their station and that of their audience.[37] The forms and practices of eloquence in this domain diverged from that of the republican citizen. This was the eloquence that had been perfected by court poets and the exchange between Hobbes and Davenant helps us to understand the rules and expectations of this domain, and how they would have applied to Hobbes and to *Leviathan*. It was the work, the building itself as Davenant would put it—and the architectural theme was also a key part of Hobbes's self-understanding—that reflected most upon its maker and this was something larger than the virtuous use of rhetorical technique.[38]

Davenant's *Preface* and Hobbes's *Answer* invite us to consider these works on at least two related registers, both of which must ultimately force our attention on persons. First, how does the work reflect upon the individual with a claim to a talent that could serve the crown? For example, what does the virtuosity displayed in *Leviathan* or *Gondibert* tell a potential patron about Hobbes or Davenant? Hobbes's praise for Davenant, however effusive, is instructive in this regard. In trumpeting Davenant's success, it identifies the form accomplishment and recognition sought in these contexts:

The vertues you distribute there amongst so many noble Persons [in *Gondibert*] represent (in the reading) the image but of one mans vertue to my fancy, which is your owne; and that so deepley imprinted, as to stay for ever there, and governe all the rest of my thoughts, and affections in the way of honouring and serving you, to the utmost of my power.[39]

The second register does not invite a direct focus on the particular author, but on how the author's work reflects upon the worldly and/or intellectual roles the author either possessed or claimed: poet, philosopher, historian, general, statesman, king, etc. The elevation of poetry, and therewith the

---

[37] For a discussion of gift-exchange in the context of absolutism see Mario Biagioli, *Galileo, Courtier: The Practice of Science in the Culture of Absolutism* (Chicago: University of Chicago Press, 1993), 36–59.

[38] Such works were to be monuments to the talents of their authors. See, for example, Davenant, *Preface*, Davenant (1971), 1, 15, 20, 22, 44. I have discussed Hobbes's architectural sensibility in 'Thomas Hobbes and the Constraints that Enable the Imitation of God', *Inquiry* 42 (1999), 149–76, and 'Oakeshott's Hobbes and the Fear of Political Rationalism', *Political Theory* 29 (2001), 806–32.   [39] Hobbes, *The Answer*, Davenant (1971), 55.

particular poet, Davenant, is a critical theme in the *Preface*. Davenant argues at length in the *Preface* that poetry is able to assist, and even exceed, divines, 'leaders of armies', statesman, 'makers of laws', and judges in their capacity to govern the conduct of subjects and soldiers.[40] He follows in the footsteps of earlier ambitious humanists in making such architectonic claims for his discipline.[41] Hobbes and Davenant were each claiming that their learned talents, as philosopher and poet, could make them valuable servants at court, and worthy of greater recognition.[42] Thus, when Davenant trumpeted his own virtues, he spoke of the role which poets could play in the education of noblemen and princes. Likewise, a philosophical scholar such as Hobbes could be more than a mere mathematics instructor; he could offer the prince valuable advice on how to order and rule the commonwealth.

Public contemplation of the most effective means of imparting instruction, moreover, was itself a way of claiming that one was worthy of the role of advising these lofty audiences. This helps explain why *Gondibert*'s *Preface* and Hobbes's *Answer* were published ahead of the poem itself. Moreover, as Hobbes's and Davenant's contemplations make clear, this was only in part a question of technique (for example, of what fancy is, and how it works on the minds of readers). It was also a question of decorum. Davenant and Hobbes gave consideration to the genre(s) best suited to their audience. Where the audience was an absolutist sovereign, or would-be absolutist sovereign, this was no small concern.[43] Consideration of the social and political rank of the person being addressed (and implicitly, the typically subordinate rank of the author) was a part of these concerns, and this extended to the genre chosen by his advisor.

On questions of genre, Davenant and Hobbes proved unique: neither were content to pick and choose between established learned forms. Both remain conscious of established genres and the scholarly roles and identities associated with them, but out of this consciousness they sometimes deliberately combine, and therefore cross boundaries between, identities and genres. This

---

[40] Davenant, *Preface*, Davenant (1971), 27–41. Davenant boasts: 'Poets (who with wise diligence study the People, and have in all ages, by an insensible influence govern'd their manners) may justly smile when they perceived that *Divines, Leaders of Armies, Statesman* and *Judges* think *Religion*, the *Sword* or . . . *Policy*, or *Law* . . . can give, without the helpe of the *Muses*, a long and quiet satisfaction in government' (ibid. 32).

[41] See, e.g. Sir Philip Sidney, *The Defense of Poesy* (1595), in *Sir Philip Sidney*, ed. Katherine Duncan-Jones (Oxford: Oxford University Press, 1989), 212–50.

[42] For a recent treatment of Hobbes's philosophy and *Leviathan* in the contexts of patronage relations see Lisa Sarasohn, 'Was *Leviathan* a Patronage Artifact', *History of Political Thought* 21 (2000), 606–31. Rhetoric and patronage dynamics are also discussed in Ted Miller and Tracy Strong, 'Meanings and Contexts: Mr. Skinner's Hobbes and the English Mode of Political Theory', *Inquiry*, 40 (1997), 323–56.

[43] Biagioli (1993). On this question in the Stuart context see Sharpe (1987).

is how we should understand the poet–philosopher combination, but Hobbes also supplies us with a more evident example in his *Behemoth*. It is at once a history of the English Civil War, and an instructive dialogue between two interlocutors, 'A' and 'B'.[44]

Davenant consciously elected to incorporate the characteristics of other poetic genres into *Gondibert*.[45] It was a poem that would echo the structure of a play; his poem would have five books, just as a play had five acts. He boasts of 'this new Building's' form, and asks Hobbes to consider 'if I have methodically and with discretion dispos'd of the materialls, which with some curiosity I had collected'.[46] The purpose of his heroic poems is to present 'great actions' that would teach and inspire their readers to virtue by lively example. In surveying his collection of poetic 'materialls' Davenant remarks:

I cannot discern . . . that any Nation hath in presentment of great actions (either by *Heroicks* or *Dramaticks*) digested Story into so pleasant and instructive a method as the English by their *Drama*: and by that regular species (though narratively and not in Dialogue) I have drawn the body of an Heroick Poem: proportioning five bookes to five *Acts*, and *Canto's* to *Scenes* . . . [47]

In the *Answer* Hobbes notes with approval Davenant's use of the first to introduce his characters, and remarks: 'me thinkes the Fable is not much unlike the Theater. . . . I could not but approve the structure of your Poeme, which ought to be no other then such as an imitation of human life requireth'.[48] This is not all Hobbes approved of in Davenant's poem. He was keen to differentiate it from the vices he associated with forms of eloquence he found damaging to civic order. Both Hobbes and Davenant illustrate a prejudice against popular oratory.

Davenant's *Preface*, like earlier defenses of poetry, undertakes to assert a set of new standards concerning what should count as great eloquence, and

[44] Thomas Hobbes, *Behemoth or the Long Parliament*, ed. Ferdinand Tönnies (Chicago: University of Chicago Press, 1990). Interestingly, this was another work in which Hobbes sought, and was denied, royal approval. In this case, approval meant being granted a license to publish the work. See Stephan Holmes, 'Introduction', ibid. p. vii.

[45] David Gladish, 'Introduction' to Davenant (1971).

[46] Davenant, *Preface*, Davenant (1971), 14.   [47] Ibid. 15–16.

[48] Hobbes, *Answer*, Davenant (1971), 50. For Davenant, a part of the instructive power of poetry resides in its capacity to offer a vivid imitation of life, even as it (unlike the works of historians) need not restrict itself to a narrative that purports to tell the story of actual peoples or events. The purpose, as Hobbes notes, is not to escape all bounds of truth, but to use the fictions available to the poet to better represent the virtues and vices of nature. Hobbes writes: 'Beyond the actuall workes of nature a Poet may now go; but beyond the conceaved possibility of nature never' (ibid. 51). Cf. Davenant, *Preface*, ibid. 24. It was, nevertheless, this fictional quality which won Davenant some of his criticism. See Martin E. Blaine, 'Epic, Romance, and History in Davenant's "Madagascar"', *Studies in Philology*, 95 (1998), 293–319.

what not.[49] In cataloguing the mistakes of others he takes note of the great mistakes committed by 'the people'. These

> think Orators (which is a title that crowns at riper years those that have practis'd the dexterity of tongue) the ablest men; who are indeed so much more unapt for governing, as they are more fit for Sedition; and it may be said of them as of the Witches of *Norway*, which can sell a storme for a *Doller*, which for Ten Thousand they cannot allay.[50]

The sorcerer's apprentice trope is echoed in Hobbes's own survey of deficient forms of eloquence where he takes aim at contemporary divines (at this time the most common source of popular rhetoric for most persons) for inadvisably following the lead of ancient poets who claimed to write by divine inspiration. Hobbes allows that the ancients must be allowed this as it is merely, 'an accessory to their false Religion'. However,

> in the spiritual calling of Divines there is danger sometimes to be feared, from want of skill, such as is reported of unskillfull Conjurers, that mistaking the rites and ceremonious points of their art, call up such spirits, as they cannot at their pleasure allay againe; by whome stormes are raysed, that overthrow buildings, and are the cause of miserable wrackes at sea. Unskillful divines doe oftentimes, the like, For they call unseasonable for *Zeale* there appears a spirit of *Cruelty*; and by the like errors instead of *Truth* they rayse *Discord*; instead of *Wisedome, Fraud*; instead of *Reformation, Tumult*; and *Controversie* instead of *Religion*.[51]

As is well known, the assault on popular oratory is not merely a part of the works that preceded *Leviathan*, but also a part of *Leviathan* itself.[52] It is therefore suggested that Hobbes must have reversed himself, in spite of his reservations, because this anti-rhetorical work is itself so thoroughly rhetorical. If, however, we account for the fact that Hobbes and his contemporaries were content to attack some forms of eloquence while lauding—and practicing—others in light of specific goals, audiences, and genres, then a different picture must emerge.[53]

This disdain for popular seditious oratory finds its converse in Davenant's *Preface*. Although Davenant had the arrogance to suggest that his poem might some day be sung at 'Village-feastes',[54] he makes it clear that his epic is not directed towards a popular audience. It is not that there wasn't a form of poetic eloquence fit for teaching the people virtues necessary for a commonwealth. Indeed, Davenant engaged in a number of attempts at civic

---

[49] Cf. Sidney (1989 [1595]); George Puttenham, *The Arte of English Posie*, ed. Gladyse Willcock and Alice Walker (Cambridge: Cambridge University Press, 1936 [1588]).

[50] Davenant, *Preface*, Davenant (1971), 19.   [51] Hobbes, *Answer*, Davenant (1971), 48.

[52] *Leviathan*, 11:20, 19:4–5, 8; 22, 30; 25:12, 15; 29:14–15, 20–1; 30:8.

[53] I address this question at greater length with Tracy Strong in Miller and Strong (1997).

[54] Davenant, *Preface*, Davenant (1971), 17.

education in theatrical form,[55] and one of the central strands of Davenant's argument in his *Preface* is that poetry (as he defines it) is better able to judge the means of creating an obedient and properly ordered state than those offices that have been traditionally charged with the task, namely divines, statesman, generals, and magistrates. Nevertheless, his epic is primarily concerned with the education of princes, not peoples, and as such its effects on the people can be indirect. The prince made virtuous by his poem will then set an example that guides the people:

I have profes'd not to represent the beauty of vertue in my Poem, with hope to persuade common men; . . . In my despare of reducing the mindes of Common men, I have not confest any weaknesse of Poesy in the generall Science; but rather infer'd the particular strength of the Heroick [i.e. epic]; which hath a force that overmatches the infancy of such mindes as are not enabled by degrees of Education, but there are lesser forces in other kinds of Poesy, by which they may traine, and prepare their understandings; and Princes, and Nobles being reforme'd and made angelicall by the Heroick, will be predomanant lights, which the People cannot chose but use for direction; as Glowormes take in, and keep the Sunns bemes till they shine, and make day to themselves.[56]

These passages certainly allow us to hear the snide voice of a disappointed and defeated royalist. If we see this as nothing more than the ranting of an elitist angry at the rabble, however, we make a mistake. Davenant's and Hobbes's shared disdain for demagogic oratory as well as their concern for the relationship between a learned work and the social standing of its audience are useful clues in teasing out the characteristics that make *Leviathan* a unique work of philosophy.

LEVIATHAN'S AUDIENCE, COURT MASQUES, AND THE CHALLENGE OF PRINCELY ADVICE-GIVING

Although Hobbes defends absolutism, his political philosophy makes a break with the absolutism, and concomitant notions of legitimacy, embraced by the Stuarts. According to Stuart doctrine, kings ruled because

---

[55] He notes that the Divines have failed in their charge, who were 'ordain'd to temper the rage of human power by spirituall menaces' (*Preface*, Davenant (1971) 28). As regards popular disobedience, they have allowed 'their Christian meeknesse [to deceive] them in taking this wilde Monster the People'; and Davenant 'rebuke[s] them for neglecting the assistance of Poets' (ibid. 30). Indeed, a key point in Davenant's preface is to emphasize that poetry better performs the functions assigned not only to divines, but also to statesman, generals, and magistrates, and in this he follows in the footsteps of earlier defenses of poetry. See also ibid. 37–8. On Davenant's more popular works see Sharpe (1987); Alfred Harbage, *Sir William Davenant, Poet Venturer, 1606–1668* (Oxford: Oxford University Press, 1935); James Jacob and Timothy Raylor, 'Opera and Obedience: Thomas Hobbes and *A Proposition for Advancement of Moralitie*, By Sir William Davenant', *The Seventeenth Century*, 6 (1991), 205–50.   [56] *Preface*, Davenant (1971), 38.

God placed them on the throne.[57] For Hobbes, famously, it is the people themselves who must transfer their right to everything in the brutal state of nature to their sovereign. The sovereign ensures that the conditions for a peaceful and prosperous commonwealth are maintained by threat of over-whelming force against those who are tempted to reclaim the rights they forfeited. It is therefore not surprising that those interested in *Leviathan*'s rhetorical characteristics have assumed that the persuasive burden faced by Hobbes is that of convincing the audience of would-be subjects. It is the people, on this reading, who must be persuaded to accept the rule of the absolutist sovereign and to transfer their rights as individuals to escape the state of nature. This is the assumption that underlies both Skinner and Johnston's reading.

Johnston draws from the passage from Hobbes's *Answer* quoted above concerning Fancy taking 'the Philosophers part upon himself'. He concludes that Hobbes's statement 'is an indictment of the limitations of his own pre-vious efforts of political philosophy'. It is not that Hobbes was acknowl-edging that he had failed to discover political truths, but on Johnston's reading he is acknowledging that he failed to communicate and 'imprint them in the minds of those people who must be taught to act in accordance with the dictates of moral virtue'.[58]

Skinner weighs several possibilities to account for why Hobbes may have changed his mind concerning rhetoric, but concludes that the critical reason is best revealed in Hobbes's bitter complaints after the fact, in his later work *Behemoth*. Here Hobbes lays much of the blame for the English Civil War on the Presbyterian ministers and members of the House of Commons. They account for the failure of science and reason (i.e. Hobbes's own doctrine) to win its proper place in the minds of the people; these rhetorically skillful individuals were able to pull the wool over their eyes. These culprits preached disobedience and seditious doctrines. Not only did the 'democratical' gentlemen in the House of Commons make their weak arguments appear stronger, the theatrics of the Presbyterians in the pulpit lead Hobbes, accord-ing to Skinner, to the 'crucial conclusion . . . that this degree of eloquence was

---

[57] Historians of political thought have rightly emphasized the cutting edge of James I's abso-lutism: kings cannot be held accountable for the deficiencies of their rule by their subjects, but by God alone. The most immediate contrast is between those who claim a right for either church or the people publicly to criticize or depose a monarch. See Johann P. Sommerville, 'Introduction,' *King James VI and I: Political Writings* (Cambridge: Cambridge University Press, 1994). Stuart doctrine, however, also speaks to the question of how kings should appear (especially before their subjects) in light of their having been appointed by God. In his mirror for princes, *Basilicon Doron*, James tells his son that God 'made you a little GOD to sit on his Throne, and rule ouer other men . . . Remember then, that this glistering worldly glorie of Kings, is giuen them by God, to teach to preasse so to glister and shine before their people, in all workes of sanctification and righteousnesse, that their persons as bright lampes of godlinesse and vertue, may, going in and out before their people, giue light to all their steps' (ibid. 12–13).   [58] Johnston (1986), 90.

sufficient in itself to seduce the multitude'.[59] I am not convinced that Hobbes ever had great faith in the 'multitude's' capacity to understand his scientific reasoning but have made this argument elsewhere.[60]

Without questioning that Hobbes thought that would-be subjects would have to be persuaded to accept the dictates of his doctrine (if not necessarily the scientific arguments), I want to suggest that Hobbes's task in writing *Leviathan* was more complicated and that his foremost audience for this text was not 'the people'. The logic of both Skinner's and Johnston's argument is that Hobbes learned that he had to fight fire with fire: if the popular orators had seduced the multitudes with their eloquence, then the only way to respond was to return to the rhetorical toolbox to insure victory for science in the popular mind. I suggest that when we take Hobbes's immediate contexts into account another possibility emerges. It was not merely the people who needed to be persuaded to accept Hobbes's conception of sovereignty. Although Hobbes's political philosophy speaks of sovereignty in general terms, Hobbes's circumstances were such that he expected that the next sovereign of Britain would be his student Prince Charles. Charles would also need to be convinced. Hobbes's immediate rhetorical task was to convince Charles that he should accept sovereignty not by divine right but by the consent of the governed. I think that *Leviathan*'s unique rhetorical characteristics are in large part attributable to this challenging task.

It is in light of this that we should see Hobbes's decision to combine the role of poet and philosopher. Poets such as Davenant had achieved remarkable success in inserting themselves as learned servants and advisors in these courtly contexts. *Gondibert* is an example of an attempt to advise a monarch in narrative form, but there were other poetic means of taking up the subject of courtly life and monarchical ideals.

Although Hobbes offers a classification of poetic genres by subject (court, city, and country life) and manner of representation (dramatic or narrative) in his *Answer*,[61] he was also aware of another, more collaborative, genre. This was the aforementioned court masque.[62] The settings for these events

---

[59] Skinner (1996), 434, but see also 431–7.

[60] Miller and Strong (1997).

[61] Hobbes, *Answer*, Davenant (1971), 45–6.

[62] Davenant's predecessor, Ben Jonson, classified the masques as poetry, and therefore essentially a thing of his own invention. This became a point of contention between himself and Inigo Jones, appointed the King's surveyor, who as ingenious and innovative stage, set, and costume designer played a significant role. Jones won this battle, and Jonson fell out of favor while Jones's influence over the enterprises continued to grow. Hobbes's patron, the Earl of Newcastle, used Jonson as author of the Entertainment for Charles I at Welbeck and Bolsilver in a less than successful attempt to rehabilitate Jonson. Davenant and those that followed were not as assertive in claiming credit for poetry in this genre. We should not assume, however, that Hobbes would have been discouraged from borrowing from the masque form because it had been reconceived as a collaborative project between poet and a material artificer. The opposite assumption seems in order. On the conflict between Jones and Jonson see D. J. Gordon, 'Poet and Architect: The Intellectual Setting of the

were not necessarily fixed, and were often far-fetched flights of fancy in which monsters and gods made regular appearances. In recent years the literature on court masques has grown immensely, and a key strand has emphasized the political salience of these works.[63]

Court masques combined the talents of many arts. Music and dance were essential components, but as the genre developed on stage it was the combined (and sometimes combative) imaginations of a poet and an architect (Inigo Jones designed the elaborate sets and mechanical special effects as well as costumes for the masques) that competed and captured the most attention.[64] Translating all of these elements to the printed page would have been a challenge, although the written portions of the masques were themselves published, and these came to include long descriptions of the scenery, costumes, and the noblemen and women who took roles in their presentation. There are elements of these dramatic presentations that I believe have been made a part of *Leviathan*.

Although the masque was a flexible form, one that invited variations, discerning the elements that make an appearance in *Leviathan* necessitates a review of what most consider the basic structure or pattern of actions that typically unfolded before the audience in its late Tudor and Stuart manifestations.[65] What makes the masque interesting from the perspective of political theory is that it presents a story of moral and political order challenged and ultimately restored. These presentations, moreover, could exhibit the characteristics of an elaborately staged didactic exercise. Specifically, they had the capacity to function as a dramatic equivalent to a mirror for princes, and they were able to do this in a remarkably inventive way that took advantage of the settings for these performances.

Unlike a play, a masque was crafted with advance knowledge (or at least expectation) of who would be in the audience. These were typically noblemen and the crown's invited guests, but the most significant member(s) of the audience were the king, or queen, or both. The stage players, moreover, were a mix of designated aristocrats and professional actors. Masque

Quarrel between Ben Jonson and Inigo Jones', *Journal of the Warburg and Courtauld Institutes*, 12 (1949), 152–78; Stephen Orgel and Roy Strong, *Inigo Jones: The Theatre of the Stuart Court* (Berkeley: University of California Press, 1973), esp. i. 53, 58) which emphasizes Jones's role and collaboration with Charles I; and for a historical account of the conflict David Riggs, *Ben Jonson: A Life* (Cambridge: Harvard University Press, 1989). For an alternative reading, suggesting that Jonson fell out of favor because Jones found a new collaborator in Charles I himself, see Sharpe (1987), 179–87. Again, this would not have been a reason for Hobbes to shy away from the genre.

[63] This view has been contested. For a useful review of current literature, including this controversy, see Suzanne Gossett, 'Recent Studies in the English Masque', *English Literary Renaissance (ELR)*, 26 (1996), 586–627.

[64] Stephen Orgel, *The Jonsonian Masque* (Cambridge, Mass.: Harvard University Press, 1965), 3–36; Orgel and Strong (1973).

[65] On the development of the form prior to this stage see Orgel (1965), 3–36.

performances not only acknowledged the monarch's presence in the audience, but the final moment or action of the masque incorporated the monarch or royal couple into the masque's resolution. In many cases, this meant that the king or queen appeared on stage as well.[66]

One of Davenant's first masques, *The Temple of Love*, is illustrative of these characteristics. As noted, the Caroline monarchy (Henrietta Maria in particular) used court masques to craft a self-image that emphasized themes of Platonic love. Monarchs were to be loved by their subjects. This ideal was quite obviously to become less and less of a reality for the Caroline monarchy, but *The Temple of Love* does not question that this ought to be the order of things. Rather, as an entertainment commissioned by the queen, it addresses the question of what kind of love subjects should show, and what might properly be the reason of their affection, loyalty, and admiration. According to the logic of this masque, the royal couple's virtues were their true beauty, and the proper object of their subject's affections. This was a love that was chaste, not bodily, spiritual rather than corporeal, divine rather than earthly. I will not discuss all the details of the masque, but emphasize the dramatic progress through this genre's typical phases: 'masque', 'anti-masque', and resolution that ends the performance and initiates the 'revels', the concluding celebratory dance.

This orientalist work's 'masque' begins with words from a costumed woman playing the role of 'Divine Poesy'. She is identified as the 'secretary of nature' and we are informed that she has been 'sent by fate' to Indiamora, 'Queen of Natsinga' (the role taken by Henrietta Maria). Fate has determined that it is time for Indiamora to be called upon to 'use the influence of her beauty' to re-establish the 'Temple of Chaste Love' on earth.[67] Divine Poesy is accompanied by reincarnated Greek poets (Demodocus, Phemius, Homer, Hesiod, Terpander, and Sappho, themselves recently reformed by Divine Poesy's Platonic influence). They also act as a chorus. Divine Poesy first announces that Indiamora shall return 'from above | To guide those lovers that want sight | To see and know what they should love'.[68] Before this can happen, however, Divine Poesy and Indiamora must deal with a band of magicians, 'the enemies of chaste love'.

The magicians make their entrance from underground caves. They wear strange dress and reveal deformed bodies. The magicians have heard that

---

[66] James I himself refused to walk on stage, but this was not true of his predecessors, or of Charles I or Henrietta Maria. In all cases, however, the performance recognized and made their presence a part of the resolution.

[67] William Davenant, *The Temple of Love*, in *Dramatic Works*, ed. James Maidment and W. H. Logan, i. 2 vols. (London: H. Sotheran, 1872–4), 286. Although I will quote text from Davenant's works, see also Orgel and Strong (1973), ii. 598–629: this includes Jones's sketches of costumes, scenery, and stage design.   [68] Ibid. i. 289.

Indiamora is to come, and express their doubts about the new doctrine of love which 'must not woo or court the person, but the mind'. Comments one magician, 'Your spirit's a cold companion at midnight.' They nevertheless confess that they have, 'mis-lead and entertained | The youthful of the world, | I mean their bodies.'[69] However, their efforts at deception are now failing. Some Persian youths first drawn to the baser pleasures promised by the magicians are approaching. They have spied a small corner of the true temple of love previously concealed, and they appear to be on their way to becoming converts to the ideals of 'Platonical lovers'.[70]

The magicians are determined to 'wake our drowsy art, and try, | If we have power to hinder destiny'. They marshal the forces of the spirits of fire, air, water, earth, and a 'sect of modern devils' in the hope that if they are not able to 'uphold the faction of | The flesh, yet to infect the queazy age | With blacker sins.'[71] This initiates the second typical phase of this genre, the anti-masque.

In this phase the magicians' parts are not performed by aristocrats, but professional actors. Professional actors also played the part of the various spirits who bring in wave after wave of persons engaged in unsavory, anti-Platonic, conduct: 'debotched and quarrelling men' accompanied by a 'loose wench'; 'amorous men and women in ridiculous habits'; 'drunken Dutch skippers'; 'witches, usurers, and fools'; and finally 'a modern devil, a sworn enemy of poesy'.[72] The magicians' efforts fail. A Persian page comes to announce that his once lusty masters are already converts to Indiamora's cult: 'For I must tell you, that about them all | There's not one grain, but what's Platonical'.[73]

Following the entrance and a dance by these reformed masters, Jones and Davenant arrange for supernatural intervention to clear the way for Indiamora's arrival and the performance's conclusion. Divine Poesy sends Orpheus over the seas accompanied by Brahmins ('Brachmani'). So begins the performance's resolution. Orpheus uses his power to calm the rude winds and troublesome waves as the Brahmins sing his praises:

> No winds of late have rudely blown,
> Nor waves their troubled heads advance!
> His harp that made the winds so mild,
> They whisper now as reconcil'd
> The waves are sooth'd into a dance.[74]

---

[69] Davenant, Dramatic Works, ed. Maidment and Logan, 292–3.   [70] Ibid. 294.

[71] Ibid. 295.

[72] Ibid. 295–6. It is noteworthy that the 'modern devil' is also a sworn enemy of 'music, and all ingenious arts, but a great friend to murmuring, libelling, and all seeds of discord' and that such devils are 'Fine precise fiends, that hear the devout close | At ev'ry virtue but their own, that claim | Chambers and tenements in heaven . . .'. This is generally understood as a reference to William Prynne, puritanical author of *Historiomastix*, a trenchant criticism of stage players, and of woman stage players in particular ('notorious whores'). He was severely punished by Charles I, who took Prynne's criticisms as an assault on Henrietta Maria: ibid. and 283–5.

[73] Ibid. 297.   [74] Ibid. 300–1.

Chaotic nature, and those who would whip up such storms, having been subdued and ordered by divine force, Indiamora arrives over the sea in a chariot. At this point the queen would have left her seat in the audience to become a part of the action on stage. A song proclaiming her presence is performed, and the queen and the noblewoman attending her then 'descended into the room'.[75] Another song begins which instructs the masquers to dance with the noblemen playing the Persian visitors. These new converts to Platonic love, 'Now offer willing sacrifice | Unto the virtues of the mind'.[76] As this dance concludes, the queen is reseated next to Charles I, and the temple of love is revealed. Inside the temple two ethereal figures emerge, Sunesis and Thelema, representing 'Understanding' and 'Will'.[77] These two form a union, and state together, 'When perfect Will, and strengthened Reason meet, | Then Love's created to endure'.[78] Finally, 'Amianteros' (chaste love) comes flying out of a cloud floated from the top of the set and proclaims: 'Y'ar the emblem of my Diety'. Sunesis salutes Charles I:

> To Charles, the mightiest and the best,
> And to the darling of his breast,
> (Who rule b'example as by power)
> May youthful blessings still increase,
> And in their off-spring never cease,
> Till time's too old to last an hour.[79]

What is noteworthy in the masque is that the key audience member—in this case the queen—enters the performance. This convention meant that monarchs, or as in this case queens, became what they saw.[80] A masque such as *The Temple of Love* therefore not only offered Charles and Henrietta Maria and the audience of assembled notables a vision of a divinely sanctioned order on earth, but gave the queen herself a role in bringing this symbolic order into being. A concept of legitimacy is not merely announced. Those who would wish to find themselves so legitimated are afforded the opportunity symbolically to enact it. Moreover, recent work on the political character of the masque has suggested that poets such as Davenant were not simply writing to reiterate and reinforce established royal doctrines concerning how and why subjects should submit to sovereign rule. It has been argued that they were more than merely pens for hire, but took the opportunity as authors of these works subtly to suggest modifications in the basis for political order. It has been argued that Davenant—who lost his nose to

---

[75] Ibid.   [76] Ibid. 302   [77] Ibid. 286.   [78] Ibid. 303.   [79] Ibid. 304.
[80] On this see Orgel (1965), Orgel and Strong (1973), and for a somewhat different perspective on the uniformity of political views within the masque, Sharpe (1987).

syphilis—had his doubts about Platonic love, and gave voice to these doubts in the speeches made by the magicians and the Persian visitor's page.[81]

For our purposes, however, there are two items of importance. The first is that the masque genre allowed a monarch to self-enact his or her own representation before the eyes of the audience. It was for the monarch a highly stylized and fantastic way to see, and become, oneself. Secondly, it offered the monarch and the masque's authors a way to suggest why that self was worthy of loyalty, admiration, and obedience. In a court that emphasized the divine sanction behind its rule the enacted intervention and approval of particular gods and spirits became a way to give this expression.

As Hobbes and his contemporaries make clear, *Leviathan* was meant to be presented to Charles II.[82] A very elaborate work 'in a marvellous fair hand' was prepared, and Hobbes went to deliver the text personally to Charles in France. His way was blocked—the Earl of Clarendon boasted, upon his recommendation—and very soon thereafter Hobbes felt the need to flee France for England.[83]

Was the *Leviathan* a text in which Charles was to see himself? It has been suggested that he would have seen himself in the frontispiece of the edition intended for him,[84] but if we are to consider Hobbes's eloquence then we will need to look for other signs. I would not wish to suggest that all that is eloquent in *Leviathan* is dedicated to the goal of allowing its reader to find a self-reflection, but there are strong suggestions in several parts of *Leviathan* that indicate that this was one of his goals. In what remains of this essay I will review these aspects of Hobbes's work, and illustrate the ways in which Hobbes's work was, in effect, a pointed counterpart to—and thereby an echo of—the court masques that the Stuart court once employed as a means of articulating its legitimacy.

Hobbes did not paint an admiring picture of human nature, and in making his break with the Aristotelian tradition, he understood that his vision of human nature would require a robust defense. As a part of this

---

[81] If the suggestion by Sharpe (1987) is correct, however, it is not merely Davenant's personal habits that are protesting against the ideal of Platonic love. Davenant's advocacy for a more bodily form of love is read by Sharpe as a subtle suggestion that Charles I's aloof personal rule be altered in favor of a regime with a more visible and passionate affection for the body politic, including Parliament.

[82] Verse Autobiography, lines 207–14, 233–46, in Curley's edn. of *Leviathan*, pp. liv–lxiv.

[83] Ibid. Edward Hyde (Earl of Clarendon), *A Brief View and Survey of the Dangerous Errors of Church and State in Mr Hobbes's Book, entitled Leviathan* (Oxford: Printed at the Theatre and Richard, 1676), 8; and Tuck, who reviews the evidence for the date of presentation in 'A note on the text' in Thomas Hobbes, *Leviathan*, ed. Richard Tuck (Cambridge: Cambridge University Press, 1991), pp. xxxii–xxxiii; on this see also Burgess (1990) and Sarasohn (2000).

[84] Keith Brown, 'The Artist of the *Leviathan* Title-Page', *British Library Journal*, 4 (1978), 24–36.

defense, he derives the conflict between men in the state of nature from the consequences that follow from the first law of nature. But this is not the only evidence that he musters. He notes in both *De Cive* and *Leviathan* that persons who are not satisfied with such abstract proofs need only observe their own actions to verify the truth of his pessimistic observations. Do we not lock our chests at night, do we not travel with arms?[85] Hobbes's remarks in the Introduction to *Leviathan* have been read in much the same spirit. Here he notes: 'whosoever looketh into himself and considereth what he doth, when he does *think, opine, reason, hope, fear,* &c, and upon what grounds, he shall thereby read and know, what are the thoughts and passions of all other men upon the like occasions.'[86] This is not to suggest that a man may know what all other persons make the objects of their desire, but we can at least know what it is for our fellow human beings to have such objects, and find the similarity in our own experience. But Hobbes does something in this Introduction which differentiates *Leviathan* from *De Cive*. In the Introduction, Hobbes also writes:

But let one man read another by his actions never so perfectly, it serves him only with his acquaintance, which are but few. He that is to govern a whole nation must read in himself, not this or that particular man, but mankind, which though it be hard to do, harder than to learn any language or science, yet when I shall have set down my own reading orderly and perspicuously, the pains left another will be only to consider if he also find not the same in himself. For this kind of doctrine admitteth no other demonstration.[87]

It is not merely individuals who must find their acquaintances, but sovereigns who must find themselves in this text. Moreover, what the sovereign reads when he finds himself in this text will be 'mankind'. Self-identification is a complex thing for 'He that is to govern a whole nation'; he must find in mankind a reflection of himself, and Hobbes's claim is to have made this difficult task less burdensome. What is left for the sovereign is to affirm that he in fact sees himself in this text. The passage is enough to suggest that *Leviathan* can function as a philosophical mirror for a prince, but what connection can be made between this and mirroring and the mirrors that poets offer?

Hobbes introduces the question of how persons are to know themselves by way of a phrase, *nosce teipsum*, which he notably translates as 'read thyself' rather than the more conventional translation 'know thyself'. He states that this phrase is 'not of late understood'. It should not, says Hobbes, be taken 'to countenance either the barbarous state of men in power towards their inferiors, or to encourage men of low degree to a saucy behavior

---

[85] *De Cive*, 1: 2 (annotation); *Leviathan*, 13: 10.   [86] *Leviathan*, 'Introduction', 3.
[87] Ibid. 4.

towards their betters'. It ought instead to become a source of unification, 'to teach us . . . the similitude of the thoughts and passions of one man to the thoughts and passions of another'.[88]

Nosce teipsum, however, was not merely a phrase, and there is good reason to believe that Hobbes was making an oblique reference. *Nosce Teipsum* was the name of a poem written by Sir John Davies (1569–1626), dedicated to Queen Elizabeth and first published in 1599.[89] It was the first English work to combine poetry and a systematic philosophical doctrine. Davies reaped the rewards of his tribute. Elizabeth made him her servant, and this began a long and successful career that included being made a member of Parliament, James I's Attorney General for Ireland, being knighted, and shortly before his death being made Lord Chief Justice.[90] On the basis of these accomplishments alone it is safe to assume that Hobbes would have known of Davies, but there are other reasons for making a still closer connection to the poem itself. I noted above that *Gondibert* deliberately combined the aspects of multiple genres. One element was choice of stanza, and, as David Galdish has noted, *Nosce Teipsum* was the model for *Gondibert*'s stanza form: four rhyming lines of iambic pentameter, *abab*.[91] Last, and most interestingly, Davies treats subjects of central concern to Hobbes: materialism, sense, the fear of death, and the mortality of the soul.[92] On these questions, their conclusions are in many respects diametrically opposed. Davies insists that the soul is spiritual, not material, that it is immortal, and that the (reasonable) indifference of noble souls to the death of their bodies stands as evidence. This is not the place to inventory the differences between Hobbes and Davies, but that so many are diametric

---

[88] *Leviathan*, 'Introduction': 3. Not all interpreters agree on the significance of this phrase. See Tracy B. Strong, 'How to Write Scripture: Words, Authority, and Politics in Thomas Hobbes', *Critical Inquiry*, 20 (1993), 128–59; Gary Shapiro, 'Reading and Writing in the Text of Hobbes's *Leviathan*', *Journal of the History of Philosophy*, 18 (1980), 147–57.

[89] Alexander B. Grosart, *The Complete Works of John Davies of Hereford*, New York, AMS Press, 1967 [1878], vol. i, 31–157.

[90] E. Hershey Sneath, *Philosophy in Poetry: A Study of Sir John Davies's Poem 'Nosce Teipsum'* (New York: Greenwood Press, 1969 [1903]), 26–31. Anthony-à-Wood tells the story of James's recognition of Davies: 'he, with Lord Hunsdon, went into Scotland to congratulate K. James as her [Elizabeth's] lawful successor; and being introduced into his presence, the king enquired the names of those gentlemen who were in the company of the said lord, and he nameing John Davies among, who stood behind them, the king straightway asked, whether he was *Nosce Teipsum*? And being answered that he was the same, he graciously embraced him, and thenceforth had so great a favour for him, that soon after he made him his solicitor, and then his attorney-general in Ireland' (*Athenae Oxonienses*, ed. Philip Buss (New York: B. Franklin, 1967 [1691–2]), ii. 401, cited in Sneath (1969), 29).

[91] Gladish, 'Introduction', Davenant (1971), p. xvi.

[92] For a treatment see Sneath (1967). Cf. David Johnston 'Hobbes's Mortalism', *History of Political Thought* 10 (1989), 647–63. Understanding *Leviathan* as a masque for a mortal god also allows us to see that he was not merely a mortalist when it came to individual souls, but also as regards the commonwealth's soul.

suggests that Hobbes may have been subtly suggesting his desire to compete with the famous self-reading of a previous courtly poet-philosopher.

If we next ask how the sovereign is to find 'mankind' in himself we are again driven to the parts of *Leviathan* where poetry makes a contribution to Hobbes's philosophy. These are the parts of *Leviathan* that offer the most concrete discussion of how the sovereign is to find a multitude in himself. Hobbes does this in two ways. The first is essentially static. He considers the prospect as a matter of definition, and this takes us to Chapter Sixteen, 'Of Persons, Authors and *Things Personated*'. This chapter has been a source of irritation to philosophers, some finding fascinating half-truths about representation, some finding inconceivable claims about agency, and others inspiration.[93] I do not propose to solve these dilemmas or reconcile competing views; I will narrowly focus on the question of how the sovereign is taught to see himself. What is perhaps most remarkable in this chapter is how thoroughly Hobbes integrates the language of a poetic domain, stage representation, into his understanding of these matters.

A person, according to Hobbes, 'is he *whose words or actions are considered either as his own, or as representing the words or actions of another man, or of any other thing to whom they are attributed, whether truly or by fiction*'.[94] There are two types of persons, natural and artificial. The natural person represents words and actions 'considered as his own'. The artificial or 'feigned' person represents the actions of another.[95] There is, notably, a stage sensibility embedded in Hobbes's approach that is prior to the division between natural and artificial persons. Thus natural persons are not so much themselves, but 'persons' representing themselves. Hobbes reinforces this impression when he notes that 'person' in Latin (*persona*), 'signifies the *disguise* or *outward appearance* of a man, counterfeited on stage, and sometimes more particularly that part of it which disguiseth the face (as a mask or visard)'. Out of these theatrical contexts, the terms 'person', or its equivalent, 'actor', and the verb 'personate' have been 'translated to any represeter of speech and action'. We now speak, says Hobbes, of persons as actors, and this is done 'both on the stage and in common conversation'.[96] We may either 'personate' ourselves, as natural persons, or 'personate' others as artificial persons.

But Hobbes does not simply appropriate the stage terminology. He politically and philosophically refines the language by delineating natural and

---

[93] See, for example, Hanna F. Pitkin, *The Concept of Representation* (Berkeley: University of California Press, 1967), 14–37; Strong (1993); Gauthier (1969); Jean Hampton, *Hobbes and the Social Contract Tradition* (Cambridge: Cambridge University Press, 1986), esp. 114–31, 208–20; A. P. Martinich, *The Two Gods of* Leviathan, (Cambridge: Cambridge University Press, 1992), 161–75.   [94] *Leviathan*, 16: 1.

[95] Ibid. 16: 2.

[96] Ibid. 16: 3, and as Hobbes notes, this translation has reached the courts, in which context Cicero spoke of bearing three persons in himself: his own, his adversaries, and the judge's.

artificial persons, and goes on to discuss the relationship between the authorship, personation, and ownership. Some artificial persons perform actions or speak words that are 'owned' by those they represent.[97] That is, we may 'author' acts or words and commission the actor or person to perform these on our behalf. This is what it means to act 'by authority'. The fictive nature of these arrangements—that they are the stagecraft of our everyday commerce—makes them the subject of suspicion, and Hobbes reflects this distrust by noting that it is necessary to take precautions when dealing with actors who claim authority. Those who engage in transactions with persons purporting to be the representatives of others, i.e. artificial persons, must insure that those persons are in fact acting by the authority they claim. Likewise, we must attribute the actions or words, including commitments, to the legitimate authors—the owners—and not the artificial persons themselves.[98]

It is from within this framework that Hobbes also speaks of the capacity of one person to become the artificial person who represents a multitude:

A multitude of men are made *one* person, when they are by one man, or one person, represented so that it be done with the consent of every one of that multitude in particular. For it is the *unity* of the representer, not the *unity* of the represented, that maketh the person *one*. And it is the representer that beareth the person, and but one person, and *unity* cannot be otherwise understood in multitude.[99]

Here the concern is not so much one of trickery and fraud, as insuring that individuals understand what it means to authorize the words and actions of a sovereign. Thus, the last qualification concerning the unity of the representer reflects Hobbes's efforts to dissuade those who assign sovereignty to a representative assembly from making the assumption that their authorization is contingent upon the unanimity of representatives or subjects. Even the disappointed minority must abide by the sovereign assembly's decision as a command. For our purposes, however, it is key that Hobbes allows that a single person may represent a multitude. He goes on to assert that these members of the multitude are each 'authors of everything their representative saith or doth in their name, every man giving their common representer authority from himself in particular, and owning all the actions the representer doth, in case they give him authority without stint'.[100] It should be noted that Hobbes's contemporaries would not have needed the lesson in Latin etymology to understand 'personation'. It was not merely Romans who used this terminology, but Davenant and Jonson as well. Davenant, for

---

[97] Some do not. Hobbes notes that things or persons incapable of authorship and ownership of words and actions (churches, lunatics, children, etc.) may also be personated when the owners of the thing, or the guardian of the person, so charges them with the role. *Leviathan*, 16: 9–10.

[98] *Leviathan*, 16: 5–8.   [99] Ibid. 16: 13.   [100] Ibid. 16: 14.

example, speaks of Henrietta Maria 'personating the chiefe Heroin' in the masque *Salmacida Spolia.*[101]

If chapter XVI of *Leviathan* illustrates the importation of stage language and categories into everyday conversations, chapter XVII, 'Of the Causes, Generation, and Definition of a Commonwealth', works in the opposite direction. It imports the fictive stage action of the masque into the authorization of the sovereign. Moreover, this reflection is not static, a matter of definition. Here Hobbes offers an active self-reflection very much like the masque's presentation of the sovereign to himself.

I am not suggesting that Hobbes's understanding of the sovereign's power is simply a product of his desire to emulate the masque form. I am suggesting, however, that Hobbes's poetic contributions reach their head in this chapter, and that he employs his eloquence to enable and encourage Charles to see himself in making out the multitude.

First on this stage is man himself. This chapter reiterates in brief man's flustered attempts at self-preservation. The laws of nature may call for justice, equality, modest, mercy, and the like, but they are not self-enforcing. They may be the dictates of right reason, and they may be the rules that God places upon the consciousness of men, but they require the sword and not merely the will and rationality of men to insure that they are made commands and not merely council. In cataloguing the reasons why a power to 'awe them all' is indispensable, Hobbes takes the opportunity to illustrate the misery and disorder of peoples who are not restrained by fear of such power.

Against the Aristotelian view of man the *polis* animal, Hobbes reminds his readers that human beings, unlike naturally social creatures, compete for honor and dignity, and this gives rise to envy, hatred, and war.[102] He does not pretend to show his reader the deformed and imperfect bodies that disturb the desired order, but Hobbes's anti-masque is an itemization of the conclusions that illustrate our proclivity to bring about our own ruin. We are prideful. Rather than see the common good served, men would prefer to see themselves honored in comparison with others. Each knowing himself to be wiser than the rest, we are constantly finding fault in the administration of common business.[103] We can use our tongues to 'represent to others that which is good in the likeness of evil, and evil in the likeness of good, and augment or diminish the apparent greatness of good and evil, discontenting men, and troubling their peace at their pleasure'. Unlike animals, we take and give offense to one another.[104]

Whereas the masque celebrated the order brought about by the monarchy through divine intervention, Hobbes resolves the story by dramatizing the

---

[101] Davenant (1872) vol. 2, *Salmacida Spolia*, 'The Subject of the Masque'. Plays, of course, referred to *Dramatis Personae*.   [102] *Leviathan*, 16: 6–7.

[103] Ibid. 16: 8–9.   [104] Ibid. 16: 10–11.

creation and authorization of a mortal god. Instead of making the sovereign divine, or fortify his rule by divine assistance, Hobbes puts poetic skill to work and allows the sovereign to see himself in the making as a product of the covenant between men in the state of nature. Hobbes's sovereign is the object of obedience not because he is the object of their love, and not because legitimacy comes from divine forces from above to grant or affirm virtues worthy of such affection and allegiance. An essential part of Hobbes's persuasive task was to convince the sovereign to accept legitimation from below. Instead of seeing themselves as a gift from above (or even aspiring to be thought one), they had instead to see themselves as the artificial, man-made, god who comes into being as a necessary means of insuring that those who have made themselves miserable can improve their condition. This, of course, is the prelude to the creation of the *Leviathan*, or mortal god.

The only way to erect such a common power . . . and thereby to secure them in such sort as that by their own industry, and by the fruits of the earth, they may nourish themselves and live contentedly, is to confer all their power and strength upon one man, or upon one assembly of men, that may reduce all their wills, by plurality of voices, unto one will . . . to appoint one man or assembly of men to bear their person, and every one to own and acknowledge himself to be author of whatsoever he that so beareth their person shall act, or cause to be acted . . . to submit their wills, every one to his will, and their judgments to his judgment.[105]

Hobbes echoed the structure of the masque to create a mortal and material God. This represents a fusion of poetry and philosophy designed to convince Charles to see himself in this artificial creation, i.e. as the personator of the multitude. Hobbes, nonetheless, allows that a sovereign assembly may also assume this role. I would suggest that this is best read as an implicit threat. If one does not come to see oneself as the multitude's mortal god, it will be possible for an assembly of men to assume this role.

The assembly might 'personate' the multitude, but Hobbes had long since made his preferences clear. He preferred the unity of a sovereign monarch over a sovereign assembly.[106] In offering a masque-like form of self-reflection, and making the image that of a god, however, Hobbes was making a gesture to Charles and by echoing the masque he makes the gesture suited to Charles. If sovereigns had been taught by poets and scholars to see themselves as gods, Hobbes was ready to use poetic skill to craft a god for Charles to become. This god was an artificial, man-made by initial '*pacts* and *covenants*'. As he notes in the Introduction: this act of covenanting 'resemble [s] that *fiat*, or the *let us make man*, pronounced by God in the creation'.[107]

---

[105] *Leviathan*, 16: 13.
[106] *Elements of Law*, II. ch. 24; *De Cive*, 'Preface', ch. 10, cf. *Leviathan*, ch. 19.
[107] *Leviathan*, 'Introduction', 1.

Thus, the fictions of the old state find their counterpart in the fictions of the new, and therewith Hobbes offers his advice on how to see and conceive of the sovereign self. In the masque the key member of the audience is called upon to participate in the making of his own legitimate image. In Hobbes's masque, *Leviathan*, the legitimate image is made in a hypothetical act:

It is a real unity of them all, in one and the same person, made by covenant of every man with every man, in such manner as if every man should say to every man *I authorise and give up my right of governing myself to this man, or to this assembly of men, on this condition, that thou give up thy right to him, and authorize all his actions in the like manner.* This done, the multitude so united in one person is called a Commonwealth, in Latin Civitas. This is the generation of that great Leviathan, or rather (to speak more reverently) of that *Mortal God* to which we owe, under the *Immortal God*, our peace and defense.[108]

Hobbes's remark in the Introduction that 'the pains left another will be only to consider if he also find not the same in himself. For this kind of doctrine admitteth no other demonstration'[109] suggests that it is the would-be sovereign who must, by accepting himself, insure the truth of his political philosophy. Not unlike a god, or a geometrician, the truth of Hobbes's doctrine is made true because the absolute sovereign must make the properties of the commonwealth himself.

Leviathan's uniqueness is rooted in its poetic-philosophical innovations. They reflect Hobbes's practical need to speak to a would-be sovereign in a poetic language familiar to the Stuart kings yet sufficient to his desire to advise the monarch to adopt his alternative conception of legitimacy. If the text speaks to the question of Hobbes's uniqueness it does so by testifying to the degree to which this philosopher found himself engaged in the thick of political life, and the unusually intricate political imagination of his historical contexts.

[108] *Leviathan*, 16: 13.   [109] Ibid. 'Introduction', 4.

Leviathan's *Theory of Justice*

LUC FOISNEAU

The theory of justice is not a recent invention. On the contrary, many philosophers since Aristotle have contributed to it, and the success of *A Theory of Justice* is owed not so much to a novel concept as to the renewal of an old idea that fell into disuse in political thought. In fact, the history of political thought has gone through a series of episodes similar to the one that preceded the publication of John Rawls's innovative work. The theory of justice suffered neglect just at those moments when it was being seriously questioned. It is to one of those periods that I am going to turn in this essay, for one of the distinguishing features of *Leviathan* is its revision of an earlier concept of justice, including the view of justice put forward by Hobbes himself in *De Cive* and *The Elements of Law*. Not only are certain elements of the theory of justice in *Leviathan* missing in his two earlier works, but each of the earlier works reflects a major crisis in the understanding of the concept of justice at the time. Hobbes's impatience with Aristotle's concepts of commutative and distributive justice, and the irony with which he criticizes them, show the contempt he had for them in the 1640s.

The loss of confidence in the theoretical relevance of justice went hand in hand with the emergence of the free market as a new means for determining value in seventeenth-century England. Although one must beware of the kind of oversimplification that may arise when interpreting a political work within the context of a complex economic and social situation, it does help to see Hobbes's theory of justice in the context of a new social and economic order based on the free market. The rejection of the theory of justice in *The Elements of Law* and *De Cive* hinges largely on a new principle of valuation, which replaces the principle of fair exchange with the law of supply and demand as a price-fixing mechanism. No need any longer to ask whether an exchange is fair: the matter is settled if there is a willing buyer. No need to ask whether a distribution of goods is fair, since it is supposed to result from a system that takes into account the evaluations of each participant in the market. Whether fair or unfair, the mechanism of the distribution of goods is seen as resulting from the collective will of the innumerable players in the exchange.

What I set out to do here, is not so much to raise a historical question about the social and economic reasons for the crisis in the concept of justice in the 1640s, as to reflect on the philosophical aspects of Hobbes's recasting of the theory of justice in *Leviathan*. The first aspect of this recasting is the emergence of a new definition of justice as keeping valid covenants; the second aspect is a new understanding of distribution and exchanges; and the third aspect is a criticism of alternative forms of justice, which is to be found in the famous refutation of the fool, in chapter XV of *Leviathan*. The peculiarity of the third of Hobbes's political treatises is thus that it simultaneously presents the crisis in the concept of justice and resolves it, in the form of a theory based on a novel conception of contractual exchanges and political authority.

I. A THEORY OF JUSTICE IN PROGRESS

Although the idea of fulfilling contracts plays an essential part in the natural law theory of *The Elements of Law*[1] and *De Cive*,[2] it is not explicitly connected with a definition of justice. The nearest Hobbes comes to such a definition is when he says, in *The Elements of Law*, that the 'breach or violation of covenant, is that which men call *injury*, consisting in some action or omission, which is therefore called *unjust*'.[3] What is being stressed in the latter passage is the fact that breaking a contract is an unjust action, but this doesn't amount to a definition of justice. Such an act is unjust, because it is contrary to the *jus*, or right, which has been transferred in the contract, but it is not opening the way to a general theory of justice, which is more than a theory of injury. Not until *Leviathan* does Hobbes genuinely formulate the theory, formally identifying justice in the third law of nature as keeping contractual agreements. In the English version, the law requiring people to perform their covenants is presented as 'the Fountain and Originall of Justice'.[4] In the Latin original, the formulation is even clearer: 'It is in this

---

[1] 'Therefore the law of nature mentioned in the former chapter, sect. 2, namely, *That every man should divest himself of the right, &c*, were utterly vain, and of none effect, if this also were not a law of the same Nature, *That every man is obliged to stand to, and perform, those covenants which he maketh*' (*The Elements of Law*, I. xvi. 1, ed. F. Tönnies (London, 1889), 82). References throughout are for *The Elements of Law* (EL) to the Tönnies edition, for the *De Cive*, Latin and English, to the Warrender editions, for the English *Leviathan* (*Lev*) to the Macpherson edition and for the Latin *Leviathan* (*Lev* Latin) to the Molesworth edition (I indicate chapter numbers and paragraph numbers).

[2] 'Legum naturalium deriuatarum altera est, *Pactis standum* esse, siue fidem seruandam esse.' (*De Cive, The Latin Version*, cap. III, i, ed. H. Warrender (Oxford: Clarendon Press, 1983), 108).

[3] EL, I. xvi. 1, p. 82.

[4] *Leviathan*, XV. 2, ed. C. B. Macpherson (Harmondsworth: Penguin Books, 1968), 202. This theory undoubtedly has Epicurean origins. See Grotius's criticism of the conventionalist theory of justice in Epicurus, *De jure belli ac pacis*, II. XX. 4. For more details on the origin of the formula

law that the nature of justice is found'.[5] These two statements in *Leviathan* constitute an advance in Hobbes's theory of justice.

Indeed, in *The Elements of Law* and in the first edition of *De Cive* (1642), Hobbes does not bother to establish a link between injury and justice. It is not until 1647, in the second edition of *De Cive*, that he attempts to expand his reasoning to include a definition of injustice, distinguishing between *injustice* and *injury*:

The word injustice (*injustitia*) relates to some Law: Injury (*injuria*) to some Person, as well as some Law. For what's unjust, is unjust to all; but there may an injury be done, and yet not against me, nor thee, but some other; and sometimes against no private person, but the Magistrate only; sometimes also neither against the Magistrate, nor any private man, but onely against God.[6]

Although this distinction undoubtedly helps to reveal a relationship between abiding by one's contracts and the institution of justice in the state, it is not sufficient to reduce the gap between a universal theory of justice and a theory of personal injury or tort. The unilateral violation of a covenant is an injury against the person with whom the agreement is made, but not necessarily an injury against the person of the magistrate. And it is not clear whether the injury done to the magistrate must be understood as an injustice done to all, or as an injury done to a single person. The reference to God tends to make the political point of the passage less clear. The distinction between injustice and injury is more clearly expressed in *Leviathan*, thanks to the personification of the state allowed by the novel theory of political representation.[7] If it is still true that 'the Injustice of an Action, (that is to say Injury,) supposeth an individuall person injured',[8] the injury done to the person of the commonwealth acquires a meaning that it could not have had in *De Cive*. Although private men can remit their debts to one another, they cannot do the same with violent acts, because such acts are an injury to the person of the state. The political notion of injustice appears, then, when the person to whom an injury is done is not a private man, but the person of the commonwealth.

In *Leviathan*, Hobbes establishes the unity of the theory of justice, specifically emphasizing not only the legal, but also the political, nature of the

---

Pacta sunt servanda, see Johannes Bärmann, 'Pacta sunt servanda. Considérations sur l'histoire du contrat consensuel', *Revue internationale de droit comparé* (janvier–mars 1961), 18–53.

[5] 'Atque in hac lege consistit natura justitiæ' (*Leviathan*, XV. 2, in *Opera Philosophica*, iii, ed. W. Molesworth (London, 1841), 111).

[6] *De Cive. The English Version*, III. 4, ed. H. Warrender (Oxford: Clarendon Press, 1983), 63–4.

[7] 'A Multitude of men, are made *One* Person, when they are by one man, or one Person, Represented; so that it be done with the consent of every one of that Multitude in particular. For it is the *Unity* of the Representer, not the *Unity* of the Represented, that maketh the Person *One*. . . . And *Unity*, cannot otherwise be understood in Multitude' (*Lev*, XVI. 13, p. 220).

[8] *Lev*, XV. 12, p. 207.

theory. He states his thesis—glaringly absent from his first two political works—in the third paragraph of chapter XV of *Leviathan*: 'So that the nature of Justice, consisteth in keeping of valid covenants: but the Validity of Covenants begins not but with the Constitution of a Civill Power, sufficient to compell men to keep them.'[9] In order to understand the relationship established here between justice and the state, it is necessary to analyse the reasons for keeping a covenant. The main reason, as we all know, for voiding a contract is usually fear of the other party not performing. If justice resides in keeping one's word, it is important that this fear does not become a hindrance. This is a particularly delicate issue in the case of those contracts called covenants, in which one party has to perform first and trust the other, because such agreements are rendered void 'where there is a feare of not performance on either part'.[10]

In chapter XIV of *Leviathan*, Hobbes points out the reason why this type of covenant cannot hold in a condition of mere nature, but only in a civil state:

For he that performeth first, has no assurance the other will performe after; because the bonds of words are too weak to bridle mens ambition, avarice, anger, and other Passions, without the feare of some coercitive Power; which in the condition of meer Nature, where all men are equall, and judges of the justness of their own fears cannot possibly be supposed.[11]

Hobbes does not argue here that the existence of the state is enough to dispel fear and distrust in human relations; nor does he claim that fear, in and of itself, renders contracts void. To take the first point, the existence of the state does not dispel fear because it is itself the source of another specific type of fear called 'terrour', which comes from its exclusive right to pass sentences and inflict punishment. Terror has an effect of its own on the fear of seeing a covenant broken. When exercised in the name of the law, terror serves 'to compell men equally to the performance of their Covenants, by the terrour of some punishment, greater than the benefit they expect by the breach of their Covenant'.[12] So fear of the state should counteract the fear that covenants will be violated by those performing second. Concerning the second point—that fear might make contracts void—Hobbes indicates that, in the condition of mere nature, agreements made out of fear create an obligation.[13] A covenant to pay a ransom is therefore valid, since it is a contract, 'wherein one receiveth the benefit of life; the other is to receive mony, or service for it'.[14] The same is true of a disadvantageous peace made by a weaker prince with a stronger one, since the weakness creates an obligation to respect the conditions of peace. If fear can be a good enough reason for

---

[9] *Lev*, XV. 3, p. 202–3. [10] *Lev*, XV. 3, p. 202. [11] *Lev*, XIV. 19, p. 196.
[12] *Lev*, XV. 3, p. 202. [13] *Lev*, XIV. 27, p. 198. [14] Ibid.

breaking a covenant, it is also a good enough reason to enter into one, and therefore to contract an obligation. As long as men are 'judges of the justness of their own fears',[15] there can be no reason for not breaking covenants, and for not entering into covenants out of fear of the contractor. Since only the law can free us from obligations contracted under conditions of violence, the state appears simultaneously as the product of a political contract based on fear, and as the condition for voiding covenants entered into through fear. Since justice is embodied in keeping covenants, and the state guarantees that these covenants will be honoured, Hobbes is right to say that the state gives meaning to the terms 'just' and 'unjust'.[16]

Thus, behind the theoretical deduction of the sovereign state lies the state as guarantor of private contracts, and particularly of private property. In renouncing his *jus in omnia*, according to the terms of the second law of nature, man does indeed acquire new, artificial rights, which result from the contract agreed upon with everyone else. A man's laying down his right to all things is the absolute condition for the existence of private property, because it allows him to acquire the right to own certain things 'in recompense of the universall Right [he] abandon[s]'.[17] The existence of a state capable of guaranteeing this mutual renunciation is the precondition for the existence of private property. Behind this philosophical justification of property rights in a political society based on contracts, there is, it might be thought, the state as a political mechanism for developing a domestic market founded on contracts. The examples that Hobbes gives in *The Elements of Law* illustrate the extension of this market to the realm of labour, which had for a long time been protected by corporations, and to the realm of landed property, which was the foundation of feudal society.[18] In this way a Commonwealth based on contract serves as the foundation of a contractual society, in which the virtue of justice tends to be replaced by the justice of commercial exchanges. What, then, is left of the virtue of justice, or justice of manners, in the new commercial society?

II. JUSTICE OF CONTRACTORS AND VIRTUE OF JUSTICE

To take further the idea that neither justice nor private property can exist without the State, Hobbes uses the well-known scholastic adage, 'Justice is

---

[15] *Lev*, XIV. 19, p. 196.

[16] 'Therefore before the names of Just, and Unjust can have place, there must be some coercitive Power, to compell men equally to the performance of their Covenants, by the terrour of some punishment, greater than the benefit they expect by the breach of their Covenant' (*Lev*, XV. 3, p. 202). [17] *Lev*, XV. 3, p. 202.

[18] *Elements of Law*, I, XVI, 3, p. 82–3; *De Cive, The English Version*, II. 4, p. 54.

the constant Will of giving to every man his own'.[19] He could also have referred to Cicero's *De inventione*, which says 'justitia est habitus animi, communi utilitate conservata, suam cuique tribuens dignitatem'.[20] or, just as legitimately, to the Roman lawyer Ulpian, who defines justice as 'the constant and perpetual will to render everyman his right'.[21] The use of the adage as the premiss of a demonstration is, however, partly ironic,[22] since Hobbes omits from his definition any reference to a man's worth (*dignitas*), turning it into a kind of tautology. What is distributive justice good for, if it means that each person must be given what is owed him according to what he already has? To avoid this absurdity, Hobbes interprets the *suum cuique* formula in terms of private property. The difference may seem negligible, but it is indeed essential, since the formula now means that each person must be given what is owed him according to his own property rights guaranteed by the state: 'And therefore where there is no *Own*, that is, no Propriety, there is no Injustice; and where there is no coërcitive Power erected, that is, where there is no Common-wealth, there is nothing Unjust.'[23] In other words, there is no justice (or injustice) where there is no private property, and there is no private property where there is no state to warrant it. But, inside the state, each man's private property must be respected, regardless of the owner's merit or virtue.

More exactly, merit and virtue must be redescribed in the framework of the new theory of justice. Merit is now defined as what is to be received by a contractor who has performed first;[24] and the virtue of justice, according to which a man is called righteous or just, is now the disposition of manners 'by which a man scorns to be beholding for the contentment of his life, to fraud, or breach of promise'.[25] Hobbes acknowledges the classical distinction between just and unjust as applied to men, but, here again, redescribes it in terms of contractual agreements, that is, in terms of just and unjust actions which consist of keeping and breaking of covenants. Whereas the just man takes care 'that his Actions be all Just',[26] that is, that he keep all his contracts, although he might break a few, the unjust man can keep some contracts he makes, but 'his Will is not framed by the Justice, but by the apparant benefit of what he is to do'.[27] According to

---

[19] *Lev*, XV. 3, p. 202. In the same passage, Hobbes refers the formula to the 'ordinary definition of Justice in the Schooles'.

[20] *De Inventione*, II. 53. See also *Ad Herennium*, III. 2.

[21] The formula, *constans et perpetua voluntas ius suum cuique tribuere*, is quoted in Justinian's *Institutiones* (I. 1).

[22] D. Hüning has remarked that Kant 'transforms the [*suum cuique*] formula into the precept which marks the entry into civil society', thus following Hobbes's criticism of this formula ('From the Virtue of Justice to the Concept of Legal Order: The Significance of the *suum cuique tribuere* in Hobbes' Political Philosophy', in I. Hunter and D. Saunders (eds.), *Natural Law and Civil Sovereignty* (Palgrave-Macmillan, 2002), 148).

[23] *Lev*, XV. 3, p. 202.   [24] *Lev*, XIV. 17, p. 195.   [25] *Lev*, XV, 10, p. 207.

[26] Ibid. p. 206.   [27] Ibid. p. 207.

Hobbes, a righteous man may sometimes be guilty, since the guilt lies in the injustice of action, but this occasional guilt doesn't make his actions lose the 'relish of Justice', which implies 'a certain Noblenesse or Gallantnesse of courage'.[28] This acknowledgement of justice as a virtue does not imply that this virtue be required by the theory of justice as a precondition. If it were the case, one could not understand how Hobbes could also declare that this 'justice of manners' be 'rarely found'.[29] It would be contradictory to consider the virtue of justice, being a rare disposition, as the foundation of the justice of the state. What matters is that people, whatever their motivations, respect the contracts they have made. This predominance of the justice of action over the virtue of justice clearly appears in Hobbes's criticism of the classical distinction between commutative and distributive justice.

This criticism must be carefully examined because it brings to light the gap—which Hobbes was already well aware of when he wrote his first works—between the classical theory of justice as a virtue and the Hobbesian theory of justice based on keeping covenants, and, further, on the free market which requires such covenants. Commutative justice is classically defined by an arithmetical proportion, according to which the values of goods traded in a commercial exchange must be equal. Distributive justice is defined geometrically: goods are distributed in proportion to the desert of the recipients.[30] The core of Hobbesian criticism is its rejection of the very foundation of those notions, which is a certain understanding of equality. Whereas Aristotle considered equality, arithmetical and geometrical, as central to the concept of justice as a virtue, Hobbes tends to deny the relevance of equality for a theory of justice.

What counts for him, as far as commutative justice is concerned, is not so much the equality of the value of things exchanged, since this worth is established by the agreement of the contractors according to the laws of the market, but the equality of the parties involved in the exchange. Contrary to thinking in terms of arithmetical proportions, which leads to the false assumption that in a fair exchange the goods being exchanged are equal, what is important for Hobbes is that both parties abide by their contractual agreement. Indeed, it is the mistaken belief in their natural superiority that can lead men to break contracts, using the high opinion they have of themselves to justify their violation of the rules of commerce.[31] In fact, in a

---

[28] Ibid.   [29] Ibid.

[30] EL, I. XVI. 5, p. 84. Cf. Aristotle, *Nicomachean Ethics*, book V, ch. 6, 1131^{a}17–24.

[31] 'Which distinction is not well made, inasmuch as injury, which is the injustice of action, consisteth not in the inequality of the things changed, or distributed, but in the inequality that men (contrary to nature and reason) assume unto themselves above their fellows' (EL, I. XVI. 5, p. 84). This belief in a natural inequality between men is contrary to the ninth law of nature, which declares 'That every man acknowledge other for his Equall by Nature' (*Lev*, XV. 21, p. 211).

transaction governed by the laws of commutative justice, the terms of exchange are not determined by considerations of equality, but by a voluntary agreement between a buyer and a seller:

And for commutative justice placed in buying and selling, though the thing bought be unequal to the price given for it; yet for as much as both the buyer and the seller are made judges of the value, and are thereby both satisfied: there can be no injury done on either side, either party having trusted, or covenanted with the other.[32]

Hobbes understood well the logic of supply and demand that had started governing the domestic market in his time. The value of products bought and sold was not to be determined by criteria external to the exchange, but by the market itself, that is, the collective judgement at a certain moment of a group of buyers and sellers. In Hobbes' words, the 'value of all things contracted for, is measured by the Appetite of the Contractors: and therefore the just value, is that which they be contented to give'.[33] Understood in this way, the just value of a product is nothing other than its price. Conversely, the fact that it is possible to establish the price of a good or service by a contract is sufficient proof that this good or service can be exchanged on a market. The fact that the power of a man can be the object of a contractual agreement is therefore proof enough that a man can enter some kind of market. Since the worth of a man is what a buyer is ready to pay for his power,[34] the concept of worth leads to a quite unusual definition of dignity, not as an absolute value but as the relative value set on a man by the commonwealth.[35] Dignity is therefore equivalent to social status, whose signs are 'offices of Command, Judicature, publike Employment . . . Names and Titles'.[36]

Thinking in terms of geometrical proportion encourages the assumption that in a good distribution the goods received must be proportional to the merit of the recipients. But, according to Hobbes, distributive justice should not be considered from the standpoint of the recipient, but from that of the giver. Since distribution concerns those goods that are owned by us, it is up to us what principle of distribution to use. Merit, if we don't want to reduce its meaning to the expectation of the contractor who has already performed, is not to be taken into account by a theory of justice, but to be considered by a theology of grace. In other words, there is no reason to give priority, in a theory of distributive justice, to the principle of geometric proportion—to each according to his merit—over any other principle. As long as the benefits we are distributing are our own, we can dispose of them as we

---

[32] EL, I. XVI. 5, p. 84.   [33] *Lev*, XV. 14, p. 208.

[34] 'The Value, or Worth of a man, is as of all other things, his Price; that is to say, so much as would be given for the use of his Power: and therefore is not absolute; but a thing dependant on the need and judgement of another' (*Lev*, X. 16, p. 151).   [35] *Lev*, X. 18, p. 152.

[36] Ibid.

like.[37] The only limits that may be imposed on this freedom of distribution are those that have been stipulated in a contract with the recipient in which the method of distribution has already been spelled out.

Is the concept of justice unable to keep up with a commercial order? This may have been true of the concept of justice in *The Elements of Law* and *De Cive*, which is submitted to very sharp criticism. Reiterating in greater detail than in his work of 1640 the long-established connection between methods of justice and concepts of equality, Hobbes, in *De Cive*, ends his summary with a question which sounds very much like an answer: 'But what is all this to justice?'[38] This critique explains why justice does not play an essential role in Hobbes' first two political works. It also shows why Macpherson is right to speak of Hobbes' 'discounting of justice', which, according to him, is in keeping with the criticism of societies that ignore the logic of the market.[39] However, this was not Hobbes's last word, because in *Leviathan* the discussion of justice is accompanied by a reconsideration of commutative justice and distributive justice as traditionally understood.

It is not enough to discredit commutative justice; it is also necessary to redefine it in terms of a new contractual and merchant society. Commutative justice has to be thought of as the justice of the contractor, in other words, as the justice of someone who keeps his commercial and political undertakings.[40] It is nothing other than the disposition of an economic agent, whose role is to buy and sell, to hire and let to hire, to lend and borrow, to barter and exchange. Defined in terms of contract, justice no longer appears as something external to market society; rather, it is one of its conditions. Without a readiness to respect commercial contracts, there would be no trust, and without trust, there can be no market economy. In the same way, distributive justice gets a redefinition appropriate to new social conditions. Distributive justice is redefined as the justice of the arbitrator or judge, in other words, of whoever decides what is just.[41] Making law and ruling on conflicts are essential to a competitive society in which conflicts constantly

---

[37] 'And for distributive justice, which consisteth in the distribution of our own benefits; seeing a thing is therefore said to be our own, because we may dispose of it at our own pleasure: it can be no injury to any man, though our liberality be further extended towards another, than towards him' (EL, I. XVI. 5, p. 84). [38] *De Cive. The English Version*, III. 6, p. 65.

[39] 'The received concepts of commutative and distributive justice, as Hobbes describes them, are concomitants of the model of a customary society. They suppose the validity and the enforcement of standards of reward other than those determined by the market' (C. B. Macpherson, *The Political Theory of Possessive Individualism. Hobbes to Locke* (Oxford: Clarendon Press, 1962), 63).

[40] 'To speak properly, Commutative Justice, is the Justice of a Contractor; that is, a Performance of Covenant, in Buying, and Selling; Hiring, and Letting to Hire; Lending, and Borrowing; Exchanging, Bartering, and other acts of Contracts' (*Lev*, XV. 14, p. 208).

[41] 'And Distributive Justice, the Justice of an Arbitrator; that is to say, the act of defining what is Just. Wherein, (being trusted by them that make him Arbitrator,) if he performe his Trust, he is said to distribute to every man his own: and this is indeed Just Distribution, and may be called (though improperly), Distributive Justice; but more properly Equity' (*Lev*, XV. 15, p. 208).

arise. It is the duty of the judge, or arbitrator, to reach a peaceful resolution between contracting parties in dispute. In this way he can restore the trust damaged by a failure to keep to an agreement.

This revision of the theory of justice throws light on the proverbial objection raised by the 'Foole', who 'hath sayd in his heart, there is no such thing as justice'.[42] What can be the meaning, in such a theory, of the fool's claim not to keep his covenants, when keeping his covenants contradicts his private interests? Is the fool's thesis not coherent with the ideal of a merchant society in which private interest must always predominate?

III. THE LIMITS OF JUSTICE, OR THE FOOLISHNESS OF MACHIAVELLIAN VIRTUE

The issue raised by the fool may be construed as that of whether we can really conceive of justice as the central concept of a theory of State and market economy, which makes no room, or very little, for the virtue of justice. We have just seen that, according to Hobbes, the State is the foundation of a system of exchange based simultaneously on private interest and on a strict adherence to covenants. We must now understand why he thinks it is irrational to justify the violation of covenants on the basis of private interest, although private interest is what matters, and, secondly, why there is, in Hobbes's view, no alternative to the limited theory of justice which he defends.[43]

In *The Elements of Law* and *De Cive* there is already an argument in favour of the rationality of keeping one's covenants. It is an analogical argument, which is also taken up in *Leviathan*, but plays a different role in this latter work. In all three works, the argument is that injury is similar to what the scholastics call absurdity:

And there is in every breach of covenant a contradiction properly so called; for he that covenanteth, willeth to do, or omit, in the time to come; and he that doth any action, willeth it in that present, which is part of the future time, contained in the covenant: and therefore he that violateth a covenant, willeth the doing and the not doing of the same thing, at the same time; which is a plain contradiction.

---

[42] *Lev*, XV. 4, p. 203.

[43] On the limits of Hobbes's theory of justice and the criticism of Kavka's interpretation of it, see T. Sorell, 'Hobbes and the Morality Beyond Justice', *Pacific Philosophical Quaterly*, 82, 3–4 (2001), 239: 'The most questionable step in Kavka's account [*Hobbesian Moral and Political Theory* (Princeton: Princeton University Press, 1986), 343–4] is the one taken earliest: namely that of attributing to Hobbes a broad conception of justice while admitting that this is different from justice in Hobbes's narrow sense. The fact is, that this narrow sense of justice–justice in the sense of keeping agreements—is the only sense that Hobbes relies on in *defining* "justice", and, whatever else is clear about Hobbes's scientific methodology, acts of definition are centrally important to it.'

And so injury is an absurdity of conversation, as absurdity is a kind of injustice in disputation.[44]

To say that there is an obvious contradiction in breaking a covenant is to say that it is not possible to do so rationally. Of course, it is clear that there are people who do not honour their contracts, but from the standpoint of the logic of law it is not coherent both to enter a covenant and to break it. The contractual system of exchange is like a logical system in that contractors have to maintain the relevant kind of consistency. The theory of natural law is, indeed, presented as a set of axiomatic precepts, which confer rigour on the theory of contracts. However, this logical analogy is not sufficient to ensure the consistency of the theory of justice. At most, it allows us to stigmatize those who do not keep their promises as behaving in an absurd way. *Leviathan*'s contribution consists in shifting the debate from the dogmatic affirmation of the illogicality of an unjust action to a possible refutation of the fool's argument, according to which there is no contradiction between making a contract and breaking it for one's benefit. Although the argument that injury is a kind of absurdity no longer plays a central part in justifying the rationality of keeping contracts, it is used in *Leviathan* to explain how renouncing one's rights creates an obligation,[45] and not to demonstrate, as in *The Elements of Law*, why one must keep to one's covenants.[46] Instead of this argument, Hobbes uses in *Leviathan* an argument, known as the fool's argument, which cannot be found in the two previous works.[47]

The foolish objection that has to be refuted in order for the theory of justice to be maintained begins with an indirect reference to Psalms 14:1 (in the Vulgate, 13:1), and goes on with a reflection that takes seriously the possibility, rejected in *The Elements of Law* and *De Cive*, that a man may, for his own benefit, choose not to respect some of his contractual engagements. Since justice resides in abiding by covenants, and since the aim of all covenants is the benefit of those who enter into them, can we not conclude that it is sometimes reasonable not to discharge a covenant, if it is beneficial? The objection of the fool hinges neither on the existence of covenants, which he acknowledges, nor the definition of justice as keeping covenants, which he accepts, but upon the fact that 'every mans conservation, and contentment, being committed to his own care, there could be no reason, why every man might not do what he thought conduced thereunto: and therefore

---

[44] EL, I. XVI. 2, p. 82. Cf. *De Cive. The Latin Version*, III. 3, p. 109.

[45] *Lev*, XIV. 7, p. 191.

[46] 'For what benefit is it to a man, that any thing be promised, or given unto him, if he that giveth, or promiseth, performeth not, or retaineth still the right of taking back what he hath given?' (EL, I. xvi. 1, p. 82).

[47] For a similar remark, see E. Curley, 'Reflections on Hobbes: Recent Work on his Moral and Political Philosophy', *Journal of Philosophical Research*, 15 (1989–90), 217, n. 37.

also to make, or not make; keep, or not keep Covenants, was not against Reason, when it conduced to ones benefit'.[48] The core of the argument lies in the suggestion of a contradiction between the two main elements of the new social and political order described by Hobbes, that is, between the right to pursue one's own benefit, which is the main motivation of modern man in a market economy, and the definition of justice as keeping covenants, on which rests the political and economic order in general. What the fool has very well perceived is the fact that, once the natural or theological foundation of obligation has been removed,[49] it is difficult, in an artificial social and political order, to see why it would not be rational to prefer one's own interest to keeping one's promises to others. In a theological or natural law perspective, there is a good enough reason not to break one's covenants, namely, a natural obligation, founded in God or in the world's order. But what happens when this natural obligation is omitted, when the world's order or God's omnipotence are voluntarily ignored? Does the artificial institution of the state, inspired by the modern theory of science, suffice to make individualism and justice stand together?

This is precisely the doubt raised by the fool, whose function is to question the new order of politics, just as the Cartesian *malin génie* questions the new order of science. In both cases, this questioning goes hand in hand with a theoretical doubt about the existence and goodness of God, without implying in the least that Hobbes or Descartes would be willing to ignore theological issues.[50] In other words, the hypothetical doubt about God is used by both philosophers, not as the expression of their inner belief, but as the condition of a radical questioning of the new order of things. The fool's argument is therefore central to Hobbes' thought, not so much because it has been the 'battle line' between a secular and a theological interpretation of his thought,[51] but because it raises a radical doubt about the foundations of the modern world. To be more precise, what is at stake here is not so much the natural or theological foundations, which are not questioned as such in the fool's argument, but the artificial and contractual foundations of modern society. The problem is not so much whether it is all right to

---

[48] *Lev*, XV. 4, p. 203.

[49] 'for the same Foole hath said in his heart there is no God' (ibid.).

[50] On the place of God's omnipotence in Hobbes's thought and in particular in his theory of natural obligation, see L. Foisneau, *Hobbes et la toute-puissance de Dieu* (Paris: Presses Universitaires de France, 2000), 215–55.

[51] Among the reasons why the fool's argument has drawn so much attention, K. Hoekstra singles out, first, the fact that the fool's 'answer seems unrealistic and simply wrong', and, secondly, the fact that 'Hobbes's reply to the Foole has been a battle line' between the secular and the theological interpretations of the entire work' ('Hobbes and the Foole', *Political Theory*, 25-5 (1997), 620).

proclaim, as the fool sometimes does,[52] that injustice can be compatible with private interest.[53] The question is rather whether the threat of injustice as breaking covenants is a constitutive flaw of the modern political system. In other words, what is at stake is the morality of the modern state, if that morality is reduced to the theory of justice as keeping covenants.

If in certain situations, albeit exceptional, self-interest could contradict justice, then the definition of the theory of justice as respect for covenants would not be true, as it would not be universal. Although the objection does not bear directly on the justice of exchanges, but on the justice of the arbitrator, the failure of Hobbes' political theory on this point would also imply a failure of his argument in favour of a general order of exchanges guaranteed by the state. Is it therefore conceivable that the supreme arbitrator draws his own sense of fairness from a different concept of justice or from a political rationale that is foreign to the rationale of justice as keeping covenants? This doubt is precisely the one raised by the fool, who 'questioneth, whether Injustice . . . may not sometimes stand with that Reason, which dictateth to every man his own good', not only in general, but *'particularly then*, when it conduceth to such a benefit, as shall put a man in a condition, to neglect not only the dispraise, and revilings, but also the power of other men'.[54] The particular situation which the fool addresses is undoubtedly a Machiavellian one, which is considered by Hobbes of particular relevance in the case made by the fool. If it is true that Hobbes addresses the general case in the first part of his answer to the fool, he does it in a way that is also relevant to the particular case of political injustice. The first paragraph of his answer,[55] which has been the most discussed, is indeed a sort of parenthesis in a series of Machiavellian illustrations of the fool's point, and Hobbes's critical analysis of those examples. In order to appreciate the Machiavellian setting of the fool's argument, it is therefore important to start with a precise characterization of what has been construed as the general case of this argument.

In answer to the fool's objection that when justice and self-interest conflict it is self-interest that must prevail, Hobbes first describes the kind of contracts that come under his theory of justice. He stresses that the question is not 'of promises mutuall, where there is no security of performance on either side; as when there is no Civill Power erected over the parties promising; for such promises are no Covenants',[56] but of covenants, 'where

---

[52] 'The Foole hath sayd in his heart, there is no such thing as Justice; and sometimes also with his tongue' (*Lev*, XV. 4. 203).

[53] For saving the pragmatism of Hobbes's theory, K. Hoekstra suggests that Hobbes shares indeed the position of the fool, that is, considers that in case of divergence between keeping a contract and preserving one's interest self-interest overrides justice, but that 'what Hobbes objects to is the doctrine of the Foole being publicized' ('Hobbes and the Foole', 639).

[54] *Lev*, XV. 4, p. 203. Italics are mine.   [55] Cf. *Lev*, XV. 5, p. 204.

[56] *Lev*, XV. 5, p. 204.

one of the parties has performed already; or where there is a Power to make him performe'.[57] The question is therefore the following: 'Is it contrary to reason that he who has not yet performed, does, in fact, do so?' Hobbes' well-known answer is that it is rational to perform one's contracts whenever there is an artificial obligation to do so, or a guarantee to be protected if we abide by our obligations. To understand better this position, which has often been commented upon, and frequently in very abstract ways, it is useful to notice that Hobbes' demonstration is based on two main arguments that have an anti-Machiavellian dimension. Behind the fool, and his error, lies the figure of the Machiavellian prince, and his conception of politics as immorality. This perspective throws some light on what is at stake in Hobbes' political theory of justice.

The first argument against the fool concerns the accidents or the unforeseeable events that sometimes turn an action doomed to fail into a success: 'when a man doth a thing, which notwithstanding any thing can be foreseen, and reckoned on, tendeth to his own destruction, howsoever *some accident which he could not expect, arriving may turne it to his benefit*'.[58] Such a complete change in a state of affairs, which renders the consequences of action unforeseeable, is precisely what Machiavelli, in *The Prince*, calls fortune. Because of the rapid changes introduced in Italy by the French armies of Charles VIII, many Italians had become fatalists, Machiavelli included.[59] Compared to 'a mountaine flood that beates downe all before it',[60] fortune introduces into human action an element which Hobbes describes in the passage just quoted as something that cannot be 'forseen', or 'reckoned upon'. Although he acknowledges the presence of such an irrational element as fate in human affairs, Hobbes rejects the Machiavellian solution which is to describe human virtue in the perspective of a perpetual struggle against fortune. More exactly, he considers that the success that eventually follows an action which otherwise would have led to our destruction is not itself rational, and shouldn't be invoked to justify breaking one's covenants. If it can no doubt modify the course of events, fortune cannot justify a posteriori irrational behaviour, and, consequently, virtue is not to be measured by the extent of success or failure in facing

---

[57] *Lev*, XV. 5, p. 204.   [58] Ibid. Italics are mine.

[59] 'I am not ignorante that manie have ben & presentlie are of opinion that the dispensation of worldlie matters doth hange in such sort upon god & fortune, that yt ys utterly impossible by anie humane pollicye to disappoynte it. [. . .] And for that there have ben alteracions seen, (and daylie are seen) quyte beyond the compasse of all humane coniecture, which when I had oftentymes debated in my mynde, I fell in some parte to imbrase the same opinion' (*Machiavelli's The Prince. An Elizabethan Translation*, ed. H. Craig (Chapel Hill: University of North Carolina Press, 1944), 110).

[60] Ibid. 111; Niccolo Machiavelli, *Il Principe*, ed. G. Inglese, (Turin: Einaudi, 1995), 163: 'questi fiumi rovinosi'.

fortune. One could scarcely show more clearly one's disapproval of Machiavellism.

The second element of Hobbes's refutation of the fool can similarly be related to a criticism of Machiavellian politics. This time the question raised is whether it is rational or not for a man in a state of war not to perform a covenant which he has entered into with others to get protection. The situation is one of uncertainty, as there is not yet, or no longer, a common power to keep everybody 'in awe',[61] but also of partial cooperation, as Hobbes supposes that there exists some kind of defensive covenant.[62] The associates, or 'confederates', form what is called a 'confederation', which can be understood, as in international affairs, as a pact of non-aggression and defensive cooperation between individuals in a general condition of war. The political situation Hobbes calls 'confederation' resembles the one in which supporters of the Pope and supporters of the emperor confronted one another in the Italian cities in the Renaissance, when there existed no common power strong enough to make them stop their quarrels. And the fool himself, who 'breaketh his Covenants, and consequently declareth that he thinks he may with reason do so',[63] resembles the Machiavellian prince, who similarly thinks, not only that he can break his covenants with his political associates, but that it is reasonable to do so when it is profitable. Therefore, the fool shares with the new prince, both the certainty that his protection depends on his confederates, and the idea that it is rational not to keep one's undertakings. Indeed, in chapter XVIII of *The Prince*, Machiavelli insists that it is advisable for a prince to know when it is necessary to break his covenants, and he does so in terms of profit similar to those used by the fool. Thus the Elizabethan translation of *The Prince* runs: 'Therefore a wise and prudent prince shoulde sticke noe longer to his promise then maye stande well with his *profitt*, nor thincke himself noe longer bownde, to keape his othe then the cause remaynes that moved him to sweare'.[64] One finds in this passage a prudential and moral justification for allowing a prince to break his covenants, when it is profitable for him to do so.

What makes the prince's wickedness and deceit legitimate is the wickedness and deceit of men in general: 'But seinge they are wicked and deceiptfull, it behoves a prince by discemblinge to meete with their malice, and by

---

[61] *Lev*, XV. 5, p. 204.

[62] 'Secondly, that in a condition of Warre, wherein every man to every man, for want of a common Power to keep them all in awe, is an Enemy, there is no man can hope by his own strength, or wit, to defend himselfe from destruction, without the help of Confederates; where every one expects the same defence by the Confederation, that any one else does' (ibid.).

[63] *Lev*, XV. 5, p. 205.

[64] *Machiavelli's The Prince*, ch. XVIII, p. 75. Italics are mine. The Italian version has: 'Non puo pertanto uno signore prudente, né debbe, osservare la fede quando tale osservanzia gli torni contro e che sono spente le cagioni che la ficiono promettere' (ibid. 116–17).

cunninge to overthrowe their Crafte'.[65] This anthropological justification cannot be found in the second argument against the fool, where Hobbes insists to the contrary on the fact that the fool's reasoning is erroneous, and devoid of all rationality. If men tolerate such a fool in their confederation, it is because they don't perceive the 'danger of their errour'.[66] But it is not possible to justify an error, the one made by the fool, by another error, the one made by the confederates, who don't see, or don't want to see, that the fool is willing to deceive them. If the confederates knew what was good for them, they would not contribute to the preservation of someone whose action tends to their destruction. The point is not, therefore, to know whether men are good or bad in themselves, but to know what is good for the political association. If there is a Machiavellian error in politics, it consists in considering what happens sometimes— that breaking covenants can contribute to one's profit—as a general rule of action. Hobbes refuses to make what he considers as an error the foundation of his own political theory. If justice matters in Hobbes's thought, it is therefore not because it obliges man to act contrary to the principle of self-interest, but because it gives a rational setting to such a principle.

The anti-Machiavellian interpretation of Hobbes's main answer to the fool can be strongly supported by the examples given by Hobbes before and after the fifth paragraph of chapter XV. Although they do not belong to Machiavellian literature as such, those examples can be easily interpreted in terms of Machiavellian politics. The first example is somewhat surprising in that Hobbes develops the fool's objection from a brief reference to the idea that 'The kingdom of God is gotten by violence'.[67] There are at least two opposing lines taken by interpreters of this idea. For some, violent men must either be regarded as righteous men who want at all costs to enter the kingdom of God described by John the Baptist; for others, the violent men are the enemies of Christ who bar the way to His kingdom. Hobbes is not so much interested in taking positions in this exegetical debate, as in establishing a link between the idea that violence may be a way of entering the kingdom of God and the Machiavellian theory of virtue: 'From such reasoning as this, [that the Kingdom of God could be gotten by unjust violence] Succesful wickednesse hath obtained the name of Vertue.'[68] Just as Agathocles became king of Syracuse thanks to a long series of wicked

---

[65] *Machiavelli's The Prince*, ch. XVIII, p. 75.   [66] *Lev*, XV. 5, p. 205.

[67] Ibid. This passage is not a citation, but is related to several passages of the Gospel, for example, Matt. 11:12: 'And from the days of John the Baptist until now the kingdom of heaven suffereth violence, and the violent take it by force'; and even more closely to Luke 16:16: 'The law and the prophets were until John; since then the good news of the kingdom of God hath been preached, and every one entereth it violently.'   [68] *Lev*, XV. 4, p. 203.

acts,[69] or Oliver of Firmo took control of the city of Firmo by fraud and force, some men intend to enter the kingdom of God thanks to their successful wickedness. As a matter of fact, Hobbes is not so much concerned here by the theological implications of the biblical idea as by its political meaning. The proof of this is given by the answer he gives to what appears to him as a frivolous objection: 'As for the Instance of gaining the secure and perpetuall felicity of Heaven, by any way; it is *frivolous*: there being but one way imaginable; and that is not breaking, but keeping of Covenant'.[70] But, although frivolous in itself, and thus easy to refute, this objection is useful, since it introduces the idea that getting a kingdom may seem a good enough reason to certain men for breaking their covenants. This Hobbesian discussion of Machiavellianism appears all the more clearly in the next two references. The first runs; 'And the Heathen that believed that *Saturn* was deposed by his son *Jupiter*, believed neverthelesse the same *Jupiter* to be the avenger of Injustice.'[71] Here a situation of Machiavellian politics is evoked in the framework of mythological thought, an etymological link existing between Jupiter and justice,[72] although Jupiter is supposed to have deposed Saturn. The second reference comes from the *Institutes*, a work by the jurist Edward Coke (1552–1634), in which he comments on a passage from Thomas de Littleton's *Treatise on Tenures*. Admittedly, Coke's position is at the very least ambiguous because he says that 'If the right Heire of the Crown be attainted of Treason; yet the Crown shall descend to him, and *eo instante* the Atteynder be voyd'.[73] This statement is obviously similar to that of the fool, since it says that if one's own interest is contradictory to justice, especially, if this interest is a political one, one should choose one's interest over justice.

Before we explain why the fool's 'specious reasoning is neverthelesse false',[74] it is important to note, first, that, in all those references, it is as if Hobbes takes particular pleasure in citing Machiavelli through the works of those who should have been his staunchest opponents: theologians of grace, on the one hand, and founders of the new natural law theory or jurists of Common Law, on the other. It is also important to remember that Hobbes's goal is not so much to refute Machiavelli, or a certain Machiavellian school in English law, as to discredit an idea of justice that does not incorporate a respect for covenants and contracts, and is therefore

---

[69] The title of ch. 8 of *The Prince*, in which those two examples are to be found, illustrates well the idea of a succesful wickedness: 'Of those which by wicked meanes have gotten principalities' (*The Prince*, 34); 'De his qui per scelera ad principatum pervenere' (*Il Principe*, 54).

[70] *Lev*, XV. 6, p. 205. Italics are mine.   [71] *Lev*, XV. 4, p. 203–4.

[72] Grotius refers to this etymology: 'It also appears that the Latin word *Jus*, which means right, comes from the word Jupiter' (*De jure belli ac pacis*, Preliminary discourse, § XII). For a different etymology, see Cicero, *Epist. ad famil.* B. IX, Ep. XXI.   [73] *Lev*, XV. 4, p. 204.

[74] *Lev*, XV. 4, p. 204.

exempt from the order of commercial exchanges. What concerns Hobbes is
to return positive answers to the following questions: can man's expectations be subject to a contractual order even in areas external to the exchange
of goods and services? And can politics be reduced to arbitration of disputes in a mercantile society?

The refutation of the theological, political and legal examples given in
support of the fool's argument are based on the two general answers that
we have already considered above. Since the success of such an action 'cannot reasonably be expected, but rather the contrary',[75] it is not rational to
be willing to overturn a sovereign by rebellion. Someone who thinks he can
enter Heaven by killing a tyrant, or—in the Latin version of *Leviathan*—
someone who wants to kill 'his king under the pretext of a religious war',[76]
cannot consider it a rational project, since the knowledge of man's estate
after death is not a matter of experience, but of faith. In other words, breaking one's vow to a prince cannot be a means of salvation, any more than
assassinating a prince under the pretext that he is a heretic.[77] Those
Machiavellian solutions to political problems are, in the framework of a
contractual society, highly problematic.

We can now see why Hobbes insists at the end of his refutation of the
fool's argument that there are no exceptions to the laws of justice. Although
he uses the concept of generosity to describe the truly righteous man,[78] it is
clear that for him there is no longer room for a virtue of justice whose scope
would go further than keeping contracts. No room for the justice of the
saints, no room for the paradoxical generosity of the Machiavellian prince.
Justice must now be given a restricted sense, which Montesquieu so well
describes when he refers to the 'feeling of exact justice'[79] that the spirit of
trade fosters in the minds of modern men. The uniqueness of *Leviathan* is
in its having succeeded in transforming the meaning of justice, making it fit
a world that would forever be dominated by the market.

Translated from the French by Lee Yanowitch and Tom Sorell.

---

[75] *Lev*, XV. 7, p. 205.

[76] 'Atque hi sunt, qui pietatis opus esse dicunt, reges suos praetextu religionis bello persequi,
deponere, et interficere' (*Lev* Latin, XV. 7, p. 114).

[77] 'Others, that allow for a Law of Nature, the keeping of Faith, do neverthelesse make exception of certain persons; as Heretiques, and such as use not to performe their Covenant to others'
(*Lev*, XV. 9, p. 206).

[78] 'That which gives to humane Actions the relish of Justice, is a certain Noblenesse or
Gallantnesse of courage, (rarely found,) by which a man scorns to be beholding for the contentment of his life, to fraud, or breach of promise' (*Lev*, XV. 10, p. 207).

[79] 'L'esprit de commerce produit, dans les hommes, un certain sentiment de justice exacte,
opposé d'un côté au brigandage, et de l'autre à ces vertus morales qui font qu'on ne discute pas
toujours ses intérêts avec rigidité et qu'on peut les négliger pour ceux des autres' (Montesquieu,
De l'esprit des lois (Paris: Garnier-Flammarion, 1979), XX. ii, p. 10).

PART TWO

Passions and Politics

The Utopianism of Leviathan

RICHARD TUCK

In this essay I want to ask directly a question which often lurks behind discussions of Hobbes, but which is rarely put clearly: how radical is the transformation of politics, and indeed human life in general, which Hobbes supposed would be the result of taking his theory seriously? I ask this question partly for its intrinsic interest, as it seems to me that answering it correctly gives us a great deal of insight into the overall character of Hobbes's politics, but also because it is relevant to the further question of who Hobbes's successors were, and what happened to Hobbesian politics in the eighteenth and early nineteenth centuries; in particular, we cannot address the issue of the relationship between Hobbes and Rousseau without first clarifying the extent to which both were utopians, of a kind. From the perspective which I shall be suggesting, *Leviathan* is as much of a utopian work as *The Social Contract*, and may indeed be the greatest piece of utopian writing to come out of the English Revolution.

We are all familiar with the grandiose claims which Hobbes made for the novelty of his ideas, and for their comprehensive break with all existing political theory. But these claims are mostly taken, I believe, to refer to the new *understanding* of politics which Hobbes was claiming for himself, rather than to a new kind of political *practice*. Even if it is allowed that Hobbes did have a new politics in mind, most writers on Hobbes have supposed that it would be something like the contemporary absolutisms of Europe rather than an utterly new kind of political and moral life. But one only has to read the most prominent statements which Hobbes made about his novelty, in all his works, to see that there seems to be more to it than this. For example, Hobbes presented *Elements of Law* in 1640 to the Earl of Newcastle as 'the true and only foundation' of a 'science' of 'justice and policy', and remarked of the book that

For the style, it is therefore the worse, because I was forced to consult when I was writing, more with logic than with rhetoric. But for the doctrine, it is not slightly proved; and the conclusions thereof are of such nature, as, for want of them, government and peace have been nothing else to this day, but mutual fear. And it would be an incomparable benefit to commonwealth [*sic* the Tönnies edition], if every man held the opinions concerning law and policy here delivered. (Epistle Dedicatory, p. xvi)

Already in this first expression of his ideas, Hobbes is making the surprising claim that his doctrine would rescue men from 'mutual fear'—that is, he is asserting the exact opposite of what is often casually assumed about Hobbes's ideas.

In *De Cive* of 1642, which is to a great extent a Latin version of the *Elements of Law*,[1] Hobbes gave an even more striking account of the historic significance of his book—an account worth quoting at some length.

The Geometers have managed their province outstandingly. For whatever benefit comes to human life from observation of the stars, from mapping of lands, from reckoning of time and from long-distance navigation; whatever is beautiful in buildings, strong in defence-works and marvellous in machines, whatever in short distinguishes the modern world from the barbarity of the past, is almost wholly the gift of *Geometry*; for what we owe to *Physics*, *Physics* owes to *Geometry*. If the moral Philosophers had done their job with equal success, I do not know what greater contribution human industry could have made to human happiness. For if the patterns of human action were known with the same certainty as the relations of magnitude in figures, ambition and greed, whose power rests on the false opinions of the common people about right and wrong [*jus et iniuria*], would be disarmed, and the human race would enjoy such secure peace that (apart from conflicts over space as the population grew) it seems unlikely that it would ever have to fight again. But as things are, the war of the sword and the war of the pens is perpetual; there is no greater knowledge [*scientia*] of natural right and natural laws today than in the past; both parties to a dispute defend their right with the opinions of Philosophers; one and the same action is praised by some and criticised by others; a man now approves what at another time he condemns, and gives a different judgement of an action when he does it than when someone else does the very same thing; all these things are obvious signs that what moral Philosophers have written up to now has contributed nothing to the knowledge of truth; its appeal has not lain in enlightening the mind but in lending the influence of attractive and emotive language to hasty and superficial opinions.   (Epistle dedicatory 6–7, p. 5)

Again, this is a surprising passage, in its repudiation of something which is almost always ascribed to Hobbes, namely the belief that nations will inevitably fight against one another. Instead, Hobbes appears to be predicting that there will be universal peace (except for 'conflicts over space', which in all his works he treated as a rather remote possibility),[2] and not because some political mechanism will ensure it but because deep features of human nature will have been transformed. Moreover, Hobbes is drawing

---

[1] See in particular *De Cive* XIV. 4, where Hobbes appears to say that the subject matter of the book are 'the Elements of *natural law* and *natural right*', in addition to the many parallel passages in the two works.

[2] The *locus classicus* for this is *Leviathan*, ch. 30, p. 181 original edition, on the 'Prevention of Idlenesse'.

a parallel between the extraordinary transformation of human existence brought about by natural science and the kind of transformation he is envisaging as a result of his science of natural right: it seems that we are to expect nothing less than a kind of Baconian alteration of the fundamental character of human life in both its material and its moral aspects. Hobbes's old intimacy with Bacon may indeed have had more far-reaching implications than has usually been supposed.

When in 1647 Hobbes came to revise *De Cive* and present it to a Europe-wide audience for the first time, he added a Preface which is even more Baconian in its handling of the history of moral errors. 'Prevailing moral Philosophy', he said, gave rise to general civil conflict.

I think that those ancients foresaw this who preferred that the knowledge of Justice be wrapped up in fables rather than exposed to discussion. Before questions of that kind began to be debated, Princes did not lay claim to sovereign power, they simply exercised it They did not defend their power by arguments but by punishing the wicked and defending the good. In return the citizens did not measure Justice by the comments of private men but by the laws of the commonwealth; and were kept at Peace not by discussions but by the power of Government. In fact, they revered sovereign power, whether it resided in a man or in an Assembly, as a kind of visible divinity. And thus they did not, as they do now, side with ambitious or desperate men to overturn the order of the commonwealth. For they could not be persuaded to oppose the security of the thing which gave them their own security. The simplicity of those times evidently could not understand such sophisticated stupidity. It was peace therefore and a golden age, which did not end until Saturn was expelled and the doctrine started up that one could take up arms against kings. (Preface 6, p. 9)

Earlier in the Preface, Hobbes identified Socrates as the first person who had brought 'civil science' out of 'the shadowy outlines of Allegory' (2, p. 7), to be followed by all the philosophers of antiquity and the modern age, and ultimately all the educated population, with all the moral damage which that implied. So it is in the most remote epochs of human history (apparently) that we are to find the last time when there was a well-founded commonwealth and the true science of justice was understood. This idea of an ancient wisdom taught in fables which had been lost with the coming of Greek philosophy was precisely the idea which Francis Bacon had developed in his *Sapientia Veterum*, in which (for example) the rebellion of Typhon against Jupiter was interpreted as a general theory of rebellion 'which because of the infinite calamities it inflicts both on kings and peoples is represented under the dreadful image of Typhon, with a hundred heads, denoting divided powers (*divisas potestates*)'.[3] And in all his works, Hobbes remained

---

[3] *Sapientia Veterum* was first published in 1609, but Bacon became interested in the subject again in the 1620s, and inserted expanded versions of three fables into *De Augmentis Scientiarum*

fond of the idea that fables and myths could be decrypted to reveal the principles of his science, as in the well-known passages on Medea as a symbol of rebellion (*Elements of Law* II.8.15; *De Cive* XII.13; *Leviathan*, ch. 30, p. 177 original).

In *Leviathan*, to take the last of the three great statements of Hobbes's political theory, and the one with which we are specifically concerned here, there is a similar history of error; indeed the fourth part of the work is entirely devoted to the subject. In it, Hobbes makes it entirely clear that no commonwealth in more than a thousand years has been well founded, and that the corruption of human life is not merely a political phenomenon: what he calls 'the Kingdome of Darknesse' has infected all of existence.

Whence comes it, that in Christendome there has been, almost from the time of the Apostles, such justling of one another out of their places, both by forraign, and Civill war? such stumbling at every little asperity of their own fortune, and every little eminence of that of other men? and such diversity of ways of running to the same mark, *Felicity*, if it be not Night amongst us, or at least a Mist? [W]ee are therefore yet in the Dark.   (ch. 44, p. 334 of the original)

Here again we see, surprisingly, that foreign war is as much a sign of darkness as civil war, and that psychological traits such as envy or bitterness are symptoms of intellectual failure. Moral disagreement, of course, was always treated by Hobbes as a kind of darkness, and in chapter 46, on 'Darknesse from Vain Philosophy', Hobbes depicted the conflicts of moral philosophers as in effect a continuation of the state of nature:

Their Morall Philosophy is but a description of their own Passions. For the rule of Manners, without Civill Government, is the Law of Nature; and in it, the Law Civill; that determineth what is *Honest* and *Dishonest*; what is *Just*, and *Unjust*; and generally what is *Good*, and *Evill*; whereas they make the Rules of *Good*, and *Bad*, by their own *Liking*, and *Disliking*: By which means, in so great diversity of tastes, there is nothing generally agreed on; but every one doth (as far as he dares) whatsoever seemeth good in his owne eyes, to the subversion of Commonwealth.   (p. 369 of the original)

This was a thought which was picked up by his acute French reader François Peleau, who observed that one of the best examples of a Hobbesian state of nature was indeed the 'war of minds' among philosophical schools.[4]

Leviathan also contains one of the clearest statements by Hobbes that he saw his commonwealth as very different from the corrupt institutions hitherto existing, in a passage which captures exactly the utopian spirit I am

---

(1623). He was thus reworking this material at about the time Hobbes was in close contact with him. See Bacon, *Literary Works* VI Part II, ed. James Spedding (repr. London: Routledge/ Thoemmes, 1996), 607, 631, 703.

[4] See my edition of *Leviathan*, 2nd edn. (Cambridge: Cambridge University Press, 1996), p. xxx.

tracing. In chapter 30, Hobbes answered sceptics who denied that there were any rational principles of the kind he was outlining, on the grounds that

if there were, they would have been found out in someplace, or other; whereas we see, there has not hitherto been any Common-wealth, where those Rights have been acknowledged, or challenged.[5] Wherein they argue as ill, as if the Savage people of America, should deny there were any grounds, or Principles of Reason, so to build a house, as to last as long as the materials, because they never yet saw any so well built. Time, and Industry, produce every day new knowledge. And as the art of well building, is derived from Principles of Reason, observed by industrious men, that had long studied the nature of materials, and the divers effects of figure, and proportion, long after mankind began (though poorly) to build: So, long time after men have begun to constitute Common-wealths, imperfect, and apt to relapse into disorder, there may Principles of Reason be found out, by industrious meditation, to make their constitution (excepting by externall violence) everlasting. And such are those which I have in this discourse set forth . . . (p. 176 orig.)

So we have every reason to suppose that Hobbes did believe that a proper understanding of his political principles would lead to something very different from the government of a Louis XIV or a Charles II; any recognizable modern state would be little better than a state of nature unless it succeeded in effecting a much more thoroughgoing transformation of its citizens than had been witnessed by any recorded society. To understand why Hobbes believed this to be possible, and why the citizens of his commonwealth would cease to display traits such as fear, aggression, or envy which (we might imagine) would be fundamental to a Hobbesian politics, we need, however, to turn to his psychological theory, as set out most plainly in the first part of the *Elements of Law* and (less plainly) in his last work of philosophy, *De Homine* of 1658.[6] Comparable discussions of human psychology are absent from both *De Cive* and *Leviathan*, which may in part explain why the transformative implications of Hobbes's ideas have only rarely been recognized, though it is clear that Hobbes assumed that his readers would eventually put his political writings alongside his psychological treatises.

In chapter 8 of the *Elements of Law*, Hobbes outlined the general character of human emotions, and stressed their intimate connection with not merely *natural*, but also what we might term *social* power:

all conception of future, is conception of power able to produce something; whosoever therefore expecteth pleasure to come, must conceive withal some power in himself by which the same may be attained. And . . . the passions whereof I am to

---

[5] I take this to mean 'claimed' rather than 'disputed'.

[6] I take his later works (often of great acuity and interest) such as the so-called *Behemoth* not to count as philosophy, at least on Hobbe's own understanding of the term.

speak next, consist in conception of the future, that is to say, in conception of power past, and the act to come . . . By this power I mean the same with the faculties of body and mind . . . , that is to say, of the body, nutritive, generative, motive; and of the mind, knowledge. And besides those, such farther powers, as by them are acquired (viz.) riches, place of authority, friendship or favour, and good fortune; which last is really nothing else but the favour of God Almighty. The contraries of these are impotences, infirmities, or defects of the said powers respectively. And because the power of one man resisteth and hindereth the effects of the power of another: power simply is no more, but the excess of the power of one above that of another.   (I.8.3-4)

As a consequence, Hobbes elevated *honour* to a crucial role in the foundation of the passions, locating his discussion of it not in the chapter on the individual passions but in the chapter on the nature of emotion in general. Since 'acknowledgement of power is called HONOUR' (I.8.5), any sense of one's own or another's power was a kind of honouring. To experience a passion was thus (in part) necessarily to honour someone, and Hobbes said bluntly at the end of the chapter that 'In the pleasure men have, or displeasure from the signs of honour or dishonour done unto them, consisteth the nature of the passions in particular, whereof we are to speak in the next chapter' (I.8.8).

   The best example of how this psychological theory operates is Hobbes's discussion of the various kinds of glory, at the beginning of chapter 9. He distinguished between 'glory', 'aspiring', 'false glory', and 'vain glory', among which his understanding of 'vain glory' is particularly interesting. Glory in general he defined as follows:

GLORY, or internal gloriation or triumph of the mind, is that passion which proceedeth from the imagination or conception of our own power, above the power of him that contendeth with us. The signs whereof, besides those in the countenance, and other gestures of the body which cannot be described, are, ostentation in words, and insolency in actions; and this passion, by them whom it displeaseth, is called pride: by them whom it pleaseth, it is termed a just valuation of himself.

Such glorying might be justifiable, but it might not be.

The fiction (which also is imagination) of actions done by ourselves, which never were done, is glorying; but because it begetteth no appetite nor endeavour to any further attempt, it is merely vain and unprofitable; as when a man imagineth himself to do the actions whereof he readeth in some romant, or to be like unto some other man whose acts he admireth. And this is called VAIN GLORY: and is exemplified in the fable by the fly sitting on the axletree, and saying to himself, What a dust do I raise! . . . Signs of vain glory in the gesture, are imitation of others, counterfeiting attention to things they understand not, affectation of fashions, captation of honour from their dreams, and other little stories of themselves, from their country, from their names, and the like.

Hobbes was always particularly hostile to vainglory or vanity, attacking it (for example) in the striking letter of moral advice which he sent to the younger son of the Earl of Devonshire: 'I think it no ill counsell, that you profess no love to any woman which you hope not to marry or otherwise to enjoy. For an action without design is that which all the world calls vanity.'[7] It was the fact that the imagination of the vain man was *in vain*, that is, led to no action, which he chiefly disliked. It is worth stressing that for Hobbes, the willingness to act on our desires was something to be admired, and was associated with courage, the 'contempt of wounds and death, when they oppose a man in the way to his end' (I.9.4) (though he fully acknowledged that, as he said in the moving passage on Sidney Godolphin at the end of *Leviathan*, courage sometimes 'enclineth men to private Revenges' (p. 483). It might be suggested that the transition from the state of nature to civil society itself required (in Hobbes's eyes) a degree of courage or a willingness to act on one's desires which made this trait fundamental to civil life, and, indeed, this is in effect plainly stated in *Leviathan*, chapter 15 (p. 74 orig.): 'That which gives to humane Actions the relish of Justice, is a certain Noblenesse or Gallantnesse of courage, (rarely found,) by which a man scorns to be beholding for the contentment of his life, to fraud, or breach of promise. This Justice of the Manners, is that which is meant, where Justice is called a Vertue . . .'

In the course of chapter 9 of the *Elements of Law*, Hobbes decoded each passion in this way, showing how each one was based ultimately on a belief about one's own power relative to that of one's fellow men. Even lust, which might have been thought to be the most immediately self-regarding of all passions, Hobbes perceptively located in this context

The appetite which men call LUST, and the fruition that appertaineth thereunto, is a sensual pleasure, but not only that; there is in it also a delight of the mind: for it consisteth of two appetites together, to please, and to be pleased; and the delight men take in delighting, is not sensual, but a pleasure or joy of the mind, consisting in the imagination of the power they have so much to please.

And he summarized his theory of the passions in a famous image at the end of chapter 9, in which the life of man was compared to a race which 'we must suppose to have no other goal, nor other garland, but being foremost', and in which each passion was interpreted as an episode in this competitive struggle with our fellow men.

The most important setting in which the passions were displayed was of course the most important of all competitions, the struggle of the state of

---

[7] Letter to Charles Cavendish, 22 Aug. 1638, in *The Correspondence of Thomas Hobbes*, 2 vols. (Oxford: Clarendon Press, 1994), i. 52 ff.

nature. As Hobbes said in the chapter on the state of nature in the *Elements of Law*,

> considering the great difference there is in men, from the diversity of their passions, how some are vainly glorious, and hope for precedency and superiority above their fellows, not only when they are equal in power, but also when they are inferior; we must needs acknowledge that it must necessarily follow, that these men who are moderate, and look for no more but equality of nature, shall be obnoxious to the force of others, that will attempt to subdue them. And from hence shall proceed a general diffidence in mankind, and mutual fear one of another. (I.14.3)

But it is important to read this and similar passages in the context of the theory of the passions which I have just outlined. Vainglory is *produced* by the false belief that one might enjoy 'precedency and superiority'; it does not *give rise* to it. Even at the deepest level of man's passions, he is governed by cognitive error and not by innate desires. Our entire emotional life, according to Hobbes, extraordinary as this might seem, is in fact a complicated set of beliefs about the best way of securing ourselves against our fellow men, with all the familiar complexities of love, pride, and laughter in the end reducible simply to a set of ideas about our own relative safety from other people's power.

As I have stressed in many other discussions of Hobbes, Hobbes took the warfare of the state of nature to be epistemic in character, and its solution to lie in an epistemological critique—the recognition by natural men of the fallibility of their own beliefs about the best way to secure themselves from threat. Once men 'in a quiet mind' (as he said in *De Cive*) had seen that the disagreement between them in itself implied that none of their beliefs were well founded, they could proceed to the mutual renunciation of their beliefs and their adoption of the single judgement of one man or assembly as the criterion by which they should decide their conduct. So we should now ask the question which (as I said at the beginning) lurks on the edge of this interpretation of Hobbes: what happens to our passions when a commonwealth of this kind has been constructed? The question is given particular point if we remember that the conflict of the state of nature is not purely what we would call moral in character: as the famous summary of his theory at the end of the *Elements of Law* (II.10.8) says, 'the civil laws are to all subjects the measures of their actions, whereby to determine, whether they be right or wrong, *profitable or unprofitable*, virtuous or vicious' (my italics); or as he said in the passage from chapter 44 of *Leviathan* which I quoted earlier, we are in 'darkness' if there is a 'diversity of ways of running to the same mark, *Felicity*'. So Hobbes was quite clear that our individual judgements about what is profitable to ourselves, as well as what is morally right, have to be merged in the judgement of the sovereign. Since our passions involve judgements of this kind, the natural conclusion is that they will at the very least be radically transformed.

The first point to make is that Hobbes supposed that acting on the basis of the laws of nature—that is, reflecting on the acts necessary to secure peace, including above all the renunciation of private judgement—will itself necessitate the elimination of most passion. We can see this most clearly, perhaps, if we trace through what Hobbes says about *revenge*, particularly in the *Elements of Law*. Revenge is one of the passions delineated in chapter 9.

REVENGEFULNESS is that passion which ariseth from an expectation or imagination of making him that hath hurt us, to find his own action hurtful to himself, and to acknowledge the same, and this is the height of revenge. For though it be not hard, by returning evil for evil, to make one's adversary displeased with his own fact; yet to make him acknowledge the same, is so difficult, that many a man had rather die than do it. Revenge aimeth not at the death, but at the captivity and subjection of an enemy; which—was well expressed in the exclamation of Tiberius Caesar, concerning one, that, to frustrate his revenge, had killed himself in prison: Hath he escaped me? To kill is the aim of them that hate, to rid themselves of fear; revenge aimeth at triumph, which over the dead is not. (I.9.6)

But Hobbes was quite clear that the law of nature forbids revenge, precisely on the grounds that it is 'vain': as he said in chapter 16, where particular laws of nature are enumerated,

seeing the law of nature commandeth pardon when there is repentance, and caution for the future; it followeth that the same law ordaineth, That no revenge be taken upon the consideration only of the offence past, but of the benefit to come; that is to say, that all revenge ought to tend to amendment, either of the person offending, or of others, by the example of his punishment; which is sufficiently apparent, in that the law of nature commandeth pardon, where the future time is secured. The same is also apparent by this: that revenge when it considereth the offence past, is nothing else but present triumph and glory, and directeth to no end; for end implieth some future good; and what is directed to no end, is therefore unprofitable; and consequently the triumph of revenge, is vain glory: and whatsoever is vain, is against reason; and to hurt one another without reason, is contrary to that, which by supposition is every man's benefit, namely peace; and what is contrary to peace, is contrary to the law of nature. (I.16.9)

Similarly, what he was later to call 'Compleasance' was to be fostered at the expense of our self-interested passions:

It is also a law of nature, *That every man do help and endeavour to accommodate each other, as far as may be without danger of their persons, and loss of their means, to maintain and defend themselves.* For seeing the causes of war and desolation proceed from those passions, by which we strive to accommodate ourselves, and to leave others as far as we can behind us: it followeth that that passion by which we strive mutually to accommodate each other, must be the cause of peace. And this passion is that charity defined chapt. 9, sect. 17.   (I.16.8)

And in general, if one goes through the list of particular laws of nature in chapters 16 and 17 of the *Elements* one finds them mostly concerned with purging men of the passions listed in chapter 9. Pride (9.1) is eliminated by 17.1 (with a sideswipe at Aristotle on natural slavery), in which 'we are to suppose, that for peace sake, nature hath ordained this law, *That every man acknowledge other for his equal*. And the breach of this law, is that we call PRIDE'; laughter (9.13) is eliminated by 16.11, '*That no man reproach, revile, deride, or any otherwise declare his hatred, contempt, or disesteem of any other*' (though Hobbes added, 'this law is very little practised'); and so on. If Hobbesian man were to live according to the laws of nature, he would not only renounce his individual judgement to his sovereign, but would live a strikingly passionless life; indeed, Hobbes sometimes implied that the elimination of passion might be necessary *before* one could effectively follow the laws. He seems to be saying this, for example, in 17.9:

A man that shall see these laws of nature set down and inferred with so many words, and so much ado, may think there is yet much more difficulty and subtlety required to acknowledge and do according to the said laws in every sudden occasion, when a man hath but a little time to consider. And while we consider man in most passions, as of anger, ambition, covetousness, vain glory, and the like that tend to the excluding of natural equality, it is true; but without these passions, there is an easy rule to know upon a sudden, whether the action I be to do, be against the law of nature or not: and it is but this, *That a man imagine himself in the place of the party with whom he hath to do, and reciprocally him in his ...*

Interestingly, this account of what it would be like to live in accordance with the laws of nature goes over into the sphere of international relations. It is a familiar thought that states on Hobbes's account function like individuals in a state of nature; but what Hobbes actually says about their behaviour makes clear that he had in mind individuals living by the laws of nature rather than individuals engaged in the warfare of the state of nature. Hobbes was in fact always rather wary about drawing the conclusion from his theory which Rousseau, in particular, insisted on, that as long as separate states exist in an unregulated international order, the state of war with all its implications must still continue. Rousseau, as is well known, saw the condition of modern warfare not only as exemplifying the Hobbesian state of nature but as incomparably worse that anything Hobbes had depicted. In *Leviathan*, Hobbes's only observation on this subject was the remark in chapter 13 (p. 63 orig.) that

though there had never been any time, wherein particular men were in a condition of warre one against another; yet in all times, Kings, and Persons of Soveraigne authority, because of their Independency, are in continuall jealousies, and in the state and posture of Gladiators . . . But because they uphold thereby, the Industry of their Subjects; there does not follow from it, that misery, which accompanies the Liberty of particular men.

But even this passage hints that there is something different about the way a state will behave, and in his earlier works Hobbes had said as much directly. In the *Elements of Law* (II.9.9) he said that the defence of a state

consisteth partly in the obedience and unity of the subjects, of which hath been already spoken, and in which consisteth the means of levying soldiers, and of having money, arms, ships, and fortified places in readiness for defence; and partly, in the avoiding of unnecessary wars. For such commonwealths, or such monarchs, as affect war for itself, that is to say, out of ambition, or of vain-glory, or that make account to revenge every little injury, or disgrace done by their neighbours, if they ruin not themselves, their fortune must be better than they have reason to expect.

Similarly in *De Cive*, outlining the methods by which a state might promote its citizens' prosperity, he observed that

great commonwealths, particularly *Rome* and *Athens*, at certain times so enlarged their country from the spoils of war, foreign tribute and the acquisition of territory by arms, that they did not impose taxes on the poorer citizens; in fact they actually distributed money and land to individuals. But we should not take enrichment by these means into our calculations. For as a means of gain, military activity is like gambling; in most cases it reduces a person's property; very few succeed. As there are only three things then which enable the citizens to increase their prosperity—*products of earth and water, hard work* and *thrift*—they are the only objects of a sovereign's duty. (XIII.14)

The power and industry which a state possesses give it a kind of security which no natural individual can possess, and as a result free it from ambition or vainglory, just as its citizens are freed from these passions by the power of the state over their domestic lives. It can live in accordance with the disciplined and bloodless principles of the laws of nature; it still needs to be wary and protective, but the instability which the principle of self-protection introduces into the state of nature among individuals will not (Hobbes seems to have thought) necessarily be found in the international sphere. This is in effect his answer to Rousseau's criticism. It remains an open question as to whether it is a good answer.

But while we get some idea from Hobbes's discussion of the laws of nature about what sort of men he envisaged acting out his ideas, the most vivid sense in his pages of how we shall live under the Leviathan comes from his discussions of the institutions of the society which operate below the level of the sovereign, discussions found principally in *Leviathan*, which goes into much greater detail about the nature of the new commonwealth than either of the two earlier works (and indeed this may well be one important reason why Hobbes produced this third redaction of his ideas). The appropriate comparison here is partly (again) Rousseau, but it is also More, the founder of the modern utopian tradition, in whose narrative Senecan or Stoic wise men, purged of their harmful passions by a combination of reflection and discipline, maintain 'the best state'. There are many parallels between the institutions and manners of Utopia and those recommended in *Leviathan*, in particular the stress on the management of labour and the attack on luxury; they also of course have in common (though we never think of them in this way) the subversion of private property. Luxury and conspicuous consumption are a constant target for Hobbes, as one would expect given what I have been saying, for they arise from emulation, envy, ambition, and pride, all passions which are to be eliminated. Thus Hobbes listed among the diseases of the commonwealth in chapter 29 of *Leviathan* (p. 174 orig.) 'the *Lethargy* of Ease, and *Consumption* of Riot and Vain Expence' (in addition to, at the international level, the '*Bulimia*, of enlarging Dominion'—all these traits, both of the state and of the citizens, arise from corrupt passions); while the duties of 'the Soveraign Representative' in chapter 30 include the imposition of taxation policies to ensure that 'he which laboureth much, and sparing the fruits of his labour, consumeth little' is rewarded more than 'he that living idly, getteth little, and spendeth all he gets' and that the commonwealth is not 'defrauded, by the luxurious waste of private men' (p. 181 orig.). In a familiar conjunction to this attack on luxury, Hobbes also proposed the state management of welfare, including (as I have observed in my most recent book) the use of colonialism precisely along the lines suggested by More.

Whereas many men, by accident unevitable, become unable to maintain themselves by their labour; they ought not to be left to the Charity of private persons; but to be provided for, (as far-forth as the necessities of Nature require), by the Lawes of the Common-wealth. For as it is Uncharitablenesse in any man, to neglect the impotent; so it is in the Soveraign of a Common-wealth, to expose them to the hazards of such uncertain Charity.

But for such as have strong bodies, the case is otherwise: they are to be forced to work; and to avoyd the excuse of not finding employment, there ought to be such Lawes, as may encourage all manner of Arts; as Navigation, Agriculture, Fishing, and all manner of Manifacture that requires labour. The multitude of poor, and yet strong people still encreasing, they are to be transported into Countries not sufficiently inhabited: where neverthelesse, they are not to exterminate those they find there; but constrain them to inhabit closer together, and not range a great deal of ground, to snatch what they find; but to court each little Plot with art and labour, to give them their sustenance in due season . . . (p. 239 orig.)

Hobbes also shared with More and the modern utopian tradition another familiar feature which (again) we tend not to think of in this context, which is the antagonism to what Rousseau was to term 'partial associations'—all the other institutions which governed men's lives in an *ancien régime* state, such as guilds, universities, families, and (of course) churches. This is such a familiar feature of Hobbes's work, and of one strain of Enlightenment thinking, that we tend to take it for granted, and not be struck by how unusual it was. An instructive comparison is with Jean Bodin, who though he shared with Hobbes a concept of legislative sovereignty and hostility to mixed government, was emphatic that sovereigns had to respect the other institutions in the society, from chartered cities to the Church (and of course families), and applauded the Parlement of Paris for throwing out the Pacification of Amboise and preserving the privilege of the Catholic Church against the king's will. (I take it that this is the prime reason why royalists like Filmer, who—unlike Hobbes—were seriously interested in preserving an *ancien régime* monarchy, found Bodin so congenial).

But the most strikingly utopian feature of *Leviathan* is its account of religion; indeed, it was in this context that I first began to think about the utopian strain in Hobbes. The major change in Hobbes's political theory between the first version (the *Elements* and *De Cive*) and the second version (*Leviathan*) was the transformation of his ideas about religion. The earlier version has what is essentially an orthodox Anglican theology and ecclesiology, while the later version (in the pungent words of Henry Hammond) is 'a farrago of Christian atheism'. In part, the transformation was to ensure that there was no rival to the sovereign; but it goes much farther than that, since Hobbes devoted a great deal of effort to the construction of a new kind of Christianity in which (for example) the conventional notion of the Trinity vanished, and from which the conventional account of Hell had been eliminated.

The desire for a reconstructed religion has been a common theme for the utopian writers from More down to the Utopian Socialists; it is implicit in the unChristian religion of the Utopians, and explicit in the blend of Protestantism and Judaism to which Bacon's fragmentary *New Atlantis* briefly alludes;[8] it is prominent in Rousseau and in Fourier, Owen and Saint-Simon. In all these authors, the transformation of religion is a necessary part of the transformation of human life at its deepest level, and in Hobbes, too, I think it plays the same role. The consequence of his revision was avowedly to eliminate fear from human life: hitherto, men had been terrified both by the 'fairies' whom they believed to have power over them and by the prospect of eternal torture. Under the new dispensation, men would no longer believe in any immaterial forces surrounding them on earth, nor would they believe that they faced any pains after death. If devout new

---

[8] *New Atlantis* is part of the selection of Bacon's works translated into Latin in the early 1620s by a team which probably included Hobbes.

Christians (that is to say, law-abiding citizens and believers in Christ as Redeemer), they would enjoy eternal life; if not, they would simply suffer the natural extinction which men had always faced. The effort which Hobbes put into the theological sections of *Leviathan*, which he was warned by Robert Payne would lose him friends, and which turned out to lose him his home among the exiles in Paris, is a striking illustration of the significance which the psychologically redemptive aspect of Hobbes's theory had come to possess for him by 1651.

The very title of the book also makes this point. As all of Hobbes's readers would have understood, the description of the commonwealth as a 'mortal God' or 'Leviathan' was a reference to the end of the Book of Job, in which God's reproach to Job for setting his own judgement against God's culminates in the divine ridicule of human power in the face of the strength of the elephant (Behemoth) and the whale (Leviathan). Leviathan in particular is far beyond human control; 'upon earth there is not his like, who is made without fear. He beholdeth all high things; he is a king over the children of pride.' God wishes Job to learn that he is as nothing compared with the Leviathan, and to renounce his own pride and confidence in his own judgement; the humble condition of Job at the end of the book, when he 'abhors himself', is the model for the citizen of the Leviathan state. The fact that the Leviathan is 'without fear' is critical, for that corresponds to what Hobbes (as we have seen) says repeatedly, that his commonwealth would rescue men from fear. By incorporating themselves into this artificial man who feels no fear, the citizens are themselves able to live a life freed from it. But they are also going to live a life without pride, their sense of their own individual importance reduced to nothing in the face of their commonwealth. We have to recognize the strangeness and the radical character of this vision, if we are properly to understand the role which Hobbes's theory played in the construction of modern politics.

Hobbes and the Classical Theory of Laughter

QUENTIN SKINNER

———◆———

I

Hobbes assured John Aubrey 'that Aristotle was the worst teacher that ever was, the worst politician and ethick', but he conceded at the same time that 'his rhetorique and discourse of animals was rare.'[1] It is certainly evident that Aristotle's *Rhetoric* was a work by which Hobbes was deeply impressed. One sign of its impact on his thinking has frequently been remarked. When Hobbes first turns to examine the character of the 'affections' in chapters 8 and 9 of *The Elements of Law*, he enunciates a number of his definitions in the form of virtual quotations from book 2 of Aristotle's text.[2] But a further and connected influence of the *Rhetoric* has been much less discussed. When Hobbes asks himself in chapter 9 of *The Elements*, and again in chapter 6 of *Leviathan*, about the nature of the emotions expressed by the phenomenon of laughter, he proceeds to outline a theory of the ridiculous closely resembling Aristotle's analysis in the *Rhetoric* and the *Poetics*. It is with the Aristotelian tradition of thinking about the laughable, and Hobbes's peculiar place in that tradition, that I am principally concerned in what follows. Like the ancient and early modern writers I discuss, I shall focus on two specific questions. What emotion does the phenomenon of laughter express? And how is the phenomenon of laughter to be understood and appraised?

II

Aristotle's most frequently quoted observation about laughter comes from the text known to Latin antiquity as *De partibus animalium*, in which he notes that human beings are the only creatures that laugh.[3] This may well have been the text that Hobbes had in mind when he spoke admiringly to

---

[1] Aubrey 1898, vol.1, p. 357.
[2] For discussions of the parallels see Strauss 1963: 36–41; Zappen 1983, Skinner 1996 38–9.
[3] Aristotle 1961, III. 10, p. 281. For a discussion see Screech 1997, pp. 1–5.

Aubrey of Aristotle's 'discourse of animals'. For my present purposes, however, Aristotle's most relevant observations can be found in the passage from book 2 of the *Rhetoric* in which he discusses the manners of youth. Hobbes was a profound student of this text, of which he produced a Latin paraphrase in the early 1630s.[4] It was from this paraphrase that someone (but not Hobbes)[5] made the translation that was published in *c*.1637 as *A Briefe of the Art of Rhetorique*, the earliest version of Aristotle's text to appear in English.[6] If we turn to this version, we find Aristotle saying that one of the characteristics of young people is that they are 'Lovers of Mirth, and by consequence love to jest at others'.[7] This leads him to enquire into the feelings expressed by their mirth, to which he replies that *'Jesting* is witty Contumely', having earlier assured us that contumely 'is the disgracing of another for his own pastime'.[8]

Aristotle's basic suggestion is thus that the mirth induced by jesting is always an expression of contempt, a suggestion already present in his earlier observation that among the sources of pleasure are 'ridiculous Actions, Sayings and Persons'.[9] As he points out himself,[10] he had already pursued these implications in his *Poetics*, especially in the brief section in which he had discussed the type of mimesis manifested in comedy.[11] Comedy deals in the risible, and the risible is an aspect of the shameful, the ugly, or the base. If we find ourselves laughing at others, it will be because they exhibit some fault or mark of shame which, while not painful, makes them ridiculous. Those who are chiefly risible are accordingly those who are in some way inferior, especially morally inferior, although not wholly vicious in character.[12]

It is possible that Aristotle was indebted for some of these observations to the remarks that Plato makes about laughter in several of his dialogues. In the *Philebus* Plato considers the nature of the ridiculous,[13] and in the *Republic* he foreshadows the central principle of Aristotle's analysis when he declares that laughter is almost always connected with the reproving of vice.[14] It would be fair to say, however, that Plato's observations remain scattered and unsystematic by comparison with Aristotle's direct engagement with the

---

[4] Hobbes's paraphrase is preserved at Chatsworth as Hobbes MS D.1: *Latin Exercises* (bound MS volume with *Ex Artistot: Rhet.*, at pp. 1–143).

[5] As Karl Schuhmann's forthcoming edition will show, the English version of Hobbes's paraphrase contains a number of anomalies and mistranslations which suggest that it cannot be by Hobbes. (I have therefore bracketed Hobbes's name in referring to this text.)

[6] [Hobbes (?)]1986, pp. 33–128.   [7] [Hobbes (?)]1986, p. 86.

[8] [Hobbes (?)]1986, pp. 70, 86.   [9] [Hobbes (?)]1986, p. 57.

[10] Aristotle 1926, I. XI. 28, p. 128, and III. XVIII. 7, p. 466.

[11] It may be, however, that Aristotle is referring to a fuller discussion in the now lost book 2 of his *Poetics*.   [12] Aristotle 1995, 1449ᵃ, p. 44.

[13] See Plato 1925 48c–50b, pp. 332–40 and cf. Plato 1926, 935d–936a, vol. 2, pp. 462–4, where he discusses the need to regulate comic writers in their use of ridicule.

[14] Plato 1930–5, 452d, vol. 1, p. 436.

topic, and it is perhaps not surprising that it was Aristotle's analysis that exercised the greatest influence in antiquity.

We find Aristotle's theory taken up in two distinct but convergent strands of thought. One was medical, and appears to have originated with the apocryphal letter of Hippocrates about Democritus, the laughing philosopher. Hippocrates reports that he was summoned by the people of Abdera—the city to which Democritus had retired in old age—because of their anxiety about the sage's apparent insanity. One of the citizens had paid Democritus a visit and 'began to weep in a loud voice in the manner of a woman weeping at the death of her child'.[15] But even in the face of this seemingly tragic outburst Democritus merely laughed. Hippocrates writes that at first he took Democritus to task for his insensitivity, but Democritus explained that 'I am only laughing at mankind, full of folly and empty of any good actions'[16] and at a world in which men occupy themselves 'with matters of no value, and consume their lives with ridiculous things'.[17] Hippocrates was greatly impressed, and on leaving Abdera thanked the people for enabling him to talk with 'the very wise Democritus, who alone is capable of giving wisdom to everyone in the world'.[18]

The other group of writers who explored the connections between laughter and contempt were the rhetoricians, and in this case they drew their inspiration directly from Aristotle's texts. The most elaborate analysis is Cicero's in book 2 of *De oratore*, in which the figure of Caesar is persuaded to discourse about the concept of the laughable.[19] Caesar begins by offering a restatement and elaboration of Aristotle's argument:

The proper field and as it were the province of laughter is restricted to matters that are in some way either disgraceful or deformed. For the principal if not the sole cause of mirth are those kinds of remarks which note and single out, in a fashion not in itself unseemly, something which is in some way unseemly or disgraceful.[20]

Caesar goes on to explain that the unseemliness can be either moral or physical in nature. He first suggests, again in strongly Aristotelian vein, that 'materials for ridicule can be found in the vices observable in people's

---

[15] Joubert 1579, Appendix, p. 358: 'voulant ancor mieus expliquer sa follie, se mit à pleurer à haute vois, comme une fame qui pleure la mort de son anfant'.

[16] Joubert 1579, Appendix, p. 363: 'Je ne me Ris que de l'homme, plein de folie, & vide de toutes accions droites.'

[17] Joubert 1579, Appendix, pp. 363–4: 'choses de nulle valeur, consument leurs vies an choses ridicules'.

[18] Joubert 1579, Appendix, p. 375: 'le tres-sage Democrite, qui seul peut randre sages tous les hommes du monde'. [19] Cicero 1942, II. 57. 233, vol. 1, p. 370.

[20] Cicero 1942, II. 58. 236, vol. 1, p. 372: 'Locus autem et regio quasi ridiculi . . . turpitudine et deformitate quadam continetur; haec enim ridentur vel sola, vel maxime, quae notant et designant turpitudinem aliquam non turpiter.'

behaviour, provided that the people concerned are neither especially popular nor figures of real tragedy'.[21] To which he adds that 'further materials especially suitable for making jokes are provided by ugliness and physical deformity'.[22]

The other leading rhetorician to examine the relations between laughter and contempt is Quintilian in book 6 of his *Institutio oratoria*, a discussion that appears to be indebted in equal measure to Aristotle's and Cicero's accounts. Quintilian reiterates that laughter 'has its source in things that are either deformed or disgraceful in some way',[23] adding that 'those sayings which excite ridicule are often false (which is always ignoble), often ingeniously distorted and never in the least complimentary'.[24] Neatly juggling *ridere* and *deridere*, he concludes that 'our mirth is never very far removed from derision', since the overriding emotion expressed by it will generally be one of disdainful superiority.[25] When we laugh, we are usually glorying or triumphing over others as a result of having come to see that, by comparison with ourselves, they are suffering from some contemptible weakness or infirmity. As Quintilian summarizes, 'the most ambitious way of glorying is to speak derisively'.[26]

III

With the recovery of the classical theory of eloquence—one of the defining achievements of Renaissance culture—the classical theory of laughter was likewise revived. It seems to have been in the early decades of the sixteenth century that a number of leading humanists first took it upon themselves to enquire into the meaning and significance of laughter, the most important discussions being those of Baldessare Castiglione in his *Libro del cortegiano* of 1528 and Juan Luis Vives in his *De anima & vita* of 1539. Later in the century, for the first time since antiquity, a specialized literature began to appear on the physiological as well as the psychological aspects of the phenomenon.[27] Here the pioneer was Laurent Joubert, a physician from Montpellier, whose

---

[21] Cicero 1942, II. 59. 238, vol. 1, p. 374: 'materies omnis ridiculorum est in istis vitiis quae sunt in vita hominum neque carorum neque calamitosorum'.

[22] Cicero 1942, II. 59. 239, vol. 1, p. 374: 'est etiam deformitatis et corporis vitiorum satis bella materies ad iocandum'.

[23] Quintilian 1920–2, VI. 3. 8, vol. 2, p. 442, quoting Cicero *De oratore*, II. 58. 236, vol. 1, p. 372: '[Risus] habet sedem in deformitate aliqua et turpitudine.'

[24] Quintilian 1920–2, VI. 3. 6, vol. 2, p. 440: 'ridiculum dictum plerumque falsum est (hoc semper humile), saepe ex industria depravatum, praeterea nunquam honorificum'.

[25] Quintilian 1920–2, VI. 3. 8, vol. 2, p. 442: 'A derisu non procul abest risus.'

[26] Quintilian 1920–2, XI. 1. 22, vol. 4, p. 166: 'Ambitiosissimum gloriandi genus est etiam deridere.'

[27] For fuller lists of Renaissance theorists of laughter see Screech 1997, p. 58 n., and especially Ménager 1995, pp. 7–11. Ménager's is an excellent study and I am much indebted to it.

Traité du ris was first published in Paris in 1579.[28] Soon afterwards several comparable treatises appeared in Italy, including Celso Mancini's *De risu, ac ridiculis* in 1598,[29] Antonio Lorenzini's *De risu* in 1603,[30] and Elpidio Berrettario's *Phisici, et philosophi tractatus de risu* of the same year.[31]

As in the case of the classical theorists, all these writers assume that the most important question to ask about laughter is what emotions give rise to it.[32] Some of them approach the puzzle by way of considering the phenomenon of laughter in conjunction with the shedding of tears. Francisco Vallesio, one of Philip II's physicians, included a chapter entitled *De risu et fletu* in his *Controversiae* in 1582,[33] while Nicander Jossius published an entire treatise under the same title in 1580.[34] Timothy Bright, a London physician, similarly juxtaposes laughter and weeping in his *Treatise of Melancholie* in 1586,[35] as does Rodolph Goclenius the elder in his *Physica commentatio de risu & lacrymis* in 1597.[36] Hobbes likewise links laughter and tears in his *Critique* of Thomas White's *De Mundo*, as does Descartes in *Les Passions de l'âme*.[37]

Among the elements common to laughter and weeping, these writers single out the fact that they are peculiar to humankind,[38] that they are largely uncontrollable,[39] and that they seem to be almost unnaturally vehement reactions to some inner movement of the soul.[40] They find it easy to agree that the main emotion expressed by weeping must be dejection and sadness,[41] perhaps accompanied on some occasions by fear.[42] But as Bright explicitly

---

[28] See Joubert 1579 and on its publishing history Ménager 1995, pp. 7–8. On the place of Joubert's work in the medical literature see Machline 1998, pp. 251–64.

[29] Mancini 1598. According to Ménager 1995, p. 9, Mancini's text was originally published in 1591. But Ménager appears to confuse the publishing history of Mancini's book with that of Antonio Lorenzini (on which see n. 30 below).

[30] Lorenzini 1606. Lorenzini's text had already been published, together with a reprint of Nicander Jossius's 1580 treatise on laughter, in Lorenzini 1603. [31] Berrettario 1603.

[32] This contrasts with some of the most interesting scholarship on the history of laughter, which has concentrated on genres of comedy and their potential for the subversion of elites. See, for example, Bakhtine 1970, Thomas 1977. [33] Vallesio 1582, V. 9, pp. 220–2.

[34] Jossius 1580, pp. 44–144.

[35] Bright 1586, ch. 28, p. 161: '*Howe melancholie causeth both weeping and laughing, and the reasons how*'. [36] Goclenius 1597.

[37] See Hobbes 1973, p. 360 on the 'affectus ridentium & flentium' and cf. Descartes 1988, Article 128, p. 156 linking 'le Ris' and 'les larmes'.

[38] Jossius 1580, pp. 91, 94–5; Vallesio 1582, p. 220. See also Goclenius 1597, pp. 21, 37, 45, who anticipates a possible objection by adding (p. 54) that the tears of the crocodile are not real but 'quasi' tears.

[39] Jossius 1580, pp. 52, 57; Vallesio 1582, p. 220; Goclenius 1597, p. 22.

[40] For the claim that 'risus et fletus praeter naturam fiunt' see Vallesio 1582, p. 222. Cf. Jossius 1580, p. 52, on how laughter 'oritur . . . ob vehementem occasionem' and Goclenius 1597, p. 21, on the 'animi commotio' involved.

[41] Jossius 1580, p. 99 claims that 'dolor seu dolorificium esset subiectum & materia fletus'. Cf. Vallesio 1582, p. 222, on 'tristitia' as the cause. See also BL Harl. MS 6083, fo. 177, Hobbes's fragment *Of Passions*, in which he likewise observes (fo. 177ʳ) that 'sudden deiection, is the passion; that causeth weeping'.

[42] Vallesio 1582, p. 222 argues that weeping can arise out of 'tristitia aut timore'.

concedes, the cause of laughter 'is of more difficultie to finde out, and the reason not so manifest'.[43] What passion of the soul could possibly be so complex and powerful as to make us 'burst out', as Vallesio puts it, in this 'almost convulsive' way?[44]

One of the feelings involved, everyone agreed, must be some form of joy or happiness. Among the humanist writers, Castiglione stresses in his *Cortegiano* that (in the words of Sir Thomas Hoby's translation of 1561) 'laughing is perceived onlie in man, and (in maner) alwaies is a token of a certein jocundenesse and meerie moode that he feeleth inwardlie in his minde'.[45] Vives similarly maintains in *De anima & vita* that 'laughter is born of happiness and delight',[46] and this doctrine was widely repeated by the humanists of the next generation and beyond.[47]

We encounter the same assumptions in the medical literature, the pioneer in this instance being the physician Girolamo Fracastoro in his *De sympathia & antipathia rerum* of 1546.[48] The cause of mirth, Fracastoro declares, must always be some form of 'internal happiness'.[49] Laurent Joubert agrees, arguing that the passion moving us to laughter must always be related in some way to joy,[50] while Francisco Vallesio more straightforwardly affirms that 'it is my belief that men laugh whenever something joyful takes place'.[51] Within a generation, everyone writing on the topic had come to take this assumption for granted. Descartes simply notes in *Les Passions de l'ame* that 'the Laugh seems to be one of the principal signs of Joy',[52] while Hobbes still more briskly concludes in *The Elements of Law* that laughter 'is alwayes joy'.[53]

It was generally acknowledged, however, that this joy must be of a peculiar kind, since it appears to be connected in some way with feelings of scorn, contempt, and even hatred. Among the humanists, Castiglione mounts one of the earliest arguments to this effect. Whenever we laugh, we are always 'mockinge and scorninge' someone, always seeking 'to scoff and mocke at vices'.[54] Thomas Wilson enlarges on the suggestion in his *Arte of*

---

[43] Bright 1586, p. 162.

[44] Vallesio 1582, p. 222 speaks of the 'quasi motus quidam convulsionis' that accompanies laughter. Jossius 1580, p. 57 similarly speaks of the passions that 'erumpunt in risum'.

[45] Castiglione 1994, p. 154.

[46] Vives 1550, p. 206: 'ex laetitia & delectatione risus nascitur.'

[47] See, for example, Jossius 1580, p. 57, Lorenzini 1606, p. 95.

[48] Ménager 1995, p. 8 notes that Fracastoro was one of the physicians appointed by the Vatican to attend the Council of Trent. He was also well-known as a poet, and received the praise of Sir Philip Sidney. See Sidney 1912, p. 35. On Hobbes as a reader of Fracastoro see Leijenhorst 1996.

[49] Fracastoro 1546, fo. 23ᵛ states that, when we laugh, 'laetitia interna in facie manifestetur'.

[50] Joubert 1579, pp. 72–3, 87–8.

[51] Vallesio 1582, p. 220: 'sentimus, homines ridere quum occurrit res iocunda'.

[52] Descartes 1988, Article 125, p. 153: 'il semble que le Ris soit un des principaux signes de la Joye'. [53] Hobbes 1969, p. 41.

[54] Castiglione 1994, pp. 155–6.

Rhetorique of 1554, the earliest full-scale neo-classical treatise on eloquence in the English language. Wilson includes a long section in book 2 entitled 'Of delityng the hearers, and stirryng them to laughter' in which he maintains that we experience feelings of contempt whenever we perceive 'the fondnes, the filthines, the deformitee' of someone else's behaviour, with the result that we are prompted to 'laugh him to skorne out right'.[55]

If we turn to the medical writers, we find the same theory laid out at greater length. Perhaps the subtlest analysis is that of Laurent Joubert, although he acknowledges a debt to the earlier work of François Valleriola, a fellow physician from Montpellier.[56] Suppose we ask, Joubert writes in the opening chapter of his *Traité*, 'what is the subject-matter of laughter?'[57] Drawing on Valleriola's discussion,[58] Joubert answers that we laugh at 'everything which is ridiculous, whether it is something done or something said'.[59] But anything we find ridiculous, Joubert goes on to explain in chapter 2, will always 'be something that strikes us as ugly, deformed, dishonest, indecent, malicious and scarcely decorous'.[60] So our laughter will always arise from the contemplation of deeds or sayings 'which have an appearance of ugliness without being pitiable'.[61] This in turn means that the joy we experience can never be unalloyed. We can never avoid some measure of scorn or dislike for baseness and ugliness, so that 'the common style of our laughter is contempt or derision'.[62] Joubert goes further and adds that, in consequence of these complex feelings, laughter can never be wholly unconnected with sadness. 'Given that everything which is ridiculous arises from ugliness and dishonesty',[63] and given that we can never contemplate such unpleasantness with equanimity, it follows that 'anything ridiculous gives us pleasure and sadness combined'.[64]

Joubert's emphasis on *tristesse* was rarely taken up, but his contention that laughter is basically an expression of scorn for ridiculous things was much reiterated,[65] especially by those who aspired to connect the insights of the humanists with those of the burgeoning medical literature. Perhaps the most important writer to forge these links was Robert Burton, who

---

[55] Wilson 1554, fos. 74ᵛ, 75ʳ.

[56] Valleriola 1588, p. 134 in turn speaks warmly of Joubert's *Traité du ris*.

[57] Joubert 1579, p. 15: 'Quelle est la matiere du Ris?'

[58] Valleriola 1554, III, IX, pp. 212–24, esp. pp. 217–18.

[59] Joubert 1579, p. 16: 'tout ce qui est ridicule . . . an fait, ou an dit'.

[60] Joubert 1579, p. 16: 'Ce que nous voyons de laid, difforme, des-honneste, indessant, malfeant, & peu convenable.'

[61] Joubert 1579, p. 16: the 'fais ou dis' that provoke laughter are those 'qui ont apparance de laideur, & ne sont pitoyables'.

[62] Joubert 1579, p. 30: '[le] commum geanre . . . e[s]t le mepris ou derision'.

[63] Joubert 1579, pp. 87–8: 'pour ce que tout ridicule provient de laideur & meffeance'.

[64] Joubert 1579, p. 87: 'la chose ridicule nous donne plaisir & tristesse'.

[65] For a similar account see Goclenius 1597, ch. 2, pp. 9, 15.

declares in the Introduction to his *Anatomy of Melancholy* of 1621 that
there has never been 'so much cause of laughter' as we encounter in our
present distempered world. He goes on to explain that in laughing we
'contemne others, condemne the world of folly', and that the world has
never been so full of folly to scorn and condemn, so full of people who are
'Fooles & ridiculous'.[66] Sir Thomas Browne, another physician steeped in
humanist learning, speaks in comparable vein in his *Pseudodoxia
Epidemica* of 1646. Discussing the passion of laughter in book 7, he agrees
that 'a laugh there is of contempt or indignation', adding that even God
himself is described in the Scriptures as laughing the wicked to scorn.[67]

So far, the account of laughter we have encountered in the humanist and
medical literature of the Renaissance presents a purely neo-classical appearance. It is true that the Renaissance writers are generally content, at least
initially, to repeat and embroider the classical case. Any suggestion, however, that they slavishly follow their ancient authorities would be seriously
misleading, and needs to be qualified in at least two important respects.

It first needs to be emphasized that, in a number of Renaissance writers,
we encounter two significant additions to their inherited arguments. First of
all, they place a new emphasis on the role of suddenness, and hence of surprise, in the provocation of mirth. Cicero in *De oratore* had alluded to the
significance of the unexpected,[68] but his Renaissance followers greatly
embroider the point. Castiglione stresses that 'certein newlye happened
cases' are particularly apt to 'provoke laughter', especially if we surprise
our hearers by speaking 'contrary to expectacyon'.[69] Vives further elabo-
rates the insight, arguing that our mirth 'arises out of a novel sense of
delight', and that 'sudden and unexpected things have more effect on us
and move us more quickly to laughter than anything else'.[70]

For a fuller analysis we need to return to the medical writers, who first
introduce into the argument the key concept of *admiratio* or wonderment.[71]
The pioneering discussion appears to be that of Girolamo Fracastoro in his
De sympathia of 1546. 'The things that generally move us to laughter', he
begins, 'must have a certain novelty about them' and must appear before us
'suddenly' and 'unexpectedly'.[72] When this happens, we instantly experience

---

[66] Burton 1989, pp. 37, 57, 101.   [67] Browne 1928–31, vol. 3, p. 312.
[68] Cicero 1942, II. 63. 255, vol. 1, p. 388; cf. also II. 71. 289, vol. 1, p. 418.
[69] Castiglione 1994, pp. 188, 190.
[70] Vives 1550, p. 207: 'insperata vera & subita plus afficiunt, citius commovent risum'. On
this assumption see Skinner 1996, p. 392. The claim was frequently reiterated by humanist
writers of the next generation. See, for example, Mancini 1598, p. 217, arguing that anything
which causes laughter must always happen *statim*, suddenly and all at once.
[71] The point was quickly taken up by the humanist writers. See, for example, Jossius 1580,
p. 58, Lorenzini 1606, p. 95.
[72] Fracastoro 1546, fo. 23ᵛ: 'Nova quoque ea sunt, quae risum movere solent.' See also fo. 24ʳ
on the need for the *res* to be *subita* and *repentina*.

a sense of wonderment, which in turn creates in us a feeling of delight. The emotional sequence is thus that 'the sudden and the unexpected give rise to *admiratio*, which in turn gives rise to *delectatio*, which in turn provokes the movement of the face we call laughter'.[73] Francisco Vallesio fulsomely acknowledges Fracastoro's analysis and goes on to appropriate it.[74] 'As a result of experiment', he reports, 'I am led to believe that men laugh when something happens which is at once pleasant and new . . . the novelty gives rise to *admiratio*, the pleasure gives rise to joy' and the combination is what makes us laugh.[75]

Fracastoro's emphasis on *admiratio* was quickly taken up by the humanists, and in particular by a number of commentators on Aristotle's *Poetics*. Here the pioneer seems to have been Vincento Maggi in his *In Aristotelis Librum de Poetica Communes Explicationes* of 1550.[76] Speaking in the special tone of vehemence that humanist scholars liked to affect, Maggi declares that 'I cannot sufficiently express my astonishment as to why it is that Cicero should have failed to say a single word about the subject of *admiratio*, which is one of the causes of laughter, when the fact is that in the absence of *admiratio* it is never possible for laughter to occur.'[77] The reason why the presence of *admiratio* is indispensable is that we laugh only when we encounter new and surprising things. It is the presence of *novitas* that induces wonderment, and it is our sense of wonderment that makes us laugh.[78]

The other important addition made by the Renaissance theorists to the classical theory of laughter arose out of their perception of a lacuna in Aristotle's original account. Aristotle's thesis in the *Poetics* had been that laughter reproves vice by way of expressing and soliciting feelings of contempt for those who conduct themselves ridiculously. As Maggi points out in his commentary on the *Poetics*, however, Aristotle had uncharacteristically failed to supply a definition of the ridiculous,[79] and had failed in consequence to indicate which particular vices are most susceptible of being held up to derision and thereby laughed to scorn.

To the medical writers this issue was of little significance, but to the humanists it often seemed the most interesting question of all. They found a clue to the answer in Aristotle's contention that wholly vicious characters

---

[73] Fracastoro 1546, fo. 24ʳ: 'Subitam & repentinam etiam admirationem ac repentinam etiam delectationem faciunt [et ex delectatione] . . . motum oris, qui risus dicitur.'

[74] Vallesio 1582, p. 220 acknowledges both Valeriola and Fracastoro.

[75] Vallesio 1582, p. 220: 'Experimento sentimus, homines ridere, quum occurrit res iocunda, & nova . . . nova faciunt admirationem, iocunda gaudium.'

[76] Maggi 1550, pp. 301–27.

[77] Maggi 1550, p. 305: 'Mirari satis non possum cur Cicero . . . de admiratione, quae est una risus causa, ne verbum quidem fecerit . . . cum risus nunquam sine admiratione fieri possit.'

[78] Maggi focuses on the importance of *novitas* in part 2 of Maggi 1550, pp. 310–22.

[79] Maggi 1550, part 3, esp. p. 325.

are not properly the subject of ridicule.[80] Castiglione enlarges on the insight
by suggesting that the vices specifically deserving of our contempt are those
which exhibit 'affectation' rather than outright wickedness, and especially
those which 'passe the degree' and thereby lead to extravagant behaviour.
'Those Affectations and curiosities that are but meane, bringe a lothsomnesse with them, but whan they be done oute of measure they much provoke laughter.' Those people who visibly 'passe the degree' when behaving
discreditably reduce themselves to absurdity, which is why they 'doe rather
provoke laughter then lothsomnesse'.[81]

Among the vices resulting from a failure to observe this ideal of *medioc-
ritas*, one of the most contemptible was generally agreed to be avarice.
Nicander Jossius singles out this weakness as one of the most obvious
'characteristics of body and soul' in which 'matters of ridicule lurk'.[82] Celso
Mancini ends his *De risu, ac ridiculis* by specifying in similar vein that one
of the failings 'most worthy of derision' is 'the miserliness of old men,
because any man is deformed and rendered monstrous by avarice'.[83] So too
Paolo Beni, who notes in his *Commentarii* on Aristotle's *Poetics* that the
figure of the miser always makes one of the best subjects for comedy.[84] The
suggestion was not lost on the comic dramatists of the age, as Ben Jonson's
Volpone and Moliere's *L'Avare* are there to remind us.

Of all the vices open to derision, however, the most flagrant were said
to be hypocrisy and vaingloriousness. If we glance forward to post-
Renaissance theories of comedy, we generally find the figure of the hypo-
crite singled out as pre-eminently worthy of contempt. This is Henry
Fielding's argument in the theoretical essay that prefaces his comic novel
Joseph Andrews of 1742. Echoing Hoby's translation of Castiglione,
Fielding begins by laying it down that the vices most open to ridicule are
those which exhibit 'affectation'. He goes on to assert that 'affectation
proceeds from one of these two causes, vanity or hypocrisy', and that 'from
the discovery of this affectation arises the ridiculous—which always strikes
the reader with surprize and pleasure'. But he adds that this happens 'in a
higher and stronger degree when the affectation arises from hypocrisy, than
when from vanity', and he concludes by noting that 'our Ben Johnson, who
of all men understood the *ridiculous* the best, hath chiefly used the hypo-
critical affectation' in his comedies.[85]

Among the Renaissance theorists, by contrast, we encounter a weightier
emphasis on the affectations of pride and vaingloriousness. It is possible

---

[80] Aristotle 1995, 1449ᵃ, p. 44.   [81] Castiglione 1994, pp. 163–4.

[82] Jossius 1580, p. 75, offers 'quodam avaritiae genus & actiones' as his first example of the
fact that 'in moribus quoque corporis, atque animi latent ridicula'.

[83] Mancini 1598, pp. 22–30: 'Ridendo avaritiam senum [quod] ab avaritia hominem fieri
deformem & monstrum.'   [84] Beni 1613, p. 162.

[85] Fielding 1985, pp. 28–9.

that they may have been directly influenced by Plato at this point, for when Socrates examines the nature of the ridiculous in the *Philebus* he not only argues that those who render themselves absurd must be suffering from some kind of vice, but adds that the vice in question will generally be lack of self-knowledge, especially in the form of self-conceit.[86] It is more likely, however, that the Renaissance writers were drawing on a suggestion of Cicero's in book 2 of *De oratore*, in which the figure of Caesar begins his analysis of the ridiculous by declaring that the people most worthy of being laughed to scorn are 'those who act in a particularly boastful way'.[87]

Whatever the source, the suggestion is one that the humanist writers of the Renaissance develop at much greater length. It is when people 'bragg and boast of them selves and have a proude and haughtye stomake', Castiglione maintains, that we are justified 'in mockinge and scorninge such a one' to raise a laugh.[88] He offers the example of men who 'speake of their auntientrye and noblenesse of birth' and of women who praise their own 'beawtie and handsomenesse'.[89] Celso Mancini singles out 'the would-be boastful soldier' as yet another type of person 'whose boastings make us laugh' because 'we know that such vaingloriousness is ridiculous and because such lack of measure irritates us'.[90] Speaking in a loftier register, Lodovico Castelvetro—yet another learned commentator on Aristotle's *Poetics*—suggests that the principal cause of laughter arises from the fact that our fallen and corrupted natures have left us 'stuffed with vanity and pride'.[91] Once again, these insights were not lost on the comic dramatists of the age, who often exhibit a special detestation of those who act without 'measure' and try to pass beyond their degree. The overweening self-love of Malvolio in Shakespeare's *Twelfth Night*, the vainglorious boasting of Puntarvolo in Jonson's *Every Man Out of his Humour*, the ridiculous social climbing of M. Jourdain in Molière's *Bourgeois Gentilhomme* are all variations on the same satirical theme.

IV

So far I have considered the two main ways in which the classical theory of laughter was extended and developed in the course of the Renaissance. Far more important, however, is the fact that a number of Renaissance writers

---

[86] Plato 1925, 48c–49c, pp. 332–6.

[87] Cicero 1942, II. 58. 237, vol. 1, p. 374, singles out the absurdity of those who 'se forte iactant'.

[88] Castiglione 1994, p. 155.   [89] Castiglione 1994, p. 163.

[90] Mancini 1598, pp. 229–30: 'Provocat nos ad risum iactantia militis gloriosi [quod] cognoscimus dementiam esse illam inanem gloriam . . . carens mensura nos vexat.'

[91] Castelvetro 1570, fo. 53ᵛ, speaks of 'la natura nostra corrotta per lo peccato originale' and the fact that 'si riempie d'alegrezza, & di superbia'.

began to express doubts about the governing assumption of the classical theory, the assumption that laughter is invariably an expression of contempt for vice. They began to ask themselves whether this argument, if not entirely mistaken, may not be considerably exaggerated. Is it really true that our laughter is always an expression of scorn? Surely some laughter—for example, the laughter of infants—is an expression of unalloyed delight?[92]

A number of medical writers, no doubt anxious to throw off the weight of scholastic learning, particularly emphasize the point. Fracastoro insists that 'the things which are said about the ridiculous are not properly said', for the truth is that 'laughter is composed out of joy and wonderment combined'.[93] Vallesio refers us to Fracastoro's anti-Aristotelian analysis and proceeds to adopt it. He begins by declaring that 'men laugh when something happens which is at once pleasant and new', but adds that 'our mirth ceases either when the feeling of novelty, or else the feeling of pleasure, wears off'.[94] From this he infers that our laughter need have nothing to do with contempt, since it can equally well be a simple response to a pleasing and surprising event. Developing the insight more systematically, the Pisan physician Elpidio Berrettario in his *Tractatus de risu* introduces a sharp distinction between what he takes to be two distinct *genera* of mirth.[95] One is the *genus* discussed by Aristotle in the *Poetics*, in which our laughter is provoked by seeing vices successfully held up to ridicule.[96] But the other is unconnected with derision, and simply arises 'when we are enticed into laughter by something that is joyful or precious to us'.[97]

Nor were these doubts confined to the medical literature. Castelvetro in his commentary on Aristotle's *Poetics*[98] opens his analysis of the passage in which, as he translates it, Aristotle had argued that 'the laughable is a subdivision of the base'[99] by retorting that 'laughter can be provoked in us by purely pleasurable things'.[100] Beni in his still more comprehensive

---

[92] One might expect to find in addition some *moral* objections to contemptuous laughter, and especially to its use (in accordance with Cicero's instructions) to mock other people's weaknesses and infirmities. But such scruples are rarely voiced in this period. Sir Thomas More is the only leading humanist to make this kind of anti-Aristotelian point. See More 1965, p. 192. But see Cockagne 2000, pp. 79–82, 89–91 for later moral anxieties about laughter as an expression of ridicule.

[93] Fracastoro 1546, fos. 23ᵛ–24ʳ: 'Verum haec non proprie ea sunt, quae ridicula dicuntur . . . Est autem risus, compositus ex admiratione & letitia.'

[94] Vallesio 1582, p. 220: 'Homines ridere, quum occurrit res iocunda, & nova . . . atque quamprimum cessat aut iocunditas, aut novitas, cessare risum.'

[95] Berrettario 1603, fos. 7ʳ and 22ʳ also singles out the laughter provoked by tickling, insisting (against Fracastoro) that this too is a 'real' and distinct *genus* of the phenomenon.

[96] Berrettario 1603, fo. 7ʳ.

[97] Berrettario 1603, fo. 19ʳ: 'Alterum vero, quando iucunditate & caritate quadam allicimur ad risum.'   [98] See Ménager 1995, pp. 32–3 for a discussion of this text.

[99] Castelvetro 1570, fo. 50ᵛ: 'Il ridevole è particella della turpitudine.'

[100] Castelvetro 1570, fo. 51ʳ: 'Il riso si muove in noi per cose piacentici.'

Commentarii on the *Poetics* similarly questions Aristotle's claim that comedy is always preoccupied with reproving vice, pointing out that 'it is not at all rare for comedy to portray good men and to represent them in a praiseworthy way'.[101]

These observations were sometimes underpinned by an anti-Aristotelian vision of the joy and delight out of which laughter can arise. The underlying emotion, some theorists argue, can often be simple *joie de vivre*, unconnected with any feelings of superiority or scorn. Fracastoro observes that 'we often laugh and show our joy when we meet our friends and acquaintances, or else our children, and more generally those who are dear to us'.[102] Castelvetro illustrates the same *mise-en-scène*, picturing a situation in which 'a father and mother receive their little children with laughter and festivity, while in a similar way a lover greets his beloved with a laugh'.[103] Referring with approval to Fracastoro's analysis,[104] Berrettario adds with a flourish that we laugh not only when we encounter our children and friends, but also when we contemplate a beloved mistress or a precious stone.[105]

A further way in which laughter can sometimes arise, according to these writers, is when we experience a sudden defeat of our expectations, whether in the form of a surprising juxtaposition or some other kind of incongruity. Nicander Jossius, although in general a close follower of Aristotle, illustrates the possibility at considerable length. He invites us to consider how we would react 'if a woman were to put on male attire, or gird herself with a sword and set out for the forum, or if a boastful soldier were to settle down with boys learning their grammar at school, or if a prince were to dress himself up as a peasant'.[106] We would certainly laugh, but the reason for our mirth would be the utter incongruity of it all, the failure to pay due respect 'to time, place, moderation or appropriateness'.[107] While these situations would undoubtedly be ridiculous, Jossius appears to suggest that we would laugh at them less in contempt than in sheer astonishment.

These insights were eventually developed in Augustan culture into a general defence of the claim that there can be purely good-natured laughter.[108]

---

[101] Beni 1613, p. 103: 'Comoedia non raro bonos exprimit . . . [et] cum laude represententet.' Cf. also pp. 162, 197.

[102] Fracastoro 1546, fo. 23ᵛ: 'Quum aut amicis & familiaribus, aut filiis, & universaliter charis occurrimus . . . ridere solemus, & laetitiam ostendere.'

[103] Castelvetro 1570, fo. 51ʳ: 'Il padre & la madre con riso & con festa riceve I figlioletti piccioli . . . & parimente l'amante raccoglie la donna amata con riso.' See also the tabulation at the end of this section of Castelvetro's commentary, which is headed (fo. 54ᵛ) 'cose piacenti che ci muovono a riso'. The first is said to be 'carita di persone prossime o amate o di cose desiderate'.

[104] Berrettario 1603, fo. 20ᵛ. [105] Berrettario 1603, fos. 19ʳ, 21ᵛ.

[106] Jossius 1580, pp. 71–2: 'si mulier induat habitum virilem, aut accincta ense proficiscatur ad forum . . . [aut si] miles gloriosus . . . sedeat cum pueris in schola discens grammaticam . . . [aut] si princeps ut rustica gens vestiat'.

[107] Jossius 1580, p. 71: 'ad locum, ad tempus, ad modum, aut occasionem'.

[108] On this development see Tave 1960, esp. pp. 43–87.

We encounter the suggestion in Joseph Addison's articles on laughter in the *Spectator* of 1711,[109] in Francis Hutcheson's explictly anti-Hobbesian *Reflections upon Laughter* in 1725,[110] and perhaps most interestingly in Fielding's Preface to *Joseph Andrews*. As we have seen, Fielding's analysis at first sight looks thoroughly classical, for he accepts that comedy aims to ridicule certain types of affectation, and he agrees that the vices most susceptible to ridicule are avarice, hypocrisy, and vanity. At the same time, however, he draws a strong distinction between the comic and what he describes as the burlesque. While the latter genre 'contributes more to exquisite mirth and laughter than any other', it never does so by seeking to arouse contempt. Rather it works by conveying a sense of the 'surprizing absurdity' of some situation, 'as in appropriating the manners of the highest to the lowest' or by producing other 'distortions and exaggerations'. The effect, if successful, will be to make us laugh, but our mirth in these cases will be 'full of good-humour and benevolence'.[111]

These later arguments were undoubtedly of great importance in the evolution of modern theories of comedy. As we have seen, however, it had come to be widely accepted as early as the opening decades of the seventeenth century that the classical theory of laughter had only succeeded in capturing one element in the explanation of this protean phenomenon. For a summary of the more complex theory that had by then become orthodox, we can hardly do better than turn to that fount of conventional sentiment, the French *conseilleur* Louis Guyon, who includes a chapter on laughter in the third edition of his *Diverses Leçons* of 1617.[112]

Guyon continues to cleave to a number of classical arguments. He agrees with Aristotle that 'man alone is capable of laughter'.[113] He adds that 'something sudden and unexpected' must happen if laughter is to be provoked.[114] And he feels bound to accept the basic Aristotelian contention that 'the cause of laughter must be a certain deformity, because we laugh only at those things which are unsuitable in themselves and appear to be badly formed'.[115]

---

[109] [Addison] 1965, no. 249 (15 Dec. 1711), vol. 2, pp. 465–9, refers us back to an earlier article (no. 49, 24 Apr. 1711, vol. 1, pp. 200–4) about Hobbes's theory of laughter. Addison maintains (pp. 466, 468) that while Hobbes's account 'seems to hold in most cases' we need to recognize a form of laughter 'in it self both amiable and beautiful'.

[110] Hutcheson 1750, originally published as three articles in the *Dublin Review* for 1725. (For the printing history see Tave 1960, p. 56.) Hutcheson 1750, pp. 6, 29 denounces the 'palpable absurdity' of Hobbes's failure to recognize that laughter frequently 'evidences good nature'.

[111] Fielding 1985, pp. 26–8. On the evolution of the contrast between laughter produced by satire (contemptuous and ridiculing) and by the burlesque (sympathetic), see Paulson 1988.

[112] Guyon 1617, I. 3. 3, pp. 434–42.

[113] Guyon 1617, p. 442: 'l'homme seul est capable [de rire]'.

[114] Guyon 1617, p. 442: 'quelque chose de soudain: & non attendu'.

[115] Guyon 1617, p. 435: 'les causes du rire sont, une certaine deformité, pource qu'on rid seulement des choses qui ne conviennent en soi, & semblent mal feantes . . . je ne le puis pas declarer autrement'.

As he makes clear, however, his intellectual allegiances are far from strictly Aristotelian, and he goes on to develop a more complex although still conventional account. He begins by stressing that it is possible to laugh 'in a civil style',[116] and explains that 'anyone who reflects properly will see that what makes us laugh is almost always something which, while it is in some way unsuitable, nevertheless need not be badly-formed'.[117] He declares that 'everything which provokes laughter gives pleasure',[118] and is very insistent that 'laughter is highly agreeable to everyone, so that anyone who provokes it in a good way, and in its proper season, is greatly to be commended'.[119] His own aspiration—as he explains in line with much Renaissance sentiment—is thus 'to show what methods a discreet personage should use to move laughter'[120] if the aim is 'always to guard one's dignity' at the same time.[121]

V

The idea that laughter can be pleasant as well as contemptuous, and can therefore form a part of a properly 'civil' life, had come to be widely accepted by the early decades of the seventeenth century. So it comes as something of a shock to find that, in the two best-known discussions of laughter in the next generation—those of Hobbes and Descartes—these assumptions are explicitly set aside in favour of a return to an unambiguously classical point of view.

This is not to say that Hobbes and Descartes restate the Aristotelian theory in its most blinkered form. They both pick up and reiterate the two developments of Aristotle's argument I have already discussed. First of all, they lay considerable emphasis on the concept originally introduced by Fracastoro into the discussion, the concept of surprise or wonderment. Descartes, for whom *admiratio* is a fundamental passion,[122] opens his analysis of laughter in *Les Passions de l'ame* by stressing the importance of novelty and suddenness, arguing that we laugh only when something happens 'to cause the lungs suddenly to inflate' so that 'the air they contain is forced out through the

---

[116] Guyon 1617, p. 434 speaks of provoking others to laugh 'bien à point & civilement'.

[117] Guyon 1617, pp. 435–6: 'qui pensera bien en soi-mesme, verra que quasi tousjours ce dont on rid, estre une chose qui ne convient pas, & toutefois n'est malfeante.'

[118] Guyon 1617, p. 434: 'tout ce qui provoque le rire ... donne plaisir'.

[119] Guyon 1617, p. 435: 'le rire est tres agreable à tous, & est bien loüable celui qui le provoque de bonne sorte, & en sa saison.'

[120] Goyon 1617, p 436: 'Je veux monstrer de quels moyens doit user un personage discret: pour mouvoir le rire'.

[121] Guyon 1617, p. 437: 'gardant tousjours la dignité d'une discrette personne'.

[122] On the place of wonder in Descartes's theory of the passions see James 1997, pp. 169–70, 187–9.

windpipe with impetuosity, forming an inarticulate and uncontrolled voice'.[123] He adds that these distinctive physiological changes take place only when a new and sudden event is associated with feelings of wonderment. The blood coming from the spleen must be 'pushed towards the heart by some light emotion of Hatred, aided by the surprise of *l'Admiration*' if the outcome is to be the form of dilation with which laughter is associated.[124]

Hobbes brings the same features together in his first and fullest discussion of laughter, which he presented in chapter 9 of his *Elements of Law* in 1640. He too stresses the importance of novelty and surprise, arguing that 'for as much as the same thinge is noe more ridiculous, when it groweth stale, or usuall. Whatsoever it be that moveth Laughter, it must be new and unexpected.'[125] He likewise agrees that the cause of laughter must be something that gives rise to admiration, especially in the form of 'a suddaine conception of some ability in himself that laugheth'.[126] It is when we experience 'the suddaine Imagination of our owne odds and eminence' that we find ourselves bursting out with mirth.[127]

Hobbes also agrees about the specific vices most open to being ridiculed or scorned. It is striking that neither he nor Descartes gives an explicit account of this aspect of the Renaissance theory of laughter in the manner of Beni, Mancini, or Castelvetro. But when Hobbes chooses to write in satirical vein—as he does above all in book 4 of *Leviathan*—the failings he takes as the targets of his ridicule are, recognizably, the three vices that the Renaissance theorists had singled out: vainglory, avarice, and hypocrisy. It is pride and vaingloriousness, especially among those whom he mockingly praises as the egregious Schoolmen,[128] that he attacks in book 4 under the heading of 'vain philosophy'.[129] It is clerical avarice that he satirizes in his withering passage about the 'profitable' doctrine of purgatory.[130] And it is clerical hypocrisy that he wittily urges us to acknowledge in his comparison between the Roman Catholic priesthood and the kingdom of the fairies: 'The *Fairies* marry not; but there be amongst them *Incubi*, that have copulation with flesh and bloud. The *Priests* also marry not.'[131]

What is striking, however, is that neither Hobbes nor Descartes ever mentions the direct challenge to the Aristotelian theory that had arisen in the course of the Renaissance, an omission all the more surprising when one reflects that they usually go out of their way to express their scorn for

---

[123] Descartes 1988, Article 124, p. 153: 'enflant les poumons subitement . . . fait que l'air qu'ils contienent, est contraint d'en sortir avec impetuosité par le sifflet, où il forme une voix inarticulée & esclatante'.

[124] Descartes 1988, Article 124, p. 154: 'poussée vers le coeur par quelque legere émotion de Haine, aydée par la surprise de l'Admiration'.

[125] Hobbes 1969, p. 41.   [126] Hobbes 1969, p. 41.   [127] Hobbes 1969, p. 42.

[128] Hobbes 1996, ch. 8, p. 59.   [129] Hobbes 1996, ch. 46, p. 458.

[130] Hobbes 1996, ch. 44, p. 426.   [131] Hobbes 1996, ch. 47, p. 481.

Aristotle's philosophy. Descartes's principal claim about laughter in *Les Passions de l'ame* remains a purely Aristotelian one. 'Although', as he explains, 'the Laugh may seem to be one of the principal signs of Joy, joy cannot be the cause of laughter unless the joy is only moderate, and is at the same time mixed with an element of hatred or wonderment.'[132] The connection of laughter with hatred and contempt is one on which he lays particular emphasis, and he later returns to it in his discussion of *la moquerie*: 'Derision or Mockery is a kind of Joy mixed with Hatred, and when this feeling arises unexpectedly the result is that we burst out with laughter.'[133]

That Hobbes returns to the same classical argument is yet more remarkable, since he opens his discussion in *The Elements* by proclaiming that his own analysis is an entirely novel one:

There is a passion, which hath noe name, but the signe of it, is that distortion of the Countenance we call LAUGHTER, which is alwayes joy; but what joy, what we thinke, and wherein we tryumph when we laugh, hath not hitherto bene declared by any.[134]

Despite this characteristic flourish, the account Hobbes goes on to give is a wholly classical one. His oft-quoted definition, initially formulated in *The Elements*, runs as follows:

The passion of Laughter is nothyng else but a suddaine Glory arising from suddaine Conception of some Eminency in our selves by Comparison with the Infirmityes of others, or with our owne formerly.[135]

The invocation of glory, and the emphasis on glorying over others, have often been singled out as quintessentially Hobbesian sentiments. As will by now be evident, however, they amount to little more than unacknowledged quotations from Hobbes's ancient sources, and in particular from the analysis of laughter in book 6 of Quintilian's *Institutio oratoria*.

Hobbes further underlines his classical allegiances by emphasizing that the feelings of glory he is describing are invariably contemptuous and derisory: 'Men Laugh at the infirmityes of others by comparison of which their owne abilityes are sett off, and illustrated.'[136] This being so, 'it is no wonder therefore that men take it heanously to be laughed at', for in becoming objects of laughter they are being 'derided, that is, tryumphed over'.[137] He summarizes still more brutally at the end of the chapter, where he

---

[132] Descartes 1988, Article 125, p. 153: 'Or encore qu'il semble que le Ris soit un des principaux signes de la Joye, elle ne peut toutefois le causer que lors qu'elle est seulement mediocre, & qu' il y a quelque admiration ou quelque haine meslée avec elle.'

[133] Descartes 1988, Art. 178, p. 195: 'La Derision ou Moquerie est une espece de Joye meslée de Haine . . . Et lors que cela survient inopinement . . . on s'esclate de rire'.

[134] Hobbes 1969, p. 41.   [135] Hobbes 1969, p. 42.   [136] Hobbes 1969, p. 41.

[137] Hobbes 1969, p. 42.

presents his 'comparison of the life of man to a race' and explains the role in this competition of the different passions of the soul:

> To fall on the suddaine, is disposition to Weepe
> To see another to fall, disposition to Laugh[138]

As in the case of Descartes, Hobbes's basic suggestion is thus that laughter expresses a joyful and contemptuous sense of our own superiority.[139]

Hobbes and Descartes enunciate similar theories, but Hobbes's analysis is a more elaborate one, embodying as it does a number of distinctive elements. One is the suggestion, put forward at the end of his discussion in *The Elements*, that we sometimes laugh not because we feel contempt for any particular person, but rather because we have been made aware of some general absurdity. This possibility allows for what Hobbes describes as 'laughter without offence', which is said to take place when we laugh 'at absurdityes and infirmityes abstracted from persons, and where all the Company may laugh together'.[140] Such laughter will still be an expression of our scorn, but instead of mocking other people to their faces we join together in ridiculing some ludicrous feature of the world and its ways.

Curiously, Hobbes never reverts to this suggestion in any of his subsequent discussions of laughter. But he introduces a further distinction in *The Elements* which he subsequently reiterates in both versions of *Leviathan*. A contrast needs to be drawn, he suggests, between two different ways in which the sense of superiority evinced by laughter can arise. Sometimes people laugh 'at the infirmityes of others by comparison of which their owne abilityes are sett off, and illustrated', and in particular 'at Jests, the witt whereof always consisteth in the Elegant discovering, and conveying to our mindes some absurdity of another'.[141] But at other times people laugh 'at their own Actions, performed never so little beyond their owne expectations, as also at their owne Jests'.[142] They laugh, that is, when they make the sudden and pleasing discovery that they are even more superior than they had supposed.

After this discussion in *The Elements*, Hobbes next returns to the subject of laughter in his manuscript fragment *Of Passions* in 1650. This includes a trenchant restatement of his basic argument, beginning as it does with the declaration that 'sudden imagination of a mans owne abilitie, is the passion that moves laughter'.[143] As this observation makes clear, Hobbes does not

---

[138] Hobbes 1969, p. 48.

[139] Heyd 1982, in an otherwise excellent discussion, makes the questionable suggestion (p. 289) that this may be due to the direct influence of Descartes. But this is because Heyd supposes (p. 286) that Hobbes first discusses laughter in 1650, whereas his principal discussion (in *The Elements of Law*) in fact dates from 1640, eight years before the publication of Descartes's *Les Passions de l'ame*.   [140] Hobbes 1969, p. 42.

[141] Hobbes 1969, pp. 41–2.   [142] Hobbes 1969, p. 41.

[143] Hobbes, *Of Passions*, BL Harl. MS 6083, fo. 177^r.

think of laughter itself as a passion, although he does speak elliptically at one moment in *The Elements* of 'the passion of Laughter'.[144] Rather, as he indicates at the outset of that discussion, he regards the occurrence of laughter as the natural 'signe' of a passion.[145] He adds in *The Elements* that the passion in question 'hath noe name',[146] but in the manuscript of 1650 he goes on to name it with confidence, remarking that it centres on the feeling of superior power—or 'imagination of abilitie'—that he particularly singles out.

Hobbes's final pronouncements on laughter can be found in the two versions of *Leviathan*, although the relevant passage from the Latin edition of 1668 amounts to little more than a translation of the English version of 1651. Hobbes begins by reverting to the definition he had already furnished in *The Elements of Law*. '*Sudden Glory*', he again declares, 'is the passion which maketh those *Grimaces* called LAUGHTER'.[147] He likewise reverts to his earlier claim that the sense of superiority prompting people to laugh can arise in one of two ways. They may succeed in accomplishing something beyond their expectations, with the result that they laugh 'because of some sudden act of their own, that pleaseth them'.[148] Alternatively, their sense of superiority may stem more directly from their perception of some contemptible weakness or 'deformed thing' in someone else.[149]

Hobbes now passes over the interesting possibility he had raised in *The Elements* to the effect that the sense of 'eminency' that makes us laugh can arise not merely from comparing ourselves 'with the Infirmityes of others', but also 'with our owne formerly'.[150] The implication that we may sometimes laugh at our previous selves finds no echo in either version of *Leviathan*. Perhaps Hobbes had come to believe, as he sometimes seems to imply, that our previous selves can be regarded as equivalent to different persons, so that there is no distinction to be made.[151] Or perhaps he had come to feel that such self-mockery is less common than he had earlier implied, especially as he stresses in *The Elements* that no one ever laughs 'at the follyes of themselves past' unless they can be sure of doing so without 'any present dishonour'.[152] 'For when a Jest is broken upon our selves or friends of whose dishonour we participate, we never Laugh thereat.'[153] Whatever the reason for the omission, the outcome is that in *Leviathan* Hobbes focuses exclusively on what he had always taken to be the principal cause of people's laughter, namely 'the apprehension of some deformed thing in another, by comparison whereof they suddenly applaud themselves'.[154]

---

[144] Hobbes 1969, p. 42.   [145] Hobbes 1969, p. 41.   [146] Hobbes 1969, p. 41.
[147] Hobbes 1996, ch. 6, p. 43. Hobbes 1841, p. 46 translates the definition, although without offering a rendering of 'grimaces'.   [148] Hobbes 1996, ch. 6, p. 43. Cf. Hobbes 1841, p. 46.
[149] Hobbes 1996, ch. 6, p. 43.   [150] Hobbes 1969, p. 42.
[151] It seems, that is, to be Hobbes's view that, even when our laughter is directed at our own former infirmities, this is an instance of our present ascendancy over others.
[152] Hobbes 1969, p. 42.   [153] Hobbes 1969, p. 42.   [154] Hobbes 1996, ch. 6, p. 43.

Before turning to the second main question I want to consider, I need to pause to ask what might have prompted Hobbes to revert to this older and partly discredited way of thinking about laughter, while at the same time laying such strong claim to the novelty of his own account. Did he think that the challenge to the Aristotelian theory mounted by so many Renaissance writers was simply misguided? Perhaps, but it seems strange that he never mentions any of the prevailing doubts or in any way makes it clear that he is writing with the aim of responding to them. Was he simply unaware that the Aristotelian theory had been so extensively criticized for its obvious one-sidedness? I confess that I do not know, but my hypothesis is that what caused the Aristotelian view to remain irresistible for Hobbes was his more general view of human nature. It is one of Hobbes's most fundamental beliefs that, as he expresses it in *Leviathan*, we need to 'put for a generall inclination of all mankind, a perpetuall and restless desire of Power after power, that ceaseth onely in Death'.[155] Not only do we find that men 'naturally love Liberty, and Dominion over others'.[156] We also find that in man 'Joy consisteth in comparing himselfe with other men', so that men 'can relish nothing but what is eminent'.[157] According to the classical theory of laughter, however, we laugh both as an expression of joy and at the same time as a means of conveying a scornful and contemptuous sense of our own superiority. This suggests that Hobbes's special interest in laughter, as well as his adherence to the classical account, may stem from the fact that, on this analysis, the phenomenon of laughter provides a perfect illustration of his more general views about the nature of humankind.

VI

I turn to the other issue generally raised by the writers I have discussed. As I mentioned at the outset, the further question they ask is concerned with how we should appraise the phenomenon of laughter, what we should think of it. For those who thought of laughter as being—or at least as capable of being—a pure expression of joy and delight, there was little difficulty here. It was possible to accept the phenomenon, at least in some of its manifestations, as uncomplicatedly worthy of being cultivated. We have already encountered this defence of laughter in such humanist writers as Castelvetro, Beni, and Guyon, and we find a noble restatement of it in book 4 of Spinoza's *Ethics*, in which laughter is treated as an element in the lighter side of life which it is part of Spinoza's purpose to commend to us.[158]

---

[155] Hobbes 1996, ch. 11, p. 70.   [156] Hobbes 1996, ch. 17, p. 117.
[157] Hobbes 1996, ch. 17, p. 119.   [158] Spinoza 1985, IV. P. 45, pp. 571–2.

Even for those who thought of laughter as invariably an expression of scorn for certain vices, it was still possible to think of it as valuable and worthy of being encouraged. One reason had been given by Aristotle himself when he had insisted that the vices deserve to be reproved, and thus that laughter, one of the most effective means of reproving them, has a moral role to play in our lives. A very different reason had been put forward by the medical writers I have discussed, for whom a disposition to laugh at the follies of mankind was taken to be a valuable means of preserving one's health. As Laurent Joubert explains in detail, the encouragement of this kind of mirthfulness is exceptionally valuable in the case of those with cold and dry complexions, and hence with small and hard hearts.[159] Anyone cursed with this temperament suffers from an excess of *atra bilis* or black bile in the spleen, which in turn gives rise to feelings of rage and, unless treated, to loss of *esprit* and eventual melancholia.[160] The example to which the physicians constantly recur is that of Democritus, whose bilious temperament made him so impatient and irritable that, as Burton reports in *The Anatomy of Melancholy*, he eventually became almost suicidally depressed.[161] Democritus's decision to cultivate the habit of laughter provided him with a remedy for this dangerous predicament.[162] By making himself a constant spectator of human absurdity, he was able to overcome his splenetic disposition by laughing at everything that excited his contempt. Not only did this improve the flow of his blood, thereby making him temporarily more sanguine; it also helped him to expel the black bile that would otherwise have brought a return of his melancholia. As Joubert concludes, we must be sanguine and light-hearted to remain 'civil', and the medical virtue of laughter stems from the fact that its violent action enables us to correct a threatening imbalance in our temperament.[163]

During the seventeenth century, however, each of these defences of laughter began for different reasons to run into difficulties. First of all, we find the belief in laughter as a form of medicine gradually losing credibility. One of the achievements of seventeenth-century physiology was to undermine the standing of humoral psychology, and with its rejection the seemingly intimate connection between laughter and good-humour was reduced to nothing more than a metaphor. Still more strikingly, we find the belief that laughter should be encouraged as a means of scorning vice, or even as an innocent expression of delight, likewise falling into disrepute in the latter part of the seventeenth century. This development, however, is less easy to

---

[159] Joubert 1579, pp. 251–4, 258–9.   [160] Joubert 1579, pp. 81–3, 273–6.
[161] Burton 1989, p. 2.
[162] Joubert 1579, Appendix, p. 363, speaks of this 'remede et cure'.
[163] Joubert 1579, p. 259, speaks of the value of laughter in helping to sustain 'la symmetrie & moderacion de la temperature ou complexion humaine'.

understand, and I should like to end by trying to outline and if possible to explain this cultural shift.

We already encounter a marked disapproval of laughter among a number of moralists' writings in the middle years of the century. Hobbes himself always expresses considerable misgivings and doubts. He refers with distaste in *The Elements of Law* to those who 'thinke the Infirmityes of another sufficient matter for his tryumph', declaring that this 'is vaine-glory, and an argument of little worth'.[164] Subsequently he speaks in yet more dismissive tones in *Leviathan*, adding that 'much Laughter at the defects of others, is a signe of Pusillanimity'.[165] The impression he always conveys is that laughter is something that needs to be eliminated or at least controlled.

If we turn to the next generation, and especially to the courtesy-books that began to proliferate around that time, we encounter an even deeper hostility. Consider, for example, the discussion of laughter in Lord Halifax's *Advice to a Daughter* of 1688. No lady, Halifax maintains, should seek to cultivate the character of 'a good-humoured woman', thereby presenting herself as someone who 'thinketh she must always be in a laugh, or a broad smile', for this alleged 'necessity of appearing at all times to be so infinitely pleased' involves 'a grievous mistake'.[166] If we glance forward a further generation to Lord Chesterfield's *Letters to his Son* of 1748, we find that laughter has been absolutely proscribed. 'I could heartily wish', the earl assures his son, 'that you may often be seen to smile, but never heard to laugh while you live.'[167]

Why did laughter fall into such disfavour with these writers on polite behaviour? Perhaps the chief source of their hostility can be traced to the demand for higher levels of decorum and self-control. An important aspect of this so-called 'civilizing' process took the form of a call for mutual respect and restraint, and more particularly for the control of various bodily functions previously classified as involuntary.[168] Laughter came to be seen as a form of incivility, and at the same time as an obvious instance of an uncontrolled reaction that needed, in polite society, to be governed and preferably eliminated.

We encounter almost nothing of this animus against laughter even in the most exacting courtesy-books of the sixteenth century. Consider, for example, the attitude adopted by Castiglione in his *Libro del cortegiano*. He is certainly anxious to ensure that our mirth should never be vulgar, nor of such a kind as to give rise to blasphemy or dangerous hostilities.[169] But he is so far from viewing laughter as inherently uncivilized that, in book 2 of the *Cortegiano*, he makes the irreproachable figure of Lady Emilia call on

---

[164] Hobbes 1969, p. 42.   [165] Hobbes 1996, ch. 6, p. 43.   [166] Halifax 1969, p. 298.
[167] Chesterfield 1901, Letter 144, vol. 1, p. 213.
[168] Elias 1994, pp. 110–17; Thomas 1977, p. 79.   [169] Castiglione 1994, pp. 155, 159–60.

M. Bernarde, after a particularly high-spirited exchange, to 'leave nowe makynge us laugh wyth practisynge of Jestes, and teache us howe we should use them'.[170] Nor do we ever find Hobbes saying that his reason for disapproving of laughter is that he sees it as indecorous. He duly notes in *The Elements of Law* that men laugh at indecencies,[171] and he emphasizes in the Latin version of *Leviathan* that we laugh not merely at other people's vices, but also at their indecorous behaviour.[172] But he never suggests—even in the case of such coarse and vulgar mirth—that we need for this reason to control or eliminate it.

Within a few decades, however, such lack of concern for the social niceties was beginning to seem ill-bred. If we ask, for example, what reason Lord Halifax gives for warning his daughter against indulging in 'senseless merriment', we learn that he regards such a 'boisterous kind of jollity' as contrary not merely 'to wit and good manners', but also 'to modesty and virtue'.[173] The reason why laughter must be avoided is that it is 'a coarse kind of quality, that throweth a woman into a lower form, and degradeth her from the rank of those who are more refined'.[174] A generation later, we find Lord Chesterfield expressing the same commitment in yet more vehement terms. So peremptory is his demand for decorum that laughter, that great vehicle of contempt, is turned into an object of contempt itself. The reason given by the earl for insisting that laughter must be altogether avoided is that 'there is nothing so illiberal, and so ill bred'. To indulge in laughter is something that 'people of sense and breeding should show themselves above'. To laugh is 'low and unbecoming', especially in virtue of 'the disagreeable noise that it makes, and the shocking distortion of the face that it occasions' whenever we succumb to it.[175]

The imperative of decorum was no doubt the principal source of the growing movement in the early modern period to outlaw laughter from polite society. To anyone living in a post-Freudian culture, however, it will seem natural to suggest a further and strongly contrasting reason for treating laughter, and especially contemptuous laughter, as something to be avoided or controlled. Such outbursts are liable to be interpreted not merely as highly aggressive, but at the same time as obvious strategies for dealing with feelings of inadequacy and self-doubt. They are liable, in other words, to be viewed as signs of psychic weakness of a kind that any self-respecting person will want to control or cover up.

Did any of the writers I have been considering attain this level of insight? The answer, perhaps unsurprisingly, is that in general they seem not to have

---

[170] Castiglione 1994, p. 153. [171] Hobbes 1969, p. 41.
[172] See Hobbes 1841, p. 46 on laughing both at 'conceptum turpitudinis alieni' and at 'facti indecori'. [173] Savile 1969, p. 298.
[174] Ibid. [175] Chesterfield 1901, Letter 144, vol. 1, p. 212.

done. To this generalization, however, there is at least one exception, and that is Hobbes.[176] As early as *The Elements of Law*, we find Hobbes observing that it is generally those who 'are greedy of applause, from every thinge they doe well' who enjoy laughing 'at their own Actions, performed never so little beyond their owne expectation'.[177] He also notes that such laughter consists in effect of 'the recommending of our selves to our owne good opinion, by comparison with another mans Infirmityes or absurditie', and it is at this juncture that he adds his scornful comment to the effect that 'it is vaine-glory, and an argument of little worth to thinke the Infirmityes of another sufficient matter for his tryumph.'[178]

For Hobbes's first explicit suggestion, however, that laughter betokens lack of self-esteem, we need to turn to his *Answer* of 1650 to Sir William Davenant's Preface to *Gondibert*:

Great persons that have their mindes employed on great designes, have not leasure enough to laugh, and are pleased with the contemplation of their owne power and vertues, so as they need not the infirmities and vices of other men to recommend themselves to their owne favor by comparison, as all men do when they laugh.[179]

Here Hobbes brings together two equally stern thoughts about laughter, namely that great minds will not merely lack any motive but any time to indulge in it.

If we turn to *Leviathan*, published a year later, we find Hobbes concentrating his main attention on the suggestion that laughter reveals a weakness of character, and expressing the thought in still more forbidding tones:

[Laughter] is incident most to them, that are conscious of the fewest abilities in themselves; who are forced to keep themselves in their own favour, by observing the imperfections of other men. And therefore much Laughter at the defects of others, is a signe of Pusillanimity. For of great minds, one of the proper workes is, to help and free others from scorn; and compare themselves onely with the most able.[180]

Since this is Hobbes's last word on the subject, it is striking to find him introducing two entirely new elements into his basic theory that laughter is an expression of contempt. One is that, because it is appropriate for great minds to compare themselves only with the most able, they will have no occasion to entertain such feelings of superiority or scorn. His other and still more demanding suggestion is that gifted people have in addition a positive moral duty to help others to cultivate similar feelings of magnanimity and respect.

---

[176] There is a hint of the same idea in Descartes 1988, Art. 179, p. 196.
[177] Hobbes 1969, p. 41.   [178] Hobbes 1969, p. 42.   [179] Hobbes 1971, p. 53.
[180] Hobbes 1996, ch. 6, p. 43.

Although Hobbes had never previously expressed these ideas in print, they were by no means new commitments on his part. He had held these views for a considerable time, as is evident from a remarkable letter of admonition and advice he had addressed to Charles Cavendish, the younger son of the second earl of Devonshire, at the time when he had taken up residence in Paris in 1638:

To encouradge inferiours, to be cheerefull with ones equalls & superiors, to pardon the follies of them one converseth withall, & to help men of, that are fallen into yᵉ danger of being laught at, these are signes of noblenesse & of the master spirit. Whereas to fall in love with ones selfe upon the sight of other mens infirmities, as they doe that mock & laugh at them, is the property of one that stands in competition with such a ridiculous man for honour.[181]

Here the duty to exhibit and help others to cultivate a proper sense of magnanimity is so much emphasized that Hobbes comes close to the traditional humanist claim that *virtus vera nobilitas est*.

Hobbes is clear, then, that laughter is fundamentally a strategy for coping with feelings of inadequacy. But is this his reason for thinking that it ought to be controlled? It is not perhaps his principal reason, for he chiefly emphasizes his dislike of the aggression he also takes to be involved. To understand his dislike, we need to begin by recalling the most basic principle of his political philosophy: that we must '*seek Peace and follow it*'.[182] When he goes on to itemize the lines of conduct we must follow if peace is to be preserved, he declares that one of these 'Articles of Peace' ('which otherwise are called Laws of Nature')[183] is that '*no man by deed, word, countenance, or gesture, declare Hatred, or Contempt of another.*'[184] The reason why the observation of this precept is indispensable to peace is that 'all signes of hatred, or contempt, provoke to fight; insomuch as most men choose rather to hazard their life, than not to be revenged.'[185] As we have seen, however, Hobbes invariably treats laughter as a sign of contempt. The main reason for his hostility is thus that he considers it an obvious threat to peace.

There are several indications, however, that Hobbes is also moved by the thought that, if scornful laughter betokens lack of self-esteem, this gives us a further reason for avoiding it. He turns to this argument at the end of chapter 9 of *The Elements of Law*, in which he lays out his fullest account of laughter and its significance. He brings his chapter to a close with his image of life as a race, adding that 'this race we must suppose to have no other goal, nor other garland, but being foremost'.[186] The achievement of felicity comes from managing 'continually to out-go the next before', while

[181] Hobbes 1994, letter 28, vol. 1, pp. 52–3.   [182] Hobbes 1996, ch.14, p. 92.

[183] Hobbes 1996, ch. 13, p. 90.   [184] Hobbes 1996, ch. 15, p. 107.

[185] Hobbes 1996, ch. 15, p. 107.   [186] Hobbes 1969, p. 47.

misery comes from being continually 'out-gone'.[187] Among the means of courting misery, one will consequently be to act vaingloriously, for those who suffer from this weakness 'lose ground with looking back'; another will be to exhibit pusillanimity, for this weakness causes us to 'lose ground by little hindrances'.[188]

These features of the race take on a special significance when we recall what Hobbes says about the failings disclosed by those who enjoy laughing derisively. As we have seen, he declares that laughter 'is vaine-glory' and that 'much Laughter at the defects of others, is a signe of Pusillanimity.'[189] He now adds that, if we give in to these weaknesses, we shall lose ground in the race of life, since vainglory causes us to look back and pusillanimity causes us to suffer hindrances. But he also believes that losing ground in this particular race is the worst thing that can happen to us. All this being so, we have strong reasons for controlling any disposition to laugh, since we have strong reasons for controlling the feelings of vainglory and pusillanimity that find their expression in laughter. We cannot afford to indulge in any such weakness while running to keep up in an emulative and hostile world.

REFERENCES

[Addison, Joseph] (1965), *The Spectator*, ed. Donald F. Bond, 4 vols. (Oxford).

Aristotle (1926), *The 'Art' of Rhetoric*, ed. and trans. J. H. Freese (London).

—— (1961), *Parts of Animals*, ed. and trans. A. L. Peck, rev. edn. (London).

—— (1995), *Poetics*, ed. and trans. Stephen Halliwell (London).

Aubrey, John (1898), *'Brief Lives', chiefly of Contemporaries, set down by John Aubrey, between the years 1669 & 1696*, ed. Andrew Clark, 2 vols. (Oxford).

Bakhtine, Mikhaïl (1970), *L'Œuvre de François Rabelais et la culture populaire au Moyen Age et sous la Renaissance*, trans. Andrée Robel (Paris).

Beni, Paolo (1613), *In Aristotelis poeticam commentarii* (Padua).

Berrettario, Elpidio (1603), *Phisici, et Philosophi Tractatus de Risu* (Florence).

Bright, Timothy (1586), *A Treatise of Melancholie* (London).

Browne, Sir Thomas (1928–31), *Pseudodoxia Epidemica*, in *The Works of Sir Thomas Browne*, ed. Geoffrey Keynes, 6 vols. (London), vols. 2 and 3.

Burton, Robert (1989), *The Anatomy of Melancholy*, i: *Text*, ed. Thomas C. Faulkner, Nicholas K. Kiessling, and Rhonda L. Blair (Oxford).

Castelvetro, Lodovico (1570), *Poetica d'Aristotele vulgarizzata et sposta* (Vienna).

Castiglione, Baldassare (1994), *The Book of the Courtier*, trans. Thomas Hoby, ed. Virginia Cox (London).

Chesterfield, Earl of (1901), *The Letters of the Earl of Chesterfield to his Son*, ed. Charles Strachey and Annette Calthrop, 2 vols. (London).

---

[187] Hobbes 1969, p. 48.   [188] Hobbes 1969, pp. 47–8.
[189] Hobbes 1969, p. 42; Hobbes 1996, ch. 6, p. 43.

Cicero (1942), *De oratore*, ed. and trans. E. W. Sutton and H. Rackham, 2 vols. (London).

Cockagne, Emily Jane (2000), 'A Cultural History of Sound in England 1560–1760', (PhD thesis, University of Cambridge).

Congreve, William (1981), *The Double-Dealer*, ed. J. C. Ross (London).

Descartes, René (1988), *Les Passions de l'ame*, ed. Geneviève Rodez-Lewis (Paris).

Elias, Norbert (1994), *The Civilising Process*, trans. Edmund Jephcott (Oxford).

Fielding, Henry (1985), *Joseph Andrews*, ed. R. F. Brissenden (London).

Fracastoro, Girolamo (1546), *De sympathia & antipathia rerum* (Venice).

Goclenius, Rodolph [the elder] (1597), *Physica Commentatio De Risu & Lacrymis* (Marburg).

Guyon, Louis (1617), *Les Diverses Leçons*, 3 vols. (Lyons).

Heyd, David (1982), 'The Place of Laughter in Hobbes's Theory of the Emotions', *Journal of the History of Ideas* 43: 285–95.

Hobbes, Thomas (1841), *Leviathan, sive De Materia, Forma, & Potestate Civitatis Ecclesiasticae et Civilis*, in *Opera philosophica*, ed. Molesworth (London), vol. 3, pp. v–viii and 1–569.

—— (1969), *The Elements of Law Natural and Politic*, ed. Ferdinand Tönnies, 2nd edn., introd. M. M. Goldsmith (London).

—— (1971), *The Answer of Mr. Hobbes to Sir Will. D'Avenant's Preface Before Gondibert* in *Sir William Davenant's Gondibert*, ed. David F. Gladish (Oxford), 45–55.

—— (1973), *Critique du De Mundo de Thomas White*, ed. Jean Jacquot and Harold Whitmore Jones (Paris).

[Hobbes, Thomas (?)] (1986), *A Briefe of the Art of Rhetorique*, in *The Rhetorics of Thomas Hobbes and Bernard Lamy*, ed. John T. Harwood (Carbondale and Edwardsville), 33–128.

Hobbes, Thomas (1994), *The Correspondence*, ed. Noel Malcolm, 2 vols. (Oxford: The Clarendon Edition), vols. 6 and 7.

—— (1996), *Leviathan, or The Matter, Forme, & Power of a Common-wealth Ecclesiasticall and Civill*, ed. Richard Tuck (Cambridge).

Hutcheson, Francis (1750), *Reflections upon Laughter* (Glasgow).

James, Susan (1997), *Passion and Action: The Emotions in Seventeenth-Century Philosophy* (Oxford).

[Jones, Erasmus] (1737), *The Man of Manners*, 3rd edn. (London).

Jossius, Nicander (1580), *De risu et fletu*, in *Opuscula* (Rome), 44–144.

Joubert, Laurent (1579), *Traité du ris, contenant son essance, ses causes, et mervelheus essais, curieusemant recherchés, raisonnés & observés* (Paris).

Leijenhorst, Cees (1996), 'Hobbes and Fracastoro', *Hobbes Studies* 9: 98–128.

Lorenzini, Antonio [*alias* Poliziano] (1603), *Tractatus Novus, Utilis et Lucundus* (Frankfurt).

Lorenzini, Antonio [*alias* Poliziano] (1606), *Dialogus pulcherrimus et utilissimus, de risu: eiusque causis et consequentibus* (Marburg).

Machline, Vera Cecília (1998), 'The Contribution of Laurent Joubert's *Traité du Ris* to Sixteenth-Century Physiology of Laughter', in Allen G. Debus and Michael T. Walton (eds.), *Reading the Book of Nature: The Other Side of the Scientific Revolution* (Kirksville, Mo.), 251–64.

Maggi, Vincento (1550), *De ridiculis*, in *In Aristotelis Librum de Poetica Communes Explicationes* (Venice), 301–27.

Mancini, Celso (1598), *De risu, ac ridiculis*, in *Moralis Philosophi Libri III* (Frankfurt), 160–231.

Ménager, Daniel (1995), *La Renaissance et le Rire* (Paris).

More, Thomas (1965), *Utopia*, in *The Complete Works of Sir Thomas More*, vol. 4, ed. Edward Surtz and J. H. Hexter (New Haven, Conn.).

Paulson, Ronald (1988), *Don Quixote in England: The Aesthetics of Laughter* (Baltimore, MD).

Plato (1925) *Philebus*, ed. and trans. Harold N. Fowler (London).

—— (1926) *Laws*, ed. and trans. R. G. Bury, 2 vols. (London).

—— (1930–5) *The Republic*, ed. and trans. Paul Shorey, 2 vols. (London).

Quintilian (1920–2), *Institutio oratoria*, ed. and trans. H. E. Butler, 4 vols. (London).

Savile, George, Marquis of Halifax (1969), *Advice to a Daughter*, in *Halifax: Complete Works*, ed. J. P. Kenyon (London), 269–313.

Screech, M. A. (1997), *Laughter at the Foot of the Cross* (London).

Sidney, Sir Philip (1912), *The Defence of Poesie*, in *The Prose Works of Sir Philip Sidney*, ed. Albert Feuillerat, 4 vols. (Cambridge), vol. iii, pp. 1–46.

Skinner, Quentin (1996), *Reason and Rhetoric in the Philosophy of Hobbes* (Cambridge).

Spinoza, Benedict de (1985), *Ethics*, in *The Collected Works of Spinoza*, ed. Edwin Curley, vol. 1 (Princeton, NJ).

Strauss, Leo (1963), *The Political Philosophy of Hobbes: Its Basis and its Genesis*, trans. Elsa M. Sinclair, Phoenix edn. (Chicago).

Tave, Stuart M. (1960), *The Amiable Humorist* (Chicago, Ill.).

Thomas, Keith (1977), 'The Place of Laughter in Tudor and Stuart England', *The Times Literary Supplement* (21 Jan.), 77–81.

Valleriola, François (1554), *De risus natura, & causis*, in *Enarrationum Medicinalium Libri Sex* (Lyons).

—— (1588), *Observationum Medicinalium Libri VI* (Lyons).

Vallesio, Francisco (1582), *De risu et fletu*, in *Controversiarum Medicarum et Philosophicarum Libri Decem* (Frankfurt).

Vives, Juan Luis (1550), *De anima & vita libri tres* ('ex ultima autorum eorundem recognitione') (Lyons).

Wilson, Thomas (1554), *The Arte of Rhetorique, for the use of all suche as are studious of Eloquence* (n.p.).

Zappen, James P. (1983), 'Aristotelian and Ramist Rhetoric in Thomas Hobbes's *Leviathan*: Pathos versus Ethos and Logos', *Rhetorica* 1: 65–91.

The Political Subject

YVES CHARLES ZARKA

———◆———

1. THE MAN WITH NO FACE AND THE SOVEREIGN WITH NO NAME

There are many points of entry into the ethical and political work of Hobbes. It can be read on various levels and with different emphases. One can read it as a quasi-deductive treatise of political philosophy which unfolds from universal elementary principles of human nature in order to show the necessity, the structure, and the inevitability of the state. Or it can be read as the story of the formation of humanity—the story of the transition from the state of nature to the civil state. Again, one can read it as involving a redistribution of the relationships between the order of nature and that of morality and politics. Finally, one can connect its message with the striking descriptions which are everywhere to be found in it: historical examples, descriptions of human types, individual portraits, ironic criticisms, and so on.

I should like to illustrate this multi-faceted character of Hobbes's text by way of a reading which is back-to-front. A back-to-front reading is obviously a reading which does not proceed in the usual fashion—that is, it does not go in the direction a commentary would ordinarily take—but it is also a reading which does not go in the direction Hobbes himself seems explicitly to have followed. To understand the sense of such a back-to-front reading, I should first say what the direct method of reading *Leviathan* is. This direct method consists, as we know, in the analysis of the life of the mind and passions, both of the individual and of human beings collectively, which leads to the institution of political sovereignty by way of that crucial event, the social covenant.

Now in this direct-method reading, we are confronted with a procedure that is impersonal in all its parts:[1] the natural man has no face and the

---

[1] It goes without saying that the point of view I adopt here in talking of an impersonal procedure is in no way in contradiction with the use Hobbes makes of the notion of the natural person, and particularly of the civil person. The individual as a natural person is in fact, by definition, some one particular person or other, just as the sovereign is some particular civil person or other.

political sovereign has no name. If the man Hobbes describes has no features which mark his individuality and if the sovereign has no name, this is because of a necessity internal to the very project of *Leviathan's* author. This project consists in making political philosophy into a field fundamentally distinct from that of historiography, developing at the level of those principles which constitute man and society. To put this in other terms, 'Leviathan' is not the name of a particular sovereign—despite speculation about the frontispiece of the work, where some people think they recognize Cromwell—but the common name of the state and of sovereignty in general. The man with no face who emerges from the direct-method reading is the man of whom Hobbes says he is always affected by the same passions, the only variation being in the objects of his passions. He is also the one who is moved, in the dynamic of human relations where political power is absent, by what Hobbes defines in chapter XI of *Leviathan* as 'a general inclination of all mankind, a perpetual and restless desire of power after power, that ceaseth only in death'. This universal man with no face, moved by the same passions and the same inclination, is, in a way, the result of the programme which Hobbes gave himself when commenting on the adage *Nosce teipsum* in the introduction to *Leviathan*:

But there is another saying not of late understood, by which they might learn truly to read one another, if they would take the pains; and that is, *Nosce teipsum*, *Read thy self*: which was not meant, as it is now used, to countenance, either the barbarous state of men in power, towards their inferiors; or to encourage men of low degree, to a sawcie behaviour towards their betters. But to teach us, that for the similitude of the thoughts, and passions of one man, to the thoughts and passions of another, whosoever looketh into himself, and considereth what he doth, when he does *think, opine, reason, hope, feare* etc., and upon what grounds; he shall thereby read and know, what are the thoughts and passions of all other men, upon the like occasions. . . . And though by mens actions we do discover their design sometimes; yet to do it without comparing them with our own, and distinguishing all circumstances, by which the case may come to be altered, is to decyfer without a key, and be for the most part deceived by too much trust, or by too much diffidence; as he that reads, is himself a good or evil man.[2]

To read the thoughts and passions of other men in oneself is thus to find in oneself the key to deciphering humanity, that is, human nature, or again the universal man with no face. This programme which is valid for knowledge of the individual is equally valid for the ruler:

He that is to govern a whole Nation, must read in himself, not this or that particular man; but Man-kind: which though it be hard to do, harder than to learn any language or science; yet, when I shall have set down my own reading

---

[2] *Leviathan*, ed. C. B. Macpherson (Harmondsworth: Penguin Classics, 1968), 82–3.

orderly, and perspicuously, the pains left another, will be onely to consider, if he also find not the same in himself.[3]

Such, then, is the universal knowledge which ought to be possessed by the sovereign with no name.

We could show how Hobbes's discourse on the sovereign with no name is a break with Machiavelli and his discourse on the man with no face is a break with Montaigne. I will just say a few words on these two points. As we know, Montaigne makes self-knowledge the object—the sole object, in a way—of his *Essays*:

Je veux qu'on m'y voie en ma façon simple, naturelle et ordinaire, sans étude et artifice: car c'est moi que je peins. Mes défauts s'y liront au vif, mes imperfections et ma forme naïve, autant que la révérence publique me l'a permis. Que si j'eusse été parmi ces nations qu'on dit vivre encore sous la douce liberté des premières lois de nature, je t'assure que je m'y fusse très volontiers peint tout entier, et tout nu. Ainsi, Lecteur, je suis moi-même la matière de mon livre.[4]

I wish to be seen in my simple, natural, and ordinary way, understated and without artifice, because it's me I'm painting. My defects will be clearly visible, my imperfections and my naïve form, as much as public respect permits it. For if I had been among the nations said to live still under the first laws of nature, I assure you that I would willingly have painted me whole and naked. Thus it is, reader, that I am the subject of my book.

Nonetheless, these themes of knowing, reading and depicting the self resonate in a very different way than in Hobbes. Self-knowledge here is, precisely, self-depiction, a depiction which has a double meaning: (1) it is a description of one's own self in terms of its singular features ('Il n'est personne, s'il s'écoute, qui ne découvre en soi, une forme sienne, une forme maîtresse, qui lutte contre l'institution: et contre la tempête des passions, qui lui sont contraires': 'There is no one who, if he listens to himself, will not discover in himself an authentic, master quality that struggles against the institution: and against the tempest of countervailing passions');[5] (2) it discovers what knowledge of the individual self can contain of the unexpected ('Je ne me trouve pas où je me cherche: et me trouve plus par rencontre, que par l'inquisition de mon jugement'—'I don't find myself where I look, and I find myself more by encounter than by interrogating my judgement').[6] To put it another way, the whole of Montaigne's procedure is situated on the level of singularity, of the singular features of a face. So much so that when the universal is discovered starting from the singular, it is more a matter of a discovery of the singularity of the other, of his unique and irreplaceable character, than of a homogeneous form which is common

---

[3] Ibid. p. 83.   [4] Montaigne, *Les Essais*, ed. Jean Céard (Paris: Le Livre de Poche, 2002), 53.
[5] Ibid. III. 2, p. 1266.   [6] Ibid. I. 10. p. 96–7.

to all humanity. This, it seems to me, is the proper way to interpret the famous phrase 'Chaque homme porte la forme entière de l'humaine condition'.[7] Now the singularity of Montaigne's object of inquiry seems totally removed from Hobbes's individual in general, which I call the man with no face.

A comparable difference seems also to be valid in relation to Machiavelli. The prince, or rather princes, both ancient and modern, of whom Machiavelli writes are individual princes, either historical or mythical. He describes their actions as a function of a particular conjunction of time, place, relationships of power, and accidental circumstances. In each case the relationship between *fortuna* and *virtù* is singular and explains their success or their failure. Sovereigns in Machiavelli have names: they are called Alexander the Great, Francesco Sforza, Cesare Borgia, or whatever. The sovereign in Hobbes is on the contrary a civil person with no name.

If I may be allowed to transpose onto Hobbes the analysis Michel Foucault made in his lecture on the subject of the relationship between knowledge of the self and concern for the self in the modern period (Collège de France, 1982),[8] I will say that Hobbes is situated at the sensitive point which defines that modernity: that of a disqualification of concern with the self (present, obviously, in Montaigne) and of a re-qualification of knowledge of the self. For the singular self which refers to itself and modifies its being in order to accede to the truth, is substituted a universal self which discovers the truth of humanity in itself on the gnoseological plane.

Such is the result of a direct-method reading of Hobbes. But Hobbes often holds surprises in reserve, and resists the overly unilateral character of the reading I have just given. Indeed, in the passage cited earlier on the *Nosce teipsum*, Hobbes already showed that despite the similarity of human passions, there is a diversity in the objects of those passions and even a diversity in the constitution and education of the individual. This latter diversity produces such important variations from one individual to another that the text of the human heart becomes muddled and confused to the point where it remains almost unreadable for human beings:

I say the similitude of *passions*, which are the same in all men, *desire*, *feare*, *hope*, etc., not the similitude of the *objects* of the passions, which are the things *desired*, *feared*, *hoped*, etc.: for these the constitution individual, and particular education do so vary, and they are so easy to be kept from our knowledge, that the characters of man's heart, blotted and confounded as they are, with dissembling, lying, counterfeiting, and erroneous doctrines, are legible onely to him that searcheth hearts.[9]

---

[7] Montaigne, *Les Essais*, ed. Jean Céard (Paris: Le Livre de Poche, 2002), III. 2. p. 1256.

[8] Michel Foucault, *L'Herméneutique du sujet*, Lectures given at the Collège de France, 1981–2 (Paris: Gallimard/Le Seuil, 2001), 15 ff.

[9] *Lev.*, ed. Macpherson (Harmondsworth: Penguin, 1968), Introduction, pp. 82–3.

The reference to the individual constitution and to education seems to make human singularity, the face or the portrait we thought we had lost, re-emerge. Now *Leviathan* contains descriptions, if not of veritable human singularities, at least of differentiated human types. Reading these types which reintroduce variety into humanity is what I call reading Hobbes back-to-front.

Let me give an example. In *Leviathan*, Hobbes describes two strange types of men whose behaviour could be characterized, in a way, as anti-political: the melancholic and the inspired.

Dejection, subjects a man to causeless fears; which is a Madness commonly called MELANCHOLY, apparent also in divers manners; as in haunting of solitudes and graves; in superstitious behaviour, and in fearing some one, some another particular thing.[10]

Now for the inspired: Though the effect of folly, in them that are possessed of an opinion of being inspired, be not visible always in one man, by any very extravagant action, that proceedeth from such passion; yet when many of them conspire together, the rage of the whole multitude is visible enough. For what argument of madness can there be greater, than to clamour, strike and throw stones at our best friends?[11]

These types of behaviour are classed under the general heading of 'madness'. 'But of the several kinds of Madness, he that would take the paines, might enrowle a legion.'[12]

We can see how the diversity of human figures, if not of individual faces, is shown by means of descriptions of human types and individual and collective behaviour. The ones I have considered are anti-political in the sense that they are opposed to the inter-individual dynamic which will lead to the social covenant. But even the melancholic and the inspired cannot long remain outside the relational dynamic which leads to that covenant. I cannot explain the reasons for this here.

It is just such a back-to-front reading which I should like to apply to the political subject. What is the political subject in Hobbes? To answer this question I shall undertake a double reading, both direct-method and back-to-front. Hobbes's political philosophy tells us something about the political subject when we read it directly, i.e. that the subject is always subjected, submitted, or obligated. He is not an actor in politics. The function of actor is assumed by the sovereign alone. In this sense, Hobbes seems to efface any figure of the individual as a political subject in order to confer the status of political subject (in the sense of political actor) solely on the civil person of the sovereign. The consequence of this position will make itself felt directly in the definition of the word 'citizen'. The principal

---

[10] Ibid. VIII, p. 140.   [11] Ibid. VIII, p. 140–1.   [12] Ibid. VIII, p. 140.

characteristics which defined the citizen from antiquity to the end of the Renaissance, as a political subject who is also an actor in the city, are emptied of all content in Hobbes.

The question is whether that is Hobbes's last word. I think it is not. For, on the reverse side of the subject who is subjected or submitted, there is another figure which comes into view. This other figure of the subject has a political content. We shall see that it is more of an outline of a subject than a real subject, but that outline of the political subject will attest to the establishment of a different relationship between the individual and power: the individual, not as a being who is submitted to power, but as one who resists.

2. THE SUBJECTED SUBJECT AND THE SOVEREIGN AS SOLE POLITICAL ACTOR

In a general way the political meaning of the notion of 'subject' in Hobbes is, as I said before, that of the subject who is submitted or subjected to the political power, the law, obligation, and so on. It is in chapter XXI of *Leviathan*, entitled 'Of the Liberty of Subjects' (the Latin is 'De libertate civium'), that this meaning of the subject appears most clearly:

In relation to these bonds [the civil laws] only it is, that I am to speak now, of the *Liberty* of *Subjects*. For seeing there is no Commonwealth in the world, wherein there be rules enough set down, for the regulating of all the actions, and words of men (as being a thing impossible) it followeth necessarily, that in all kinds of actions, by the laws prætermitted, men have the liberty, of doing what their own reasons shall suggest, for the most profitable to themselves.[13]

The notion of the liberty of subjects is paradoxical because the two terms which compose it seem to be in contradiction with each other. Civil liberty is defined in opposition to civil obligations—civil laws, that is, which are 'Artificial chains'. To give some content to the notion of 'Liberty of Subjects', we must therefore define the classes of action in which the subject can be said to be free, that is to say where the subject is not prevented from doing what reason suggests, whilst still remaining submitted or subjected to the political power. There are two classes of action which relate to this definition. First, the class of actions which result from 'Corporal liberty'. If, indeed, we consider liberty in the proper sense of the term, it appears that '*A FREE MAN, is he, that in those things, which by his strength and wit he is able to do, is not hindered to do what he has a will to*'.[14] Here one is free as long as one is not in chains or in prison. Now this is the case with individuals in the

---

[13] *Lev.*, ed. Macpherson (Harmondsworth: Penguin, 1968), XXI, p. 264.
[14] Ibid. XXI, p. 262.

state. The subjected subject in Hobbes is a subject who possesses corporal liberty; the subjected subject is not a slave. Secondly, there is the class of actions which have not been made the object of laws or regulations on the part of the sovereign. In domains where the sovereign has remained silent, the subject is free to act as he wishes: 'Such as is the liberty to buy, and sell, and otherwise contract with one another; to choose their own aboad, their own diet, their own trade of life, and institute their children as they themselves think fit; and the like.'[15]

We can understand that Hobbes could draw two consequences from this definition of the liberty of subjects: (1) the liberty of subjects does not limit the power of the sovereign in any way. Hobbes, indeed, does not balk at an extreme example: the sovereign can without injustice order the death of an innocent subject. The liberty of subjects really is a liberty of those who are subjected, and the limits of whose subjection are set by the sovereign alone. (2) One must not confuse the liberty of subjects with the liberty of the state or of the commonwealth: 'Every Commonwealth, (not every man) has an absolute liberty, to do what it shall judge (that is to say, what that man or assembly that representeth it, shall judge) most conducing to their benefit.'[16] The liberty of the state is clearly the liberty of the sovereign as subject-actor and not in any way the liberty of individual subjected subjects. This is what Hobbes appears to say clearly in the interpretation he gives of the liberty of the city of Lucca:

The *Athenians*, and *Romanes* were free; that is, free Commonwealths: not that any particular men had the liberty to resist their own representative; but that their representative had the liberty to resist, or invade other people. There is written on the Turrets of the city of *Luca* in great characters at this day, the word LIBERTAS; yet no man can thence inferre, that a particular man has more liberty, or immunity from the service of the Commonwealth there, than in *Constantinople*. Whether a Commonwealth be Monarchical, or Popular, the Freedom is still the same.[17]

The content of this notion of the individual submitted or subjected to power can be precisely analysed in terms of three modes of the constitution of 'dominion over many'.[18] Here is the formulation given in the *Elements of Law*:

Considering men therefore again in the state of nature, without covenants or *subjection* one to another, as if they were but even now all at once created male and female; there be three titles only, by which one man may have right and dominion over another; whereof two may take place presently, and those are: *voluntary offer of subjection*, and yielding by compulsion; the third is to take place, upon the supposition of children begotten amongst them.[19]

---

[15] Ibid. XXI, p. 264. [16] Ibid. XXI, p. 266. [17] Ibid.
[18] *The Elements of Law (= EL)* II, III, 1, ed. F. Tönnies (London: Frank Cass, 1969). Cf. also *De Cive*, VIII, 1 ed. Molesworth, *Opera Latina* (London, 1845), ii. 249. [19] Ibid. II. III. 2.

The right of dominion can therefore be constituted according to three different modes: voluntary submission, forced submission, and generation. These three titles of dominion give rise, respectively, to the commonwealth of institution, the commonwealth of acquisition, and dominion of children.

1. Let us consider first of all the third title, which *De Cive* calls *dominium paternum*, dominion over children. As we know, this dominion belongs first to the mother. It is she who originally has the right of dominion over the child. The father or any other man can only obtain it if the mother abandons the child or if she transfers to a man the right which she has herself. Since every dominion over a person is supposed to stand on a juridical act, the child is considered to make an act of submission or of obedience to its mother, its father, or whoever else it may be. What is the content of this submission on the part of children? In the name of the virtual pact which they make, children are, Hobbes says, 'in most absolute subjection to him or her, that so bringeth them up, or preserveth them'.[20] In clear terms, this means:

They may alienate them, that is assign his or her domination, by selling or giving them in adoption or servitude to others; or may pawn them for hostages, kill them for rebellion, or sacrifice them for peace, by the law of nature, when he or she, in his or her conscience, think it to be necessary.[21]

In order to measure the terrifying extension Hobbes allows to the *dominium paternum*, it will be enough to compare his position with that of Grotius.[22] For Grotius, the father only has the right to govern the child (this right includes the right to chastise, but only with a view to constrain the child to complete its duties or to correct it). But this right of the father disappears as soon as the child acquires the capacity of judgement which is necessary for the conduct of its actions, and leaves the father's house. The child, now become adult, is the absolute master of his/her actions and totally independent of the rights of others. What is more, the child has a right of property over things which belong to him/her, except that the use of this right is delayed. We can see, then, how Grotius, in opposition to Hobbes, limits the paternal right to the provisional governance of the actions of the child.

2. The second title of domination defines the *dominium despoticum*. This supposes, first of all, victory over one or more men and the fear of death which that victory inspires in the defeated. However, the pre-eminence of force cannot by itself constitute a right of dominion. For such a title to be constituted would require in addition a promise or a pact by which the

---

[20] *The Elements of Law (= EL)* II, III, 1, ed. F. Tönnies (London: Frank Cass, 1969), II. IV. 8.
[21] Ibid.
[22] Cf. *De Jure belli ac pacis*, critical edition by B. J. A. De Kanter-Van Hettinga Tromp (Aalen: Scientia Verlag, 1993), II. V. 1–7.

weaker committed to serve the stronger, who would already have allowed him not just his life, but also his corporal liberty. This pact makes the relationship of submission into a juridical one, whereby the master–servant relationship is established. When corporal liberty is not accorded by the master, so that the defeated is either in chains or in prison, another relationship is established: that of master–slave. In this latter case domination is by pure constraint; there is no mutual confidence between the master and the slave.

By virtue of his pact—tacit or virtual—the servant owes an unreserved obedience and submission to the master, who correlatively has a right of *absolute dominion*[23] over him. This submission, in the version of it given in *Elements of Law* and *De Cive*, is very extensive since it concerns not only the governance of the actions of the servant but also his physical person, his goods, and even his children.

A master therefore is to be supposed to have no less right over those, whose bodies he leaveth at liberty, than over those he keepeth in bonds and imprisonment; and hath absolute dominion over both; and may say of his servant, that he is *his*, as he may of any other thing. And whatsoever the servant had, and might call *his*, is now the master's; for he that disposeth of the person, disposeth of all the person could dispose of; insomuch as though there be *meum* and *tuum* amongst servants distinct from one another by the dispensation, and for the benefit of their master; yet there is no *meum* and *tuum* belonging to any of them against the master himself, whom they are not to resist, but to obey all his commands as law.[24]

Here we can see to what point the submission of the subjects of a *despotical kingdom*, which Hobbes was to call a *Commonwealth by Acquisition* in *Leviathan*, is extreme. It knows only one limit: if the servant is deprived of his corporal liberty (which can only happen if he is in prison or in chains or, what comes down to the same thing, in peril of his life), he is then freed from all submission and all obligation towards the master. He can exercise his natural right to defend his life by running away or even by killing the master.

To measure the submission of the subject in a *Commonwealth by Acquisition*, it will help to compare that submission with the status of perfect voluntary servitude in Grotius.[25] Perfect servitude consists in serving a master all one's life in exchange for food and the other necessities of life, which the master must provide to the servant. Thus conceived and 'kept within the bounds of nature, this subjection has nothing about it that is too hard', says Grotius. Indeed, not only does the master have no right to kill the servant, nor to inflict cruelty on him (which Hobbes would allow, with certain reservations), but in addition he has no right over his children.

---

[23] *EL*, II. III. 4.   [24] Ibid.   [25] Cf. *De jure belli ac pacis*, II, V, 27.

This would be unacceptable to Hobbes: '*The children of the servant are the goods of the master in perpetuum*'.[26]

So we can see the point to which the figure of the political subject is that of a subjected subject, of a subject practically turned into a thing, from which it would seem that there is no way in which we could expect to see the birth of the figure of a subject who is a political actor.

3. The last title which constitutes domination or submission is, in the words of *Elements of Law*, a '*voluntary offer of subjection*'.[27] Does this submission have the same effects as the previous two? It is an important question, because this mode of the constitution of domination defines a *Commonwealth by Institution*. To determine the content of the right of domination by the sovereign and his subjects' obligation of submission, we must return to the wording of the social covenant. Now the clause of the social covenant which everyone makes with everyone else is limited to the transfer of the right of use (*jus utendi*) of the power of each individual. The right of the sovereign must therefore be limited to directing the actions of subjects (or citizens). This can happen when individuals' wills are included in the will of a sovereign individual or of a sovereign council.[28]

In the space of this essay I cannot examine all the difficulties posed by the government of the actions of subjects in *Elements of Law* and *De Cive*. Nonetheless, it is clear that the individual subject remains a subjected subject and never becomes an actor-subject. The inclusion of the wills of individual subjects in the will of the sovereign simply means that the sovereign is the only political actor.

Does the theory of authorization and representation in *Leviathan*, which involves precisely the establishment of a relationship between an author and an actor, change things fundamentally on this point? I do not think so. The theory of authorization in *Leviathan* admittedly does profoundly modify the nature of the social covenant, something I have endeavoured to show on various occasions.[29] But its object is precisely and explicitly to make the sovereign the only political actor, in virtue of the unlimited mandate of individual subjects. These subjects have to recognize the will of the sovereign as their own, that is to say they must submit without contest. It is from this, moreover, that we can deduce the rights of the sovereign and the submission of subjects. Subjects cannot: (1) change the form of government, (2) remove the sovereign from power, (3) protest against the sovereign's institution, (4) denounce certain of his actions as unjust, etc.

The rights of sovereignty are all defined in terms of the same argument founded on the act of authorization. This argument consists in saying that

---

[26] *EL*, II. IV. 4.   [27] *EL*, II. III. 2.   [28] *EL*, I. XIX. 6.
[29] See *Hobbes et la pensée politique moderne* (Paris: PUF, 1995; 2nd edn. 2001), 197–227.

each time a subject opposes the will of the sovereign he enters into contradiction with himself, and in particular with the act by which he authorized the sovereign to govern all his actions with a view to peace and public security. By instituting the sovereign as the only actor, subjects deprive themselves of all status as political subject-actors. Recognition by subjects of the sovereign's actions as their own is the counterpart of this deprivation. Or rather, we ought to say that if the individual is an actor-subject, it is by virtue of a single act: that of the social convenant. Now this act is precisely the one by which he gives up the status of actor in order to recognize the sovereign henceforth as the only actor.

Over against the subjected subject, the only political actor is, therefore, the sovereign.

3. THE DESTITUTION OF THE CITIZEN

The most direct consequence of the sovereign's status as the only political actor and, by consequence, the only political subject, is found in Hobbes's destitution of the citizen. This point has often been highlighted,[30] which is why for my own part I shall consider it from a particular point of view: that of the relation between Bodin and Hobbes on the notion of citizenship.

However, in order to understand the principle I shall simply recall that, at least since Aristotle, the citizen has been defined as being at once free of all subjection with regard to a master, and as a participant in the political life of the city:

That which is a citizen is thus manifest on the basis of these considerations: of the one who has the faculty to participate in deliberative or judiciary power, we say that he is a citizen of the city concerned, and we call a city, in short, all the people of this kind when they are sufficient to live in autarchy.[31]

This definition of the citizen by notions of liberty and participation was to constitute a permanent tradition in political thought. What is Bodin's position in this respect?

In his *Six Books of the Republic*, Bodin re-elaborates the distinction between the subject, the citizen, and the foreigner in terms of his doctrine of sovereignty. What is particularly significant here is that Bodin does not draw the same consequences as Hobbes from his doctrine of sovereignty regarding the status of the citizen. Bodin defines the citizen as 'le franc

---

[30] Recently in Quentin Skinner's book, *Reason and Rhetoric in the Philosophy of Hobbes* (Cambridge: CUP, 1996), 287 f.sq.   [31] Aristotle, *Politics*, III. 1. 1275^b.

subject tenant de la souveraineté d'autruy'.[32] This is how he comments on this definition:

Voilà l'origine des Républiques, qui peut esclaircir la définition de Citoyen, qui n'est autre chose que le franc sujet, tenant de la souveraineté d'autrui. Je dis franc subject: car combien que l'esclave soit autant ou plus subject de la République que son seigneur, si est-ce que tous les peuples ont toujours passé par commun accord, que l'esclave n'est point citoyen, et en termes de droit est compté pour rien.[33]

There is no pure and simple identification between the notion of the citizen and that of the subject in Bodin. Indeed, even if every citizen is a subject of the republic, not every subject is a citizen. The citizen is a free subject, who is only called a subject because his liberty is partly diminished by sovereignty:

De sorte qu'on peut dire que tout citoyen est subject estant quelque peu de sa liberté diminuée par la majesté de celuy auquel il doit obéissance: mais tout subject n'est pas citoyen, comme nous avons dit de l'esclave.[34]

One can say that every citizen is a subject, as some of his liberty is diminished by the majesty of the one to whom he owes obedience; but not all subjects are citizens, as we have said of the slave.

When we compare Hobbes's position with that of Bodin, we see how far Hobbes modified the notion of citizenship. Note first of all that Hobbes uses the word 'citizen' very little. It is absent from *Elements of Law* and is only used in three marginal occurrences in the English *Leviathan*.[35] On the other hand, Hobbes uses the term *civis* quite often in *De Cive*, which is perfectly reasonable, and in the Latin version of *Leviathan*, often in the place of the English 'subject'. What is the content of this notion of the citizen? What will show this best is a central text from chapter V. 11 of *De Cive* where there is a definition of sovereignty (*summa potestas*, *summa imperium*) and of the citizen (*civis*). As to the latter, Hobbes says:

Civium unusquisque, sicut etiam omnis *persona civilis subordinata*, ejus, qui summum imperium habet, SUBDITUS appelatur.

Each of the *citizens*, and every *subordinate civil person*, is called a SUBJECT of him who holds the *sovereign power*.

The citizen is thus unilaterally reduced to the subject. The content of this operation is given in paragraph 12 of chapter V:

Hinc est quod duo sint genera civitatum, alterum *naturale*, quale est *paternum* et *despoticum*; alterum *institutivum*, quod et *politicum* dici potest. In primo

---

[32] Jean Bodin, *Les Six livres de la République*, édition de 1576, livre I, chapitre VI (Paris: Fayard, 1986), p. 112. Chapter VI of book I is titled 'Du citoyen, et de la différence d'entre le subject, le citoyen, l'estranger, la ville, cité et République'.   [33] Ibid. p. 113–14.

[34] Ibid. p. 114.

[35] *Lev.*, XIII, p. 187, a reference to citizens who close their shutters; XXVII, p. 265, a reference to the citizens of Athens; XXXIX, p. 497, where it concerns the definition of the notion of Churches.

dominus acquirit sibi *cives* sua voluntate; in altero *cives* arbitrio suo imponunt sibimet ipsis *dominum*, sive is sit *unus homo*, sive *unus coetus* hominum cum *summo imperio*.

Hence there are two kinds of *commonwealths*; one kind is *natural*, like the *Paternal* and *Despotic*; the other is the kind of commonwealth which is *by design*, and which may also be called *political*. In the first case a *Lord* acquires *citizens* for himself by his own will; in the second, the *citizens* impose a *Lord* upon themselves by their own decision, whether that be *one man* or *one group* of men with *sovereign power*.

Here we can see clearly the operation which enables Hobbes to reduce the notion of citizen completely to that of subject: the citizen is no longer a free subject, he is defined in terms of his submission to a *dominus*.

Such, then, is the result of the direct-method reading: in the individual subject we cannot find the least suggestion of an individual subject-actor. The traditional figure of the actor-subject, that is to say the citizen, is emptied of its content.

4. AN OUTLINE OF AN INDIVIDUAL POLITICAL SUBJECT: RESISTANCE TO POWER

Must we leave it at that? Is the destitution of the citizen Hobbes's last word on the relationship between the individual and power? If that were so, we should have to admit the traditional conclusion which has been drawn: Hobbes's politics confers political responsibility, restricted to public defence and security, on the sovereign alone, and turns individuals away from all interest in the political by pointing them exclusively towards the realization of private ends.

Now, I do not think that this is the case. There is another figure of the political subject which is the reverse side, as it were, of the subjected subject. To uncover this other figure of the subject, even if it is really only an outline of the political subject, we need to turn again to chapter XXI of *Leviathan* on the liberty of subjects.

In our earlier considerations we examined two meanings of the liberty of subjects: corporal liberty and the liberty which is due to the absence of civil laws or regulations. Now these two liberties are negative, certainly; the first is defined by the absence of external obstacles, and the second by silence on the part of the law. Is there not a third form of liberty, which is no longer negative but, in a certain sense, positive? It would indeed appear that one ought to give a positive response to this question. When Hobbes examines what he calls 'the true liberty of a Subject'[36] he indicates right away what

---

[36] Ibid. XXI, p. 268.

he means by it: 'that is to say, what are the things, which though
commanded by the Sovereign, he [the subject] may nevertheless, without
injustice, refuse to do'.[37] This formula is not insignificant: it is a matter of
knowing what the subject can refuse to do despite the order of the sovereign, that is, what is called a little further on the 'Liberty to disobey'[38] or
'Liberty to refuse'.[39] These expressions must not of course be taken in
isolation, but in the theoretical context of chapter XXI which gives them
their meaning. But we can already note that it is no longer a question of
negative forms of liberty: disobedience or refusal are particular positive
effects of the right or liberty to resist. It is, as we shall see, a different relationship between the individual and power which is being outlined here.

To give an account of the liberty to refuse, or the liberty to disobey, we
need to return to the terms of the social convenant, whose wording and
finality define the subjects' rights and obligations. Now there is a right which
can never be the object of a transfer, and this is the right of resistance. It is
important to define both its meaning and its extent.

The right of resistance is a subjective right[40] possessed by every human
individual, whatever the relational context in which his existence is lived
out. This is as true in the state of nature as in the civil state: 'a man cannot
lay down the right of resisting them, that assault him by force, to take away
his life; because he cannot be understood to ayme thereby, at any Good to
himselfe'.[41]

This right, then, attaches to the natural person of a human being, and is
founded on the fundamental ethical principle according to which: 'every
man, not onely by Right, but also by necessity of Nature, is supposed to
endeavour all he can, to obtain that which is necessary for his conservation'.[42] It goes without saying that to give up our right to resist would be to
contravene this ethical principle. Let me add three remarks to this.

First, the right of resistance does not consist merely in resisting that which
could put one's life directly in danger, but also that which could put it indirectly in danger and that which, without putting it directly or indirectly in
danger, could affect people whose injury or death would cause us suffering.[43] So we have the right to resist anyone who seeks to attack us by force
to kill us, to cause us injury, or to imprison us; but also anyone who seeks to
prevent us benefiting from air, water, movement, or safe passage from one
place to another; and, further, anyone who seeks to have us testify against
ourselves or against anyone 'by whose Condemnation a man falls into misery; as of a Father, Wife or Benefactor'.[44]

---

[37] Ibid.   [38] Ibid. p. 269.   [39] Ibid.
[40] Cf. Grotius, *De jure belli ac pacis*, I, I, IV–V, pp. 31–2.
[41] *Lev*. XIV, p. 192; *De Cive*, II, 18; cf. also *EL*, I. XVII. 2.   [42] *Lev*. XV, pp. 209–10.
[43] Cf. Ibid. p. 202.   [44] Ibid. XIV, p. 199.

Secondly, it is an absolutely inalienable human right. A convention under which a man undertook to give up his right of resistance to someone else (whoever it might be) is always null and void. The alienation of the right of resistance, indeed, would contravene reason, or the cause which is the foundation of every transfer of rights: that is, the *consideration* of a certain benefit for oneself.[45] To alienate one's right of resistance would consist, for the person who alienated it, in placing the object of his will in contradiction with the cause which governs it. The act would thus be contradictory and could only result from error or ignorance. And it goes without saying that rights cannot be founded on error or ignorance.

Thirdly, the right of resistance, being absolutely inalienable, is not one of the rights we transfer to the sovereign in the social covenant. It defines, that is, the part of natural right (or liberty) which the individual keeps in the state, even when he has given up his right to everything. Recall that the right to everything is not to be identified with natural right, but constitutes the enhanced form which that right has in a state of war.[46] Within the state, the right of resistance constitutes the sphere of human rights in whose name an individual can always legitimately oppose the political power. The application of this principle to punishment, that is to a penalty legally pronounced by a tribunal which has established guilt, is clear: punishment 'being Force, a man is not obliged not to resist'.[47] A man, become citizen, therefore keeps (because he is a man) a right of resistance which he cannot transfer to the state and which he does not receive from the state. Subjective human rights can neither be lost nor received.

The right of resistance defines, from now on, the proper sphere on which the political power cannot encroach. It is precisely when the political power interferes with it that the right of resistance becomes the liberty to disobey or the liberty to refuse. We cannot, then, limit the scope of the right of resistance simply to the private dimension; it also has political implications. Hobbes draws out some of these, touching on the limits of civil obedience. We must recall, however, that these limits do not in any way limit the rights of the sovereign, but they do imply the possibility of being in conflict with the sovereign.

The most notable consequence of the right of resistance concerns the right to punish. Contrary to what is often thought, the hardest thing to consider in Hobbes's work is probably penal law.[48] Hobbes does not manage to provide a foundation for penal law, because even when such law is in

---

[45] Ibid. p. 192.
[46] On the *jus in omnia* as an enlarged form of the *jus naturale*, see. my book *La Décision métaphysique de Hobbes* (Paris: Vrin, 1987; 2nd edn. 1999), 312–17.
[47] *Lev.* p.199; cf. *D.Ci.*, II, 18.
[48] Cf. Zarka, *Hobbes et la pensée politique moderne*, 228–50.

conformity with legal procedure, when it is exercised by means of violence it calls into question the sphere of natural subjective rights. Everyone, therefore, has the right to oppose and resist it, although this obviously does not mean that such resistance would be victorious: 'No man is supposed bound by Covenant, not to resist violence; and consequently it cannot be intended, that he gave any right to another to lay violent hands upon his person.'[49]

5. CONCLUSION

We can see, then, that a different relationship between the individual and power can be outlined on the basis of a reinterpretation of the right of resistance. This outline is that of a figure of the political subject which is very different from that of the submitted subject, since the individual begins to constitute a subject from the moment he resists power. But of course we should not go too far in this direction: Hobbesian doctrine has as its main object the foundation of obedience on the part of subjects. But we also know that his political doctrine often contains surprises and that, looked at back-to-front, it can say things which are both different from, and more profound than, what it yields to a direct-method reading.

Translated from the French by Edward Hughes.

[49] *Lev.* XXVIII, p. 353.

The Burdensome Freedom of Sovereigns

TOM SORELL

Hobbes's political philosophy calls for a donation of obedience from the many to the few, or from the many to a single person. The many agree to transfer to the few or to the one person the right to decide what will secure the safety of the many, and the man or body of men to whom this right passes acquires sovereignty over the many. The sovereign decides what each of the many must do or omit to do in order to stay secure, and the many must act accordingly or be guilty of injustice. The many fall in with the sovereign's decisions by keeping his laws. This is what subjection means in Hobbes's political philosophy, and while Hobbes says that the laws could never prescribe each man's actions or omissions down to the last detail (cf. *L*, ch. 21, Tuck, p. 147),[1] there is scope in theory for a pretty definite channelling of the behaviour of subjects across many departments of life. What Hobbes calls 'the liberty of subjects' is the range of action that is not prohibited by the sovereign's laws. Compared to the range of action permitted to agents before they submit to the sovereign, the scope of the liberty of subjects can be very small.

It is completely different for the sovereign. He submits to no one, transfers the right of deciding how to secure himself to no one; and when he accepts the right to choose the means of safety for the many, he does not do so in return for the promise to them that he will secure the peace. He enters into no agreement with the many at all, and he is not subject to the laws that bind his subjects. He is a uniquely free agent in a commonwealth, and though he can in principle become the subject of another sovereign, in domestic politics he seems to be a law unto himself. Is there any respect, then, in which the sovereignty of a Hobbesian sovereign can be constrained or limited other than by another sovereign? So long as constraint is identified with obligation to individuals or groups within the state, the answer would seem to be 'No'. I am going to argue, however, that there is more to constraint than obligation. In some perfectly clear senses the Hobbesian sovereign is far from free to do what he likes, though he retains the right of

---

[1] I use Richard Tuck's edition of *Leviathan* (Cambridge: Cambridge University Press, 1991).

nature that his subjects give up when they leave the state of nature. Concentrating on the case of sovereignty vested in a single person rather than in an assembly, I will point out that the burdens of securing what Hobbes calls 'peace' are great, both where the peace is domestic and where it is international. Even if the sovereign is not strictly *answerable* to his subjects or to law or to other sovereigns for what he does, he does not have the luxury of ruthlessness that is open to ordinary individuals in the state of nature. One reason is that he is a potential enemy of all of the men he represents; another is that he is an actual enemy of other sovereigns. But a third and less obvious reason is that to carry out the duties of sovereign he has to desert the persona of an individual and identify with the interests of his subjects. The more he acts out of narrow self-interest, and at the expense of the interests of his subjects, the more he stands to lose the power that makes such acts tempting; while the less he acts on behalf of the self, the less his freedom to act attaches to him individually. Instead, it attaches to the union he personifies.

I

An important source for Hobbes's views about the freedom of sovereigns is *Leviathan*, chapter 21, paragraph 8:

The Libertie, whereof there is so frequent, and honourable mention in the Histories, and Philosophy of the Antient Greeks, and Romans, and in the writings, and discourse of those that from them have received all their learning in Politiques, is not the liberty of Particular men; but the Libertie of the Common-wealth: which is the same with that, which every man then should have, if there were no Civil Laws, nor Common-wealth at all. And the effects of it are also the same. For as among masterless men, there is a perpetual war, of every man against his neighbour; no inheritance, to transmit to the Son, nor to expect from the Father; no propriety of Goods, or Lands, no security; but a full and absolute Libertie in every Particular man: So in states, and Common-wealths not dependent on one another, every Common-wealth, (not every man) has an absolute Libertie, to do what it shall judge (that is to say, what that Man, or Assemblie that representeth it, shall judge) most conducing to their benefit. But withall, they live in the condition of perpetuall war, and upon the confines of battle, with their frontiers armed, and canons planted against their neighbours round about. The *Athenians*, and *Romanes* were free; that is, free Common-wealths; not that any particular man had the Libertie to resist their own Representative; but that their Representative had the Libertie to resist, or invade other people.   (Tuck, p. 149)

Hobbes's message here is complicated. First, there is an echo of the famous point made earlier in *Leviathan* that the state of liberty is the state of war. When every individual man is free to see to his own security and well-being, freedom means the end to all possessions, all goods. This unprofitable liberty does not deserve the praise that the ancients have heaped on liberty, and indeed, according to the passage, the ancients were referring to something else when they spoke well of liberty: namely, the liberty of commonwealths or of sovereign representatives or of whole peoples. The liberty of a commonwealth can be a valuable thing, because even a limited and local peace allows all of the good things in life to be pursued with some hope of attaining them. But this liberty resides in the sovereign representative, and not in each of his subjects. Like the liberty of individuals, the liberty of sovereigns always coexists with war; but it relocates and shrinks war-zones. Instead of having to defend a frontier that starts at the surfaces of one's body, as in the state of nature, the free agent in the shape of the sovereign representative has frontiers determined by the land and forces he controls, frontiers that make room for individual and collective well-being. As Hobbes says in *Leviathan*, the reason that the misery of the freedom of individuals does not attend the freedom of sovereigns is that the latter sustains the industry of subjects domestically (*L*, ch. 13, Tuck, p. 90). But war—and Hobbes means cold war as well as hot—remains in the international arena.

When Hobbes identifies the liberty of sovereigns with the unprofitable liberty of the state of nature, he seems to be implying that liberty in any form is only an apparent good; but when he distinguishes the liberty that the ancients were genuinely praising—liberty in the form of the liberty of sovereigns—from the liberty that they are wrongly but popularly taken to praise, at least *that* form of liberty appears to be a genuine good. I think this latter implication fits in better with other things Hobbes says than the wholesale dismissal of the good of liberty. But, to the extent that the liberty of sovereigns is a genuine good, it does not involve quite the perfect discretion to judge what is necessary for security as Hobbes's theory extends to the individual in the state of nature. In other words, to the extent that the liberty of sovereigns is a good kind of liberty, Hobbes is not entitled to the strong analogy he wishes to draw between the liberty of sovereign representatives and the liberty of particular men in the state of nature.

Leviathan contains two general arguments leading to the conclusion that the liberty of sovereigns is a genuine good. First, there is an argument to the conclusion that one source of decision-making is better than many in relation to collective security and well-being, and the effect of instituting a sovereign is that one man or body of men decides for all. This argument implies that monarchy is better than democracy or aristocracy, that a system of checks and balances is worse than a single, unbroken line of command from the top, and that unanimity between independent interests is worse than a fusion of the different interests. Second, there is an argument setting out what one man or a body of men needs to do in order to see effectively to collective security and well-being, an argument with the strong implication that the requirements of collective security and well-being require very great latitude for action. Taken together, the arguments are to the effect that if a sovereign asserts himself in the ways required, that is, makes a certain definite use of the unlimited latitude that he has when the many submit to him, he and they will enjoy peace and the fruits of peace indefinitely. The first argument comes, in among other places, chapter 17, paragraph 5, and, in another form, toward the end of chapter 18, where Hobbes is discussing the indivisibility of the rights of sovereigns. The second argument stretches over the whole of chapter 30.

The second argument is the more perplexing of the two, for chapter 30 is full of precepts for the exercise of sovereignty, and yet the essence of sovereignty seems to be that, whichever man or body of men the many submit to, that man or that body of men is the sole judge of what must be done to secure internal peace and defence from foreign attack. The individual in the state of nature retains the right of nature—the right to see to his well-being and security by whatever means he chooses; and the sovereign acquires the same right with respect to the commonwealth (*L*, ch. 30, last para., Tuck, p. 244). Just as, according to Hobbes's theory, there is no gainsaying the individual in the state of nature in respect of what he thinks necessary for his security and well-being, so there is no gainsaying the sovereign with respect to the safety and well-being of the commonwealth. If the point about the right of nature is taken seriously, then isn't the sovereign incorrigible, so that whatever the sovereign thinks is right to do *is* right to do? What, then, if the sovereign decides to do something other than, or in conflict with, the set of things chapter 30 of *Leviathan* tells him to do? Surely in that case, by the lights of Hobbes's theory, he makes a mistake in statecraft, so that he is not incorrigible after all.

The difficulty we are considering arises from connecting the right of nature with incorrigibility. It disappears if individuals or sovereigns with the right of nature are taken to be fallible about means to the end of peace, but can be excused for their mistakes because they are making judgements *in extremis*. I take it that this is how Hobbes invites us to think about individuals in the state of nature. He surely does not want to claim that all men in the state of nature are above criticism in their choice of means or ends. He shows obvious disapproval for those who kill because they love fighting, or those who attack and dispossess out of vanity or greed. Again, his theory commits him to saying that anyone who would rather go on fighting than submit with the majority of others to government is irrational, and has not thought through the consequences of making himself a target for those who join together in a commonwealth. These implied criticisms of some of those who are caught up in the war of all against all do not undercut the claim that these very people can blamelessly use any means they like to secure themselves against their fellows if they genuinely think they will otherwise be unsafe.

Sovereigns, too, are capable of misjudging the ends served by government and the appropriate means to those ends. To the extent that they are involved in threatening international relations, tantamount for Hobbes to war, they are making judgements *in extremis*, and so long as they genuinely think public safety depends on it, they cannot be blamed for adopting measures that turn out to be inappropriate. In this respect, they are exactly like individuals in the state of nature. From the angle of domestic arrangements, too, sovereigns can in a sense be above criticism. The reason this time is not that they are acting in the face of emergency, but because they have had transferred to them the prerogative of making judgements about safety and security, which transfer is undone when those the sovereign is charged with protecting make judgements of their own about what should have been done, and criticize the sovereign for behaving differently. The effect of submission to the sovereign is for the many to say to the one: 'You be the judge of the means to my well-being and security instead of me', and it is injustice to take back one's right to judge except where one's life genuinely seems to depend on it. Nevertheless, although a certain kind of *popular* criticism is ruled unjust by the terms of submission, the possibility of a sovereign doing something that disagrees with the purpose of the commonwealth is not. For example, it is possible for a sovereign to impoverish one of his subjects so as to enrich a favourite (*L*, ch. 19, Tuck, p. 132). It is also possible for a sovereign to pass a law that benefits him personally, say by requiring everyone to give him a present on his birthday, without this contributing to the collective well-being or adding to any military defence. This is where chapter 30 comes in. It tries to derive from the purpose of the commonwealth the principal kinds of activity that sovereigns should engage in, and this purpose excludes certain things actual sovereigns do, or might do, even where they are things sovereigns are within their rights to do.

So chapter 30 does not conflict with the freedom of sovereigns. On the other hand, it shows that the freedom of sovereigns is very different in many respects from the freedom of individuals. According to Hobbes, a free individual—an individual in the state of nature—displays a pattern of behaviour determined by appetites and aversions of the moment and the entrenched likes and dislikes of a lifetime. Some of his tastes are formed by what is admired by others with whom he lives, but there has to be some prospect of personal gratification in the courses of action he selects. Where each has the right of nature and can adopt any means he likes to defend himself or pursue felicity, no one can be sure of his success in attaining or keeping anything he has an appetite for; no good can be enjoyed securely, not even survival. This means that doing what comes naturally—pursuing what pleases one and avoiding what one dislikes—is a strategy that is likely to be unsatisfying or fatal. Realizing as much—and this is the main benefit to individuals of a science of politics—makes one revalue upwards the good of security. Acting on this revaluation means freely submitting with others to a sovereign. This exercise of freedom—the one recommended by appetite corrected by the science of politics—is the best that the state of nature offers at the level of individuals. It is an exercise of freedom to end or severely limit one's freedom.

Now chapter 30 also indicates how freedom is to be exercised where the appetites of *sovereigns* are corrected by political science. But the style of correction is very different in the two cases. At the level of individuals the correction of appetite works by identifying something people always have reason to pursue but are unlikely to value very highly—personal security—and making whatever is necessary for security obligatory. An appetite everyone has—the appetite for security—is made overriding, because its satisfaction is a condition of the satisfaction of other appetites. Or, in other words, Hobbes shows that what *really* ought to matter above all to individuals, because everything that seems to matter is unattainable without it, is the thing they should pursue before they pursue other things. In the case of sovereigns, civil science works in a different way. It takes powers conferred by the submission of the many, powers that are likely to be directed by sovereigns toward personal or partly personal ends, or to short-term public ends, and shows why they are *mis*directed if directed toward these ends. First, personal ends are different from the ends that a sovereign has as representative of the people; and the ends that a sovereign has to pursue as a representative of the people are prior to those he ought to pursue personally. Moreover, allowing personal ends to dominate the ends of the office of sovereign representative is a way of frustrating those personal ends. Although there is a parallel between the case put to individuals and the case put to sovereigns—Hobbes argues for the dominance of an end that wouldn't otherwise be recognized as dominant or as a condition of other ends—the notion of representativeness is crucial to the proper exercise of sovereign freedom. To use the terms Hobbes introduces in chapter 16 of *Leviathan*, the sovereign has to forget the natural person he is—the individual he is—and concentrate on the artificial or feigned person he is, the one that represents the union of the many who covenant together for peace.

A representative is someone who acts or speaks on behalf of others; and a sovereign representative is someone who decides on behalf of the many how their 'strength and means' (*L*, ch. 28, Tuck, p. 121) may best be used for their 'peace and common defence' (ibid.). The many say to the sovereign: 'Use us and our possessions in whatever way you think will secure us and allow us to live as agreeably as possible.' The many do not say: 'Do with us and our means as you like.' Even if they did say this, according to Hobbes, they could not be understood to give up their right to self-protection. But they do not say anything like this in forming a commonwealth, and the sovereign representative does not act on behalf of the union of the many if the things he does cannot be understood as helping to make or maintain the peace. If taxes collected by a king are spent on lavish parties, or if the land and houses of some subjects are seized only to allow the king to hunt game more conveniently, then, though the expenditure or seizure is not strictly *unjust* by the terms of Hobbes's theory, and cannot justly be used as a pretext for rebellion or law-breaking by subjects, neither action uses the means of the public for public defence. So each is a misuse of the authority the sovereign is given.

Chapter 30 of *Leviathan* points to many other things that would count as misuses or mistaken uses of the office of the sovereign. One of the most striking of these is making unnecessary laws (*L*, ch. 30, Tuck, pp. 239 f.); another is making laws that are not perspicuous (ibid. 240). A third is applying the laws more leniently to the rich and aristocratic than to the poor and lowly (ibid. 237); a fourth, possibly a corollary of the third with respect to tax law, is taxing income rather than consumption (ibid. 238–9); a fifth is punishing any crimes that proceed from provocation, even great crimes, as severely as crimes that show contempt for justice or for the sovereign's authority. Many of these misuses of sovereign authority proceed from a very broad interpretation of the public safety that the commonwealth in the person of the sovereign is supposed to procure. It isn't the simple protection of life and limb, but the creation of conditions in which subjects can work to provide for themselves some of the contentments of life. Too much law can get in the way of this; that is why Hobbes makes it a condition of a law being good that it is necessary, rather than that it be (for example) enforceable.

Since public safety and the latitude to provide for oneself sometimes require conflicting things, Hobbes involves every sovereign in a balancing act. If the sovereign restricts the liberty of subjects for the sake of public security, he may take away the conditions necessary for a modicum of economic well-being. And if he pursues a laissez-faire policy with respect to work for the sake of prosperity, he may create a class of economically powerful and politically ambitious subjects. It helps to reduce the tensions between reasonable liberty and security if subjects themselves want whatever is required to keep the peace, rather than having to be deterred from disturbing the peace. This is why duties of public instruction are high on Hobbes's list of requirements of the sovereign's office (cf. ibid. 233–5). People are to be taught not to prefer foreign nations and their forms of government to their own nation and its government. People are to be taught not to desire change of government, not to back popular men, not to dispute about the sovereign power, and many other things. Then there are groups of duties in relation to the choice of advisers and officials, and the maintenance of effective armed forces.

Hobbes arrives at the requirements of sovereign office in chapter 30 in the light of three things: a theory of the rights of sovereigns (ch. 18); a survey of the known inconveniences of different forms of government (ch. 19); and an account of the things that tend to weaken commonwealths (ch. 29). Chapter 19 comes out in favour of monarchy, not because it has no inconveniences, but because it has fewer than other forms of government, and none that it does not share with the alternatives. Chapter 30 spells out the the ways in which the rights have to be exercised so as to avoid the things that weaken the commonwealth. Foremost among the things that tend to weaken a commonwealth is the sovereign's failing to assert all his powers consistently enough. A right that is put aside can be hard to reassert, Hobbes says, because it will look to subjects with no historical knowledge to be an opportunistic adjustment of the balance of power in the sovereign's favour. In chapter 29 Hobbes gives examples of English kings who allowed their powers over churchmen and over barons to be eroded. The other major sources of weakness of the commonwealth derive from seditious popular opinions, against which public instruction as described in chapter 30 is effective. So chapter 30 is no deduction of the things that sovereigns should do from the concept of public safety in the abstract. It is historically informed, realistic about the shortcomings even of monarchy, and a sort of confirmation, in the face of the incredulity he expects from some readers, that nothing less than all of the rights of sovereignty are needed in practice.

The office of the sovereign representative is burdensome, but how, if at all, is the sovereign limited by forces within the commonwealth? It is the strength and means of the many, to the extent that the sovereign can marshal them through laws, that constitute the sovereigns's power, and the wrong laws can reduce the resources of his subjects, and so *his* power. *Leviathan* makes the point often. At the end of chapter 18, Hobbes says in passing that the sovereign's 'strength and glory' consists in the 'vigor' of his subjects (Tuck, pp. 128–9). A few paragraphs later, he says the same thing in an argument for monarchy as the preferred form of government:

[W]here the publique and private interest are most closely united, there is the publique most advanced. Now in monarchy, the private interest is the same with the publique. The riches, power, and honour of a Monarch arise onely from the riches, strength and reputation of his Subjects. For no King can be rich, nor glorious, nor secure; whose Subjects are either poore, or contemptible, or too weak through want, or dissention, to maintain a war against their enemies.   (ch. 19, Tuck, p. 131)

Because the monarch draws his power from his subjects, he cannot afford to weaken or impoverish them too much. To what extent is this a limitation on the sovereign's freedom? Hobbes distinguishes (*L*, ch. 21, Tuck, p. 146) between limitations on freedom and limitations on power: a limitation is a limitation on freedom when it is an external impediment to action; but an inherent disability or internal weakness is a limitation on power. Hobbes's metaphor of the union of the many into a commonwealth impersonated by the sovereign, and his metaphor of the commonwealth as artificial man whose soul is sovereignty and whose strength is the wealth and power of the individual subjects (*L*, intro., para. 1, Tuck, p. 9) may make it seem as if the state of subjects is strictly a limitation on power rather than freedom; for in a sense subjects are always internal to the body politic. This, however, is to take the metaphor too literally. Faced with subjects who are unwilling to do his bidding even when it is for their own security, or who straightforwardly resist or turn on the sovereign, even when they are a weak faction and can be overcome, the sovereign can straightforwardly be obstructed from without.

There is no incoherence, then, in the idea of a sovereign's freedom being limited by the resistance of a few of his subjects. (Incoherence is threatened if the resistance is general; for then sovereignty is lost.) But what about limitations in the form of balancing acts necessary for securing the public safety in the sense of chapter 30? The sovereign must not impose too much on his subjects, nor give them too much latitude; he must use ministers, counsellors, and military commanders, but not lose control over the things he delegates to them or gets advice about. The task of balancing is made considerably easier if subjects and subordinates are on the sovereign's wavelength: if they make keeping the peace as central an aim as the public safety is for the sovereign. Public instruction can in principle see to some of this. But there are limits. Subjects are not public officials. They keep the peace not by thinking about peace in the abstract or its general requirements but by going about lawful business, preferably gainful business, since it is to the advantage of the commonwealth that the assets of each subject be as great as possible. The goals of this gainful, lawful activity are supposed to be uppermost in the minds of subjects; the requirements of security are left to the sovereign. This is one of the few things that distinguishes the subject in a Hobbesian commonwealth from a soldier in a standing army. Although every subject can in principle be called upon to contribute to military action that defends the commonwealth, and although subjection is tied to a project of collective self-defence, not every subject is supposed to be occupied in a full-time military role, or to live as a self-conscious member of a national peacekeeping force. The demands of peacekeeping are fulfilled by staying within the law on non-peacekeeping business: a lawful trade, for example. The fact that subjects are not only permitted but required by Hobbes's theory to invest themselves in private projects can work against a willingness to go further in peacekeeping than law-abidingness. People may be reluctant to leave their trade for military service. Or, even if they are not asked to join the army, they may be unwilling to donate what they regard as 'their' assets to a public project of defence, or any other public project. Ordinary subjects have at the very least divided attention and loyalty even when they break no laws and are gainfully employed. Public ministers, for their part, may be pursuing specific public goals that make competing demands on public resources even when all are authorized by the sovereign. So even they may pull against one another, or against the sovereign if his priority is a public goal other than the one they are responsible for. In any case, they, like the sovereign himself, are dependent on the cooperation of ordinary subjects, cooperation that may not be forthcoming where the public goals being pursued are being frustrated at the top, or where pursuing them takes away from other things that people are lawfully doing or even commanded to do.

In the conditions just described, people who are carrying out the roles assigned to them by Hobbes's theory have reasons deriving from how they carry out those roles for being reluctant to do the sovereign's bidding. This is unlike the reluctance of the naturally or congenitally lazy, or those whose own ambitions set them against the sovereign. It is a reluctance that Hobbes's theory justifies, since it concedes that, in pursuing the public safety, the sovereign can strike the balance between sometimes conflicting desiderata in the wrong way. The reluctance of normally law-abiding subjects, or of conscientious ministers, to fall in with the sovereign's plans, is a sign of the balance being struck in the wrong way. The potential for a problem of cooperation of this kind is hidden in Hobbes's writings; for he often writes as if problems of cooperation only arise where sovereignty is divided, as in a representative assembly, or in a monarchy where certain essential powers of sovereignty are delegated. It is true that divided sovereignty presents its own problem of cooperation. The many members of a representative assembly, or those in charge of different branches of government in a system with checks and balances, may retain the right of nature or something close to it; and this means that no one is authoritative. Where the legitimate judges of what is best to do are reduced to one, the prospect of stalemate in government is more remote. But because sovereignty even in one person is a balancing act, and because the work of carrying out the sovereign's decisions is necessarily distributed among many people, there can be a problem of cooperation even where no powers that Hobbes thinks essential to sovereignty are delegated.

II

I have been trying to suggest that although sovereignty and thoroughgoing freedom are supposed to go together in Hobbes's political philosophy, and *do* go together to the extent that being free means being the sole local retainer of the right of nature, the makings of legitimate obstruction of the sovereign by his underlings, or at least legitimate reluctance to cooperate with the sovereign, are also present in the theory. These things can constrain the sovereign just as much as the delegation or division of sovereign powers. The problem would be curtailed significantly or excluded altogether if the sovereign had no conflicting public objectives, or if he were able to rule with no ministers and if there were no legitimate private objectives that subjects could pursue that conflicted with the sovereign's. But stipulations to this effect would leave Hobbes's political philosophy hopelessly removed from the real world.

I come now to a second area of difficulty for Hobbes's theory of the sovereign. We can broach it by asking what incentive anyone has for *accepting* responsibility for the public safety from the many, even when that responsibility is taken on the condition that each member of the public submits absolutely to whoever is sovereign. The answer cannot be that accepting the responsibility is a means to acquiring things anyone might self-interestedly seek, like riches, deference, fame, or personal power itself. For to the extent that someone accepts the office of the sovereign, he accepts the considerable means, deference, and so on that go with the post as a means of protecting the many and not as so many contributions to his personal gratification. What is more, even if using these public resources as personal property has a peacekeeping use, because it commands the admiration or awe of the many, and promotes their obedience to laws intended to secure the public safety, it is clear that (for example) the king's jewels are secure as personal property only as long as the sovereign is effective at staving off civil or international war. There is always the risk of being deposed and killed, or of being deposed and exiled to a life of poverty and obscurity. The more resources are made unavailable for the public safety because they are used for frivolous personal consumption, the more the sovereign weakens his people and makes them a target for conquest, or courts their resentment or jealousy. Someone who accepts to be sovereign knowing that the rights and duties are those set out in *Leviathan*, will see that using the office for personal enrichment is a misuse of the office. One does not act on behalf of the many by making oneself rich, unless making onself rich is a means of securing the public safety, which is implausible.

Hobbes famously says that no one does anything voluntarily unless he forsees some good to himself (cf. e.g. *Leviathan*, ch. 14, Tuck, p. 93). This principle has an unclear application where someone is both a representative person and a natural person, as a king is. Someone who is in a position to accept the transfer of the right of nature from the many is, at the point of deciding, a natural person only: so for it to be in his self-interest to accept, he must see some benefit to his natural person of becoming sovereign. But he can also see, if he has Hobbes's science of politics, that to discharge the office of the sovereign is to rule in the interests of his subjects, and only where *that* interest permits, in his own interest. Moreover, as already said, the science of politics gives reasons why, even where the public interest seems to permit significant personal enrichment, it may be better for a king *not* to enrich himself. A scientifically informed, clear-headed decision to accept the office of the sovereign, then, is probably more selfless than selfish. But it cannot be too selfless: otherwise Hobbes's theory of voluntary action cannot make sense of the acceptance of sovereignty being voluntary. But the more prudent someone who accepts it is, the less it will look as if there is anything in it for him if he accepts.

For Hobbes's theory to work, there ought to be something about sovereignty in any form that gives to whomever it is offered a reason for accepting it. Perhaps what is crucial is that sovereignty is the *gift* of the many, and there is always reason to accept a gift, since a gift is a benefit. This suggestion seems less than compelling, however: *Leviathan* denies that a gift is given with no expectation of return to the giver; so every gift has strings attached, and because owning the gift of power can confer onerous and even dangerous responsibilities, it is always possible that it is not beneficial on balance.

Chapter 10 of *Leviathan* suggests that the power of sovereignty and the honour shown to sovereignty are reasons for accepting it. To be the sovereign is not just to be *more* powerful than one was before becoming sovereign, or to be relatively powerful: it is to have the greatest of human powers (Tuck, p. 62). And since whatever is a sign of power is honourable (Tuck, p. 65), sovereignty is supremely honourable. Moreover, although human beings differ in many kinds of behaviour—what Hobbes calls 'manners'—and many kinds of motivation, according to Hobbes, they all want power, the more of it the better. And the reason is that human life is never without some goal or other still to be pursued, for which means, the more the better, are always welcome. There is a revealing passage in chapter 11 of *Leviathan* in which Hobbes both illustrates the universal human desire for more and more power, and hints at a solution to our problem of how the responsibilities for public safety could be combined with projects gratifying to the natural person of the sovereign:

And the cause of this [restlesse desire of Power after power], is not always that a man hopes for a more intensive delight, than he has already attained to; or that he cannot be content with a moderate power; but because he cannot assure the power and means he hath to live well, which he hath at present, without the acquisition of more. And from hence it is, that Kings, whose power is greatest, turn their efforts to the assuring it at home by Lawes, or abroad by Wars, and when that is done there succeedeth a new desire; in some, of Fame from new Conquest; in others, of ease and sensual pleasure; in others, of admiration, or being flattered for excellence in some art, or other ability of the mind.   (Tuck, p. 70)

This passage suggests that the maintenance of peace at home and abroad is not necessarily a permanent project, but one that can be concluded and followed by projects geared to the natural person the sovereign is. In that case, according to the passage, fresh power is required for the pursuit of those personal projects. But some power, the passage suggests, can be directed by the sovereign at whatever goal he likes, so long as peace is assured. It is not as if all or most of the power that the sovereign is given is earmarked for public protection, but only as much as public protection requires, with the excess being available for anything else the sovereign pleases.

Hobbes *can*, then, motivate the acceptance of sovereignty by institution. It is always worth accepting, because it carries with it so much power, power that can be channelled into anything the sovereign finds personally gratifying so long as peace is assured. In the case of sovereignty by acquisition, the reason for accepting sovereignty is even more intelligible. In that case, someone who has been directing a war of conquest succeeds in probably a long and hard competition, and has the satisfaction of his opponents' surrender, as well as the fresh resources of the conquered people.

Is there a residual problem over the relationship between the natural and representative person of the sovereign? Someone who gives himself over to ease and sensual pleasure after a period of legislation and wars of foreign conquest might seem to take his eye off the ball. Perhaps he can afford a holiday from the work of lawmaking and military command, but can he contemplate out-and-out retirement? If not, because the maintenance of peace is more plausibly held to be a permanent project than something that is got out of the way once and for all, the question of whether sovereignty is personally beneficial *on balance* arises again with full force. I do not think there is a complete solution to this problem in Hobbes's writings. He needs either an account of voluntary action that does not require purely self-interested action, or an account of sovereignty that, in addition to emphasizing the requirements of office, gives latitude to the sovereign to indulge himself to any extent that does not incapacitate him for carrying out the duties of the sovereign. This would be a way of acknowledging that the sovereign by institution is a natural person before he becomes a representative person. However, there is no guarantee that the permission to indulge himself will ever be able to be taken advantage of. It is possible that someone who accepts sovereignty will be overwhelmed by the demands of office and find it unsafe to permit himself much of a life outside government and military command.

In a way this difficulty is useful for Hobbes, since it underlines the point that people who envy the sovereign, and wish for his power, misunderstand that the safe uses of that power are narrowly circumscribed. The sovereign's army is not a personal bodyguard; the wealth a sovereign has access to is unwisely used on private indulgence. It is probably better for someone who wants power and a reasonable discretion to use it as he likes to aim at being a relatively rich, private person, rather than the most powerful public person. Although the gift of sovereignty is a great gift, it can burden its recipient or make him vulnerable to the terrible revenge of those who are disappointed in a bargain for protection. These risks and others limit the sovereign's freedom. Appreciating the limits ought to make the prospect of kingship more fearful than exhilarating.

PART THREE

Biblical and Political Authority

The Covenant with God in Hobbes's Leviathan

EDWIN CURLEY

Hobbes's Christian critics attacked *Leviathan* both for affirming and for denying the possibility of a covenant between God and man. Filmer attacked Hobbes for affirming that possibility. Clarendon attacked him for denying it. And both writers did this in the name of the Christian religion.[1]

How can this be? Is Hobbes's text really so ambiguous as to permit a doubt about his position? How is it possible that two intelligent readers should have attributed diametrically opposed views to him? And how is it possible that both the supposed affirmation and the supposed denial should prove offensive to Christian readers? Is the Christian tradition so ambiguous on this point as to permit both views to be regarded as heretical? These are the questions I wish to address in this essay.

We may divide our subject into questions of fact and questions of right. *What in fact did Hobbes say* on this subject in *Leviathan*? Did what he said leave him open to radical misunderstanding? And *what ought he to have said*, in order not to offend Christian sensibilities? What ought a faithful Christian to think about the possibility of a covenant with God? Let us take the questions of fact first and turn to the texts to see what they say.

I

Prima facie, it would seem clear that Hobbes *is* committed to affirming the possibility of a covenant between God and man, not to denying it. Midway

I presented an earlier version of this essay at the University of Chicago in April 2001. I am indebted to the audience at that session for a number of helpful comments (and particularly to Richard Strier).

[1] For Filmer, see his *Observations on Mr. Hobbes's* Leviathan (London, 1652); for Clarendon, see his *A Brief View and Survey of the Dangerous and Pernicious Errors to Church and State in Mr. Hobbes's Book, Entitled Leviathan* (1676). Both of these works have recently been reprinted in *Leviathan: Contemporary Responses to the Political Theory of Thomas Hobbes*, ed. G. A. J. Rogers (Bristol: Thoemmes Press, 1995). In that edition the relevant passages may be found on pp. 12–14 and 210.

through *Leviathan* he speaks of God's having a 'twofold kingdom' (XXXI. 4).[2] One kingdom is natural; the other, prophetic. Earlier in *Leviathan* he had made the same distinction in slightly different terms: 'God is king of all the earth by his power'—this is God's natural kingdom, or kingdom by nature—'but of his chosen people he is king by covenant' (XII. 22). The latter is God's prophetic kingdom. Hobbes has extended discussions of God's kingdom by nature in *L* XXXI, and of God's kingdom by covenant in *L* XXXV and XL.[3] Given this, how could there be any doubt about Hobbes's commitment to the possibility of a covenant between God and man?

Nevertheless, Clarendon does accuse him of denying that possibility. The context is a discussion of Hobbes's doctrine that the power of the *human* sovereign is not based on a covenant between him and his subjects, but on a covenant of the subjects among themselves. Clarendon observes that if the right of the sovereign were based on a covenant, in which the subjects promised obedience and the sovereign promised to rule justly,

This had been a more natural and equitable institution, and more like to have lasted, having in it the true essential form of contracts, in which it will never be found that one party covenants, and the other not; which is the reason Mr. Hobbes himself gives, why no covenant can be made with God, and that . . .

Here Clarendon quotes from Hobbes:

the pretence of covenant with God is so evident a lie, even in the pretenders' own consciences, that it is not only an act of an unjust, but also of a vile and unmanly disposition.   (*L* XVIII. 3)

To this Clarendon replies that this assertion is 'destructive of our religion and against the express sense of Scripture'.

In a sense Clarendon is right to complain here. The idea of a covenant between God and man is central to both the Jewish and the Christian religions. The Hebrew Bible records numerous instances of covenants between God and man. Modern biblical scholars distinguish between two main types of covenant: what David Noel Freedman has called the covenant of divine commitment, best exemplified by the covenant with Abraham in Genesis 15, and what he calls the covenant of human obligation, best exemplified by the Mosaic covenant at Mt. Sinai in Exodus 19–24.[4] On Freedman's

---

[2] I cite the text of *Leviathan* by chapter and paragraph number, as given in my edition (Indianapolis: Hackett, 1994).

[3] These discussions parallel fairly closely the discussions of the Kingdom of God by nature in *De Cive* XV, and of the Kingdom of God by (the old) covenant in *De Cive* XVI. But *Leviathan* does not have anything comparable to *De Cive*'s discussion of the Kingdom of God by the new covenant in *De Cive* XVII. There is very little on our topic in *The Elements of Law*. For these works I use the editions of Warrender (2 vols., Oxford, 1983) and Tönnies (London: Frank Cass, 1969).

[4] See David Noel Freedman, 'Divine Commitment and Human Obligation: the Covenant Theme', *Interpretation* (October 1964), 419–31.

analysis, the principal difference between them is that in covenants of divine commitment, God takes upon himself certain obligations by making a unilateral and unconditional promise to his people,[5] a promise which remains in force until God fulfills its terms. In Genesis 15 this commitment is to give Abraham innumerable offspring and to give those descendants an extensive territory.[6] In covenants of human obligation, God also incurs an obligation to his people; but his obligation is conditional on their fulfilling their part of the covenant. His promise is conditional: *if* the people are obedient, they will be his 'treasured possession out of all the peoples'; the people promise unconditionally that they will do everything the Lord commands them to do. So there are mutual promises in the covenant of human obligation, and only a divine promise in the covenant of divine commitment.

In Christianity the very terms Christians use to designate the two major divisions of their Bible reflect the importance of this idea: the term 'testament' is to be interpreted via the notion of a covenant;[7] the 'Old Testament' is the history of the covenantal relationship God formerly had with the people he originally chose, the Jews. The 'New Testament' announces a new covenant between God and all men, a more universal covenant, 'not of letter, but of spirit' (2 Cor. 3:6). So if Hobbes had really denied the possibility of a covenant between God and man in the passage Clarendon quotes, he would have been striking at something quite fundamental both to Judaism and to the Christian religion.

But did he deny that possibility? If we consider the context of the quote, we may have some doubt about Clarendon's fairness as a controversialist. His quotation comes from a passage in *L* XVIII, where Hobbes is arguing that the covenant which institutes the commonwealth presupposes that the people who covenant are free to do so, that they are not bound by any prior covenant which would be inconsistent with the obligations they undertake in establishing the commonwealth. So they cannot allege a prior covenant as a ground for legitimate disobedience to the sovereign. Nor, Hobbes adds, can they allege a new covenant:

Whereas some men have pretended for their disobedience to their sovereign a new covenant, made (not with men, but) with God, this also is unjust; for there is no covenant with God but by mediation of somebody that representeth God's person, which none doth but God's lieutenant, who hath the sovereignty under God. But this pretence of covenant with God is so evident a lie, even in the pretenders' own consciences, that it is not only an act of an unjust, but also of a vile and unmanly disposition. (XVIII. 3)

---

[5] Or in the exceptional case of the Noachic covenant, to all mankind.

[6] 'From the river of Egypt to the great river, the river Euphrates.' Unless otherwise noted, quotations from Scripture come from *The New Oxford Annotated Bible*, ed. Bruce Metzger and Roland Murphy (Oxford: OUP, 1991), hereafter NOAB.   [7] See NOAB, NT iii.

Here Hobbes seems to deny only the possibility of *a certain kind of covenant* with God: no one can covenant with God *directly*; but people can covenant with God via a mediator, who in this case is the civil sovereign. So on the evidence of this passage we do not have an unqualified denial of the possibility of any covenant whatsoever between God and man.

Let's call the idea that covenants with God must involve a mediator *the mediation doctrine*. It is not obviously antithetical to Scripture. The covenant at Mt. Sinai involved Moses as a mediator, and the accounts of this covenant in Exodus and Deuteronomy suggest that it may have been necessary for him to act in that role. Exodus, for example, portrays the people as saying to Moses prior to the covenant: 'You speak to us and we will listen; but do not let God speak to us, or we will die' (20:19).[8]

On the other hand, not every biblical covenant involves a mediator. The various covenants God makes with Abraham in Genesis[9] are cases prima facie contrary to Hobbes's requirement. And sometimes Hobbes seems to acknowledge this, as when he writes:

at the making of this covenant God spake only to Abraham, and therefore contracted not with any of his family or seed, otherwise than as their wills (which make the essence of all covenants) were before the contract involved in the will of Abraham, who was therefore supposed to have had a lawful power to make them perform all that he covenanted for them.   (XL. 2)

So Hobbes's commitment to the mediation doctrine sometimes seems to waver.

Why, in the face of the biblical counterexamples, does Hobbes advance the mediation doctrine? The passage from which Clarendon quotes sheds no light on this question. Clarendon represents Hobbes as saying in that passage that a covenant with God would lack 'the true essential form of contracts', because it would not involve a mutual exchange of promises. But Hobbes did not say that. And in fact, when he discusses Freedman's paradigmatic covenant of human obligation, the covenant at Mt. Sinai, which does involve a mutual exchange of promises, he correctly represents it as involving, not only a divine promise, but also a promise on the part of the people to obey, and claims that this promise shows that God's kingdom by covenant is founded on the consent of the people of Israel. (*L* XXXV. 5). On the other hand, when he discusses Freedman's paradigmatic covenant of divine commitment, which involves only a unilateral promise, he misrepresents the scriptural situation, assimilating that covenant to a covenant of human obligation by attributing to Abraham a promise of obedience which appears nowhere in the text (*L* XXXV. 4).

---

[8] Similarly, in Deuteronomy Moses, remembering the covenant, says to the people: 'The Lord spoke with you face to face at the mountain, out of the fire. At that time I was standing between the Lord and you, to declare to you the words of the Lord; for you were afraid because of the fire and did not go up the mountain' (Deut. 5:4–5).   [9] e.g. at 12:1–3; 15: 1–16; 17:1–22.

Why does Hobbes think it evident that if anyone claims to have made a covenant with God without the mediation of his sovereign, he is lying? Why is this *so* evident that even the person who makes the claim must recognize it as a lie? I don't know. But I can observe that the mediation doctrine which appears in XVIII. 3 is a variant of an earlier version of that doctrine which Hobbes had articulated in *L* XIV. There he wrote:

To make covenant with God is impossible, but by mediation of such as God speaketh to (either by revelation supernatural or by his lieutenants that govern under him and in his name); for otherwise we know not whether our covenants be accepted or not. (XIV. 23)

This earlier passage is interesting in at least two ways: first, it has a less restrictive set of conditions under which someone may qualify as a mediator; not only the civil sovereign may fulfill this role; so may anyone who has had a direct revelation from God, such as a prophet;[10] second, it does give a reason why a mediator is necessary; without a mediator we cannot know whether or not our covenant is accepted.

But this reason is rather puzzling. It doesn't square with those biblical texts which support the need for a mediator; they suggest that (ordinary) humans cannot be in the presence of God and survive the experience.[11] Hobbes suggests rather that we have an epistemological problem in dealing with God directly: we cannot know whether or not God has accepted our covenant unless a mediator has informed us of his acceptance.[12]

This is a curious doctrine, which goes back to Hobbes' earliest discussion of covenants with God in *The Elements of Law*. There Hobbes had argued that it was an essential feature of all covenants, and indeed, of transfers of right generally, that

It is impossible to make a covenant or donation to any that by nature, or absence, are unable, or if able, do not actually declare their acceptation of the same. First

[10] The narrowing of the conditions for qualifying as a mediator in *L* XVIII is curious. One explanation suggested at the discussion of this essay in Chicago was that in *L* XVIII Hobbes is talking only about covenants at the present time; since it was standard Protestant doctrine in Hobbes's day that miracles have ceased, and since miracles are a necessary criterion for qualifying as a prophet, Hobbes may have thought that the possibility of mediation by a prophet was a thing of the past.

[11] The qualification about *ordinary* humans is implicit in the biblical narrative. We must understand some such qualification, if mediation is to work: the mediator must be able to survive the experience of communicating directly with God. According to Exodus 19:7–25 Moses alone enjoys this privilege; if the people or the priests were to go up the mountain to look upon the Lord, they would perish.

[12] I note here one puzzle about this doctrine which I will not attempt to deal with now. The doctrine that we need a mediator to be sure that our covenant has been accepted makes sense only if we suppose that man, not God, initiates the covenant. This is not the biblical situation. As Freedman points out, both in covenants of divine commitment and in covenants of human obligation, God, as the superior party, takes the initiative in making the covenant. Hobbes may be thinking, not of any biblical covenants, but of the various Scottish covenants which Martinich describes in *The Two Gods of* **Leviathan** (Cambridge: CUP, 1992), 143–6.

of all, therefore, it is impossible for any man to make a covenant with God
Almighty, farther than it hath pleased him to declare who shall receive and accept
of the same covenant in his name. Also it is impossible to make covenant with
those living creatures of whose wills we have no sufficient sign, for want of common language. (I. XV. 11)

I observe that the chapter summary at the head of this chapter represents
this section as maintaining that there can be no covenant of men except
with other men. If that were what the passage says, Clarendon would be
vindicated. But the chapter summary seems to be at variance with the section it summarizes. The text disallows the possibility of any covenant
between men and non-human animals, on the ground that there can be no
communication between the parties. But it allows the possibility of a
covenant between God and man *provided* that God has designated someone to accept the covenant in his name. We are still left with a puzzle,
though: if God can solve our epistemological difficulty by declaring that
someone is authorized to accept our covenant in his name, why can he not
solve it more simply, by just declaring his acceptance?

Hobbes does not explain how having a mediator helps us out of this epistemological difficulty. If *we* cannot know, without a mediator, whether our
covenant has been accepted, how can *the mediator* know? If the mediator
himself required a mediator, we would generate an infinite regress. But if
the mediator can know, without his own mediator, why can we not know
without a mediator? In the case of the covenant at Mt. Sinai, the answer
might plausibly be that the mediator, Moses, had a unique relationship with
God. When Miriam and Aaron challenged Moses' authority at Hazeroth,
proclaiming that God spoke to them too, the Lord came down in a pillar of
cloud, called Aaron and Miriam to him, and said:

> When there are prophets among you,
> I the Lord make myself known to them in visions,
> I speak to them in dreams.
> Not so with my servant Moses;
> He is entrusted with all my house.
> With him I speak face to face – clearly, not in riddles;
> And he beholds the form of the Lord.
>
> (Numbers 12:6–8)

So even among the prophets, Moses enjoys a special position. God commu-
nicates with him much more clearly than he does with other prophets, and
in a way which leaves no doubt that it is God he is speaking with.[13] But if
we emphasize that Moses had a uniquely close relation to God, then it may

---

[13] Elsewhere, however, it is suggested that even Moses cannot see God's face and live, though
he can see God's back (Exodus 33:17–23).

be awkward to explain why Hobbes allows the civil sovereign to play the role of mediator.

Even if there is a good solution to that problem, we have a further question: how can ordinary humans *know* that the mediator has been communicating with God when they can't themselves know that *they* have been communicating with God? So far as I can see, Hobbes's answer to this further question is: they can't. In his discussion of divine positive law, those commandments which are given not to all men, but only to some, Hobbes asks how we can know that the person whom God has authorized to declare these positive laws (Moses, say) can be known:

God may command a man by a supernatural way to deliver laws to other men. But because it is of the essence of law that he who is to be obliged be assured of the authority of him that declareth it, which we cannot naturally take notice to be from God, *how can a man without supernatural revelation be assured of the revelation received by the declarer?*

His answer is that it is 'evidently impossible' for one man to be sure of another's revelation without his own special revelation.

For though a man may be induced to believe such revelation from the miracles they see him do, or from seeing the extraordinary sanctity of his life, or from seeing the extraordinary wisdom, or extraordinary felicity of his actions, all which are marks of God's extraordinary favour, yet they are not assured evidences of special revelation. Miracles are marvellous works, but that which is marvellous to one may not be so to another. Sanctity may be feigned; and the visible felicities of this world are most often the work of God by natural and ordinary causes. And therefore, no man can infallibly know by natural reason that another has had a supernatural revelation of God's will, but only a belief (every one, as the signs thereof shall appear greater or lesser, a firmer or a weaker belief). (*L* XXVI. 40)

So, according to this passage, all of the signs you might rely on to determine whether or not someone else has had a divine revelation are unreliable. Ergo, you have to have a special revelation from God to know that someone who purports to bring you laws from God is what he claims to be.

But the rationale for the mediation doctrine was that ordinary humans need a mediator because without one they cannot be sure that their covenant has been accepted. Direct communication with God is too uncertain. But it's precisely direct communication with God which is required to be sure that the mediator has been in communication with God. The uncertainty which makes the mediation doctrine necessary also makes it impossible for the mediator to give us the assurance he is supposed to give us.[14]

---

[14] This is also, I believe, the message of *L* XXXII. 5–6. I note in passing that in *De Cive* XVI, which does not seem to have the mediation doctrine, Hobbes discusses the various appearances of God to Abraham, and concludes that it was a matter of faith, not of reason, that Abraham believed that the voice and promises he heard were the voice and promises of God.

I conclude from this that Clarendon may be right in the end, even though he seems at first to misrepresent Hobbes's position. Although Hobbes may not explicitly deny the possibility of a covenant between God and man,[15] his insistence that the covenantal relationship be mediated does, if followed to its logical conclusion, lead to that denial, when combined with Hobbes's skepticism about our being able to know that a particular revelation has occurred.

II

Let us turn now from these epistemological worries about covenants with God to Filmer, whose concerns arise more from what we might call the metaphysics of morals. Filmer does not question that Hobbes *is* committed to the existence of a covenant between God and man. But he does question whether Hobbes *should be* committed to the existence of such a covenant, both given the biblical record and given Hobbes's own philosophical theology.

The first point Filmer attacks is Hobbes's claim that Scripture most commonly uses the phrase 'the kingdom of God' to signify:

a kingdom properly so named, constituted by the votes of the people of Israel in peculiar manner, wherein they chose God for their king by covenant made with him, upon God's promising them the possession of the land of Canaan.   (L XXXV. 2)

Filmer contends that if we look at the scriptural text Hobbes relies on for this claim,[16]

it will be found that the people did not constitute by votes, and choose God for their king; but by the appointment first of God himself the covenant was to be a God to them: they did not contract with God, that if he should give them Canaan, they would be his subjects, and he should be their king . . .   (Filmer, p. 12)

This round, I think, goes to Hobbes on points. It's true that in the passage in question it is God who takes the initiative, offering to bestow blessings on the people of Israel if they obey his voice and keep his covenant. Moreover, the people do not respond to this offer by taking anything like what we would think of as a vote. There is no slate of opposing candidates and no counting of the votes. It's worse than Florida in the last American presidential election. But Moses, as mediator, does lay God's offer before the people: 'If you obey my voice and keep my covenant, you shall be my treasured possession out of all the peoples.' This is a reaffirmation of the original

---

[15] I put this somewhat cautiously because I am uncertain how much weight to put on the chapter summary of *The Elements of Law* I. xv. 11.

[16] i.e. (or so I believe) Exodus 19:3–8. Hobbes does claim, in XXXV. 2, that the explanation he gives of 'the kingdom of God' articulates the sense in which the phrase is most commonly used in Scripture. But so far as I can see, the strongest passage in support of this claim is that one passage in Exodus 19.

promise made to Abraham, though with the difference that now the promise is conditional on the people's obedience.[17] And if the people do not exactly *vote*, they do nevertheless express their will: 'The people all answered as one: "Everything that the Lord has spoken we will do." ' (Exodus 19:8). This *is* a promise of obedience, made in return for a conditional promise of great rewards. We have an offer and an acceptance. The essential elements of a contract seem to be present. If it's an exaggeration to describe this situation as the people choosing God to be their king, it does not seem too much to describe it as the people entering into a covenant with God.

The second round, however, and the bout, I think, go to Filmer on a technical knockout. The passage I quoted above continues as follows:

> It was not in their power to choose whether God should be their God, yea, or nay: for it is confessed He reigned naturally over all by his might.

This is an apt invocation of Hobbes's doctrine of the kingdom of God by nature, according to which God has a natural right to man's obedience in virtue of his omnipotence (XXXI. 5). Filmer proceeds to drive the point home:

> If God reigned naturally, He had a kingdom, and sovereign power over his subjects, not acquired by their own consent . . . If a contract be the mutual transferring of right, I would know what right a people can have to transfer to God by contract. Had the people of Israel at Mount Sinai a right not to obey God's voice? If they had not such a right, what had they to transfer?

This seems to me a very acute line of questioning. Let me amplify the thought, to make it crystal clear.

What is a covenant, in Hobbes's philosophy? It is a special kind of contract, in which one person performs his part of the contract at one time and trusts the other to perform later. (*L* XIV. 11) And what is a contract? It's a mutual transfer of right (*L* XIV. 9), in which one party delivers up *his* right to something (say, a piece of land) in return for the other party's delivering up *her* right to something else (say, a sum of money).

Can there be a mutual transfer of rights between God and man in Hobbes's philosophy? I do not see how, so long as Hobbes adheres to the theory of God's sovereignty which he advances in *L* XXXI. For according to that theory, God has a right to all things in virtue of his omnipotence:

> The right of nature whereby God reigneth over men, and punisheth those that break his laws, is to be derived, not from his creating them (as if he required obedience, as

---

[17] See Genesis 15, where God simply and unconditionally promises numerous offspring and possession of a large territory. The alternative version of this covenant in Genesis 17 is not, it seems to me, a pure example of a covenant of divine commitment. Though the promise is not explicitly conditional, God clearly has expectations of Abraham and his descendants, since he goes on to command that Abraham and all the males in his household be circumcised. We might regard the promise as tacitly conditional on obedience to the accompanying command. Although there is also no explicit acceptance of the offer in Genesis 17, we might regard Abraham's immediate obedience to the command as tacit acceptance.

of gratitude for his benefits), but from his *irresistible power* . . . To those . . . whose power is irresistible, the dominion of all men adhereth naturally, by their excellence of power; and consequently, it is from that power that the kingdom over men, and the right of afflicting men at his pleasure, belongeth naturally to God Almighty, not as Creator and gracious, but as omnipotent. (XXXI. 5)

If God has an absolute right of dominion over all men, stemming from his omnipotence, I do not see what rights he might still have to acquire by entering into a covenant with man. What could he have *after* the contract which he did not have before? This consideration excludes the possibility of a covenant of human obligation, involving mutual promises between God and man. This is the other side of Filmer's line of questioning, looking at the contract from the divine side rather than the human.

Similar considerations exclude the possibility of a covenant of divine commitment, with its unilateral divine promise. If God's omnipotence *entails* that he has those rights, and if his omnipotence is an essential property he has, which he cannot lose without ceasing to be God, then God cannot cease to have those rights. What could he have had *before* the contract which he does not retain afterward? If it's a necessary property of God that he has an absolute right to all things, he can neither gain nor lose rights by contract. The contract model implies that God's rights over man are contingent on man's agreement to obey him, that God acquires new rights over man, in exchange for others which he surrenders in the contract. But the model of God's absolute sovereignty implies that God's rights are not contingent on anything man does or can do. If God's rights follow from his omnipotence, then they cannot come and go depending on what man does.

Moreover, it seems that we could generalize this result. In a certain sense, it doesn't matter that the particular divine attribute Hobbes appeals to, in explaining God's sovereignty, is his omnipotence. Suppose God's sovereignty was a consequence of some other essential property he has (say, supreme perfection). So long as this property entails that God has an absolute right over all things, and so long as it is a property God cannot lose, then God will have nothing to acquire by entering into a contract, and nothing he could surrender in exchange for newly acquired rights.

Now, it might be objected that the alternative theory of God's sovereignty which Hobbes considers in XXXI. 5, is that God's sovereignty is based on his being our creator. It may be said that being our creator, unlike being omnipotent, or being supremely perfect, is not an essential property of God. If we assume that the creation was an event occurring at some point in past time, prior to which only God existed, then there was a time when God was not our creator. He has that property now, according to the dominant view in Christian philosophical theology, because he freely chose to bring into existence a world of finite beings. So it's a contingent fact about God that he is our creator. If his rights follow from a contingent property, then prima facie he could lose them through a promise.

This may not be a tenable view of the creation, from a Christian point of view. Leibniz may be right that, for a morally perfect being, not creating beings other than himself is not an option. But to pursue that line of argument here would take us too far afield. And for present purposes, it doesn't seem to matter. If we think, as most theologians have, that even the power of God cannot alter the past, then we have a different version of the same problem—even if we take God's absolute right over his creation to follow from the contingent fact that he created us. If it follows from God's having created us that he has a right over us which is not conditional on our consent, and if the fact of his having created us, once it has become a fact, cannot be altered, then God will have no right which he could surrender for the sake of entering into a contract with us.

So it looks to me as though there are going to be difficulties in any philosophical theology which holds that God has an absolute, unconditional right to our obedience, even if that theology differs from Hobbes's in the explanation it offers of this right. Whether the divine attribute which grounds the right is omnipotence or something else, even some contingent property of God's, it will be difficult to understand how God could enter into a contract with his creatures.

Now in some ways this is a welcome result. For the God of the Hebrew Bible was issuing commands, and punishing people for disobeying them, long before he entered into any covenants with man. The first biblical covenant is with Noah, in Genesis 9, many generations after the crimes and punishments of Adam, Eve, and Cain. And that covenant, like the other covenants in Genesis, is a covenant of divine commitment. We do not get a covenant of human obligation until the Mosaic covenant in Exodus. So it would be awkward if God's right to obedience depended on a covenant of human obligation. On the other hand, if God's right to obedience does not depend on covenant, what is the point of making covenants? What right can a promise of obedience give God which he did not already have?

III

Hobbes addresses this problem, though with what seems to me indifferent success. In *Leviathan* he first confronts it[18] in a passage in the chapter 'Of

---

[18] Hobbes had raised the issue earlier, in De Cive XVI. 4–5, where the problem is, not that God's kingdom by nature is incompatible with a kingdom by covenant, but that it makes the kingdom by covenant superfluous, and the 'solution' seems to be that Abraham acquired no new obligations in his covenant, because the only commandment given to him in connection with it

religion', writing that where God has introduced religion by a supernatural revelation,

there he also made to himself a peculiar kingdom and gave laws, not only of behavior towards himself, but also towards one another; and thereby in the kingdom of God, the policy and civil laws are part of religion; and therefore the distinction of temporal and spiritual domination hath there no place. It is true that God is king over all the earth; yet may he be king of a peculiar and chosen nation. For there is no more incongruity therein than that he that hath the general command of the whole army should have withal a peculiar regiment or company of his own. God is king of all the earth by his power; but of his chosen people he is king by covenant . . . (*L* XII. 22)

Can Hobbes seriously think that there is no incongruity, i.e., no contradiction, between God's being king over all the earth by nature and his being king over a particular people by covenant? Or is this an ironic passage, one in which we may reasonably suspect that Hobbes's implicit doctrine is in conflict with his explicit doctrine?

Consider the analogy Hobbes offers us, in his effort to show us that there is no contradiction between God's being king over all by nature and his being king over a particular people by covenant. Certainly a general may be the commander of a whole army and at the same time have a special relationship with a particular regiment, which he commands more directly than he commands other regiments, whose day-to-day command he delegates to subordinate officers. But is the general's special relationship to that particular regiment contingent on their consenting to it? Hardly. If the general has command over the whole army, and wishes to enter into a special relationship with one particular regiment, he may choose the regiment at his own discretion. They will be obliged to obey him regardless of their wishes. Their consent is not necessary. The analogy Hobbes uses, in an apparent attempt to persuade us that there is no contradiction, breaks down at precisely the point where it needs to hold firm.

Hobbes returns to the problem in *L* XL, where he begins by describing Abraham as 'first in the kingdom by covenant'. Abraham, he says, was the first to oblige himself,

and his seed after him, to acknowledge and obey the commands of God—not only such as he could take notice of, as moral laws, by the light of nature, but also such as God should in special manner deliver to him by dreams and visions. For as to the moral law, they were already obliged, and needed not have been contracted

was the commandment of circumcision and this was part of the covenant itself, the sign of Abraham's having accepted it. (Hobbes is thinking, not of the covenant in Genesis 15, but of the alternative version of that covenant in Genesis 17.) What God contracted for was not obedience, but recognition that the being whose voice and promises Abraham had heard in his visions and dreams was God. The discussion is muddied by Hobbes's tendency to assimilate covenants of divine commitment to covenants of human obligation.

withal, by promise of the land of Canaan. Nor was there any contract that could add to or strengthen the obligation by which both they and all men else were bound naturally to obey God Almighty.[19] And therefore, the covenant which Abraham made with God was to take for the commandment of God that which in the name of God was commanded him in a dream or vision, and to deliver it to his family, and cause them to observe the same.   (XL. 1)

This is peculiar. First, it's a conspicuous feature of the Abramic covenant that Abraham makes no explicit promises to God in any of the versions of the covenant (Gen. 12, Gen. 15, or Gen. 17). This makes it rather hard to say what, if anything, Abraham has committed himself to. Hobbes treats the Abramic covenant as if it were a covenant of human obligation rather than a covenant of divine commitment. Second, Hobbes concedes here, as explicitly as we might wish, that in a covenant of human obligation, like the one at Mt. Sinai, where the people do promise to obey God, their promise adds nothing to their natural obligation. So he construes their promise as committing them only to use certain procedures for determining what the will of God is, as a promise to treat certain kinds of evidence as evidence of God's will. I can find no scriptural basis for this odd interpretation. Finally, in the Latin *Leviathan* Hobbes omits the sentence which says most clearly that the people's promise of obedience does not add to their natural obligation. All in all, Hobbes's treatment of this issue amounts to a confession that it is not possible to reconcile God's kingdom by nature with his kingdom by covenant.

Now it may be suggested[20] that the covenant at Mt. Sinai at least does add to human obligations by committing the people of Israel to various practices which are not part of natural law and are not binding on all men: e.g., to keep the seventh day as the sabbath, to make an altar of earth for God, to sacrifice sheep and oxen on it, as burnt offerings, to free male Hebrew slaves after six years of service, not to permit female sorcerers to live, etc. And it's certainly true that most of the commandments the Israelites received at Mt. Sinai are not part of natural law. The problem with this way out, I think, is not that *some* of the commandments *are* part of natural law—though that's surely true—but that what the people promise to do is simply to obey God, to do whatever he commands. And that *ought to be* an obligation they had prior to entering into the covenant, not one which was created by their promise.

The upshot of all this, I think, is that in the two passages in *Leviathan* in which Hobbes explicitly takes account of the problem of reconciling the

---

[19] In *Opera Latina* the sentences underlined are replaced by: 'For he was already bound by natural laws, so that there was no need to covenant concerning them.'

[20] Martha Nussbaum made this suggestion in the discussion of an earlier draft of this essay at the University of Chicago.

kingdom of God by nature with the kingdom of God by covenant, he shows no signs of having a solution to that problem. And the inadequacy of his attempts to do so seems rather transparent.

IV

Let's take stock now. At the beginning of this essay I asked the following questions: is Hobbes's text really so ambiguous as to permit a doubt about his position regarding the possibility of a covenant between God and man? How is it possible that two intelligent readers should have attributed diametrically opposed views to him? I hope my answer to these questions will be clear: Hobbes's readers attribute those opposed views to him because his text really is quite ambiguous. His formal position is clear enough: that it is possible for there to be a covenant between God and man, and that there have in fact been such covenants. But he attaches odd conditions to this possibility, conditions which make it inoperable: we can covenant with God only through a mediator; but we cannot really be obliged by this covenant if we cannot be assured of the mediator's authority to deliver God's word to us; and we cannot really be assured of the mediator's authority.

Moreover, it is deeply problematic that there should be any covenant between God and man, understanding a covenant as a mutual transfer of rights, given the absolute sovereignty Hobbes attributes to God when he analyses his kingdom by nature. We do not see how Hobbes could maintain the possibility of such a covenant and at the same time hold that in virtue of his nature God has absolute sovereignty over his human creatures.

Let's turn now to the next question I asked: how is it possible that both affirming and denying the possibility of a covenant between God and man should prove offensive to Christian readers? One answer might be that Filmer has a political motive for criticizing Hobbes's affirmation of the covenant between God and man. He favors the absolute sovereignty of human kings, and is uncomfortable with any theological doctrine which might deny him a divine model for that sovereignty.[21] Analogously, we

---

[21] For Filmer the covenant at Mt. Sinai is an awkward fact, which must be explained away. He says: 'The covenant mentioned at Mt. Sinai was but a conditional contract, and God but a conditional King, and though the people promised to obey God's word, yet it was more than they were able to perform, for they often disobeyed God's voice, which being a breach of the condition, the covenant was void, and God not their King by contract' (see *Leviathan: Contemporary Responses*, ed. Rogers, 12) This seems to imply that God was the people's king by contract just so long as they obeyed him and he lived up to his part of the bargain. But if absolute sovereignty is incompatible with kingship by covenant, it does not matter how long the kingship by covenant lasts. And it's a strange contract which one of the parties can void simply by failing to comply with the terms of the contract. Filmer may think that this is acceptable, because God is always king by nature, before, during, and after the period of the covenant's validity. But that just illustrates the

might say, Clarendon favors a constitutional monarchy, and therefore is anxious to retain the theological doctrine of a covenant between God and man as a model of the proper relations between human sovereigns and their subjects. But explaining the theological positions of these critics by appeal to their political preferences does not go deeply enough into the issue. Why is the Christian tradition they share so open to this kind of political use?

We already have the beginnings of our answer to this question. Denying the possibility of a covenant is troublesome because historically Christianity has been strongly committed to the broad accuracy of the biblical narrative, with its stories of frequent *actual* covenants which were central to the relationship between God and man. Christianity is as committed as Judaism is to the idea that *originally at least* the Jews were God's chosen people, and that God's special relationship to the Jews was formalized in a series of covenants. But affirming the possibility of a covenant is also troublesome because, when we spell out the implications of this possibility in the way that Hobbes does, it appears that the covenant gives God a moral authority over his human creatures which is merely contingent, and indeed, contingent on man's acceptance of that authority. This is hard to square with the fact that the Bible frequently portrays God as issuing commands which are independent of any covenant. And it seems to diminish God's authority. Why should the ruler of the universe need man's consent to issue prohibitions on murder, theft, and adultery?

What I am suggesting, then, is that the tension in Hobbes's philosophy between the kingdom of God by nature and the kingdom of God by covenant reflects a tension within the Christian tradition between absolutist and covenantal conceptions of God's authority. ('Tension' is the polite word for it. It is the word we use when we do not wish to be so rude as to accuse a thinker or a tradition of being self-contradictory.) We can see the tension in the biblical tradition portrayed quite forcefully in the book of Job. Job was an upright and perfect man, who prospered until one day the Satan[22] persuaded God to test Job's faith, to make sure that Job was not obeying God for the sake of the rewards he received, but out of a true loyalty to God. So God gave the Satan permission to inflict horrible sufferings on Job. When Job's wife told him to 'curse God and die', Job maintained an attitude of unconditional loyalty: 'The Lord giveth and the Lord taketh away; blessed be the name of the Lord.' But then his 'friends' appeared on the

---

problem: if God's sovereignty is absolute, a logical consequence of his nature, there is no room for a covenant.

[22] The Hebrew, *ha-satan*, has a direct article. So, as Marvin Pope observes, 'the term is a title, and not yet a proper name.' (*Job*, ed. and tr. Marvin Pope (Garden City, NY: Doubleday/Anchor, 1985), 9). The Satan of this work is not the Satan of later Christian tradition, not an enemy of God, a fallen angel, but a member in good standing of God's heavenly court, whose role is to assist God by bringing him intelligence of what is happening on earth.

scene: 'God is just. He would not permit these terrible things to happen to you unless you deserved them. So however innocent you may appear to be, however innocent you may think you are, you must have done something to deserve what is happening to you.' These 'friends' are sometimes called Job's 'comforters'. Some comfort. Job then begins to insist on his innocence, and in response to the provocation of the comforters, demands a hearing before God, in which his fault should be made clear to him.

In this dialogue the comforters represent the covenantal strand in biblical thought: God is just; being just, he is bound by his promises to reward and punish people in proportion to their obedience to his commands. If God causes or permits us to suffer, there must be a reason, and it must somehow be our fault. In the beginning Job's attitude is quite different. He accepts the suffering he receives without questioning God's justice or his own loyalty to God. This represents the absolutist strand in biblical thought. In his dialogue with the comforters Job comes, in some measure, to take their point of view. He does not concede that he has done wrong, or that there is a general correlation between virtue and reward. But he begins to feel that his suffering is not merely *suffering*, but given his innocence, *unjust suffering*. And he demands that God tell him what he has done wrong, that God justify his treatment of him. Job does hear from God, near the end of the work. But it cannot be said that he receives an *answer* from him. Instead, God responds to Job's question with a series of questions of his own: 'Who is this that darkens counsel by words without knowledge? . . . Where were you when I laid the foundation of the earth? . . . Have you commanded the morning since your days began; and caused the dawn to know its place? . . . Do you know when the mountain goats give birth? Do you observe the calving of the deer?' And why shouldn't God answer a question with a question? The point of this remarkable discourse, I think, is that this God does not need to answer to anyone. That's what Job learns when God speaks to him out of the whirlwind.

I suggest that Hobbes shows his awareness of this tension by weaving a discussion of the book of Job into his explanation of God's kingdom by nature. In *L* XXXI, immediately after the passage I quoted earlier, in which Hobbes had argued that God's absolute sovereignty is based on his omnipotence, Hobbes connects this claim with the problem of evil:

This question, *Why evil men often prosper, and good men suffer adversity*, has been much disputed by the ancient, and is the same with this of ours, *By what right God dispenseth the prosperities and adversities of this life*; and is of that difficulty as it hath shaken the faith, not only of the vulgar, but of philosophers, and which is more, of the Saints, concerning the Divine Providence . . . *Job*, how earnestly does he expostulate with God, for the many afflictions he suffered, notwithstanding his righteousness?

This question, in the case of *Job*, is decided by God himself, not by arguments derived from *Job's* sin, but his own power. For whereas the friends of *Job* drew their arguments from his affliction to his sin, and he defended himself by the conscience of his innocence, God himself taketh up the matter, and having justified the affliction by arguments drawn from his power, such as this, *Where wast thou, when I laid the foundations of the earth* (*Job* 38:4), and the like, both approved *Job's* innocence, and reproved the erroneous doctrine of his friends [*Job* 42:7] . . .

I do not agree with every detail of Hobbes's analysis of the book of Job. God does not argue only from his power that he has a right to afflict Job, no matter what Job has done. Many of the rhetorical questions concern the differences of knowledge between God and Job, not merely differences of power. But Hobbes is deadly accurate when he points out that at the end of Job God rejects the doctrine of the comforters. He says to them: 'You have not spoken of me what is right, as my servant Job has.' In rebuking the comforters, God is rejecting the covenant theology they espoused and endorsing Job's return to an attitude of total submission to God.

So the conflict in Hobbes's philosophy between the kingdom of God by nature and the kingdom of God by covenant mirrors a conflict in the religious tradition between God's absolute sovereignty and his entrance into covenants with the people of Israel. And Hobbes seems to have been aware of this conflict in the tradition. Could he have intended to bring his readers to that awareness? Could his elaborate and puzzling discussion of the covenant with God be a subtle way of making that point?

It's tempting to answer these questions with a question: why not? But that would be to usurp the prerogative of God. Let me close by trying to offer a more positive reason for saying 'yes' to these last questions. It's a central doctrine in Hobbes's political philosophy that the civil sovereign cannot be a party to the social contract without compromising his sovereignty. If we viewed the social contract as an agreement between the people and their sovereign, in which the sovereign's right to rule depended on his living up to his part of the bargain by ruling justly, who would adjudicate disputes between the sovereign and the people over his performance? The sovereign's function is to be the ultimate arbiter of disputes. Hobbes sees clearly, in the civil case, that sovereignty is incompatible with basing the sovereign's right to rule on a contract between the sovereign and his people. I cannot believe that he failed to see the same thing in the religious case. Moreover, the disparity between the human sovereign's authority over his subjects and God's authority over his creatures is sufficiently obvious, once you think about it, that Hobbes might, quite reasonably, have expected some of his readers to notice it. Filmer in fact did notice it, and complained that Hobbes was being inconsistent, both with sensible religious doctrine and with his own philosophy, in allowing the possibility of a covenant between God and man. And Clarendon in his way noticed it, when he accused Hobbes of denying the possibility of such a covenant. Clarendon did not see clearly why Hobbes could not allow a covenant between God and man. But his instincts were right. No such covenant is possible in Hobbes's philosophy. It is only, I think, an attachment to textual literalism, and a reluctance to probe beneath the surface, which has prevented Hobbes's other readers from seeing this.

APPENDIX[23]

In the final sentence of the essay I was thinking particularly of Martinich, who (so far as I am aware) is the only recent writer on Hobbes to pay any attention to this issue. Martinich is aware that there is a problem here, but he doesn't seem to grasp the problem in its full generality.[24] He sees that it would be incompatible with God's sovereignty for him to incur obligations to his people. But he thinks that this is a problem only in Hobbes, and not in the biblical tradition. And he does not see that there is any problem about humans having rights which they could transfer to God.

According to Martinich, Hobbes could have made his view consistent if he had had at his disposal the fruits of modern biblical scholarship, and deployed the distinction between parity covenants and suzerainty covenants. Following Ernest Nicholson,[25] Martinich identifies parity covenants as ones in which equal parties incur mutual obligations to one another. In suzerainty covenants the parties are unequal; the inferior party incurs obligations to the superior party, but the superior party does not incur any obligations to the inferior party; he merely expresses an intention to perform some action for the benefit of the inferior party. Martinich identifies the Abramic covenant of Genesis 15 as a parity covenant, and the Abramic covenant of Genesis 17 as a suzerainty covenant.

There are a number of problems with this proposed solution: (1) it will not work if it is admitted that any of the biblical covenants are parity covenants, since those are conceded to involve mutual obligations; (2) it will not work if suzerainty covenants are wrongly characterized when it is said that they do not involve obligations on the part of the superior party; and (3) it does not deal with Filmer's question: how, consistently with God's sovereignty, can human obligations to obey God be contingent on their promising to do so? I might add that the selection of Genesis 15 as an example of a parity covenant and the neglect of the covenant at Mt. Sinai are deeply puzzling.

---

[23] The material in this appendix was not read at the conference, but constituted a footnote to the copy of the essay I gave to Prof. Martinich at the conference.

[24] Cf. *Two Gods*, 181–2 and 291–4.   [25] *God and His People*, Oxford: OUP, 1986

The Interpretation of Covenants in
Leviathan

A. P. MARTINICH

———◆———

Theist interpreters of Hobbes, that is, those who think that Hobbes was a theist, and nontheist interpreters, that is, those who think he was not, agree on at least this, that the most conspicuous difference between *Leviathan* and his other two treatises on political theory is the extensive treatment of religion. While it may appear that they agree about little else, that is not true. They agree about an infinite number of things, to use 'infinite' as Hobbes does (3.12).[1] They agree that Hobbes was born in 1588 and attended Magdalen Hall, that he wrote *Leviathan* and many other works, . . . that he was a materialist and determinist, . . . that he engaged in disputes with John Bramhall and John Wallis, among others. The dots of ellipsis indicate that the specification of beliefs common to theist and nontheist interpreters could go on indefinitely. This is not an idle remark. We could, if we needed to, state for virtually every sentence in each of Hobbes's published books or those in Molesworth's edition of Hobbes's works that the sentence is one that Hobbes authored. We would also agree about the meaning of almost all of the sentences, even though for some sentences we would disagree about what Hobbes meant by them.

I am emphasizing the amount of agreement initially so that we do not in the end exaggerate the difference between my theist interpretation of Hobbes's treatment of divine covenants and many nontheist ones. In sections, I and II, I discuss the nature of interpretation because I think the chances of agreement or disinterested evaluation of the competing views will be increased if the nature and standards of interpretation are made explicit. In sections III–V, I criticize Edwin Curley's nontheist interpretation of Hobbes's doctrine of covenants.

I. INTERPRETATION AND NETWORKS OF BELIEF

Seeing that the disagreements between theist and nontheist interpreters are built upon a broad base of shared beliefs may lead one to wonder what the

---

[1] References to *Leviathan* within the text will be to chapter and paragraph, and quoted from Edwin Curley's edition (Indianapolis: Hackett, 1994).

prospect is for something close to full agreement. My guess is that it is infinitesimally small. The reason has to do with the nature of interpretation. Every interpreter comes to a text with a large and complex Network of Beliefs about the world, built from her own particular experiences.[2] The subnetwork of beliefs that relate to Hobbes's life and philosophy is at most a tiny portion of anyone's Network. Also, even though those subnetworks are very similar, the interpretation of a text is influenced by principles that may be deployed at different times in different ways. But I want to say more about the Network before going on to talk about the principles of interpretation.

The Network has several properties.[3] It seems to be a unity; that is, each belief is or can be related to every other belief. Trivially, they can all be related by conjoining beliefs of the Network. More importantly, many beliefs are logically related to other beliefs. One belief, say 'Most people are self-interested', entails others, say 'Some people are self-interested'. And some beliefs lend plausibility to other beliefs even if the former do not entail the latter. Second, some beliefs are held more tenaciously or strongly than others. Some are virtually unassailable: the world is very old and most people have lived most of their lives on or very near the surface of the earth. Third, the Network is gappy. Notwithstanding the great number of our beliefs, it is (almost) always possible to add additional beliefs that in effect would fill in gaps. For example, the belief that Jones shot Smith has gaps that could be filled in various ways. To take only three dimensions, the shooting could have been done (*a*) maliciously/accidentally, (*b*) with a pistol/rifle, (*c*) on Sunday/Monday. Fourth, beliefs are added and subtracted in groups rather than individually. A person who comes to believe that Lee has just been divorced also adds at the same time such beliefs as, that Lee has been unhappy, has hired a lawyer, needs some comforting, and so on. Not all of these beliefs may be explicit but they must be at least implicit.[4] Similarly, when beliefs are deleted, they are subtracted in clusters.

The process of textual interpretation begins when the Network is in effect disturbed by a text. People operate with something like a Principle of Maximum Intelligibility: if something can be understood to have a meaning, it will be understood to have a meaning. The process ends with respect to that text when the Network has been revised in a way that aims at being true.[5] The process of textual interpretation is just a special case of understanding

---

[2] My idea of a Network of Beliefs derives from W. V. Quine, *The Web of Belief*, 2nd edn. (New York: Random House, 1978).

[3] Only normal Networks (and other concepts) will be described. Diseases and various malfunctions may cause a Network to lose one or more of the described properties.

[4] I hold to a moderate holism, according to which the meaning of any word or sentence depends to some extent on its relation to other words and sentences. It is not possible to have a language in which all the words and sentences were logically independent of each other.

[5] The process of updating the Network in general does not end until death.

the world in general. The latter principles have proven reliable in the past. They could not be other than reliable since survival has depended on it. Nevertheless, the process is not obviously mechanical or deterministic. It is partly *ad hoc* but not predominantly so.

Interpretations are guided by general principles—they might just as accurately be described as maxims or rules of thumb—that are widely accepted, usually without respect to a specific side in a debate. (I will return to this matter below.) My point here is that because interpreters come to a text with a Network of Beliefs and each person's experience is different from that of every other, it is not surprising that the way one person interprets a significant text will differ from that of another. And it is unlikely that universal agreement can be achieved because one's pre-existing Network will dispose one person to understand it one way and another person to understand it another.

There is something of an irony in the situation within which people try to determine the best interpretation from a class of interpretations. An interpretation can be judged to be better or worse than another only when an initial Network of Beliefs is the same for both of them. To judge a text T_1 with respect to a Network N_1 and T_2 with respect to N_2 is to vary the independent variables. Suppose interpreters P_1 and P_2 disagree about whether interpretation I_1 is better than I_2. Since better and worse interpretations are always relative to the Network from which the interpreter begins, it may be the case that, according to the maxims of interpretation, for P_1, I_1 is a better interpretation than I_2, and for P_2, I_2 is a better interpretation than I_1. And given the varying prior experiences of P_1 and P_2, there may be no way to arbitrate between them.

This in short explains why it is highly unlikely that even the best theist and nontheist interpreters could reach a consensus on the crucial issue that divides them: Hobbes's beliefs about revealed religion. To say that each is the 'best' is to concede that each uses the broadly shared principles of interpretation in a highly skilled way.

The fact that the chances of complete consensus are remote does not mean that debate is pointless. One interpreter may have made a mistake about some matter that the other interpreter can show to be a mistake, for example, about what the evidence is or about how a principle should be deployed. Also, the process of debate often forces an interpreter to clarify the issues and to organize her arguments better. In addition, the fact that there is often not one correct, determinable interpretation does not mean that every interpretation is acceptable. A proponent of one interpretation can recognize that from among the competing interpretations I_1 is better than I_2 even when I_2 is closer to her interpretation than I_1.

It must also be noted that just as there may be irresolvable disputes between theists and nontheists, there may be equally irresolvable disputes between the nontheists, for example the deist and atheist interpretations. And the nomenclature of disputes is always relative to an issue. A theist and nontheist interpreter may agree on some other significant issue, say, Hobbes's belief in absolute sovereignty, that would pit them against intepreters who think that Hobbes was a secret revolutionary and that *Leviathan* was intended as a rebel's catechism.

My focus on the possibility of irresolvable debates should not raise the fear of anarchic relativism. Because each person's Network is causally and functionally connected to a common world, Networks are very similar in most respects. These similarities allow there to be an idealized, public Network or subnetwork relevant to the community of interpreters that functions as a base from which to judge the merits of competing interpretations.[6]

II. PRINCIPLES OF GOOD INTERPRETATION

Let's now consider some of the principles of a good interpretation that I alluded to. While philosophers are inclined to be monists or dualists and never, let us say, 'trivialists', I think that it is better to begin an inquiry with more principles than ultimately may be necessary rather than fewer. Simplicity is a virtue, but not to the exclusion of others (cf. principle 5 below). At least a dozen principles of interpretation operate, of which I will mention only ten here.

1. Conservatism: A Network should be updated by changing as few of one's existing beliefs as possible. Theories that require enormous changes in the pre-existing Network should be resisted. This property of a good interpretation sometimes interferes with getting the right interpretation. As Hobbes says:

But for those that by Writing or Publique Discourse, or by their eminent actions, have already engaged themselves to the maintaining of contrary opinions, they will not be so easily satisfied. For in such cases, it is naturall for men, at one and the same time, both to proceed in reading, and to lose their attention, in the search of objections to that they had read before.   ('Review and Conclusion', 13)

Since each principle, if misapplied, can interfere with arriving at the correct interpretation, I will not mention this fact for the others.

2. Frugality: Some beliefs are held more strongly than others; so given a choice between deleting a stronger one and a weaker one, the weaker one should go. By 'strength' here I mean the quantity of good evidence, not logical strength, which I refer to in the next principle.

---

[6] Because the community is not homogeneous but consists of subcommunities, the public Network is a 'fuzzy set' of beliefs.

3. *Palpability*: A palpable interpretation is the one most obvious or closest at hand. (It may not ultimately be the best interpretation, but it is one that is more likely to be true *ceteris paribus*.) If A is holding a smoking gun and is standing over B who is prone and bleeding, the interpretation that holds that A shot B is more palpable than the one that holds that C, not present, shot B and A took the gun from C.

4. *Generality*: Explanations that apply to a broader range of phenomena are better than ones that apply to a narrower range. The thesis that stock epithets in Homer's work serve the purpose of giving the oral poet an easy way to keep to the meter and time to think about the next line is attractive because of its generality. It is even more attractive because the thesis can be generalized to explain the practice of oral poets in, say, Serbia in the twentieth century.

5. *Simplicity*: The fewer principles or entities required for an interpretation the better. 'Ockham's Razor'—entities should not be multiplied unnecessarily—is a corollary of logical simplicity. Misapplications of this principle are both numerous and interesting. The serpent in Eden, Satan, and the devil are traditionally identified. In fact, each has an independent origin and hence different properties.

6. *Coherence*: An interpretation should (be able to) show how each part of the text coheres with the others (horizontal coherence), and how the interpretation coheres with what it is reasonable to hold that the author and his audience believed (vertical coherence).

7. *Completeness*: An interpretation should account for the entire text. What counts as 'the entire text' is relative. It could refer to a sentence, paragraph, or chapter of the whole work. It would be fair, of course, for a critic to object that the interpretation is not acceptable as part of a larger text, several sentences, paragraphs, or chapters.

8. *Consistency*: Propositions added to a Network should be consistent with the existing Network, not necessarily with the statements of the text itself.[7]

9. *Proportionality*: Each sentence, paragraph, and chapter should be given its appropriate weight. Each part of a text should be given its proper weight. A sentence that looks like a topic sentence should be given more weight than one that appears to be off-hand. Hobbes in effect commented on an aspect of this property when he talked about how to resolve an apparent contradiction in an author's work.[8] In the so-called 'Adulterer's Bible', a typographical error in one occurrence of the seventh commandment was "Thou shalt commit adultery." If one argued that that text proved that the affairs

---

[7] Quentin Skinner, 'Meaning and Understanding in the History of Ideas', in James Tully (ed.), *Meaning and Context* (Princeton: Princeton University Press, 1988), 41–2.

[8] *The Elements of Law, Natural and Politic*, ed. J. C. A. Gaskin (New York: Oxford University Press, 1994), 21.13.

of David, Solomon, and others in the Hebrew Bible were in fact acceptable, and that the passages that seemed to condemn adultery were ironic, satiric, or hyperbolic, one would be giving undue weight to 'Thou shalt commit adultery.'

10. Defensibility: A good interpretation is able to defend itself against criticisms. This is especially important when one interpretation is competing with another.[9]

These rules are both descriptive and normative. Most interpreters use these principles most of the time; and they ought to apply them, because they are good rules.

III. HOBBES'S THEORY OF COVENANTS AND ITS PROBLEMS

In 'The Covenant with God in Hobbes' *Leviathan*' (this volume, pp. 199–216), Edwin Curley argues as part of his general nontheist interpretation that Hobbes's treatment of covenants is designed to show that divine covenants are impossible and that Hobbes expects his audience to infer from this fact that one of the foundations of the Christian religion is destroyed.[10] Curley rests his interpretation on two main claims. First, Hobbes's doctrine about divine covenants is so ambiguous that it is plausible for a reader to think that the ambiguity is intended to cast doubt on the possibility of divine covenants. Curley writes:

Hobbes' Christian critics attacked *Leviathan* both for affirming and for denying the possibility of a covenant between God and man. Filmer attacked Hobbes for affirming that possibility. Clarendon attacked him for denying it. And both writers did this in the name of the Christian religion.

How can this be? Is Hobbes' text really so ambiguous as to permit a doubt about his position? How is it possible that two intelligent readers should have attributed diametrically opposed views to him? (p. 199)

Curley thinks the answer to the last question is that Hobbes intentionally made his text ambiguous, so that readers would infer that the idea of divine covenants is incoherent. Curley's second claim is related to the answer just described: Hobbes concocted views about divine covenants so odd that he expected his readers to see that he did not intend them to be taken seriously.[11] So Hobbes must have intended his readers to recognize that divine covenants are impossible, according to Curley.

---

[9] There are other principles that do not need to be mentioned here. See also my 'Interpretation and Hobbes's Political Philosophy', *Pacific Philosophy Quarterly* 82 (2001), 309–31.

[10] This complex description of Hobbes's intentions is necessary in order to establish that Hobbes meant that divine covenants are impossible. See H. P. Grice, 'Meaning', in A. P. Martinich (ed.), *The Philosophy of Language*, 4th edn. (New York: Oxford University Press, 2001), 92–7.

[11] Curley ('The Covenant with God in Hobbes's *Leviathan*', this volume) says that Hobbes's views are 'puzzling', 'curious', and 'peculiar' (Curley, pp. 203, 211).

In this section, I want to cast doubt on both claims by giving a number of examples from Hobbes's political philosophy that show that it was ambiguous or otherwise deficient on a large number of issues. Since the ambiguities and other deficiencies infest his general political philosophy, one cannot hold that the ambiguities in his views about religious covenants are proof that he was being nonserious, without holding that he was nonserious about his general political philosophy.

Since the theist interpreter is not committed to any particular interpretation of Hobbes's theory of covenants so long as it is consistent with the theist interpreter's other views, I will not present a separate treatment of Hobbes's theory of divine covenants.[12] I am mainly concerned here with the principle of defensibility, of defending a version of the theist interpretation. More broadly, I am interested in casting doubt on the use of 'reading between the lines' when it is not required either by the explicit meaning of the text or by the historical context.

I begin with Hobbes's general understanding of covenants. A covenant is the "mutual transferring of right"[13] (14.9). The most important kind of covenants are sovereign-making ones since they provide the stability necessary for the effective use of other covenants. Although in most covenants the only relevant parties are the contracting ones, that is, the persons who acquire an obligation in virtue of transferring their right, it should not be shocking that the most important kind have a slightly different character. As Hobbes explains sovereign-making covenants, in addition to what we may call 'the contracting parties', that is, the persons who transfer their right and acquire obligations, there is a person who is not a contracting party but has something to gain from the covenant. Borrowing from the law, I will call such a person a 'third-party beneficiary'. If persons A and B covenant to each transfer their right to \$1,000 to be paid to F, then F is a third-party beneficiary. No great importance should be assigned to the meaning of the word 'third-party'. The logic is the same if A, B, C, D, and E covenant to each transfer their right to \$1,000 to be paid to F, the third-party beneficiary. Nor need the ordinary meaning of 'beneficiary' be understood, if Hobbes is right about the woes of being a sovereign (*The Elements of Law*, 24.2).

---

[12] I think the main lines of my treatment in *The Two Gods of Leviathan* (Cambridge: Cambridge University Press, 1992) are correct.

[13] For his own purposes, Hobbes should not have required a 'mutual transferring of right', for there are possible cases in which people covenant simply to renounce their right to something. Suppose persons P_1 and P_2 each have rights to something that might injure the other one, say, a bomb. (The bombs could even be ones that could kill both, say, Doomsday Bombs, similar to the one in *Dr. Strangelove: How I Stopped Worrying and Learned to Love the Bomb*.) They might covenant to alienate their rights to use the bomb. So transfer of right should not be essential to covenants. I use 'alienate' instead of 'renounce' because, for Hobbes, when someone renounces a right, the person 'cares not to whom the benefit thereof redoundeth' (14.6). But in the case imagined, the person does care.

As applied to sovereign-making covenants, the many prospective subjects are contracting parties and the sovereign is a third-party beneficiary. Now this feature strikes many readers as odd or worse. Their reaction is the same as Clarendon's. Intuitively, it seems that the sovereign must have been a contracting party of the covenant with his subjects. If this were not the case, then the following seems to be true:

Absurdity 1: The citizens can release each other from obedience to the sovereign.
Absurdity 2: The sovereign is 'at the mercy of his Subjects'.[14]
Absurdity 3: The sovereign does not injure his subjects if he uses his 'power wantonly or tyrannically'.[15]

I am using 'Absurdity', in an artificially broad sense, to mean a proposition that is intuitively unacceptable, either because it seems to be obviously false as a matter of fact or to contradict some conspicuous element of Hobbes's theory. One of my readers objected that my use of the term 'Absurdity' was 'absurd'. His objection, however, proves the appropriateness of my term because he naturally used the word 'absurd' to express his belief that my use of it was obviously or 'intuitively unacceptable'.

In order to remind the reader of its technical sense here and to soften its pejorative connotation, I will capitalize 'Absurdity' when I mean it in the sense just described. Notice that for something to be an Absurdity it is sufficient for it to 'seem' to be either unacceptable or false; for we are interested in what the numerous, mutually inconsistent interpretations might indicate about Hobbes's philosophy. That is, I want to show that Hobbes's text is in fact so ambiguous or otherwise flawed that it is easy for multiple interpreters to have contradictory interpretations or for an interpreter to claim that Hobbes's theory is odd, puzzling, or absurd. Consequently, the fact that two seventeenth-century critics interpret a passage or doctrine in contradictory ways or that a philosopher can point out problems with the doctrine does not show that the doctrine is not Hobbes's.[16]

Absurdities 1–3 have nothing to do with 'covenants made with God' or religion in general. They are apparent consequences of Hobbes's general theory. I say 'apparent' consequences because it is possible that Hobbes or a Hobbesian could show that the alleged Absurdities do not follow from the theory. Hobbes for example claims, and David Gauthier argues,[17] that his view does not involve Absurdity 1 (see 18.3). And, although Absurdity 3

---

[14] Clarendon, in *Leviathan: Contemporary Responses to the Political Theory of Thomas Hobbes*, ed. G. A. J. Rogers (Bristol: Thoemmes Press, 1995), 210.   [15] Clarendon, ibid.

[16] I am not saying that Hobbes did not have a relatively coherent and insightful theory; only that such a theory is highly interpretative. Also, I think that Curley's criticisms of the possibility of divine covenants are (almost) completely correct.

[17] *The Logic of Leviathan* (Oxford: Clarendon Press, 1969), 157–60.

seems to entail that there are no constraints whatever on the sovereign, Hobbes himself would argue that the sovereign is bound by the laws of nature (21.7).[18] (Absurdities 1–3 will be used again in section IV of this article.)

Other Absurdities follow from other aspects of Hobbes's treatment of sovereign-making covenants. Hobbes says that each contracting party in effect says to every other one: "*I authorise and give up my right of governing myself to this man, or to this assembly of men, on this condition, that thou give up thy right to him, and authorize all his actions in like manner*" (17.13). It appears that the sovereign-making formula is contradictory, because one cannot both authorize and give up one's right to something. One can *authorize* someone to do something only with respect to things that one has ownership or legal control over. A person who owns an automobile can authorize his friend to use it. But once he *gives up* his right to it, he can no longer authorize anyone to do anything with it. A trustee (who herself is authorized) to care for and maintain a property in good condition can authorize someone else to maintain it. But once the trustee's right is given up in some way (say, by termination or removal) she can no longer authorize anyone to do anything with respect to that property. Thus, we propose:

Absurdity 4: One can authorize the use of something the right to which one has given up.

Someone might object that Absurdity 4 is a clear misinterpretation of Hobbes's theory. 'Authorize', the objection claims, means the same as 'give up'. Now this objection will not work, because Hobbes makes very clear that for X to authorize Y to do A is for X to take on the action of A; if Y does A, then X does A. (In fact, this last clause may be imprecise since Y may not be *doing* A in the proper sense since Hobbes does not consider Y responsible for A. Y's bodily movements with respect to A are the actions of X.) And it is quite clear that if X has given up X's right to Y with respect to some object O and Y does something A with O, it is not the case that X does A with O. If Xavier gives or sells his automobile to Yolanda and Yolanda hits a pedestrian, it is not the case that Xavier hits the pedestrian. Hobbes is quite clear that in authorizing the sovereign, subjects take on all the actions of the sovereign: 'they are bound, every man to every man, to own, and be reputed author of, all that he that already is their sovereign shall do and judge fit to be done' (18.3; see also, 18.4, 18.6).

---

[18] Of course the argument would not rest there. For those who hold that Hobbes's laws of nature are merely prudential, being constrained by them would not be an effective check on sovereigns. Thus, some would consider 'The sovereign is bound only by the laws of nature' to be yet another Absurdity.

So there are good grounds for attributing Absurdity 4 to Hobbes's theory. However, that does not mean that the objection considered in the preceding paragraph is completely groundless. If Hobbes's theory is inconsistent, then it may be the case that he says or implies that to authorize someone to do something is also to do something that is incompatible with the idea of authorization. In particular, Hobbes sometimes represents authorizing someone as submitting oneself to that person or putting oneself under the control of that person. In chapter 21, Hobbes tries to show that his theory of absolute sovereignty affords subjects as much freedom as citizens have according to the republican or neo-Roman political theory. Many of Hobbes's claims in that chapter are astounding:

There is written on the turrets of the city of Lucca in great characters at this day the word LIBERTAS; yet no man can thence infer that a particular man has more liberty, or immunity from the service of the commonwealth, there than in *Constantinople*. Whether a commonwealth be monarchical or popular, the freedom is still the same. (21.8)

Hobbes's claim in this passage seems so obviously false that we can add:

Absurdity 5: In the seventeenth century, Constantinople was as free as Lucca.

One might assert in Hobbes's defense that the apparent meaning of Absurdity 5 is not its Hobbesian meaning. In its Hobbesian meaning, Absurdity 5 means that both Constantinople and Lucca were in the state of nature with respect to all other civil states and in that respect equally free; so, Absurdity 5 is not really absurd. One can grant this defense but then one must observe that even if Absurdity 5 is a misnomer, Hobbes's claim is open to misinterpretation because its genuine meaning is irrelevant to the issue of whether republics and their citizens are freer than the civil states governed by absolute sovereigns. This point suggests that Hobbes's view is committed to a related absurdity:

Absurdity 6: In the seventeenth century, the citizens of Constantinople were as free as the citizens of Lucca.

Absurdity 6, it seems, is as false as his claim that there is no difference between monarchy and tyranny except the attitude of the speaker (19.2). Again, a defender of Hobbes could assert that the apparent meaning of Absurdity 6 is not its Hobbesian meaning, where 'Hobbesian' begins to be synonymous with 'Pickwickian'. In its Hobbesian meaning, Absurdity 6 means that however much political obligation one has in Lucca and however much obligation one has in Constantinople, the obligatoriness (though perhaps not the amount of obligations) of each is the same. The reply again is that this defense saves the truth of Hobbes's position by convicting it of irrelevance. Republican theorists never said or implied that in republics obligation is not obligation.[19]

The next absurdity comes from Hobbes's attempt to neutralize neo-Roman or republican theory: 'For in the act of our *submission* consisteth both our *obligation* and our *liberty*, which must therefore be inferred by arguments taken from thence'[20] .... (21.10). It is not immediately clear, I believe, what Hobbes means by this. Taking 'consisteth in' to mean 'to have its being in',[21] one might think that Hobbes is saying in part:

Absurdity 7: Liberty has its being in the act of submission.

This understanding is confirmed by what he says later in the same chapter: 'The obligation, and Liberty of the subject is to be derived . . .' The singular number of the verb 'is' suggests that obligation and liberty are identical! Hobbes wants the reader to get this impression, because it makes his theory of absolute sovereignty and alienation appear more palatable, when compared with the evident liberty in republican theory.[22] However, Absurdity 7 is inconsistent with Hobbes's view that liberty exists in the state of nature and can exist independently of laws and obligations, although it is diminished by them.

Given the main line of argument in chapter 21, my guess is that Hobbes's passage does not in fact mean what Absurdity 7 says. Hobbes wants to show that the act of submission, or at least the words uttered in performing that act, do not limit the natural freedom of a subject. Thus, 'consist' probably means 'to exist together or alongside of each other as compatible facts'. So, he probably means that liberty and obligation can exist together. This notwithstanding, his statement is ambiguous or paradoxical.

In the paragraph containing the passage just considered is another passage that also contains an Absurdity: 'And because such arguments [for the origin of obligations] must either be drawn from the express words [of submission] *I authorize all his actions*, or from the intention of him that submitteth himself to his power' (21.19). That is,

Absurdity 8: The words 'I authorize all his actions' are words of submission.

---

[19] One might accuse Hobbes of disingenuousness in asserting Absurdities 5 and 6, but if this is what it is, it does not lend support to those who want to read his text 'between the lines'. For Hobbes's technique here is to assert his own view in a misleading way; it is not to assert the opposite of his own view with the expectation that the audience will be able to pick out just those assertions from the multitude of sincere ones.

[20] The references of 'which' and 'thence' in the next clause, 'which must therefore be inferred from arguments taken from thence', are clarified by the Latin: 'In ipsa submissione consistit tum *obligatio*, tum *libertas*. Itaque ex eadem submissione obligationis, et libertatis argumenta sumi debent' (*Opera Latina*, iii 164).

[21] 'Consists in', entry 6 under 'consists', *Oxford English Dictionary*.

[22] It is no good to object that I am 'reading between the lines' here. I have no objection to identifying various implied or covert intentions in a text. I object only to the nonPalpable ones.

It is not true that authorizing a person makes one subordinate to that person and makes one submit to him. If a person P authorizes a real estate agent A to locate and bid on a house, P is not thereby subordinate to A. P is as free as she was before the authorization. If P also contracted with A not to buy any house during a certain period or to pay a commission to A for services rendered, these are obligations that are logically independent of the authorization. If P becomes obligated to buy a house because of the 'actions' of A, it is because these actions are owned by P and not because P is subordinate to A.

Other Absurdities could be drawn.[23] Indeed, it was conventional for Hobbes's critics to accuse him of inconsistency. Bramhall incorporated the claim into the ample subtitle of *The Catching of Leviathan*, which says that *Leviathan* 'abound[s] with palpable contradictions'. Clarendon gives two lists of Absurdities in *A Brief View and Survey*, pp. 190–3, 311–15.[24] And there are others. Some of Hobbes's apparent contradictions are classic, such as the dispute about whether the laws of nature are moral laws, whether moral obligation exists in the state of nature, and whether his treatment of sovereignty by acquisition is compatible with his treatment of sovereignty by institution.[25]

One reason that Hobbesian scholarship has been a growth industry for the last thirty years is that his texts are replete with ambiguities. These ambiguities allow the clever scholar to uncover novel, but textually based, interpretations of Hobbes's philosophy that run against the conventional, but equally textually based, interpretations. The former include the views that in *Leviathan* he was for toleration, was a utopian,[26] and advocated 'autonomous rational action'.[27]

---

[23] Since subjects 'own . . . all the Actions (without exception) of the man or assembly we make our sovereign', when the sovereign kills a person, that person kills himself; that is, every person killed directly or indirectly by the sovereign commits suicide (21.10).

[24] George Lawson, *An Examination of the Political Part of Mr Hobbs His Leviathan* (London, 1657), 63; and Samuel Pufendorf, *Of the Law of Nature and Nations, Eight Books*, 3rd edn., tr. Basil Kennett (London, 1717), 86. Also, in 'Hobbes and the Classical Theory of Laughter' (this volume), Quentin Skinner gives an example of an obviously false statement made by Hobbes. Hobbes claims that his theory of laughter is his own theory, when it was well known to have been expressed by Aristotle. I don't know why Hobbes makes this particular mistake, but I do think he was sometimes sloppy about the facts.

[25] Stanley Moore, 'Hobbes on Obligation: Moral and Political', *Journal of the History of Philosophy* 9 (1971), 43–62 and 10 (1972), 29–42 for a discussion of some contradictions, and Philip J. Kain, 'Hobbes, Revolution and the Philosophy of History', in C. Walton and P. J. Johnson (eds.), *Hobbes's 'Science of Natural Justice'* (Dordrecht: Martinus Nijhoff Publishers, 1987), 203–18, for a discussion of others, plus references to other works.

[26] Richard Tuck, 'Hobbes and Locke on Toleration', in Mary Dietz (ed.), *Thomas Hobbes and Political Theory* (Lawrence, Kan.: The University of Kansas Press, 1990), 153–71, and 'The Utopianism of *Leviathan*' (this volume).

[27] Quoted from an advertising brochure for David van Mill, *Liberty, Rationality, and Agency in Hobbes's Leviathan* (Albany, NY: State University of New York Press, 2001).

In addition to the textual ambiguities, some of the Absurdities arise from the fact that Hobbes's beliefs were odd. He believed that geometric points have extension, that Torricelli and Boyle did not produce good evidence for the existence of vacua, and that he had squared the circle, even after several mathematicians whom he respected pointed out his mistakes to him, sometimes the same mistakes. Rather than admit his own failings, he was flabbergasted that so many intelligent people should be mistaken about his achievements.

My general conclusions are (1) that Hobbes's theory about the nature of covenants is nonstandard in so far as he does not make the sovereign a contracting party; (2) that it is contradictory in so far as by the sovereign-making formula the subject authorizes the sovereign to act for the subject on the very thing that the subject alienates (namely, governing the subject); and (3) that Hobbes often misstates or gives a false impression of what his view is. In short, when Hobbes says something false or dubious about a topic, one Palpable explanation is that he or his theory is in some way confused or confusing. There is no need in these cases to attribute to him irony or sarcasm, and no need generally to appeal to the nonPalpable tactic of 'reading between the lines' in order to explain them. Of course, it may be appropriate to 'read between the lines' in some particular case. So let's see whether Curley has given us reason to do so as regards divine covenants.

IV. OPPOSING INTERPRETATIONS AND REPLIES

Curley thinks that the contradictory interpretations of Clarendon and Filmer are significant. I do not. Even if Hobbes's views were more conventional in form and substance, the existence of contradictory interpretations would be easy to explain. All that is needed is one correct interpretation and one false one on the very same topic. False interpretations are usually explainable for any number of mundane reasons such as the inattention, ignorance, stupidity, or personal antipathy of the interpreter, not to mention indeterminate or ambiguous texts. Are any of these possibilities actualized here? Personal antipathy is. Clarendon was alienated from Hobbes around 1650; and the irritation was aggravated in the late 1660s when Clarendon, ever loyal to the Stuart kings, had to live in bitter exile on the Continent, while Hobbes, who had made his peace with the Commonwealth, was safe in England and a friend of Charles II.

As for Filmer, though intelligent, he was not better than a second-rate thinker, one of the last notable defenders of patriarchy. Also, Curley himself thinks that Filmer's interpretation of the Mosaic covenant is suspect: 'For Filmer the covenant at Mt. Sinai is an awkward fact, which must be explained away.'[28] If Curley is right, we have more reason to trust Filmer less. So both Clarendon, as a hostile interpreter, and Filmer, as possibly a dubious interpreter of Scripture, should not inspire confidence prior to reading their interpretations of Hobbes's text. This does not mean that either or both of them are mistaken in what they say. In fact, I think Filmer is correct in understanding Hobbes to hold that there are straightforward divine covenants; and Clarendon is correct in understanding Hobbes to hold that sovereigns are not contracting parties in sovereign-making covenants. Each can be right because each can emphasize different aspects of Hobbes's account. In short, Curley's strategy of presenting the conflicting interpretations of Filmer and Clarendon as a reason to suspect Hobbes of 'writing between the lines' has nothing to recommend it. The way to determine the extent to which the interpretations of Filmer and Clarendon are right or wrong is to read their texts to find out what they say, to read Hobbes's text to find out what he said, and then to compare the two.[29]

But suppose the focus of interest is not the correctness or incorrectness of their interpretations but the meaning of Hobbes's text. How should the process be described? It may initially seem odd that we should do something similar: read Hobbes's text and, as appropriate, read the relevant texts by Filmer and Clarendon and others ('collateral texts'), and compare the tentative interpretations of each to see whether they fit well or not. But it is not. All interpretation involves the same subprocesses, which include the interpreter's having in her Network, either before the interpretation begins or while it is proceeding, nonlinguistic information about who Hobbes, Clarendon, and Filmer were and what their historical circumstances were.[30] The process of interpretation is dynamic, not linear. It requires trying out various conjectures or hypotheses about the meaning of the focal text and the collateral texts and about the beliefs of the authors and audience of each. The process is guided by the Principles described in section II and ends when the original Network has been updated with the beliefs necessary to understand the text. Let's call 'the narrow interpretation' those propositions that

---

[28] Curley, this volume p. 212, n. 21. It is not clear to me what Filmer's point is, nor am I sure that he is mistaken. The covenant on Sinai is typically understood as a conditional covenant in contrast with the covenants of Abraham (Gen. 15) and David (2 Sam. 7; Ps. 89:1–38), which are understood as unconditional (*Harper's Bible Dictionary*, ed. Paul J. Achtemeier (San Francisco: Harper & Row, Publishers, 1988), 191).

[29] Curley eventually does this. My objection is to his methodological position that the existence of contradictory interpretations of a certain philosopher gives us a reason to suspect the author of 'writing between the lines'.

[30] My debt to Quentin Skinner's works should be obvious; see his contributions to James Tully (ed.), *Meaning and Context: Quentin Skinner and his Critics* (Princeton: Princton University Press, 1988). My description of the process of interpretation is a simplification. To mention just one additional complexity, the process may require subtracting some of the beliefs that were part of the Network when the process of interpreting began.

state the meaning of the target text, and call 'the broad interpretation' those propositions that state the meaning of the target text, the collateral texts, and (putative) facts about the authors and audiences relevant to understanding the target and collateral texts. The broad interpretation may include such propositions as that one collateral text is mistaken about the meaning of the target text, that the interpretation of another collateral text is one-sided, unfair, or uncharitable, and that one collateral text is meant ironically.[31] Notice that the interpretations of the collateral texts, e.g., Filmer's and Clarendon's, play some role and provide some evidence of what Hobbes meant, but do not provide conclusive evidence.

The mere fact that the interpretations of Filmer and Clarendon are contradictory suggests that the meaning of Hobbes's text cannot be read off from theirs. One or the other may have misinterpreted Hobbes, as Curley realizes. Moreover, the collateral texts are as open to misinterpretation as the target text is. To give more weight to the collateral texts than to the primary text is one way of violating the principle of Proportionality.

This completes my discussion of the merit of Curley's example of having one's own interpretation of an historical text guided by the conflicting interpretations of the author's contemporaries. In the remainder of this article, I want to consider two related matters. One concerns the general strategy of 'reading between the lines'. The other, which I consider in section V, concerns Curley's use of the strategy in his interpretation of Hobbes's theory of divine covenants.

Concerning the first issue, recall that Clarendon (justifiably) holds that according to Hobbes no sovereign is a party to a sovereign-making covenant. That is, Hobbes is committed to

Absurdity 9: Sovereigns are not parties to sovereign-making covenants.

This counts as an Absurdity because Clarendon's belief that monarchs are contracting parties accords with the dominant view of the time, against Hobbes's. Clarendon says that because of its 'true essential form', a covenant 'will never be found . . . [in which] one party covenants, and the other not'. Clarendon notes two groups of consequences entailed by Absurdity 9: (1) The sovereign is not obliged to the subjects to 'govern righteously'; 'the sovereign hath no security for the obedience of his People'; if the people 'rebell against him, he cannot complain of injustice don [*sic*] to him, because they have broke no promise to him.' These include Absurdities 1–3, mentioned above. In short, the state is less equal and less

---

[31] I think Clarendon is being ironic when he says: 'we may believe that he [Hobbes] doth not himself believe one word in this Book that we find fault with' (*A Brief View and Survey of Leviathan* (Oxford, 1676), 254). (I have corrected a typographical error in the original.) And he is being ironic when he refers to Hobbes's geometry as 'beloved and justly esteemed' (p. 298).

secure than it needs to be. (2) Hobbes's theory is 'destructive of our Religion, and against the express sense of Scripture'.[32] Notice that the focus of Clarendon's criticisms is Hobbes's theory of covenants in general. He shows that Hobbes's theory is defective by pointing out that it has (allegedly) false consequences in two realms. As regards the secular realm, Hobbes's theory creates an inequitable and unstable state. As regards the religious realm, Hobbes's theory destroys the Christian religion and does not jibe with Scripture. Clarendon is not saying here that Hobbes had designed his theory of covenants in order to render divine covenants impossible, and to have his readers guess that that was his intention. Indeed, Hobbes appeals to biblical covenants to support his theory (20.16–18). He must know that if the biblical covenants do not jibe with his theory, it is his theory that will suffer. Moreover, if, on the basis of Clarendon's criticisms, one were justified in holding that Hobbes was using his theory of covenants surreptitiously to subvert revealed religion, then, by parity of reasoning, one would also have to hold that he was surreptitiously subverting the existence of civil states. Hobbes would be both atheist and anarchist.

Rather than asserting that Hobbes is surreptitiously subverting government and religion, Clarendon is observing that the inability of Hobbes's theory to ground both civil states and revealed religion adequately shows that his theory is fundamentally defective. John Bramhall used the same tactic when he claimed that *Leviathan* should have its name changed to *The Rebel's Catechism* because 'howsoever in words he denie all resistance to the soveraign, yet indeed he admitteth it.'[33] The same kind of reasoning induced him to call Hobbes an atheist. Hobbes objected that it was unfair to draw conclusions from an author's work that the author himself would disavow: 'So that his [Bramhall's] atheism *by consequence* is a very easy thing to be fallen into, even by the most godly of men of the Church.' Bramhall himself, Hobbes argues, could be accused of atheism by consequence, along with all the scholastic philosophers, even though 'they do not say in their hearts that there is no God.'[34] To accept Bramhall's reasoning as it applies to religion but not as it applies to politics is to engage in special pleading.

When readers are forced to choose between, on the one hand, the (assumed) fact that sovereigns actually do covenant with their subjects and that God covenanted with humans, and, on the other hand, Hobbes's nonstandard theory of covenants, readers will reject Hobbes's theory and not

---

[32] Clarendon in *Leviathan: Contemporary Responses to the Political Theory of Thomas Hobbes*, 209–10.

[33] John Bramhall, *The Catching of Leviathan*, in *Leviathan: Contemporary Responses to the Political Theory of Thomas Hobbes*, 145.

[34] 'An Answer to a Book Published by Dr. Bramhall, Called *The Catching of the Leviathan*', in *English Works*, ed. Molesworth, 11 vols. (London: John Bohn, 1839–45), iv. 384.

change their view about the facts. In general, it is a losing strategy to try to subvert belief in some well-entrenched fact by propounding a novel and counterintuitive theory.[35]

None of this is to say that novel and counterintuitive theories never undermine well-entrenched facts; but the process is different from the one to which Curley is committed. When Copernicus advanced the heliocentric theory, he openly explained why the apparent movement of the sun around the earth was not what was actually happening. He did not employ the strategy of 'writing between the lines', which would have him try to perform the following bizarre trick: to assert both (i) the sun moves around the earth and (ii) the sun rises and sets on the earth's horizon, and to expect his readers to infer that he believed (i) in order to discredit (ii), which he is to expect his audience to come to think is obviously absurd.[36]

V. THE SOURCE OF THE MEDIATION DOCTRINE

Another problem for the strategy of 'reading between the lines' is illustrated in Curley's use of it with regard to what he calls 'the mediation doctrine': 'for there is no covenant with God but by mediation of somebody that representeth God's person' (18.3). Curley thinks that what Hobbes means by this, and thus what Hobbes expects his readers to understand, is that there can be no covenant with God *simpliciter*, because it is demonstrable that there can be no mediation between God and humans. Since Curley's interpretation is inconsistent with Hobbes's extended discussion of divine covenants in chapter 35, he concludes that Hobbes did not mean the extended discussion to be taken seriously. That is, Curley is giving the single clause expressing the mediation doctrine more weight than the many paragraphs in which Hobbes discusses something (divine covenants) that readers would have taken as fact. Curley cannot object that what justifies marginalizing the many paragraphs is the fact that Hobbes wants his readers to see that the mediation doctrine expresses his genuine view, for that begs the question.[37]

I think a better interpretative practice is to understand the mediation doctrine in a way that is consistent with other parts of the text, specifically,

---

[35] This is illustrated in Clarendon, *A Brief View and Survey of Leviathan*, 285–6.

[36] Of course there are other ways of getting across a new and controversial position. One might write a dialogue, as Galileo did. But dialogues are not inherently devices for 'writing between the lines', and, in any case, *Leviathan* is not a dialogue.

[37] Also, the tactic of privileging the mediation doctrine over the many paragraphs conflicts with Hobbes's own sensible maxim about how to handle apparent contradictions in a text: 'For in contradictory significations of the will . . . that which is directly signified, is to be understood for the will, before that which is drawn from it by consequence' (*The Elements of Law, Natural and Politic*, ed. J. C. A. Gaskin, 21.13).

the extended discussions of divine covenants and consonant with related beliefs of Hobbes's contemporaries. For example: the mediation doctrine occurs in a sentence that begins: 'And whereas some men have pretended for their disobedience to their sovereign a new covenant, made (not with men, but) with God, this also is unjust' (18.3). The phrase 'some men' suggests that Hobbes is talking about a specific incident (or a few of them). The salient act of disobedience for Hobbes and his readers was that of the Scots and English in the Civil War, the causes of which included the signing of the (Scottish) National Covenant and the Solemn League and Covenant, covenants not authorized by Charles I.[38] Further, Hobbes himself quotes the sentence above in his 'Considerations Upon the Reputation, Loyalty, Manners, and Religion of Thomas Hobbes',[39] in order to criticize John Wallis's allegiance during the Civil War to the side that advocated the Solemn League and Covenant.

The proponents of the Solemn League and Covenant believed that, because of sin, human knowledge of God was radically deficient. To get the right kind of knowledge, a covenant between God and man was required; the covenant could be effected only by a mediator, specifically Jesus Christ. The Westminster Confession (1647), which formally expressed the theology of the covenanters, put the point in this way:

The distance between God and the creature is so great, that . . . [creatures] . . . could never have any fruition of him . . . but by some voluntary condescension on God's part, which he hath been pleased to express by way of covenant. . . . It pleased God, in his eternal purpose, to choose and ordain the Lord Jesus . . . to be the Mediator between God and man.[40]

These views were not distinctive of the Scottish and English covenanters; they were a prominent part of Reformed theology, as expressed famously by John Calvin in his *Institutes*. One of his favorite titles for Jesus was

---

[38] Curley wonders why Hobbes thinks it evident that 'if anyone claims to have made a covenant with God without the mediation of his sovereign, he is lying' (Curley, this volume, p. 203). I think the answer is that Hobbes is talking only about the National Covenant and the Solemn League and Covenant. However, one could argue that Hobbes is unfair because the signers of the National Covenant and the Solemn League and Covenant seem to covenant with themselves with God as their witness rather than covenanting with God as a contracting party. Hobbes either did not read the documents themselves or, more likely, read them with prejudice. (*The Constitutional Documents of the Puritan Revolution*, 3rd edn., ed. Samuel Rawson Gardiner (Oxford: Clarendon Press, 1906), 124, 126, 268, 271.)   [39] *English Works*, ed. Molesworth, iv. 432.

[40] 'Humble Advice of the Assembly of Divines . . . Concerning a Confession of Faith' (1647); quoted from *The Constitution of the Presbyterian Church, Part I Book of Confessions* (Louisville, Ky.: Presbyterian Dissertation Service, 1983), 6.037 and 6.043. The doctrine appeared in other Reformed documents: the second Helvetic Confession (ch. 5) said that the only way to invoke God is 'through the mediation of Christ alone'. And it is held today: 'The Christian faith centres on the person and work of Christ as mediator' ('mediation' in *New Dictionary of Theology*, ed. Sinclair Ferguson et al. (Downers Grove: Il.: InterVarsity Press, 1988), 418–19).

'Christ the Mediator', based on 1 Timothy 2:5: 'One mediator between God and men, the man Jesus Christ'. According to Calvin, even the 'Old Covenant' depended upon Jesus.[41] In William Ames's *The Marrow of Theology*, Christ is introduced as 'the Mediator' and is the person through whom God makes 'his will known' to humans.[42] So the doctrine of the necessity of a human mediator, of which Christ was the paradigm, was so familiar to his readers and so obviously not satisfied by the Solemn League and Covenant that Hobbes could say: 'this pretence of covenant is so evident a lie, even in the pretenders' own consciences, that it is not only an act of an unjust, but also of a vile and unmanly disposition' (18.3) and expect to be understood.[43]

It was not necessary to take a view of mediation as narrow as the covenanters. A person could have held that there were two (the Old and the New, or the covenant of works and the covenant of grace) or more than two (the covenants with Noah, Abraham, Moses, David, and others). Hobbes favors the multiple covenant view, because it invites the more general principle that 'there is no covenant with God but by mediation of somebody that represents God's person' (18.3). Given the beliefs of Hobbes's contemporaries, his view that Abraham and Moses mediated the divine covenants was sensible, and not (to his contemporaries) obviously at odds with epistemic or logical principles.

The mediation doctrine occurs in a paragraph devoted to specifying the 'rights and faculties of him, or them, on whom the sovereign power is conferred by the consent of the people assembled', in a chapter named 'Of the Rights of Sovereigns by Institution'. Hobbes's attention is fixed on protecting the rights of the sovereign against rebellious subjects who might try to undermine the sovereign's authority by claiming an independent covenant with God.

Curley might object that Hobbes makes the same claim against the possibility of covenanting with God without a mediator in his first discussion of the nature of covenants in a chapter that is not explicitly about the rights of sovereigns: 'To make a covenant with God is impossible, but by mediation

---

[41] John Calvin, *Institutes of the Christian Religion*, ed. John T. McNeill, 2 vols. (Philadelphia: The Westminster Press, 1960). See the Index for references, but especially 1.21, 2.10.1, 2.11.1, 2.12.1, and 3.2.1 n. 5.

Calvin's idea of covenants continues to be held by Reformed Christians: see *Eerdmans Dictionary of the Bible*, ed. David Noel Freedman et al. (Grand Rapids, MI: William B. Eerdmans Publishing Company, 2000), p. 878a. That Moses was a mediator between God and the Hebrews continues to be held by biblical scholars. See, for example, the comments on Ex. 20:18, Ex. 34:27–28, and Deut. 5:4–5 in *The New Oxford Annotated Bible*, 3rd edn. (New York: Oxford University Press, 2001).

[42] William Ames, *The Marrow of Theology*, John Dykstra Eusden (Durham, NC: The Labyrinth Press, 1983), ch. 12, sect. 4; see also sect. 9 and ch. 37, sects. 2, 6, and 11.

[43] Hobbes has more fundamental objections to the way biblical covenants are understood by Covenant Theology; see Luc Foisneau, *Hobbes et la Tout-puissance de Dieu* (Paris: Presses Universitaires de France, 2000), 333–58.

of such as God speaketh to, either by revelation supernatural or his lieutenants that govern under him and in his name; for otherwise we know not whether our covenants be accepted or not' (14.23).[44] My reply is based on the same principles and evidence I have presented above. Our interpretation should have the virtue of Proportionality. We need to weigh the evidence of the mediation doctrine against the numerous statements in which Hobbes says or implies that there are divine covenants. We need to consider that Hobbes often misstates or misleadingly states his own views.[45] We need to consider what Hobbes plausibly could have meant, given the beliefs of his contemporary readers, especially the beliefs that there have been divine covenants and that any theory that would entail that there could not be any must be false.[46] We need to consider how this passage might fit with other passages, to wit, the similar claim at 18.3 (Coherence and Completeness). And we need to consider the immediate context, two aspects of which are relevant here. First, the marginal summary for the relevant sentence is: 'Nor [are there Covenants] with God without Special Revelation.' Second, chapter 14 is concerned with the first two Laws of Nature, 'Seek peace', and 'Lay down your right to all things', which is done through a sovereign-making covenant. In light of all of this, I take Hobbes's comment at 14.23 to be influenced by his view of sovereign-making covenants. When he says 'otherwise *we* [my emphasis] know not whether our covenants be accepted or not', he is using 'we' to refer to those who are not mentioned in the preceding complex phrase, to wit, those who do not receive immediate supernatural revelation and those who are not sovereigns. All of this is evidence that the mediation doctrine in 14.23 is proleptic to the claim at 18.3 and means the same thing. Interpreting the two passages similarly is also justified by their similar wording: 'To make covenant with God is impossible, but by mediation of such as God speaketh to (either by revelation supernatural or by his lieutenants that govern under him and in his name)' (14.23); and 'there is no covenant with God but by mediation of somebody that representeth God's person, which none doth but God's lieutenant . . . ' (18.3). That is, the statement at 14.23, like the one at 18.3, must be understood as restricted

---

[44] I take the 'we' in the latter clause to refer to subjects who do not claim a special revelation for themselves.

[45] Examples of his misstatements about his own view of covenants have been given above. Curley also knows that Hobbes misstates some things about divine covenants. Referring to the covenant at Genesis 17, Hobbes says: 'In this covenant Abraham promiseth, for himself and his posterity, to obey as God the Lord that spake to him . . . ' Curley observes that Abraham did not promise. If we accept Curley's view for the sake of discussion, the importance of this example is that Hobbes misstates facts about religion even when there is no conceivable surreptitious motive. Hobbes was sometimes sloppy. So it's a mistake to construe instances of misstatement as prima facie evidence of subversive intent.

[46] See A. P. Martinich, 'On the Proper Interpretation of Hobbes's Philosophy', *Journal of the History of Philosophy*, 34 (1996), 273–83.

to those subjects who cannot credibly claim that God appeared to them. That this excludes for practical purposes all subjects does not mean that Hobbes thought that there had never been a revelation, since the ideology of established religions, for example, Judaism, Christianity, and Islam, makes the acceptance of new claims to revelation very difficult.[47]

Curley may say that my interpretation does not take account of the proofs he has produced that show that there are irresolvable epistemological problems with knowing whether a covenant with God has ever occurred.[48] I agree with Curley's arguments.[49] What they show is that Hobbes's theory does not justify the belief that God covenanted with any person, not what Curley asserts, namely, that Hobbes meant that God never covenanted with any person, that is, that Hobbes *intended* his audience to *recognize* that he *wanted* them to *think* that the belief that God covenanted with any person is false. [50] Showing the latter is much more difficult because of the embedded intentional attitudes. But the latter is required by the concept of meaning something.[51] The purpose of enumerating the various Absurdities is to show how difficult it is to justify the strategy of 'reading between the lines' once the odd consequences of Hobbes's theory, consequences unrelated to divine covenants, are noted.[52]

Perhaps there is some other way to motivate 'reading between the lines'. Curley quotes this passage:

God is king over all the earth . . . [and also] king of a peculiar and chosen nation. For there is no more incongruity therein than that he that hath the general command of the whole army should have withal a peculiar regiment or company of

---

[47] Clarendon too says that God 'hath discontinued immediate Communication' with humans after the Bible was completed (*A Brief View and Survey of Leviathan*, 235).

[48] Curley, this volume, pp. 203–6.

[49] At one point in his article Curley says: 'According to Martinich, Hobbes could have made his view consistent if he had had at his disposal the fruits of modern Biblical scholarship, and deployed the distinction between parity covenants and suzerainty covenants.' In fact, I said that Hobbes 'might have found a way around his dilemma' if he had known of the distinction (*The Two Gods of Leviathan* (Cambridge: Cambridge University Press, 1992), 292). I do not think that Hobbes's view could be salvaged and do think that the Bible contains many internal contradictions and many doctrines that are rationally indefensible.

[50] There are well-known procedures for judging that when someone makes-as-if-to-say that *p* she conversationally implies that *q*. When an interpretation claims that an author made-as-if-to-say-that *p* and in fact meant not-*p* through some nonspecified or unconvincing line of reasoning, as scholars who favor 'reading between the lines' usually do in my opinion, the interpretation is dubious. And this is how I judge the nontheist interpretation. See H. P. Grice, 'Logic and Conversation', and A. P. Martinich, 'A Theory for Metaphor', both in Martinich (ed.), *The Philosophy of Language*, 165–75 (Grice), 447–57 (Martinich).

[51] Grice, 'Meaning'.

[52] I am tempted to say that it is possible that Hobbes was a nontheist, but we cannot know it. And therefore I resist.

his own. God is king of all the earth by his power, but of his chosen people he is king by covenant. (12.22)

He then says:

Can Hobbes seriously think that there is no incongruity, i.e. no contradiction, between God's being king over all the earth by nature and his being king over a particular people by covenant? Or is this an ironic passage, one in which we may reasonably suspect that Hobbes' implicit doctrine is in conflict with explicit doctrine? (p. 210)

Curley's incredulity is based on the fact that a general of an army might also command a regiment but that this command is not based on a covenant among the soldiers. This is correct but irrelevant. Analogies need to fit only as far as they are intended to fit. What Hobbes wants to show is that something can be F of the whole G and also F of a part of G: king of all people (all over the earth) and king of part of all the people (the chosen people). And his military analogy fits: a general may be general of the whole army and also general of a part of the army. So far from being meant ironically Hobbes's analogy is clearly correct.

Curley gives another reason for holding that Hobbes knew that his theory of covenants made divine covenants impossible. It is his claim that Hobbes's assertion that God could have a natural kingdom of right and a special kingdom by covenant is so obviously false that Hobbes must have intended his audience to recognize it. Curley says:

If God has an absolute right of dominion over all men, stemming from his omnipotence, I do not see what rights he might still have to acquire by entering into a covenant with man. What could he have *after* the contract which he did not have before? (p. 208)[53]

I think Curley's reasoning is based on a false belief about Hobbesian rights. He seems to think that if someone is a contracting party to a covenant, then that person always ends up with more rights after the covenant is made than he had before; thus, since God always had a right to everything, he could never in fact covenant. That this line of reasoning is unsound can be shown in at least two ways. (i) Suppose A and B covenant to each give C $10 dollars. Then neither ends up with more rights. (ii) In the state of

---

[53] Richard Tuck in discussion suggested that Hobbes answered the question 'What does God have after the covenant with Abraham that he did not have before?' in the *De Cive*, 16.4. In brief, it is that Abraham acknowledged that the person talking to him was in fact God and not someone or something else.

nature, every person has a right to everything; but this does not prevent them from covenanting.[54] They do not get more rights, even when a right is transferred to them. If Adam transfers his right to apple *a* to Eve, she does not get a right she did not have before;[55] rather, one potential barrier to her exercising her right has been removed. Also, when a subject transfers his right to kill his fellow man to his sovereign, the subject loses a right but the sovereign does not get a right that he did not previously have. The sovereign already had the right to kill his fellow man in virtue of being in the state of nature (28.2).

When Curley says 'If God's omnipotence *entails* that he has those rights, and if his omnipotence is an essential property he has ... , then God cannot cease to have those rights',[56] he seems to be confusing rights with power. God's power would no more be diminished by giving up some rights than a human's power is diminished by giving up rights. A person has as much natural liberty after entering the civil state as he had before *Leviathan* (14.2 and 21.6), as much power but fewer rights. If Curley were to object that this means that giving up a right produces no effective bond against God, the reply would have to be that that is Hobbes's doctrine: 'And covenants without the sword are but words, and of no strength' (*Leviathan*, 17.2; see also 18.4; cf. 21.5).

I have been able to defend a theistic interpretation of Hobbes's treatment of divine covenants without mentioning some beliefs that influence my general approach to Hobbes. But it may be helpful if I make these beliefs explicit. Hobbes lays out such distinctions as those between faith and reason, belief and knowledge, immediate and mediate revelation and applies them ostensibly to solve problems in philosophical theology, often in novel ways. If all of this were a sham, even for the purpose of getting his audience to read between the lines, he would risk looking like a buffoon who has gone to extraordinary effort to construct a philosophical Rube Goldberg machine. Hobbes aspired to construct a science of all things, was proud, and was sensitive about criticism. I do not believe he would adopt an argumentative strategy that would tend to make him an object of

---

[54] The case is different when someone has previously given up his right to something. Then that person may reacquire the right to that thing by a transfer of right.

[55] It is not essential to a right that it belongs to a particular person. Although Adam's right to the apple is not Eve's right to the apple, Adam and Eve are equal if both have a right to the apple, and it does not matter who gave the person the right. Even if God gave Adam his right to the apple and Eve received her right from some other source, Adam and Eve are equal with respect to the apple so long as each has a right to it.   [56] Curley, this volume, p. 208.

ridicule and to persist in it after it caused him to be ridiculed. [57] He wanted his theories celebrated, not laughed at. Given this desire, it was sensible for Hobbes to show that his theory explained the possibility of divine covenants and it was not sensible for him to show that divine covenants are impossible.[58]

[57] Curley seems to think that Hobbes's misrepresentations of the biblical text are another tactic for discrediting the Bible (Curley, this volume, p. 201). This strikes me as implausible. Wildly wrong, but seriously propounded, interpretations of the Bible are easy to find in sixteenth- and seventeenth-century texts. Hobbes's critic George Lawson, for example, claims that Jephthah did not sacrifice his daughter (*An Examination of the Political Part of Mr Hobbs His Leviathan, in Leviathan: Contemporary Responses to the Political Theory of Thomas Hobbes*, 56–7; cf. Judges 11:29–40). Clarendon claims that God was not upset with the Israelites for choosing monarchy (*A Brief View and Survey of Leviathan*, 74; cf. 1 Sam. 8:4–18). In *The Institutes of the Christian Religion*, John Calvin's interpretations, which have Jesus Christ talked about throughout the Old Testament, are replete with mistakes. Without some special background, such as in satire, a misrepresentation of the meaning of a text will not lead the audience to think that there is something dubious about the text, rather than about the representation of it. Of course, I do not think that Hobbes's discussion has the air of satire about it.

[58] I want to thank Jo Ann Carson, Luc Foisneau, Kinch Hoekstra, Leslie Martinich, and Sharon Vaughan for commenting on this essay.

Leviathan, *the Pentateuch, and the Origins of Modern Biblical Criticism*

NOEL MALCOLM

————◆————

I

In chapter 33 of *Leviathan* Hobbes confidently asserted that the Pentateuch was not written by Moses. It contained, he suggested, some Mosaic materials; but '*Moses* did not compile those Books entirely, and in the form we have them'. Instead, 'the Scripture was set forth in the form we have it in, by *Esdras*'—that is, by Ezra the Scribe, the person who, according to the books of Ezra and Nehemiah, was allowed by Cyrus to go to Jerusalem and teach the Law to those Jews who had returned there from the Babylonian captivity. In support of this argument, Hobbes cited a passage from the apocryphal Second Book of Esdras, in which Ezra is portrayed as rewriting the books of the Law after they had been entirely burnt in the destruction of the Temple.[1] Jewish tradition—accepted by Christian theologians—had long accorded a special role to Ezra: it held that he and his colleagues (the men of the 'Great Synagogue') had fixed the Hebrew Bible in its present form, adding the vowel-points and other editorial features of the text. But the Second Book of Esdras went far beyond that, in its claim that Ezra had miraculously rewritten all the Scriptures; and Hobbes, in the special use he made of this claim to reinforce a denial of Moses's authorship, went further still.

This apparent reassignment of the Pentateuch from Moses to Ezra was taken up enthusiastically by Spinoza in his *Tractatus theologico-politicus*. Before long, it would become part of the common stock of polemical

I am very grateful to Edwin Curley, Franck Lessay, and Quentin Skinner for comments on this essay. A much longer version of it, with more detail on the textual-critical arguments used by Hobbes, La Peyrère, and Spinoza, and on the question of the lines of derivation between their arguments, appear in my *Aspects of Hobbes* (Oxford, 2002), 383–431.

[1] T. Hobbes, *Leviathan* (London, 1651), 200, 203. The citation is from 2 Esdras 14:21–2, 45. This apocryphal book may be referred to as 2 Esdras or 4 Ezra; it will be referred to as 'the Second Book of Esdras' in this essay. (The two canonical books entitled Ezra and Nehemiah in Protestant editions of the Bible are 1 Ezra and 2 Ezra in the Vulgate, having originally formed a single text; there is one other apocryphal book, derived from a compilation of those two canonical books but with some other inserted material, which may be referred to as 1 Esdras or 3 Ezra.)

arguments deployed by the radical Enlightenment, from Thomas Aikenhead, who was executed in 1697 for having described the Old Testament as 'Ezra's fables', to Voltaire, who would write: 'People ask me who wrote the Pentateuch. They might as well ask me who wrote "The Four Sons of Aymon", "Robert the Devil", or the tale of Merlin the sorcerer . . . My guess is that Ezra made up all those Tales of a Tub when he returned from the Babylonian captivity.'[2]

During the last decades of the seventeenth century many defenders of Christian orthodoxy, both Catholic and Protestant, reacted against the denial of the Mosaicity of the Pentateuch, which they regarded as both a dangerous threat and a new one. They were in no doubt as to where it had originated. It came from an unholy trinity of heresiarchs: Hobbes, Spinoza, and La Peyrère. In 1679 the Catholic scholar Pierre Daniel Huet, for example, penned a refutation of Spinoza's arguments, remarking that they were borrowed from Hobbes and La Peyrère; in 1684 the Lutheran theologian Johann Benedict Carpzov, discussing this 'new hypothesis', observed that Spinoza had taken it from La Peyrère and 'that propagator of atheism in England, Thomas Hobbes'; and in 1692 the Calvinist Hermann Witsius noted that the Mosaic authorship had been universally accepted until the appearance of Hobbes's *Leviathan* (1651), La Peyrère's *Prae-Adamitae* (1655), and Spinoza's *Tractatus* (1670).[3] Modern scholars, while uncertain of the precise lines of filiation linking the arguments of these three works, are generally agreed that their rejection of the Mosaic theory marked a decisive new stage in the interpretation of the Bible—a development that has been called the 'exegetical revolution'.[4] For although the details of these

---

[2] On Aikenhead see M. Hunter, ' "Aikenhead the Atheist": The Context and Consequences of Articulate Irreligion in the Late Seventeenth Century', in M. Hunter and D. Wootton (eds.), *Atheism from the Reformation to the Enlightenment* (Oxford, 1992), 221–54. Voltaire: *Examen important de Milord Bolingbroke ou le Tombeau du Fanatisme*, in his *Mélanges*, ed. J. van den Heuvel (Paris, 1965), 1019–1117; here pp. 1027–8 ('On me demande qui est l'auteur du *Pentateuque*: j'aimerais autant qu'on me demandât qui a écrit *les Quatre Fils Aymon, Robert le Diable*, et l'histoire de l'enchanteur Merlin . . . Je conjecture qu'Esdras forgea tous ces *Contes du Tonneau* au retour de la captivité'). The 'Quatre Fils d'Aymon' and 'Robert le Diable' were popular (and anonymous) verse-romances. For details of other comments by Voltaire on Moses, Ezra, and the Bible see D. Levy, *Voltaire et son exégèse du Pentateuque: critique et polémique* (Banbury, 1975), esp. pp. 98–103, and F. Bessire, *La Bible dans la correspondance de Voltaire* (Oxford, 1999), 64–6, 195–7.

[3] P. D. Huet, *Demonstratio evangelica ad serenissimum Delphinum* (Paris, 1679), 140–4, 145 ('rationes . . . quarum partem aliquam è Leviathane Thomae Hobbesii Angli mutuatus est; partem è Praeadamitico Systemate'); J. B. Carpzovius, *Historia critica Veteri Testamenti autore Ricardo Simone . . . edita, oratione inaugurali discussa* (Leipzig, 1684), 31 ('Nova etiam hypothesis de Mose Pentateuchi minimè autore conferre huc debebat plurimum, cujus bonam partem à Prae-Adamitarum architecto Isaaco Peyrerio, & illo Atheismi per Angliam propagatore Thomâ Hobbesio post maledictum Spinosam didicerat'); H. Witsius, *Miscellaneorum sacrorum libri IV* (Utrecht, 1692), I. 14, 'An Moses Auctor Pentateuchi?' (pp. 102–30), esp. pp. 104–5, 119.

[4] The phrase is Anthony Grafton's: see his *Defenders of the Text: The Traditions of Scholarship in an Age of Science, 1450–1800* (Cambridge, Mass., 1991), 205. Cf. similar comments in

authors' claims differ significantly (La Peyrère does not nominate Ezra, Hobbes does so with qualifications, while Spinoza attributes to him not only the Pentateuch, but also Joshua, Judges, and the books of Samuel and Kings), they all bring forward, as evidence for their arguments, examples of anachronisms in the biblical text. This way of distinguishing different temporal strata in the text was a style of textual analysis that seemed to point directly towards the *Quellenforschung* of the eighteenth and nineteenth centuries; these three writers (among whom Hobbes was the first to set out his arguments in print) could thus be seen as pioneers of modern biblical criticism. However, a closer study of the evidence will suggest that some distinction needs to be made between the methods of criticism they used, and the radical uses to which they put the evidence uncovered by those methods.

II

Many centuries before these writers, Jewish exegetes had considered the possibility that some of the words in the Pentateuch were not written by Moses. Even the Babylonian Talmud accepted that the last eight verses of Deuteronomy (describing Moses's death and burial) were not by him.[5] One of the leading rabbinical scholars of the Middle Ages, Abraham Ibn Ezra (1089–1164), went further than this, however: he not only denied the Mosaicity of the whole of the last chapter of Deuteronomy (twelve verses, not eight), but also hinted that some other phrases here and there in the Pentateuch were later interpolations. Examples mentioned by him included the phrase 'beyond Jordan' in Deut. 1:1, which, referring to the wilderness, could only have been written by someone who (unlike Moses) had actually reached the Promised Land.[6] The fact that Ibn Ezra's arguments were cited

---

R. Popkin, *Isaac La Peyrère (1596–1676): His Life, Work and Influence* (Leiden, 1987), 1. The question of the filiation of these arguments between the three is complex. Spinoza probably had read both La Peyrère and Hobbes, but may have originally formed his position independently; Hobbes may have heard of La Peyrère's work when it circulated in manuscript, but there is no evidence that he had read it. See my discussion of these issues in *Aspects of Hobbes*.

[5] *Baba Bathra*, tr. M. Simon and I. W. Slotki, 2 vols. (London, 1935) (= vols. 5 and 6 of *Seder Nezikin*, ed. I. Epstein, 6 vols. (London, 1935)), i. 71 [14b]: 'Joshua wrote the book which bears his name and [the last] eight verses of the Pentateuch.'

[6] A slightly abbreviated version of the key text by Ibn Ezra, with Spinoza's Latin translation, is given in Spinoza, *Opera*, C. Gebhardt, 4 vols. (Heidelberg, 1925), iii. 118. The full Hebrew text is printed in J. Buxtorf, (ed.), *Biblia rabbinica*, 2 vols. (Basle, 1618–19), i, fo. 191ʳ, and translated in F. Stummer, *Die Bedeutung Richard Simons für die Pentateuchkritik*, Alttestamentliche Abhandlungen, iii, Heft 4 (Münster in Wuppertal, 1912), 11. On Ibn Ezra's theory see W. Maier, 'Aben-Ezra's Meinung über den Verfasser des Pentateuchs', *Theologische Studien und Kritiken*, 5 (1832), 634–44, and S. Regev, ' "Ta'amei ha-mitzvot" in R. Avraham Ibn-Ezra's Commentary: Secrets', in F. Díaz Esteban (ed.), *Abraham Ibn Ezra y su tiempo: actas del simposio internacional Madrid, Tudela, Toledo 1–8 febrero 1989* (Madrid, 1990), 233–40.

by Spinoza, in support of his attribution of the Pentateuch to Ezra, completes a larger historical pattern: for the techniques of textual analysis used by Ibn Ezra may well have been learned, at least in part, from his study of Islamic anti-Jewish writings, in which (thanks partly to a knowledge of the apocryphal Second Book of Esdras, which had long been available in Arabic translations) it was commonly argued that Ezra was the real author of the Pentateuch.[7]

From writers such as Ibn Ezra, techniques for the detection of interpolations in the biblical text were assimilated into the mainstream Christian tradition. The key figure here was the Spanish theologian and Hebraic scholar, Alfonso Tostado Ribera de Madrigal (1400–55), known as 'Tostatus', who made a careful study of Ibn Ezra's writings. He agreed, for example, that the description of Moses' death and burial was a later addition: although he considered it possible that Moses could have described his own death prophetically, he thought the phrase 'no man knoweth his sepulchre to this day' (Deut. 34:6) could not have been written by him. Elsewhere he came to a similar conclusion about the phrase 'unto this day' (Deut. 3:14): 'Those are not the words of Moses, but of Ezra.'[8] Other possible cases of interpolations were also discussed by him, in some cases to be rejected. What matters, however, is not so much his particular verdict on any of these cases, as the way in which he alerted readers to the possibility of constructing such textual arguments for post-Mosaic additions and alterations. Indeed, his first thematic discussion at the beginning of his commentary on Deuteronomy was the *quaestio* 'Who wrote the book of Deuteronomy: Moses or Ezra, or Joshua?', which began: 'Doubts are raised by many people over who might have written this book.'[9] Who those 'many people' were, he never said; perhaps this was nothing more than a rhetorical device. But by countering so explicitly these 'many' unnamed opponents, and by explaining so openly the logic of their argument, Tostatus ensured that the number of people considering—or even sharing—such doubts would indeed be many in the end.

After Tostatus, the next important writer to develop these arguments was a Flemish Catholic, Andreas Masius, who was recognized as one of the most brilliant Hebrew scholars of his day.[10] In his posthumously published book

---

[7] See H. Lazarus-Yafeh, *Intertwined Worlds: Medieval Islam and Bible Criticism* (Princeton, NJ, 1992), 56–73; E. Fritsch, *Islam und Christentum im Mittelalter: Beiträge zur Geschichte der muslimischen Polemik gegen das Christentum in arabischer Sprache* (Breslau, 1930), 59–60.

[8] A. Tostatus, *Opera omnia*, 23 vols. (Venice, 1596), v, fos. 183ʳ (Deut. 34), 15ᵛ ('Ista non sunt verba Moysis sed Esdrae'). On Tostatus see P. L. Suarez, *Noematica biblico-mesianica de Alfonso Tostado de Madrigal, Obispo de Avila (1400–1455)* (Madrid, 1956).

[9] Ibid. v, fo. 2ʳ ('Quis scripsit librum Deuteronomij, Moyses an Esdras, vel Iosue'; 'Quis hunc librum scripserit apud multos in dubium vertit').

[10] On Masius, who published a Syriac grammar and helped to correct the Antwerp Polyglot Bible, see C. G. Jöcher, *Allgemeines Gelehrten-Lexicon*, 4 vols. (Leipzig, 1750–1), iii,

about Joshua (issued in 1574, one year after his death) he presented a new version of the role of Ezra in the preparation of the Bible—one that was to have far-reaching consequences. According to Masius, Ezra the Scribe had not rewritten the whole of Scripture, nor had he merely 'restored' it in the sense of tidying up the text and removing minor corruptions; rather, he had taken a group of materials which were 'dispersed, scattered and mixed together in annals' and had 'collected, arranged and united them in, as it were, a single volume'.[11] Masius did not explicitly include the Pentateuch in this list of Ezran compilations; with regard to the Mosaic books, he commented only that Ezra had inserted a few words and sentences 'here and there'.[12] However, in a later discussion of another such example (the use of the place name 'Dan'), he remarked more ambiguously: 'The Mosaic books, in their present form, were not composed by Moses, but by Ezra, or by some other godly man.'[13] Also, in presenting his theory about the use of 'diaries and annals' in the compilation of the historical books, Masius gave the example of the 'Book of the wars of the Lord' mentioned in the Pentateuch (Num. 21:14). At the very least, this seemed to be another example of an Ezran interpolation (given that that book had contained descriptions of the actions of Moses, and was presumably written not by him but by a later chronicler). But if, as Masius said, the Jews had kept such diaries and annals 'in ancient times', and if Ezra had had access to such materials going back almost to the time of Moses, the possibility might reasonably have occurred to some readers of Masius that the story of Moses himself had been compiled out of similar materials.[14] Masius's account thus formed a starting point for the textual theories of Richard Simon (who saw the Old Testament as the product of a long accumulation of material written by 'public scribes') and, ultimately, for the *Quellenforschung* of scholars such as Jean Astruc in the eighteenth century.[15]

cols. 259–60, the comments in L. Diestel, *Geschichte des Alten Testaments in der christlichen Kirche* (Jena, 1869), 311–12, and the biographical sketch by H. de Vocht, 'Andreas Masius (1514–1573)', in *Miscellanea Giovanni Mercati*, 6 vols. (Vatican City, 1946), iv. 425–41. One leading modern biblical scholar, Moshe Goshen-Gottstein, reserves special praise for Masius: see his 'The Textual Criticism of the Old Testament: Rise, Decline, Rebirth', *Journal of Biblical Literature*, 102 (1983), 365–99 (at p. 372 n.).

[11] A. Masius, *Iosuae imperatoris historia illustrata atque explicata* (Antwerp, 1574), first pagination, p. 119 ('dispersa, dissoluta, confusa in annalibus'; 'ab Ezdra collecta, dispositaque, & tamquam in uno codice compacta').

[12] Ibid. second pagination, p. 2 ('interjectis, saltem, hîc, illic, verborum, & sententiarum clausulis').

[13] Ibid. second pagination, p. 301 ('Neque Mosis libros sic, vt nunc habentur, ab illo esse compositos: sed ab Ezdra, aut alio quopiam divino viro').

[14] Ibid. second pagination, p. 2 ('priscis temporibus apud Ecclesiam fuisse diaria, & annales'; 'liber bellorum Domini'). 'Ecclesia' here is Masius's term for the religious institutions of the Jews.

[15] See J. Astruc, *Conjectures sur les mémoires originaux dont il paroit que Moyse s'est servi pour composer le livre de la Genèse* (Brussels, 1753).

While Masius's arguments may have pointed in radical new directions, their orthodoxy was apparently never in question. Indeed, they were taken up by some of the most respected Catholic commentators of the next two generations—men such as the Spanish Jesuit Benedictus Pererius (Bento Pereira), who lectured at the Collegium Romanum from the 1580s until his death in 1610, or the Flemish biblical scholar Cornelis van den Steen (universally known by the Latin version of his name, Cornelius à Lapide), who taught at Louvain before moving to the Collegium Romanum in 1616. At one point in his commentary on the Pentateuch, à Lapide even made explicit the suggestion about the Mosaic writings which had been merely implicit in Masius's account: 'Note that Moses wrote the Pentateuch in a simple way, in the form of a diary or annals; Joshua, however (or someone like him) set those Mosaic annals in order and divided them into books, adding and interpolating quite a few sentences.'[16] As this statement shows, à Lapide's prime candidate for the role of editor was not Ezra, who lived long after Moses, but Joshua, Moses's immediate successor. The last chapter of Deuteronomy, he suggested, was 'by Ezra, or rather, by Joshua'; and when discussing Tostatus's attribution to Ezra of two phrases in Deut. 3 (about Og's iron bed, and the place name 'Bashan-havoth-Jair') he wrote: 'if these things were added by someone, they were added not by Ezra, but by the person who edited these Mosaic diaries soon afterwards.'[17] Nevertheless, in his later commentary on the Book of Ezra he maintained the standard view that Ezra had ordered and corrected the whole of the Hebrew Bible, and accepted that he was probably responsible for the phrase 'unto this day' wherever it occurred.[18] His commentary on the Pentateuch was enormously popular (it was reprinted ten times between 1617 and 1661), not only with Catholics but with Protestant scholars too, who appreciated his concentration on the literal meaning of the text.[19] Thanks to à Lapide, the idea that there were post-Mosaic materials in the Pentateuch became widely diffused in early seventeenth-century Europe.

Set against the background of this tradition of textual analysis, from Ibn Ezra and Tostatus to Masius and à Lapide, the critical methods used

---

[16] C. à Lapide, *In Pentateuchum Mosis commentaria* (Paris, 1630), 23 ('Aduerte, Mosen Pentateuchum simpliciter conscripsisse, per modum diarij vel annalium; Iosue tamen, vel quem similem, eosdem hos Mosis annales in ordinem digessisse, distinxisse, & sententias nonnullas addidisse, & intexuisse'). This commentary was first published in Antwerp in 1616.

[17] Ibid. 899 ('ab Esdra, vel potiùs a Iosue'), 907 ('si haec addita sunt ab alio quopiam, non ab Esdra, sed ab eo, qui diaria haec Mosis paulò post digessit, esse addita').

[18] à Lapide, *Commentarius in Esdram, Nehemiam, Tobiam, Judith, Esther, et Machabaeos* (Antwerp, 1734), 4. This commentary was first published posthumously at Antwerp in 1645; à Lapide died in 1637.

[19] For a list of editions (all at Antwerp or Paris) see A. Williams, *The Common Expositor: An Account of the Commentaries on Genesis 1527–1633* (Chapel Hill, NC, 1948), 276; Williams also notes that the next most popular commentary was that of Pererius (p. 8).

by La Peyrère, Hobbes, and Spinoza begin to look much less innovatory. Of the three pieces of evidence brought forward by Hobbes for the non-Mosaicity of the Pentateuch, two had been discussed by à Lapide, and the third by Ibn Ezra: Hobbes could not read Ibn Ezra's Hebrew, but he certainly knew people who could. Of the thirteen arguments adduced by Spinoza, six were cited from Ibn Ezra, four had been discussed by Tostatus and two by Masius. And of the six pieces of evidence presented by La Peyrère, five had been commented on by à Lapide.[20] True, the radical conclusion drawn by the three later writers—that the anachronisms in the Pentateuch proved not merely that some passages were added, but that the text as a whole was non-Mosaic—had not been put forward by any of the earlier commentators (though the Masius–à Lapide thesis about a subsequent editor forming the text from an assortment of Mosaic raw materials might be taken to point in that direction). But La Peyrère's basic idea—that there lay behind the biblical text a collection of disparate source-materials—had already been adumbrated in this, the scholarly mainstream tradition. Indeed, the very phrase he used for Moses's original materials, *diurni commentarii* (daily commentaries), seems little more than a paraphrase of the term *diaria* (diaries), which had already been used by Masius, Pererius, and à Lapide.[21] It is not necessary, therefore, to suppose that La Peyrère's approach was either that of a revolutionary genius, or that of an autodidactic troublemaker who had just applied to the Bible his iconoclastic but home-made common sense.[22] What La Peyrère, Hobbes, and Spinoza were doing was to take some theories that were already widely available and set them off in a new direction; as so often seems to be the case in the history of ideas, the advance of radical heterodoxy came about not by means of a frontal assault on the orthodox tradition, but through a more complicated and opportunistic judo-like

---

[20] For a more detailed presentation of this evidence see my *Aspects of Hobbes*.

[21] I. La Peyrère, *Prae-adamitae* (n.p., 1655), 'Systema theologicum', IV.1, p. 153 ('Crediderim certe, diurnos commentarios Mosem confecisse'). (There are at least two different printings, in several different issues, of this book, all dated 1655. I refer to the one, probably by Janssonius in Amsterdam, in which the two parts of the book have 52 and 260 pp. respectively.) Klaus Scholder exemplifies a common overestimation of La Peyrère's originality when he writes that he was one of the first to develop a 'literary history' of the Pentateuch with his innovatory 'Fragmenten-Hypothese' (*Ursprünge und Probleme der Bibelkritik im 17. Jahrhundert: ein Beitrag zur Entstehung der historisch-kritischen Theologie* (Munich, 1966), 102–3).

[22] The first interpretation is that of Richard Popkin, who portrays La Peyrère as a 'revolutionary' thinker and the founder of modern Bible criticism (*Isaac La Peyrère*, 1–2, 48–50; on p. 50 he comments that 'Only the wildest radical enthusiasts of the Puritan Revolution and La Peyrère were willing to conclude that Moses was not the author of it all [*sc.* all the Pentateuch]'). The second is that of Anthony Grafton, who, while agreeing that 'no one did more' to make the 'exegetical revolution' happen than La Peyrère, assumes that his response to the Bible was largely unmediated: 'Two centuries later, La Peyrère might have stood at the back of a revival meeting, shouting "Hey, mister, where *did* Cain's wife come from?" ' (*Defenders of the Text*, 205, 211–12).

manoeuvre, in which the impetus set up by the orthodox thinkers played its own essential role.[23]

III

This brief survey of earlier theories about the text of the Pentateuch has answered one question—from where might Hobbes, La Peyrère, and Spinoza have derived the material for their arguments?—only to raise another. If these ideas had been current for such a long time (at least since the publication of Masius's work in the 1570s), why did the radical use of them, denying Mosaic authorship and attributing the Pentateuch to Ezra instead, spring up only in the middle of the seventeenth century? Surely the same arguments could have occurred to anyone at any time in the previous seventy-five years or so?

In fact there is one recorded example of an individual freethinker of the late sixteenth century reaching similar conclusions about Moses—though without making any reference to Ezra. In 1582 a schoolteacher from the Ardennes, Noël Journet, was burnt as a heretic in Metz; details of his errors were supplied in a subsequently published refutation. His main claims about the Pentateuch were, first, that Moses could not have written it, because it described his death; secondly, the argument from 'beyond Jordan'; and thirdly, an argument from the anachronistic use of the place name 'Hebron'.[24] The first two points could have been derived, as we have seen, from Tostatus, and the third may have been taken (directly or indirectly) from Masius; to this extent, Journet can properly be described as a forerunner of the mid-seventeenth-century writers, a radical adaptor of the mainstream textual-critical tradition.

Nevertheless, there was a considerable difference in style and purpose between Journet's approach and that of Hobbes, La Peyrère, and Spinoza. His aim was simply to portray the Bible as an absurd tissue of lies (in the

---

[23] While this background to the theories of Hobbes, La Peyrère, and Spinoza on the Pentateuch has been largely ignored by writers on those three thinkers, it has been briefly acknowledged by some historians of biblical interpretation: see Diestel, *Geschichte des Alten Testaments*, 357; Stummer, *Die Bedeutung Richard Simons*, 28; H.-J. Kraus, *Geschichte der historisch-kritischen Erforschung des Alten Testaments*, 2nd edn. (Neukirchen, 1969), 57.

[24] R. Peter, 'Noel Journet, détracteur de l'Ecriture sainte (1582)', in M. Lienhard (ed.), *Croyants et sceptiques au XVIᵉ siècle: le dossier des 'Épicuriens'* (Strasbourg, 1981), 147–56; here pp. 148–50. Journet's other arguments concerned petty inconsistencies (for example, if Moses had just turned 'all the waters' into blood (Exod. 7:20), what did the magicians of Egypt work on when they did the same?). See also F. Berriot, 'Hétérodoxie religieuse et utopie dans les "erreurs estranges" de Noël Journet (1582)', *Bulletin de la Société de l'Histoire du Protestantisme Français*, 124 (1978), 236–48 (with further examples of petty inconsistencies, p. 242). The refutation was by Jean Chassanion, *La Refutation des erreurs estranges & blasphemes horribles contre Dieu & l'Escripture saincte* (Strasbourg, 1583).

words of his indictment, 'saying that the holy Scripture is full of fables, and of all sorts of fantasies and falsehoods').[25] Theirs, on the other hand, was to treat it as a normal document, a human artefact which had a history of its own, and which could thus be subjected to historical analysis. In the accounts of Hobbes and Spinoza, the role of Ezra was therefore not some contingent extra detail; it was an essential part of their human, historical, and indeed political explanation of the nature and function of the text. These two writers in particular were drawing not only on a tradition of argument about textual interpolations in the Pentateuch, but also on other debates which had developed during the late sixteenth and early seventeenth centuries—not just about the role of Ezra, but also about the whole nature of the biblical text. Their position cannot be properly understood unless it is also set against this broader background.

The general idea of applying the methods of classical textual scholarship to sacred texts had been current since the writings of Valla in the fifteenth century and Erasmus in the early sixteenth. But its strongest stimulus came from the doctrinal warfare of Protestants and Catholics in the latter part of the sixteenth century. Although the early Reformers had shown some flexibility in their approach to the Old Testament (occasionally suggesting emendations of the Hebrew), the standard Protestant position that emerged in the second half of the century was that the Hebrew text—which meant, in practice, the Masoretic vowel-pointed text printed in Venice in 1525—was the inspired and inerrant Word of God.[26] At the fourth session of the Council of Trent, however, the Roman Catholic Church attributed a primacy of authority not to the Hebrew (or the Greek of the New Testament) but to the Vulgate. This was, on the face of it, a paradoxical position to adopt, as no one denied that the Vulgate's version of the Old Testament was itself a translation from the Hebrew. But the post-Tridentine Catholic polemicists argued that the version of the Hebrew which was used by Jerome (and which was now lost, its substance surviving only in the form of his translation) was actually superior to the present-day Masoretic text: in the centuries after Jerome, the Hebrew had been progressively corrupted by the Jews.

The Catholics' strategy was thus to undermine confidence in the Masoretic Bible, by demonstrating that it was, to some extent at least, the product of an historical process of human interventions. Inevitably, therefore, this approach promoted the application of textual-critical methods to the Hebrew Bible. Some Catholic writers, sympathetic to Hebraic scholarship, argued that precisely because the text was corrupted, it was necessary to use

---

[25] Peter, 'Noel Journet', 147 ('disant que l'Ecriture sainte est pleine de fables, de toute rêveries et mensonges').

[26] See the comments in Goshen-Gottstein, 'Textual Criticism of the Old Testament', 370–1.

rabbinical writings in order to get at its true meaning. One such was the early sixteenth-century Italian friar (of Albanian origin) Petrus Galatinus; another, writing towards the end of that century, was the French Benedictine Hebraist Gilbert Génébrard.[27] Both were enthusiastic defenders of the apocryphal Second Book of Esdras; both therefore reaffirmed the importance of Ezra as the 'restorer' of the text after the Babylonian captivity. Galatinus accepted that Ezra had rewritten the entire Hebrew Bible; he thought the vowel-points had been added a little later, and argued that the corruptions to the text had crept in during the centuries between the death of Ezra and the birth of Christ.[28] Génébrard, writing with the benefit of Levita's researches on the dating of the vowel-points, also denied that they were added by Ezra, but accepted all the other activities traditionally ascribed to him (retranscribing the text, correcting it, ordering the books and dividing them into verses).[29] This, the maximal version of the story of Ezra's restitution of the Bible, appealed to such Catholic writers because it could also function as a weapon of anti-Protestant polemics. It suggested that just as the authentication and interpretation of the Scriptures now depended on the authority and tradition of the Catholic Church, so too the priestly authority of Ezra, together with the 'tradition' embodied in the Great Synagogue, had been essential to the survival and re-establishment of the Hebrew Bible. As the leading Huguenot theologian André Rivet put it in 1627, Catholic writers, 'who leave no stone unturned to diminish the authority of the Scriptures', were using the apocryphal story of Ezra to insinuate that 'the Church had been preserved only by means of tradition, during the entire period of the Babylonian captivity.'[30]

The current of argument identified here by Rivet certainly existed on the Catholic side, but it was an extreme view, and a minority one. The mainstream Catholic position was set out by Robert Bellarmine in his lectures to the Collegium Romanum during the 1580s. Bellarmine rejected the idea that Ezra had miraculously rewritten the entire Bible; rather, he had merely collected and corrected the text, from copies which had survived throughout the captivity. Also dismissed was the claim that the Hebrew had been deliberately corrupted by the Jews. He concluded that 'the Hebrew

---

[27] See A. Hamilton, *Apocryphal Apocalypse: The Reception of the Second Book of Esdras (4 Ezra) from the Renaissance to the Enlightenment* (Oxford, 1999), 49–53, 63–5.

[28] P. Galatinus, *Opus de arcanis catholicae veritatis* (Basle, 1550), 3, 27, 32. This work was first published in 1518.

[29] G. Génébrard, *Chronographia in duos libros distincta*, 2nd edn. (Louvain, 1572), fos. 27ᵛ–28ʳ; on Lévita's arguments for the late dating of the vowel-points see G. E. Weil, *Élie Lévita: humaniste et massorète (1469–1549)* (Leiden, 1963), esp. pp. 297–313.

[30] A. Rivet, *Isagoge seu introductio generalis, ad Scripturam Sacram Veteris & Novi Testamenti*, in his *Opera theologica*, 3 vols. (Rotterdam, 1651–60), ii. 841–1040; here ch. 6, art. 18, p. 877 ('qui nullum non movent lapidem ut sacris literis derogent'; 'absque scripturis conservatam fuisse Eccles. solâ traditionis ope, toto tempore captivitatis Babylonicae').

Scriptures have not been generally corrupted by the efforts or malice of the Jews; nor, however, are they absolutely intact and pristine. Rather, they do contain some errors, which crept in partly through the negligence or ignorance of the copyists . . . and partly through the ignorance of the Rabbis who added the vowel-points.'[31]

In this way Bellarmine satisfied all the essential post-Tridentine requirements: he confirmed that the Vulgate represented a more authentic version of the text (because some corruptions had entered the Hebrew at a later stage, during the process of vocalization); he attributed just enough unreliability to the existing Hebrew to undermine the Protestant position, but not so much as to imply that the Hebrew could not be relied on at all; and he emphasized that, amid such uncertainties, Christians needed a source of authoritative judgement on the text.[32] This last argument—from the need for authority and certainty—would remain the most distinctive feature of the Catholic position, and the favourite vantage-point from which to attack the Protestants.

In response, the commonest strategy of Protestant writers was to attack the extreme Catholic claim that Ezra, acting as an embodiment of ecclesiastical authority, had rewritten the Hebrew Scripture, which had otherwise entirely perished. Often the Protestant writers would cite, in support of this aspect of their argument, the writings of Bellarmine, as if to show that the Catholic position was self-contradictory.[33] All they really demonstrated thereby, however, was that there was little disagreement between most Catholics and most Protestants on the nature of the tasks actually performed by Ezra: he had not miraculously rewritten the Hebrew scriptures, but he had collected, edited, corrected, ordered, and subdivided them. Those activities were considered to be of great importance, and one of the consequences of this whole debate was thus to give new prominence, in scholarly circles and more generally, to the role played by Ezra in the formation of the Bible.

Rashly, a few Protestants did also include among those activities the imposition of the vowel-points: the leading representative of this hard-line Protestant position was Johannes Buxtorf the elder, whose influential work

---

[31] R. Bellarmine, *Disputationes de controversiis Christianae fidei, adversus hujus temporis haereticos*, Controv. 1, 'De verbo Dei', in his *Opera omnia*, 8 vols. (Naples, 1872), i. 65 ('Scripturas hebraicas non esse in universum depravatas, opere vel malitia Judaeorum; nec tamen esse omnino integras et puras, sed habere suos quosdam errores, qui partim irrepserint negligentia, vel ignorantia librariorum . . . et partim ignorantia Rabbinorum qui addiderunt puncta').

[32] For a valuable discussion of Bellarmine's position vis-à-vis Protestant controversialists on these issues see J. C. H. Lebram, 'Ein Streit um die hebräische Bibel und die Septuaginta', in T. H. Lunsingh Scheurleer, and G. H. M. Posthumus Meyjes (eds.), *Leiden University in the Seventeenth Century: An Exchange of Learning* (Leiden, 1975), 21–63; esp. pp. 35–8.

[33] See for example Johannes Buxtorf, *Tiberias, Sive, Commentarius Masorhenicus triplex* (Basle: Jacob Dekker, 1665), 105; Rivet, *Opera theologica*, ii. 878.

Tiberias (1620) extolled Ezra and the men of the Great Synagogue as the people who, acting under divine instruction, had fixed the Hebrew Scripture in its present form.[34] But such an argument was all too vulnerable to the advances of biblical scholarship. In the second quarter of the seventeenth century Catholic writers launched a new wave of attacks on the Masoretic Hebrew text: they not only developed the existing arguments about the lateness of the vowel-points, but also made use of a new weapon, the Samaritan Pentateuch (i.e. the Hebrew Pentateuch as preserved in the archaic script of the Samaritans, who had become separated from the Jews), copies of which had just been obtained from the Levant.[35] According to one Catholic scholar, Jean Morin, the original Hebrew text, as represented by the Samaritan version, had been without vowel-points or even word-divisions, and was thus profoundly enigmatic and ambiguous; only with the divinely ordained guidance of the Church was it possible to establish its true meaning.[36]

Morin's publications caused outrage not only among his Protestant opponents, but also among Catholic Hebrew scholars in the French capital. Bitter quarrels on this subject raged throughout the 1630s and 1640s. One of Morin's supporters, a Maronite scholar from the Lebanon, Abraham Ecchellensis (Ibrahim al-Hakilani), who had come to Paris in 1640 to assist with the preparation of the Paris Polyglot, so offended one of the professors of Hebrew at the Collège Royal with his disparagement of the Hebrew Bible that the professor, Valérian de Flavigny, tried to take him to court.[37] According to a later memoir written by Ecchellensis, the main argument he deployed against de Flavigny was as follows: 'Although the Vulgate is indeed a translation, we must hold it to be as authentic as the original; for it has been declared such by the Pope, and by his general Council, in just the same way that the Hebrew text was restored and declared authentic by Ezra and his Great Synagogue after the Babylonian captivity.'[38]

---

[34] Buxtorf, *Tiberias*, 93–105; cf. the discussion in S. G. Burnett, *From Christian Hebraism to Jewish Studies: Johannes Buxtorf (1564–1629) and Hebrew Learning in the Seventeenth Century* (Leiden, 1996), 219–25.

[35] See J.-P. Rothschild, 'Autour du Pentateuque samaritain: voyageurs, enthousiastes et savants', in J.-R. Armogathe (ed.), *Le Grand Siècle et la Bible* (Paris, 1989), 61–74.

[36] See P. Auvray, 'Jean Morin (1591–1659)', *Revue Biblique*, 66 (1959), 397–414, and Lebram, 'Ein Streit', esp. pp. 30–2, 39.

[37] See P. J. A. N. Rietbergen, 'A Maronite Mediator between Seventeenth-Century Mediterranean Cultures: Ibrahim al-Hakilani, or Abraham Ecchellense [*sic*] (1605–1664) between Christendom and Islam', *Lias: Sources and Documents relating to the Early Modern History of Ideas*, 16 (1989), 13–41; esp. pp. 26–7. See also Ecchellensis's polemical reply to de Flavigny, *Epistola apologetica prima* (n.p. [Paris], 1647), esp. pp. 45–6, 54–5.

[38] Archivio di Stato, Rome, Fondo Cartari-Febei, vol. 64, fos. 70–84, 'Vita d'Abramo Ecchellense Maronita. Ab ipsomet die 16 Feb. 1657', here fos. 78ᵛ–79ʳ ('se bene la Vulgata è versione, si deue hauere, e tenere per authentica come il suo proprio originale, essendo per tale dichiarata dal sommo Pontefice, e dal suo generale Concilio, nell' istesso modo appunto, che fù

While divisions thus opened up among the Catholics, they also emerged on the Protestant side: the Huguenot scholar Louis Cappel, who had been one of the first to reject Buxtorf's claims about the antiquity of the vowel-points, composed a major work admitting—to the dismay of Protestant hardliners— that the Masoretic Hebrew text was unreliable. Cappel dismissed as a rabbinical fantasy the idea that the present text did not differ from 'the originals written by Moses or Ezra'.[39] He was building, to some extent, on Morin's work; but unlike Morin he believed that a reliable meaning could be extracted from the consonantal Hebrew by a careful application of the methods of textual criticism, without dependence on the authority of the Church.[40] Protestant scholars blocked the publication of Cappel's major treatise, *Critica sacra*, in both Holland and Switzerland; it was eventually published in Paris, thanks to the help of the Oratorian Jean Morin, the Jesuit Denis Petau, and Hobbes's close friend the Minim friar Marin Mersenne.[41]

It seems likely that Mersenne had followed these controversies over the nature and transmission of the Hebrew text very closely; he was also a personal friend of Abraham Ecchellensis. No one played a greater role in Hobbes's intellectual life in Paris in the 1640s than Marin Mersenne. So, although (or, indeed, because) Hobbes was not himself a Hebrew scholar, it is reasonable to suppose that he would have discussed these matters with his learned friend, and would therefore have been made aware of some of the latest developments in the theory of biblical interpretation—a theory which, with the transition from Morin to Cappel, had just entered a peculiarly critical phase.

The key problem was how to reconcile the text's authority, which was divine, with its history, which was more and more evidently human. Catholics depended on the authority of the Church to vouch for the divine authority of the text—an argument which could take surprisingly hyperbolic forms. A catechism published by Cardinal Sourdis included the question and answer 'To whom does it belong to define the canonical books?' 'To the Church, without whose authority I would grant no more credence to St Matthew than I do to Livy.'[42] This authority to declare the status of

---

restaurato, e dichiarato per authentico il testo Hebraico da Ezra, e dalla sua gran Congregatione doppo la Cattiuità di Babilonia'). Seen through Hobbesian eyes (with the authority of both the Pope and Ezra viewed as purely human), this formulation would bear a striking similarity to Hobbes's own position.

[39] L. Cappel, *Critica sacra* (Paris, 1650), 5 ('Mosis vel Esdrae autographis'). On his dispute with Buxtorf see Burnett, *From Christian Hebraism*, 229–39.

[40] For a valuable account of Cappel's theories see F. Laplanche, *L'Écriture, le sacré et l'histoire: érudits et politiques protestants devant la Bible en France au XVIIe siècle* (Amsterdam, 1986), 229–43.   [41] Ibid. 226–8.

[42] Cited in D. Chamier, *Panstratiae catholicae, sive controversiarum de religione adversus Pontificios corpus*, 4 vols. (Geneva, 1626), i. 148 ('Ad quemnam pertinet definire libros Canonicos?' 'Ad Ecclesiam: cuius absque authoritate non maiorem fidem adhibuerim Diuo Matthaeo: quam Tito Livio').

the text had traditionally been regarded as bound up with the authority to interpret it. Writers such as Bellarmine had thus been able to accept the idea that the text had been rendered uncertain (to some extent, at least) by a human process of transmission and corruption, because they thought this could only strengthen the need for an authoritative interpreter. But if modern research was making the Bible seem more and more similar to a human artefact such as the text of Livy, then it was also suggesting that the way to establish its meaning was simply to engage in more research and textual criticism: that, after all, is how editors of Livy resolve their textual problems, not by seeking out some superior authority.

The Protestants too had a theory of the authority of the Bible that was becoming increasingly dislocated from the practice of its textual study and interpretation. The standard Protestant view was that the Scripture was self-authenticating: every verse, every word of the Bible shared this self-evidencing divine quality, and this meant, in turn, that the only authority to be drawn on in interpreting any one passage of Scripture must be that of other passages. This approach to the Bible was especially vulnerable to the application of textual-historical methods. The problem was not merely that some words or verses might be shown to be corrupted and inauthentic—thus breaking the spell of the text's divine perfection. Rather, any internal differentiation of the text, distinguishing, for example, between primary materials and later editorial ones, or between directly inspired passages and merely historical narratives, might put at risk the belief in the Scripture's total uniformity of authority, suggesting that some parts of it were more human (and therefore less reliable) than others. This was the fundamental reason why a Calvinist such as David Pareus refused to accept the idea that some of the apparent anachronisms in the Pentateuch could be explained as later interpolations, insisting instead that they were all written prophetically by Moses:

How can Moses write about kings who lived long after him? . . . You may as well ask: how did he know about the creation of the world, the flood, the lives of Noah and Abraham, etc., which happened long before him? If you say, he knew these things because he had heard about them, it is clear that no mere rumour could have supplied him with such a precise and infallible history. Rather, one should say that he wrote that history by means of prophetic inspiration . . . For stories which are accepted merely on the basis of rumour and hearsay often contain something unreliable or fictitious.[43]

---

[43] D. Pareus, *In Genesin Mosis commentarius* (Frankfurt, 1615), col. 1683 (on Gen. 36:31) ('quomodo scribat Moses de ducibus, qui multo post eum fuerunt? . . . Pariter quaeras, vnde creationem rerum, diluuium, Noachum, Abrahamum, &c Moses nouerit, qui multo ante eum fuerunt? Si dicas, auditione eum haec habuisse, certe fama nulla tam exactam tamque infallibilem historiam ei suppeditare potuit. Potius prophetica inspiratione illam scripsisse dicendus est . . . Quae enim fama & relatione tantum accipiuntur, non raro lubricum vel fabulosum quid admixtum habent'). This work was first published in 1609.

Pareus was resisting an incoming tide of textual-historical interpretation, which was flowing through both Protestant and Catholic channels. As we have seen, the commentators on the Pentateuch may have maintained the theoretical possibility that the anachronistic passages had been written by Moses prophetically; but in many cases they thought they were actually strengthening the reliability of the text by providing a more natural and human explanation. Similarly, it was increasingly assumed that the veracity of the historical parts of the text could be defended (not weakened) by treating them as eye-witness reports, on the same basis as any other direct account of human experience. As Cornelius à Lapide put it, 'Moses received and disseminated these things partly from tradition, partly from divine revelation, and partly from knowledge as an eye-witness: for the events he narrates in Exodus, Leviticus, Numbers and Deuteronomy are events at which he himself was present, as participant or witness.'[44] In this way the miraculous uniformity of the Scriptures was subtly undone, as they were transformed into a complex artefact containing elements of different kinds and different derivations.

What this line of argument seemed to imply was that divine revelation, instead of being the condition or constitutive quality of the entire Bible, was something contained in just some of its parts: the words spoken by God or by angels, or the specifically prophetic utterances of the prophets. These might now be seen as isolated fragments of divinity, floating in a sea of human text. Admittedly, few orthodox theologians were willing to look at the Bible in that way, as they continued to believe that the human text too was written under divine guidance of a more general and providential kind. But one person who did not hesitate to push the argument to this conclusion—and, indeed, a little further—was Thomas Hobbes. He distinguished carefully between two senses of the phrase 'the Word of God': in the narrow sense it meant words spoken by God, and in the broad sense it signified merely words *about* God, the 'Doctrine of Christian Religion'. In the second sense, he observed, the whole of the Bible was the Word of God, 'but in the former sense not so. For example, although these words, *I am the Lord thy God, &c.* to the end of the Ten Commandements, were spoken by God to Moses; yet the Preface, *God spake these words and said*, is to be understood for the Words of him that wrote the holy History.'[45] The radical step taken by Hobbes (and avoided by all orthodox writers) was to point out that where a fragment of divine revelation is conveyed to us by a merely human narrative, its reliability can be no greater than that of the narrator himself—in other words, merely human.

---

[44] à Lapide, *In Pentateuchum commentaria*, 23 ('Moses haec partim traditione, partim diuina reuelatione, partim oculari inspectione didicit & accepit: nam quae in Exodo, Leuitico, Numeris & Deuteronomio narrat, ea praesens ipse vidit & gessit').

[45] Hobbes, *Leviathan*, 222, 223 (quotation).

If *Livy* say the Gods made once a Cow speak, and we believe it not; wee distrust not God therein, but *Livy*. So that it is evident, that whatsoever we believe, upon no other reason, then what is drawn from authority of men onely, and their writings; whether they be sent from God or not, is Faith in men onely.[46]

Hobbes thus adopted a position precisely opposite to the old Protestant theory about the self-evidencing, self-authenticating nature of Scripture as divine revelation. For Hobbes no revelation, once imparted to one human being, could be transmitted to any other human being in a self-authenticating way, as the means of transmission would be necessarily (and merely) human.

How God speaketh to a man immediately, may be understood by those well enough, to whom he hath so spoken; but how the same should be understood by another, is hard, if not impossible to know. For if a man pretend to me, that God hath spoken to him supernaturally, and I make doubt of it, I cannot easily perceive what argument he can produce, to oblige me to beleeve it.[47]

Traditionally it had been claimed that revelation could also be verified by the fact that it was accompanied by miracles and/or prophecies; these had been used as supporting arguments, by both Catholics and Protestants, for belief in the divine authority of the Bible. But Hobbes was able to dismiss this whole line of thought, using a devastating combination of scriptural arguments (about the ability of sorcerers to replicate miracles, and about the need to examine even successful prophets for their conformity with true doctrine) and ontological assumptions about the existence of natural causes for all such phenomena.[48]

Having thus placed the special authority of divine revelation out of human reach, and having reduced the status of the Bible to that of a human document, Hobbes might have left it there, on a par with the works of Livy, Plutarch, Thucydides, and the rest. Instead, he insisted that its composition was defined, and its interpretation regulated, by special authority—the authority of the Church, acting under that of the sovereign. Not having any direct instructions about the Scriptures from God, ordinary citizens must be guided by 'the authority of their severall Common-wealths; that is to say, of their lawfull Soveraigns. According to this obligation, I can acknowledge no other Books of the Old Testament, to be Holy Scripture, but those which have been commanded to be acknowledged for such, by the Authority of the Church of *England*.'[49] On the face of it, Hobbes was thus adopting

---

[46] Hobbes, *Leviathan*, 32.   [47] Ibid. 196.   [48] Ibid. esp. chs. 12, 36, 37.

[49] Ibid. p. 199. Hobbes's views on the relation between the authority of the Church and that of the sovereign in this context do seem to have undergone a significant development between *De Cive* and *Leviathan*: in the earlier work, the former type of authority had a different derivation from the latter, even though the exercise of it was entirely subordinate to the sovereign's authority (see L. Strauss, *The Political Philosophy of Hobbes: Its Basis and Genesis*, tr. E. M. Sinclair (Chicago, 1952), 72; H. Reventlow, *The Authority of the Bible and the Rise of the Modern World*, tr. J. Bowden (London, 1984), 213; J. P. Sommerville, *Thomas Hobbes: Political Ideas in Historical Context* (London, 1992), 119–27).

a version of the Catholic position—albeit one in which the authority of the Church was strictly subordinated to that of the political ruler. As some commentators on Hobbes have noted, there was a general congruence between his political theory and the Catholic theory of scriptural and doctrinal interpretation: in both, the need for an ultimate authority was paramount.[50] Occasionally the similarity could be quite striking. Thus Bellarmine, deriding the reliance of radical Reformation theologians on 'private inspiration' ('internus afflatus'), had exclaimed:

how much confusion and universal chaos would ensue if, in any human republic, the laws and decrees of the higher powers were taken away, and each person were allowed to do whatever seemed to him fair and just according to his own natural prudence? . . . What, then, would happen if private inspiration were the only thing to be looked for, and acted on, in that republic which is not human but divine [*sc.* the Church]?[51]

But in the writings of Catholic theologians such as Bellarmine this human, political analogy was only an analogy. The real argument was theological: Catholics claimed that the only sure place in which the gifts of the Holy Spirit (requisite for the correct interpretation of Scripture) were located throughout the ages was the Roman Catholic Church. The resemblance between Hobbes's argument and that of the Catholics was thus quite contingent; what for them was merely an illustrative analogy was for him the only real argument, because the only real authority on earth was human and political.

Hence the importance of Ezra. Hobbes's prime aim in setting out his Ezran hypothesis was not to ridicule the Scriptures, not to portray them as 'Ezra's fables', not to show that the whole Mosaic story was fictitious; rather, it was to substantiate historically his view that the only 'authority' the Scriptures could have was a human and political one. This, indeed, was what distinguished them from the works of Livy and the rest. 'By the Books of Holy Scripture, are understood those, which ought to be the *Canon*, that is to say, the Rules of Christian life. And because all Rules of life, which men are in conscience bound to observe, are Laws; the question of the Scripture, is the question of what is Law throughout all Chistendome.'[52] When people asked '*From whence the Scriptures derive their Authority*', he observed, they misunderstood the issue if they thought this was a question

---

[50] Robert Orr, for example, has commented on the 'somewhat bizarre agreement' between Hobbes and the Roman Catholic Church on the need for a sovereign interpreter: *Reason and Authority: The Thought of William Chillingworth* (Oxford, 1967), 86.

[51] Bellarmine, *Opera omnia*, i. 25 ('si in quavis humana republica, sublatis legibus institutisque majorum, id unicuique liceret, quod naturali sua prudentia aequum ac justum censeret; quanta perturbatio rerum omnium? Quanta confusio sequeretur? . . . Quid igitur fieret, si in ea republica, quae divina potius quam humana est . . . solus internus afflatus expectandus et sequuendus esset?').

[52] Hobbes, *Leviathan*, 199.

about why people believed those texts to be divine; different people had different criteria of belief (or, one might say, degrees of credulity), and there could be no general answer to such a question. Instead, 'The question truly stated is, By *what Authority they are made Law*.'[53]

Hobbes did not deny that parts of the Pentateuch (such as the 'Book of the Law' contained in Deuteronomy) were derived from Moses himself; Moses had been the legislator and civil sovereign of his people, and Hobbes had no difficulty in supposing that such utterances had had a genuine legal and historical status in the 'commonwealth' which Moses founded. What he objected to, however, was the idea that any text could have operated, through the centuries after Moses, as an independent locus of authority— independent, that is, of the political rulers of the day. Equally, therefore, he rejected the idea that when other texts were written (for example, the prophetic books) they immediately became authoritative by virtue of their own nature as divine revelation.

Accordingly, his history of the authority of the Bible was a chronicle of discontinuities, punctuated by political acts. Under Moses, and for many generations thereafter, the only canonical scripture had been the 'Book of the Law'; then, for a long time, this book had been lost, and the rulers of Israel had 'had no written Word of God, but ruled according to their own discretion'; then the Book of the Law was 'found again in the Temple in the time of Josiah, and by his authority received for the Law of God'. But, Hobbes emphasized, 'Moses at the writing, and Josiah at the recovery thereof, had both of them the Civill Soveraignty. Hitherto therefore the Power of making Scripture Canonicall, was in the Civill Soveraign.'[54] What Ezra did was in some ways just a repetition of what had happened under Josiah: a previously canonical text was reaffirmed as canonical (with, in this case, a large quantity of other texts being added to it). The key point, once again, was political:

From hence we may inferre, that the Scriptures of the Old Testament, which we have at this day, were not Canonicall, nor a Law unto the Jews, till the renovation of their Covenant with God at their return from the Captivity, and restauration of their Common-wealth under *Esdras* . . . Now seeing Esdras was the High Priest, and the High Priest was their Civill Soveraigne, it is manifest, that the Scriptures were never made Lawes, but by the Soveraign Civill Power.[55]

For Hobbes, then, the story told in the apocryphal Second Book of Esdras was simply too convenient to be disregarded: here was a ready-made foundation for the claim that the whole body of the Old Testament had been issued, at a particular time, by someone exercising sovereign power. He quoted at length, approvingly, from the passage in 2 Esdras 14 which begins

---

[53] Hobbes, *Leviathan*, 205.   [54] Ibid. 283–4.   [55] Ibid. 284.

with Ezra's address to God, 'Thy law is burnt . . .', and goes on to describe his miraculous non-stop dictation for forty days. Of course, Hobbes's own comments elsewhere on inspiration and the gifts of the Holy Spirit implied that any such story should be given a more naturalistic explanation. What exactly he thought Ezra had done, however, is not clear. One of the phrases Hobbes used, describing the Scripture as 'set forth in the form wee have it in, by *Esdras*', could have meant either that Ezra edited it (which was the orthodox view) or that he actually composed it; but he also referred to '*Esdras*, who by the direction of Gods Spirit retrived them [*sc.* 'the Bookes of the Old Testament'], when they were lost', which implies that they had previously existed in some form or other.[56] In his comments on particular books, Hobbes did argue in some cases (Kings and Chronicles, for instance) that they must have been written during or after the captivity; in other cases (the Pentateuch, Joshua, Judges, Samuel) he commented merely that they were composed 'long after' the time they described, without trying to identify the precise time of composition or the author. In several cases he accepted the traditional attributions: the Song of Songs was by Solomon, for example, and the prophet Amos did write the book which bears his name. And his general conclusion was that 'these Books were written by divers men'.[57] One might say that Hobbes was combining, in a somewhat nonchalant way, the orthodox view of Ezra as an editor of pre-existent materials with the more radical idea that he composed some of these books (including, possibly, the Pentateuch) himself. Nowhere in Hobbes's account does one find the sort of argumentation deployed by Spinoza, who insisted that most of the historical books of the Bible must be the work of a single writer, and tried to demonstrate that that writer must be Ezra.[58] Hobbes could afford to be nonchalant, even agnostic, about such matters. Questions of authorship were, for him, of secondary importance; the primary question concerned not authorship, but authority.

What Hobbes and Spinoza had in common, nevertheless, was that they were both trying to explain the development of the Bible in essentially historical and political terms.[59] Commenting on Spinoza's theory, the nineteenth-century scholar Ludwig Diestel observed that in presenting the Old Testament as something both natural and national (that is, to be understood as part of the political history of the Jews), Spinoza had broken out of the old dilemma, in which the Bible was to be viewed either as pure revelation, or as the work of impostors.[60] The same can also be said of Hobbes (with the qualification that the dilemma had not been entirely unbroken

[56] Ibid. 203.   [57] Ibid. 200–2, 204.

[58] Spinoza, *Tractatus theologico-politicus*, ch. 8, in *Opera*, iii. 126–7.

[59] See the valuable comments in J. P. Osier, 'L'Herméneutique de Hobbes et de Spinoza', *Studia Spinozana*, 3 (1987), 319–47, esp. pp. 334–41.

[60] Diestel, *Geschichte des Alten Testaments*, 359 n.

before he wrote). Unlike the radical anti-Christians who came after him, such as Aikenhead or Voltaire, he did not portray the Old Testament as a piece of outright imposture, cooked up by Ezra the Scribe. His account of its political history—of its establishment, in particular circumstances, as an authoritative text—gained more sense and solidity from supposing that the text itself had a previous history up to that point (albeit a various and uncertain one), that its narrative could be used as historical evidence, and that one component of it, the 'Book of the Law' in Deuteronomy, had been preserved from a much earlier political context, the government of the Israelites by Moses. In comparison with the orthodox tradition of biblical interpretation from which Hobbes had drawn many of his materials, his argument was, undoubtedly, heterodox and innovatory. But in comparison with the later arguments of the radical anti-Christians, it seems positively old-fashioned in its assumptions about the historical development (and therefore, in a sense, the historicity) of the text. Why, then, was Hobbes's Ezran theory so quickly and automatically assimilated to the radical tradition, by foes and friends alike?

Some commentators have felt that Hobbes's other remarks in *Leviathan* about the nature and reliability of the Scriptures, and his style of exegesis itself, were sufficient proof of a desire to ridicule and discredit the Bible entirely.[61] But the evidence here is ambiguous, at best. For example, when Hobbes states that 'although these Books were written by divers men, yet it is manifest the Writers were all indued with one and the same Spirit, in that they conspire to one and the same end, which is the setting forth of the Rights of the Kingdome of *God*', it may be tempting to argue that his choice of the word 'conspire' is a heavy-handed hint at deception and malevolence.[62] The word could have those overtones in early modern English, but it could also refer quite neutrally to the sharing of a common purpose: one sixteenth-century text declared that 'The cyvyle lyfe ys a polytyke ordur of men conspyryng togyddur in vertue and honesty.'[63] Hobbes's formulation

---

[61] For a strongly stated expression of this view see T. L. Pangle, 'A Critique of Hobbes's Critique of Biblical and Natural Religion in *Leviathan*', *Jewish Political Studies Review*, 4/2 (1992), 25–57, esp. p. 31.

[62] Hobbes, *Leviathan*, 204; cf. Q. Skinner, *Reason and Rhetoric in the Philosophy of Hobbes* (Cambridge, 1996), 412: 'There is thus a considerable *frisson* attaching to Hobbes's use of the term to describe the books of the Bible.' Professor Skinner does not argue that 'conspire' could only have had a negative sense; he cites it as an example of the rhetorical figure *aestismus*, which depended on inherent ambiguity between an acceptable meaning and a negative or satirical one. However, in most of the examples he gives (pp. 409–12), there could be little doubt that it was the negative meaning that was really intended; that, indeed, is why *aestismus* functioned as a 'mocking trope' (p. 409). My point is that in this case, given the direct precedent of Bellarmine's wording, there is a real possibility that the acceptable meaning was the one intended.

[63] Thomas Starkey, *Dialogue between Cardinal Pole and Thomas Lupset*, I. i. 19, cited in OED, 'conspire' (3).

was in fact strikingly similar to that of Robert Bellarmine, which he had almost certainly read: Bellarmine gave, as one of the proofs of the authenticity of Scripture, 'the incredible and obviously divine conspiring [*conspiratio*] and harmony of so many men, who together wrote the sacred books in different places, times, languages, and circumstances.'[64]

The point is not that such congruences with orthodox argumentation prove that Hobbes's overall purpose and meaning must have been equally orthodox. It is, rather, that the reasons why his treatment of the Bible was thought to be radically hostile to orthodox belief are to be found not in any of his particular arguments about the biblical text itself, but in the whole surrounding structure of argument—above all, in his naturalistic treatment of miracles and prophecy, and his epistemological blocking of any transmission of divine revelation from one human being to another. These surrounding arguments, after all, were the reason why his presentation of biblical texts as historically developed documents differed from the approach of those orthodox scholars who were also engaging in historical-textual analysis. Orthodox theologians such as Cornelius à Lapide or Hugo Grotius could treat the Scriptures as composite, human documents because they retained the assurance that one could know that God had been at work through those human channels. But Hobbes removed the basis for that assurance, making it unattainable and unknowable, and thus causing the Scriptures to be essentially indistinguishable from any other human writings. The fact that he regarded them as partly historical, while later radicals saw them as works of fiction, was therefore a secondary issue; the radicals were correct in supposing that, where the fundamental issues were concerned, Hobbes was on the radical, heterodox side.

Leo Strauss made a similar point in his study of Spinoza's biblical criticism, when he observed that philological-historical arguments in themselves could not destroy belief in the authenticity of revelation; for that purpose, more fundamental arguments of a theological or metaphysical kind were needed.[65] But his presentation of this point risked giving the impression that anyone who was deploying philological-historical arguments was at least trying to undermine revelation—even if the attempt, in the absence of those more fundamental arguments, was bound to be unsuccessful. As we have seen, there was a long tradition of applying philological-historical analysis to Scripture within orthodox Christianity; there was nothing

---

[64] Bellarmine, *Opera omnia*, i. 24 ('incredibilis quaedam et plane divina conspiratio atque concordia tot virorum, qui diversis locis, temporibus, linguis, occasionibus sacra volumina conscripserunt'). This is from Bellarmine's *De verbo Dei*, the first part of his *Disputationes de controversiis*. Hobbes wrote at length against the third part of that work (*Leviathan*, 300–20), and also commented on the sixth (pp. 346–7); so it seems reasonable to assume that he had read the whole work with some care.

[65] L. Strauss, *Spinoza's Critique of Religion*, tr. E. M. Sinclair (Chicago, 1997), 141–4.

implicitly or necessarily anti-Christian about it. While some of the claims made by Hobbes and Spinoza went far beyond what orthodox writers had hitherto allowed, their philological-historical arguments were, *qua* philological-historical arguments, products of that tradition. Which prompts the question: can it really be true to say that Hobbes and Spinoza (and/or La Peyrère) were the 'founders' of modern biblical criticism?

That these writers had a great impact is clear: the numerous denunciations of them, some of which were cited above, are testimony to that. To some extent they polarized opinion, pushing many people to extremes of acceptance or rejection. Thus on the one hand Hobbes's and Spinoza's theories about the Pentateuch were taken up enthusiastically by freethinkers such as Charles Blount in England and Antonie van Dale in Holland; on the other hand there were critics who insisted on the Pentateuch's Mosaicity, dismissing even the commonly accepted proofs of interpolations as a threat to true faith.[66]

Yet the most significant developments in biblical-critical thinking took place not at these extremes but, so to speak, in the middle. Most of the mainstream critics who denounced Hobbes, La Peyrère, and Spinoza (such as Huet, Carpzov, and Witsius) took it for granted that there were interpolations and editorial changes in the biblical text. Jacques Abbadie even put forward a theological argument *for* textual corruptions: the books of the Bible had undergone the vicissitudes normally suffered by all human texts, he suggested, so that wrestling with the resulting difficulties would provide good spiritual exercise for the faithful.[67] Richard Simon, while he was certainly innovatory in the contents of his philological-historical arguments, and although he was therefore denounced by many of these writers, belongs essentially to this middle ground: he defended the Mosaicity of the Pentateuch in broad terms by arguing that it was mainly compiled by 'public scribes' working under Moses's direction.[68] Simon was able to pursue his philological-historical arguments to their novel conclusions because he had worked out, at the theological level, a more subtle and advanced theory of revelation, in which divine inspiration was thought of as inhering in

---

[66] C. Blount, *The Oracles of Reason* (London, 1693), 16–17 (summarizing Hobbes); A. van Dale, *Dissertationes de origine ac progressu idololatriae et superstitionum* (Amsterdam, 1696), 686–7 (asserting Ezran authorship); A. Ross, *Leviathan Drawn out with a Hook: Or, Animadversions upon Mr Hobbs his Leviathan* (London, 1653), 35 (claiming that Moses 'writes of his death and sepulcher by anticipation'); J. Templer, *Idea theologiae Leviathanis* (London, 1673), 123–4 (insisting on Mosaic authorship of the whole text, with the sole exception of Deut. 34:6–12).

[67] J. Abbadie, *Traité de la vérité de la religion chrétienne*, 2 vols. (Rotterdam, 1684), i. 267–8 ('il a esté nécessaire aussi que la révélation des Juifs parût sugette aux accidens qui arrivent aux autres livres, pour exercer la foi encore à cet égard').

[68] R. Simon, *Histoire critique du Vieux Testament*, 2nd edn. (Amsterdam, 1685), 3 ('Ainsi l'on pourra dire en ce sens-là, que tout le Pentateuque est veritablement de Moïse, parce que ceux qui en ont fait le Recueil, vivoient de son tems, & qu'ils ne l'ont fait que par son ordre').

a whole collective process of human writing, not merely in the supernatural experiences of individual authors.[69]

After Simon, other writers were able to advance innovatory theories of their own, relying on the increasingly common assumption that the divine authority of the Scripture was not incompatible with a human textual history: thus the Remonstrant theologian Jean Le Clerc, for example, proposed that the Pentateuch was compiled neither by Ezra nor by public scribes, but by the priest sent to Samaria by the king of Assyria, and the Catholic Hebraist Étienne Fourmont suggested that it was written in the reign of David.[70] Fourmont's style of reasoning gives an especially good indication of how philological-historical arguments could be used within the theological mainstream. Responding to Calmet's reactionary defence of the Mosaicity of the Pentateuch, he noted that Calmet used the apparent anachronisms to disprove the claim that the Pentateuch was a work of imposture, on the grounds that no impostor would have left such obvious contradictions in his work. This was indeed a good argument against outright forgery, Fourmont observed, but it did not remove all doubts about when the text was written.

If one supposed that an honest man had written the Pentateuch, basing his work on the writings of Moses, and that he had done so at the behest of an enlightened prince such as David, or of the whole nation, one could follow the rules of proper textual criticism, without fearing any ill consequence, and perhaps one might even bring oneself to do so for reasons of piety.[71]

It was this principle—following the rules of textual criticism, for reasons of piety—that would lie behind the work of later scholars such as Jean Astruc; it had previously been applied by a whole series of writers, from Masius and à Lapide to Grotius, Cappel and Simon. Modern biblical criticism grew out of this tradition; it was not 'founded' by Hobbes or Spinoza, even though it may have been stimulated in some ways by their writings. It

---

[69] See R. Simon, *Lettre à Monsieur L'Abbé P., D. & P. en T., touchant l'inspiration des livres sacrés* (Rotterdam, 1687), 13–27, and the comments in J. Steinmann, *Richard Simon et les origines de l'exégèse biblique* (Paris, 1960), 209.

[70] J. Le Clerc, *Sentimens de quelques théologiens de Hollande sur l'Histoire Critique du Vieux Testament* (Amsterdam, 1685), esp. pp. 125–9 (referring to 2 Kings 17); E. Fourmont, *Lettres à Monsieur ** sur le commentaire du Père Calmet sur la Genèse* (Paris, 1709–10: two parts, continuously paginated), 24, 35. Both arguments were based on the idea that the Samaritan Pentateuch must have existed before Ezra (who were traditionally credited with replacing the Samaritan script with the 'square' Hebrew alphabet); the presumed interpolations, which were also in the Samaritan text, therefore could not have been made by Ezra.

[71] Fourmont, *Lettres*, 24 ('mais il reste toûjours un doute sur l'antiquité du livre; parce qu'il semble qu'en supposant un honnête homme qui auroit composé le Pentateuque, sur les écrits même du Législateur, & cela par l'ordre de quelque Prince éclairé comme David, ou de toute la nation, on pourroit suivre les regles de la veritable critique, sans craindre aucune conséquence, on se porteroit peut-être même à le faire par un principe de piété').

would also be an exaggeration to say that the anti-Christian tradition of the radical Enlightenment was 'founded' by those authors: it too had many other, and deeper, roots. But it can at least be said that the influence of their theories on that radical tradition was long-lasting and profound; and of all their theories relating to the Bible, none proved more congenial to radical minds, or more effective in radical hands, than the attribution of the Pentateuch to Ezra.

Hobbes's Protestantism

FRANCK LESSAY

———————◆·◆———————

De toutes les vertus morales, il n'y avait guère que la religion qui fût une matière problématique dans la personne de Hobbes.

(Pierre Bayle, *Dictionnaire historique et critique*, Hobbes entry)

Recent research on Hobbes's theology and religious thinking has made substantial progress. Writers take up questions in a spirit of tolerance and refrain from striking inquisitorial attitudes. More importantly, they acknowledge that it is impossible to ignore the subject or to treat it with any degree of credibility as peripheral to the political theory or, for that matter, to Hobbes's philosophical system. Most commentators have wisely given up pronouncing on the sincerity of the philosopher's statements. Yet they disagree considerably in their interpretations of his religion. We may distinguish three approaches taken by commentators. One was that of the Italian scholar Arrigo Pacchi. His most important studies on Hobbes have recently been collected.[1] They are those of a historian, concerned to reconstruct the coherence of a way of thinking on the basis of a genealogy of the author's views, going as far back in ancient and medieval times as necessary and excluding any a priori thesis.[2] The second approach—Aloysius Martinich's[3]—is strictly theological. Although it also aims to put Hobbes's ideas into historical perspective, the context chosen is more limited in scope. The investigation is guided throughout by a double conviction: that on no important doctrinal point does Hobbes's theology depart from the Calvinist orthodoxy dominant in the Church of England of the late Elizabethan, early Jacobean periods; and that though he was conservative-minded in that respect, Hobbes was a modernist in his unsuccessful attempt to reconcile religion with the new science of the time. The third

---

[1] Arrigo Pacchi, *Scritti hobbesiani (1978–1990)*, ed. Agostino Lupoli (Milan: Franco Angeli, 1998). Out of the ten studies in the book, seven are devoted to Hobbes's theology.

[2] This means the eventual admission of failure to establish the coherence mentioned, for example on the capital point of Hobbes's somewhat forced identification of the God of nature with the God of Revelation.

[3] Aloysius Martinich, *The Two Gods of Leviathan: Thomas Hobbes on Religion and Politics* (Cambridge: Cambridge University Press, 1992).

approach—Luc Foisneau's[4]—is a philosophical one. While it fully acknowledges the foundational significance of a central theological postulate—that of God's omnipotence—it explores its effects on Hobbes's anthropology and ethics.

Many valuable lessons can be learnt from these three lines of inquiry. But because they are largely concerned with the sincerity of Hobbes's professions of belief, they do not go as far as they might to provide a coherent or unitary understanding of the different and sometimes idiosyncratic religious views he claimed to hold. Important obstacles stand in the way of such an enterprise. We could cite Hobbes's own ambiguities on issues like the Trinity. There were also the bitter polemics in which he was caught up, which at times obscure both his own positions and those of his adversaries. Problems of definition have to be taken into account. Does it make *sense* to refer to an orthodox Protestant? Does Anglicanism mean the same sort of beliefs and sensibility at the beginning of the seventeenth century and under the Restoration? Finally, there are questions of method. The usual way of investigating such a field is by exploring sources. This can be most helpful, and recent instances of illuminating commentaries come to mind.[5] I, for one, shall first try to assemble the main pieces of the case so as to establish a tentative religious identity of Hobbes. I shall then proceed with an attempt to disentangle the various logics which seem to be at work in his doctrines. *Leviathan* will be the major focus of this survey, although other works will be cited.

I. PROBLEMS OF IDENTIFICATION

At one point in *Leviathan*, Hobbes seems to envisage the possibility that the civil sovereign might commit the care of religious affairs to the Pope, just as he might to any archbishop or assembly of bishops or pastors. Hobbes adds immediately that the men put in charge by the sovereign

---

[4] Luc Foisneau, *Hobbes et la toute-puissance de Dieu* (Paris: Presses Universitaires de France, 2000).

[5] George Wright's examination of the striking kinship between Hobbes's trinitarian doctrine and that of the Cappadocian Fathers in Antiquity; Stefano Simonetta's work on the links between Hobbes's and Marsilius of Padua's ecclesiological theories; Gianni Paganini's research concerning a likely influence of Lorenzo Valla on Hobbes with regard to the Trinity again. On grey areas of Hobbes's theology, these studies bring precious and welcome light. However, they deal with quite specific issues. Besides, although they help retracing Hobbes's probable intellectual ancestry, they are not meant to evidence the logic—if it exists—behind all the religious theses he advocated. To some extent, their partial character can be deceptive: emphasizing Hobbes's debt to humanistic modes of thinking, such as an anti-dogmatic, rationalist approach to theology, can deflect attention from various tenets he shared with extremist religious groups, starting with a radical concept of predestination.

would be subordinated to the latter's authority and would fulfil their appointed tasks *jure civili*, not *jure divino*.[6] The allusion to the Pope then appears for what it is: a thinly veiled joke. Considerations about the source and mode of authority of religious rulers directly challenge Catholic doctrine on fundamental points and confirm the true nature of the whole chapter, which is that it is to be read as one long anti-Roman pamphlet. Indeed, Hobbes's hostility to the Church of Rome is perceptible in many other passages of the book. Its grounds are summed up as early as chapter XII. They combine history and theology. As soon as the Church obtained official recognition of Christianity as the Roman empire's religion, popes set about imposing their rule on emperors, a goal they pursued in later periods with all other holders of sovereignty. The popes cited the necessity for sovereigns to be crowned by a bishop, or the legitimacy of exempting the clergy from civil jurisdiction, or again of deposing heretical princes. At the same time they acquired complete popular domination by propagating such preposterous doctrines as purgatory, which convinced people that the Church held the keys to their salvation. In their enterprise, they enlisted the priceless help of the heirs to Greek philosophy, Schoolmen, who elaborated all the theological absurdities appropriate for consolidating the Church's hold on the laity. In brief, the history of the Roman Church was one of continuous encroachments on the authority of lawful sovereigns. It was supported by an intellectual army equipped with philosophical weapons adapted to men's spiritual needs (or to their credulity). Hobbes presents a record of decadence of the original religion, due to the permeation of the faith by pagan superstitions and to the deliberate perversion of religious duties by men bent on gratifying their lust for power. In one of the few explicit references to the Reformation that *Leviathan* contains, Hobbes concludes by stating that the break with Rome was brought about in England as in other European countries by the contempt which the Roman clergy earned for themselves (just like the priests of the Gentiles many centuries before), 'by their uncleanness, avarice, and juggling between princes', and also 'partly from bringing of the philosophy and doctrine of Aristotle into religion by the Schoolmen, from whence there arose so many contradictions and absurdities as brought the clergy into a reputation both of ignorance and of fraudulent intention'.[7]

Later passages in *Leviathan* dealing with the same topics are just amplifications of those themes, which recur in other works like *De Cive* and even more so in the series of shorter treatises composed by Hobbes in the 1660s

---

[6] *Leviathan*, XLII:80. The first figure refers to chapter, the second one to paragraph. Edition used: Edwin Curley (Indianapolis and Cambridge: Hackett Publishing Company Inc., 1994).

[7] Ibid. XII:31. The whole passage includes paragraphs 31 and 32.

(the Latin version of *Leviathan*, the *Dialogue of the Common Laws of England*, the *Answer to a Book entitled the Catching of the Leviathan*, and the pamphlets on heresy). With the added denunciation of the canonization of saints as a new form of idolatry,[8] of transubstantiation as unintelligible and unfounded in Scripture,[9] of the papal claims to infallibility and to universal monarchy,[10] they are very much part of the stock Protestant arguments against the Catholic Church. They clearly suggest that Hobbes approved of the Reformation as an interruption of Roman dominance over Christendom. They find doctrinal support in several tenets which belong to what we might call a core Protestant theology, common to the major denominations derived from the Reformation—what comes closest to a form of orthodoxy in so far as this notion has any validity in a context of divided churches. Three of these tenets stand out. The most essential one is reliance on the Bible as the only acceptable rule of faith, the source of all necessary knowledge in matters of belief, and the best guide to salvation.[11] 'By the Books of Holy Scripture', Hobbes writes, 'are understood those which ought to be the *canon* (that is to say the rules) of Christian life'.[12] The Holy Scriptures 'supply the place and sufficiently recompense the want of all other prophecy' (this has been the case since the time of Jesus, who was the last true prophet) and from them, 'by wise and learned interpretation and careful ratiocination, all rules and precepts necessary to the knowledge of our duty both to God and man, without enthusiasm or supernatural inspiration, may easily be deduced'.[13] It is all the more important to determine with absolute clarity what few and simple articles of faith must be drawn from the Bible as 'eternal life and the salvation of each person are contained in Sacred Scriptures (whose reading our Church has permitted and recommended to all)'.[14] This must be achieved in such a way as to let Holy Writ produce its effects on each individual conscience without obstacles, 'because there ought to be no power over the consciences of men but of the Word itself, working faith in every one, not always according to the purpose of them that plant and water, but of God himself, that giveth the increase'.[15]

---

[8] *Leviathan*, XLV:34. This reference, like the following ones, is only to one illustration among others.

[9] Ibid. VIII:27; XXXVII:13; XLIV:11.

[10] Ibid. XLV:34; XLVII:3 (Latin text); the whole of chapter XLII for universal monarchy.

[11] One remembers William Chillingworth's proclamation: 'By the Religion of Protestants, I do not understand the Doctrine of Luther, or Calvin, . . . but that wherein they all agree, and which they all subscribe . . . as a perfect Rule of their Faith and Actions, that is, the BIBLE. The BIBLE, I say, the BIBLE only, is the Religion of Protestants!' (*The Religion of Protestants A Safe Way to Salvation* [1638] *Works*, (9th Edition, 1727), 272).   [12] *Leviathan*, XXXIII:1.

[13] Ibid. XXXII:9.

[14] Ibid. XLVII:29 (Latin text, Edwin Curley's translation as in all other quotes from that version of *Leviathan*).

[15] Ibid. XLVII:20. This statement is very largely a paraphrase of St Paul, from whom the metaphor of faith as a plant is borrowed: see 1 Cor. 3:5–8.

The second tenet, justification by faith, is suggested by the statement just quoted. Faith in Christ is what saves, to the exclusion of any other force or cause. As such, 'faith is the gift of God, and he worketh it in each several man by such ways as it seemeth good unto himself' (the 'most ordinary immediate cause of our belief concerning any point of Christian faith' being 'that we believe the Bible to be the word of God').[16] Faith does not make works (in the form of obedience to the laws, whether divine or civil) unnecessary. In fact, they are two requisites of salvation. Yet, works would be incapable, by themselves, of securing our salvation, because human nature is irremediably sinful. Thus,

all that is necessary to *salvation* is contained in two virtues: *faith in Christ*, and *obedience to laws*. The latter of these, if it were perfect, were enough to us. But because we are guilty of disobedience to God's law, not only originally in Adam, but also actually by our own transgressions, there is required at our hands now, not only *obedience* for the rest of our time, but also a *remission* of sins for the time past, which remission is the reward of our faith in Christ.[17]

In even greater conformity to the very language of sixteenth-century Reformers, Hobbes contends:

if by righteousness be understood the justice of the works themselves, there is no man that can be saved; for there is none that hath not transgressed the law of God. And therefore, when we are said to be justified by works, it is to be understood of the will, which God doth always accept for the work itself, as well in good as in evil men.[18]

Quite logically, justification by works is denounced by Hobbes as one of those doctrines—together with transubstantiation, penance, absolution, purgatory, indulgences and exorcisms—by which the Church of Rome preserved its 'kingdom of darkness' for so many centuries, in other words its illegitimate command of Christians' obedience.[19]

The gift of faith being obviously reserved for certain men, divine election is the third tenet central to Protestant theology defended by Hobbes. The occurrence of miracles (until the time of Christ, and not later) had no other purpose than 'to beget belief, not universally in all men (elect and reprobate), but in the elect only, that is to say, in such as God had determined should become his subjects'.[20] The Passion of Christ was intended to renew the alliance between God and the chosen few, Jewish at first, Gentile later: 'God, having determined his sacrifice for the reduction of his elect to their former covenanted obedience, for the means whereby he would bring the same to effect, made use of their malice and ingratitude.'[21] Granted that the soul perishes with the body, as many passages in Scripture indicate, one

---

[16] *Leviathan*, XLIII:7.   [17] Ibid. XLIII:3.   [18] Ibid. XLIII:20.
[19] Ibid. see XLVII:13–14.   [20] Ibid. XXXVII:6.   [21] Ibid. XLI:5.

must believe that only a fraction of men, and those designated from all eternity by God, will enjoy the benefit of eternal life after the resurrection. The words of Solomon—'That which befalleth the sons of men, befalleth beasts, even one thing befalleth them; as the one dieth, so doth the other; yea, they have all one breath' (Eccl. 3:19)—demonstrate this point if taken for what they evidently mean. 'By the literal sense,' Hobbes comments, 'here is no natural immortality of the soul, nor yet any repugnancy with the life eternal which the elect shall enjoy by grace.'[22] It is right, therefore, to claim that 'the elect are the only children of the resurrection, that is to say, the sole heirs of eternal life'.[23]

Giving full scope to the notion of God's incomprehensible and unchangeable decrees of salvation and reprobation, the whole of the treatise *Of Liberty and Necessity* argues for predestination. In reply to Bramhall's defence of free will in the name of God's justice and mercifulness, Hobbes paraphrases St Paul (Rom. 9:11–19) and writes:

When they, meaning Esau and Jacob, were yet unborn, and had done neither good nor evil, that the purpose of God according to election, not by works, but by him that calleth, might remain firm, it was said unto her [viz. Rebecca] that the elder should serve the younger, &c. What then shall we say? Is there any injustice with God? God forbid. It is not therefore in him that willeth, nor in him that runneth, but in God that showeth mercy. For the Scripture saith to Pharaoh, I have stirred thee up that I might show my power in thee, and that my name might be set forth in all the earth. Therefore whom God willeth, he hath mercy on, and whom he willeth he hardeneth.[24]

God's omnipotence implies predestination as an aspect of universal necessity. To worship God, which means to honour him, includes the recognition of that power of absolute and all-comprehensive pre-determination. 'He that thinketh that all things proceed from God's eternal will', Hobbes asks, 'and consequently are necessary, does he not think God omnipotent? Does he not esteem of his power as highly as possible? which is to honour God as much as may be in his heart'.[25] There is no sense in claiming that prayer is thus rendered pointless: it is also an effect of God's immovable will and must be understood both as a form of thanksgiving and as an acknowledgement of God's omnipotence. To Bramhall's objection on that count, Hobbes answers:

And for prayer, whereas he saith that the necessity of things destroy prayer, I deny it; for though prayer be none of the causes that move God's will, his will being unchangeable, yet since we find in God's word, he will not give his blessings but to those that ask, the motive of prayer is the same. Prayer is the gift of God no

---

[22] *Leviathan*, XLIV:24.   [23] Ibid. XLIV:29.
[24] *Of Liberty and Necessity*, Hobbes's *English Works*, ed. Molesworth, 11 vols. (London, 1839–45), iv. 248.   [25] Ibid. 257.

less than the blessing, and the prayer is decreed together in the same decree wherein the blessing is decreed . . . And prayer to God Almighty is but thanksgiving for God's blessings in general, and though it precede the particular thing we ask, yet it is not a cause or means of it, but a signification that we expect nothing but from God, in such manner, as he, not as we, will . . .[26]

For the same reason of God's omnipotence, which is self-justifying, the fact that men's actions result from the divine will does not mean that they must be immune from sanctions, whether or not they seem to be sinful. God's justice is its own measure. Besides, its exercise has an exemplary value:

An action therefore may be voluntary and a sin, and nevertheless be necessary; and because God may afflict by a right derived from his omnipotence, though sin were not, and because the example of punishment on voluntary sinners, is the cause that produceth justice, and maketh sin less frequent, for God to punish such sinners, as I have said before, is no injustice.[27]

All of those principles, which marked a definite departure from Roman theology, could be regarded as in accordance with the official doctrine of the Church of England, as expressed in the 39 Articles adopted in 1563 and ratified in 1572. The supremacy of the Bible as a rule of faith was stressed in Article 6 ('Of the Sufficiency of Scripture'); salvation by faith in Articles 11 ('Of the Justification of Man'), 12 ('Of Good Works') and 13 ('Of Works Before Justification'); predestination in Article 17 ('Of Predestination and Election'). To that extent, Hobbes had some cause to describe himself as an Anglican, as he did at times in *Leviathan* and much more often in later treatises when, precisely, that quality was denied him on grounds of heretical and blasphemous theological views. *Leviathan* contains few explicit professions of that sort. They deal mostly with the composition of the Bible, concerning which Hobbes writes that he can 'acknowledge no other books of the Old Testament to be Holy Scripture but those which have been commanded to be acknowledged for such by the authority of the Church of England'.[28] More numerous are the declarations of Anglican loyalty in the *Answer to the Catching of the Leviathan*. In order to defend himself against Bramhall's accusations, Hobbes even poses as a better follower of the Church of England's doctrines than the bishop, as exemplified by the exchange about the existence of a *cœlum empyraeum*: 'where is it in the Scripture', he asks, 'where in the Book of Common Prayer, where in the canons, where in the homilies of the Church of England or in any part of our religion?'[29] Pleading submission to the teachings of the Church of England, Hobbes

---

[26] Ibid. 257–8.   [27] Ibid. 260.   [28] *Leviathan*, XXXIII:1.
[29] *An Answer to a Book Published by Dr Bramhall, Late Bishop of Derry, Called the 'Catching of the Leviathan'*, Hobbes's *English Works*, iv. 347 (referred to hereafter as *Answer to the Catching of the Leviathan*). The allusion to homilies very probably refers to the Second Book of

vows to refrain from any utterance disagreeing with the Anglican creed: 'I profess still, that whatsoever the Church of England (the Church, I say, not every doctor) shall forbid me to say in matter of faith, I shall abstain from saying it, excepting this point, that Jesus Christ, the Son of God, died for my sins'.[30] Supposing, he claims, some of his theological views had appeared to belie this pledge in the past, two facts must be taken into account: the Church of England had ceased to exist and had not been replaced by any other national institution when he wrote *Leviathan*, so that no religious authority could control his opinions at the time; and it would remain to be demonstrated that his views contradicted Scripture. There again, Hobbes invokes, as it seems he can, the Anglican confession of faith: 'For the Church, though it excommunicates for scandalous life, and for teaching of false doctrines, yet it professeth to impose nothing to be held as faith, but what may be warranted by Scripture: and this the Church itself saith in the twentieth of the Thirty-Nine Articles of Religion.'[31]

To these affirmations must be added, in order to complete Hobbes's portrait as an acceptable Anglican, the vehement plea for Church government as established by law in England. *Leviathan* stresses royal supremacy in all religious matters, describing the sovereign's power in terms which seem to be borrowed straight from Elizabethan legislation. The claim—as against Cardinal Bellarmine's advocacy of the Pope's universal jurisdiction—that the civil sovereign 'hath the supreme power in all causes, as well ecclesiastical as civil' reads almost like a quote from the 1559 Act of Supremacy.[32] The whole of the exceptionally long chapter XLII can be regarded as a demonstration of that point, and one can understand why Hobbes, in the appendix to the Latin version of *Leviathan* published in the troubled year 1668, wrote in self-defence that the author of that book 'defended admirably the rights of the king, both in temporal matters and spiritual'.[33] The same object was vigorously pursued in the polemical works composed in that period, Hobbes posing once again as a more dutiful Anglican than

Homilies published under Edward VI, whose reading was recommended in the 35th of the 39 Articles ('Of Homilies') as containing 'a godly and wholesome doctrine'.

[30] Ibid. 367.

[31] Ibid. 355. Article 20 reads, as Hobbes suggests: 'The Church hath power to decree rites or ceremonies and authority in controversies of faith; and yet it is not lawful for the Church to ordain anything contrary to God's word written, neither may it so expound one place of Scripture, that it be repugnant to another.'

[32] *Leviathan*, XLII:80. See the pledge contained in the 1559 Act of Supremacy, which required acknowledgement that 'the Queen's Highness is the only supreme governor of this realm, and of all other her Highness's dominions and countries, as well in all spiritual or ecclesiastical things or causes, as temporal' (text from: *The Tudor Constitution. Documents and Commentary*, ed. G. R. Elton Cambridge: Cambridge University Press, 1984).

[33] Latin Appendix to *Leviathan*, III:1. Whether one shares the admiration expressed here by Hobbes for his own book is another matter.

his adversaries had been. He was the one who denied 'that the whole clergy of a Christian kingdom or state being assembled, are the representative of that Church further than the civil laws permit, or can lawfully assemble themselves, unless by the command or by the leave of the sovereign civil power', and asserted 'that the denial of this point tendeth in England towards the taking away of the king's supremacy in causes ecclesiastical'.[34]

The polemical texts deal with another key aspect of the issue of ecclesiastical government: namely, the internal structure of the Church. According to his reply to Bramhall, Hobbes favours episcopacy wholeheartedly, provided it is associated with the recognition of the sovereign's supreme authority. 'For my own part', he writes, 'all that know me, know also it is my opinion, that the best government in religion is by episcopacy, but in the King's right, not in their own.'[35] A system organized on the basis of such principles is declared to be the best possible one, as suggested in the idealized (or even idyllic) picture provided of the cooperation between sovereign and bishops when they are all of one mind on fundamental questions:

Where the king is a Christian, believes the Scripture, and hath the legislative power both in Church and State, and maketh no laws concerning Christian faith, or divine worship, but by the counsels of his bishops whom he trusteth in that behalf; if the bishops counsel him aright, what clashing can there be between the divine and human laws?[36]

Those are explicit and specific grounds for accepting Hobbes's self-description as an Anglican. Hobbes believed they found confirmation in biographical facts. There was his behaviour at the time of his serious illness in Paris, which had caused him first to reject courteously Father Mersenne's invitation to convert to Catholicism, then to accept Dr John Cosins's spiritual assistance.[37] His attitude on his return to England, when he had insisted on attending religious services following the Anglican liturgy, was also supposed to be telling.[38] Doubts about the *extent*—which is not to say the

---

[34] *Answer to the Catching of the Leviathan*, 337–8. This passage may well contain an implicit allusion to the 21st of the 39 Articles ('Of the authority of General Councils'), which states that 'General Councils may not be gathered together without the commandment and will of princes'.

[35] Ibid. 364. This repeated the claim, in his prose autobiography, that 'he had always approved of the government of the Church through bishops before all other forms' (in Edwin Curley's edition of *Leviathan*, p. lxiv). [36] Ibid. 364.

[37] 'A few days later, Dr John Cosins, afterward Bishop of Durham, approached him and offered to pray with him to God. Hobbes thanked him and said: 'Yes, if you take the lead in prayers according to the rite of our Church.' This was a great sign of reverence for episcopal discipline' (Hobbes' Prose Autobiography, in Edwin Curley's edition of *Leviathan*, p. lxv).

[38] 'When he returned to England, he indeed found preachers in the churches, but seditious ones; and extemporary prayers, bold, and sometimes blasphemous; but no creed, no decalogue. And so for the first three months he did not find any service in which he could participate. Finally a friend took him to a church more than a mile from his quarters, where the pastor was a good

sincerity, let alone the *reality*—of Hobbes's adherence to Anglicanism as understood by an exact contemporary of his such as John Bramhall (born in 1593 or 1594) begin to arise precisely when one considers the issue of Church government. Two points illustrate the differences between Hobbes and the established Church. One concerns the sovereign's power. Hobbes clearly ascribes full pastoral status to the ruler (whether English or not, although he asserts that his interpretation corresponds strictly to the legal position of the monarchs of England). Not only has the Hobbesian sovereign complete authority over the Church, the right to decide controversies in matters of faith and to appoint all its pastors and bishops; he can perform any of the latter's functions:

But if every Christian sovereign be the supreme pastor of his own subjects, it seemeth that he hath also the authority, not only to preach (which perhaps no man will deny), but also to baptize and to administer the sacrament of the Lord's Supper, and to consecrate both temples and pastors to God's service (which most men deny, partly because they use not to do it, and partly because the administration of sacraments, and consecrations of persons and places to holy uses, requireth the imposition of such men's hands as by the like imposition successively from the time of the apostles have been ordained to the like ministry).[39]

Putting his point even more forcefully in reply to an objection from John Bramhall to the effect that this was quite excessive, Hobbes did not hesitate to assert later that 'the King of England has all the right that any good king of Israel had'.[40] He was, in fact, going much further than English law provided, since the 37th of the 39 Articles stated:

Where we attribute to the Queen's Majesty the chief government, by which titles we understand the minds of some slanderous folks to be offended; we give not our Princes the ministering either of God's Word, or of the sacraments, the which thing the Injunctions also lately set forth by Elizabeth our Queen do most plainly testify; but that only prerogative, which we see to have been given always to all godly Princes in holy Scriptures by God himself; that is, that they should rule all estates and degrees committed to their charge by God, whether they be ecclesiastical or temporal, and restrain with the civil sword the stubborn and evil-doers.

Hobbes was aware of the unusual character of this proposition, since he admitted it would be denied 'by most men' for lack of familiarity with the practices he advocated. He also had in mind Queen Elizabeth's decision, alluded to in the 37th Article and mentioned in a later passage in

---

and learned man, who administered the Lord's Supper by the rite of the Church; with him he could participate in the service. This was another sign, not only of a man who favoured the episcopal side, but also of a sincere Christian. For at that time neither the laws nor fear compelled anyone to go to any church' (ibid. p. lxv).

[39] *Leviathan*, XLII:72.   [40] *Answer to the Catching of the Leviathan*, 345.

Leviathan, formally to renounce her pastoral functions just after the Act of Supremacy had been passed.[41] His position, however, must be correlated with the other major difference he had with the Church of England in the field of ecclesiology, which was to do with the sources of the power of bishops. The 'consolidation of the right politic and ecclesiastic in Christian sovereigns'[42] for which he argued implied that bishops—like all pastors in the commonwealth—held the whole of their right from the sovereign. They were '*his* ministers' (my italics), and their legal status was entirely identical to that of 'the magistrates of towns, judges in courts of justice, and commanders of armies', who 'are all but ministers of him that is the magistrate of the whole commonwealth, judge of all causes, and commander of the whole militia, which is always the civil sovereign'.[43] To the extent that any man could be said to rule men *jure divino*, this transcendant sanction necessarily benefited the sovereign and no one else, ruling out in the commonwealth two powers equal in dignity and equal, therefore, in their capacity to require the subjects' obedience:

All pastors, except the supreme, execute their charges in the right (that is, by the authority) of the civil sovereign, that is, *jure civili*. But the king and every other sovereign executeth his office of supreme pastor by immediate authority from God (that is to say, in God's right, or *jure divino*). And therefore, none but kings can put into their titles (a mark of their submission to God only) *Dei gratia rex, &c.* Bishops ought to say, in the beginning of their mandates, *By the favour of the King's Majesty, bishop of such a diocese*, or as civil ministers, *in his Majesty's name*. For in saying *Divina providentia* (which is the same with *Dei gratia*, though disguised), they deny to have received their authority from the civil state, and slyly slip off the collar of their civil subjection, contrary to the unity and defence of the commonwealth.[44]

Bramhall protested against this statement, which he said contradicted earlier ones by Hobbes (in *De Cive*) about the power of the keys conferred on pastors by their consecration.[45] However Hobbes's views evolved in this connection, Bramhall's indignation stemmed from his own conviction that bishops exercised their ministry *jure divino*.

In another book of controversy, *Schism Guarded and Beaten Back upon the Right Owners* (1658), Bramhall wrote that there was only one difference between Catholics and Anglicans on that issue: the former considered that the Pope alone held his special mission 'immediately' from Christ, all other bishops holding theirs mediately by papal designation; according to

---

[41] See *Leviathan*, XLII:78. Yet, Hobbes insists that Elizabeth took her decision in order to ease the conscience of members of the clergy who were reluctant to take the oath of supremacy to a woman, although not on legal grounds. [42] Ibid. XLII:79.

[43] Ibid. XLII:70. [44] Ibid. XLII:71.

[45] See *Answer to the Catching of the Leviathan*, 343–4. The relevant passages in *De Cive* are in III (part), XVII (chapter), 24–25 (paragraphs).

Anglicans, on the other hand, no such distinction applied, episcopacy proceeding uniformly from an immediate appointment by Christ.[46] Bramhall, in that respect, proved a faithful follower of Archbishop William Laud who, in 1637, had declared before the Star Chamber that, Calvin and his disciples notwithstanding, the bishops' office derived from God and Christ 'immediately'.[47] One might add—if any proof was needed in addition to the reference to Laud—that this doctrine in no way ran against the divine right of kings. James I also defended it. 'That Bishops ought to be in the Church,' he wrote in 1616, 'I ever maintained it as an Apostolic institution and so the ordinance of God, contrary to the Puritans, and likewise to Bellarmine, who denies that Bishops have their jurisdiction immediately from God.'[48]

Ecclesiology was not, however, the only area of clear disagreement between Hobbes and the Laudian Church. Theology was another, as shown by the example of sacraments. For Hobbes, they are mere signs, whose value is purely symbolic or commemorative. Neither do they carry any effective presence nor do they convey any grace. Their meaning is entirely abstract or figurative. Nothing important distinguishes them from levitical rites, whose contractual signification they share as tokens of membership of a nation or Church. One of the two that have scriptural validity, baptism, marks a person's deliberate adherence to the covenant with God, first concluded through Moses for the benefit of a single people, then renewed through Jesus Christ for the benefit of all believers:

He that is baptized is dipped or washed, as a sign of becoming a new man, and a loyal subject to that God whose person was represented in old time by Moses and the high priests, when he reigned over the Jews, and to Jesus Christ his Son, God and Man, that hath redeemed us, and shall in his human nature represent his Father's person in his eternal kingdom after the resurrection, and to acknowledge the doctrine of the apostles who, assisted by the spirit of the Father and of the Son, were left for guides to bring us into that kingdom, to be the only and assured way thereunto.[49]

The other, the Lord's Supper, commemorates this 'admission' into the community of Christ's disciples:

In the Old Testament the sign of admission was circumcision; in the New Testament, baptism. The commemoration of it in the Old Testament was the

---

[46] In Bramhall's *Works* (Oxford, Library of Anglo-Catholic Theology, 5 vols., 1842–1845), ii. 453.

[47] In *The Stuart Constitution. Documents and Commentary*, ed. J. P. Kenyon (Cambridge: Cambridge University Press, 1986), 148.

[48] James I, *A Premonition to All Most Mighty Monarchs, Kings, Free Princes, and States of Christendom, Works*, ed. James Montague, Bishop of Winchester (1616), 306.

[49] *Leviathan*, XLII:18.

eating (at a certain time, which was anniversary) of the Paschal Lamb, by which they were put in mind of the night wherein they were delivered out of their bondage in Egypt; and in the New Testament, the celebrating of the Lord's Supper, by which we are put in mind of our deliverance from the bondage of sin by our blessed Saviour's death upon the cross.[50]

What is at stake in both cases is an assumption of allegiance:

The sacraments of admission are but once to be used, because there needs but one admission; but because we have need of being often put in mind of our deliverance and of our allegiance, the sacraments of commemoration have need to be reiterated. And these are the principal sacraments, and as it were the solemn oaths we make of our allegiance.[51]

Bramhall correctly saw what those statements meant and exclaimed:

All the power, virtue, use, and efficacy, which he ascribeth to the holy sacraments, is to be signs or commemorations. As for sealing, or confirming, or conferring of grace, he acknowledgeth nothing. The same he saith particularly of baptism: upon which grounds a cardinal's red hat, or a sergeant-at-arms his mace, may be called sacraments as well as baptism, or the holy eucharist, if they be only signs and commemorations of a benefit.[52]

In this, he was relying on the doctrine he had expounded earlier, according to which the Lord's Supper is a 'commemorative, imperative, applicative sacrifice', communicating or confirming to the participants the benefit of God's grace through a 'representation' of Christ's death on the Cross. What commemoration the eucharist involved certainly did not exclude an active presence of Christ in the sacrament, whose sanctifying effect derived from the fact that in the language of the Holy Church, the things commemorated are related 'as if they were taking place'. The Lord's Supper, like baptism, depended for its efficacy as a sign on the 'analogy' between the sign and the thing signified, but this analogical dimension in no way reduced the rite to an abstract, purely reflexive process.[53]

Could it be that Bramhall was giving voice to a late, crypto-Catholic version of Anglican doctrine, somewhat removed from the original intent of the reformed Church of England, while his adversary was more faithful to the authentic heritage of that Church? The thesis of a pre-Laudian and pre-Arminian Hobbes, indelibly marked by the Calvinistic theology of late sixteenth- and early seventeenth-century Anglicanism, has attracted some commentators, notably Martinich. It does not seem to rest on very solid ground. Even though Bramhall presented a mild defence of the Thirty-Nine Articles, writing that they must not be considered as genuine articles of

---

[50] *Leviathan*, XXXV:19.　　　　　　　　　　　　　　　　　[51] Ibid.
[52] Quoted by Hobbes in *Answer to the Catching of the Leviathan*, 341.
[53] In *The Bishop of Derry's Answer to the Epistle of M. de la Milletière*, *Works*, i. 54–5.

faith, the expression of a necessary truth '*extra quam non est salus*', and that their main use was to provide a basis of unity between Anglicans,[54] it was obviously his notion of sacraments which accorded with that of the reformers of the Church of England. Article XXV appears to oppose word for word Hobbes's definition of sacraments as signs of admission or commemoration of admission, while it anticipates Bramhall's statements: 'Sacraments ordained of Christ be not only badges or tokens of Christian men's profession, but rather they be certain sure witnesses and effectual signs of grace and God's good will towards us, by the which He doth work invisibly in us, and doth not only quicken, but also strengthen and confirm, our faith in Him.'

The description of baptism in Article XXVII again rejected the idea of a mere 'badge or token' of membership of the Church and emphasized the conveyance of grace:

Baptism is not only a sign of profession and mark of difference whereby Christian men are discerned from others that be not christened, but is also a sign of regeneration or new birth, whereby, as by an instrument, they that receive baptism rightly are grafted into the Church; . . . faith is confirmed, and grace increased by virtue of prayer unto God.

The doctrine of the Lord's Supper, at last, stressed the real, although spiritual, presence involved in the two kinds of the sacrament: 'to such as rightly, worthily, and with faith receive the same, the bread which we break is a partaking of the body of Christ, and likewise the cup of blessing is a partaking of the blood of Christ. . . . The body of Christ is given, taken, and eaten in the Supper, only after an heavenly and spiritual manner.' The adverb 'only' contained in the last sentence can be explained by the explicit concern to repudiate the notion of transubstantiation. It does not mean that the presence of Christ in the eucharist is purely symbolic or commemorative. In that respect, the drafters of the Thirty-Nine Articles and— paradoxically—followers of theirs, such as Bramhall, agreed with Calvin's doctrine on the subject.

For all its figurative and metonymical value, a sacrament, Calvin contends, can be defined as 'a testimony of the divine favour toward us, confirmed by an external sign, with a corresponding attestation of our faith towards Him'.[55] To those participants who receive them with faith, 'the sacraments are truly termed evidences of divine grace, and, as it were, seals of the goodwill which he entertains toward us'; they 'sustain, nourish, confirm, and increase our faith'.[56] That is why—again—they are more than

---

[54] In *A Replication to the Bishop of Chalcedon, Works*, ii. 201.

[55] John Calvin, *Institutes of the Christian Religion*, IV (book), XIV (chapter), 1 (paragraph), tr. Henry Beveridge (Edinburgh: Calvin Translation Society, 1845). Text from the Internet at the site: http://www.bible.org/docs/history/calvin/institut/httoc.htm.   [56] Ibid. IV. XIV. 7.

simple 'badges', as Calvin writes about baptism:

those who have thought that baptism is nothing else than the badge and mark by which we profess our religion before men, in the same way as soldiers attest their profession by bearing the insignia of their commander, have not attended to what was the principal thing in baptism; and this is, that we are to receive it in connection with the promise, 'He that believeth and is baptised shall be saved'. (Mark 16:16)[57]

It is certainly true that 'the expression which is uniformly used in Scripture, when the sacred mysteries are treated of, is metonymical'.[58] But this is meant to remedy the infirmity of our minds, as can be deduced from the Lord's Supper:

as this mystery of the secret union of Christ with believers is incomprehensible by nature, he exhibits its figure and image in visible signs adapted to our capacity, nay, by giving, as it were, earnests and badges, he makes it as certain to us as if it were seen by the eye; the familiarity of the similitude giving it access to minds however dull.[59]

The 'similitude' between corporeal and spiritual things, therefore, is the most efficient means to secure access to the latter: 'by the corporeal things which are produced in the sacrament, we are by a kind of analogy conducted to spiritual things'.[60] Being 'represented under bread and wine', the body and blood of Christ, as we may learn, 'are not only ours but intended to nourish our spiritual life'.[61] Granting that 'the presence of Christ in the Supper' must be held 'to be such as neither affixes him to the element of bread, nor encloses him in bread, nor circumscribes him in any way', one will 'willingly admit any thing which helps to express the true and substantial communication of the body and blood of the Lord, as exhibited to believers under the sacred symbols of the Supper, understanding that they are received not by the imagination or intellect merely, but are enjoyed in reality as the food of eternal life'.[62]

In an exposition of his creed which reads like a commentary of Calvin, *A Reformed Catholic* (1597), the Puritan divine William Perkins is possibly even more explicit in referring to the 'real presence' of Christ in the Eucharist. Considered, on the one hand, 'in respect of the signs', this presence is relational: 'when the elements of bread and wine are present to the hand and to the mouth of the receiver, at the very same time the body and blood of Christ are presented to the mind.' Considered, on the other hand, 'in respect of the communicants', Christ's presence is experienced through faith: as there occurs in the believers' souls 'a real union, and consequently a real communion between us and Christ . . ., there must needs be such a kind of presence wherein Christ is truly and really present to the heart of

---

[57] Ibid. IV. XV. 2.   [58] Ibid. IV. XVII. 22.   [59] Ibid. IV. XVII. 1.
[60] Ibid. IV. XVII. 3.   [61] Ibid.   [62] Ibid. IV. XVII. 19.

him and receives the sacrament in faith.' As a consequence, Perkins writes, true Protestants do not differ at all from Catholics 'touching the presence itself, but only in the manner of the presence. For though we hold a real presence of Christ's body and blood in the sacrament, yet we do not take it to be local, bodily or substantial, but spiritual and mystical, to the signs by sacramental relation and to the communicants by faith alone.'[63]

Not only does there seem to be little sense in contrasting an archaic, Puritan-leaning Anglican Hobbes with more modern, crypto-Catholic Arminians like Bramhall: on the central issue of sacraments, it appears that Hobbes stood apart from a solid theological group which included Puritans and Arminian Anglicans alike, not to mention other Protestant groups. Another aspect of this opposition which is too well known to be dwelt on concerns the question of heresy. What must be stressed here as an indication of the distance between the contending parties is not the content of their respective doctrines, but the significance of Hobbes's main argument, whose effect is to strip all established Churches of their historical legitimacy. Whether Hobbes's own theological views were heretical or not, and whether his self-defence against the numerous and virulent accusations he was subjected to was convincing or not, what appears relevant here is his attempt to invalidate the very notion of heresy. The fact that the basis of his demonstration is provided in *Leviathan* (in the English version), i.e. long before the great wave of controversies he became involved in, strengthens the impression that the point was of crucial theoretical importance to him.

Just as *tyranny* is the name given to monarchy by men who are hostile to it,[64] *heresy* is a disparaging word applied to a private opinion. Due to 'ignorance of the signification of words, which is want of understanding',

men give different names to one and the same thing from the difference of their own passions: as they that approve a private opinion, call it opinion; but they that mislike it, heresy; and yet heresy signifies no more than private opinion, but has only a greater tincture of choler.[65]

Being nothing more than a disliked private opinion, heresy never justifies a disloyal attitude towards the man who holds it (an obvious implicit attack against Catholic policies, but one which could also be targeted against all those who had a disposition for heresy-hunting, and therefore a daring and perilous statement on the part of Hobbes, despite the rhetorical skill displayed in its wording):

Others, that allow for a law of nature the keeping of faith, do nevertheless make exception of certain persons (as heretics and such as use not to perform their

---

[63] William Perkins, *A Reformed Catholic* (Cambridge, 1597). Text from the Internet at the site: http://www.apuritansmind.com/WilliamPerkins/WilliamPerkinsSalvationMainPage.htm.

[64] *Leviathan*, XIX:2. The parallel between tyranny and heresy is suggestive by itself.

[65] Ibid. XI:19.

covenant to others); and this also is against reason. For if any fault of a man be sufficient to discharge our covenant made, the same ought in reason to have been sufficient to have hindered the making of it.[66]

In legal terms, heresy still amounts to a private opinion, one that is publicly defended although it is contrary to an official doctrine. 'Heresy', therefore, cannot logically apply to an opinion held by a sovereign, who determines public doctrines. Again, however, one must note that its intrinsic content is not what makes a claim heretical but its authoritative public prohibition:

heresy is nothing but a private opinion, obstinately maintained, contrary to the opinion which the public person (that is to say, the representant of the commonwealth) *hath commanded to be taught.* By which it is manifest that an opinion publicly appointed to be taught cannot be heresy, nor the sovereign princes that authorize them heretics. For heretics are none but private men that stubbornly defend some doctrine prohibited by their lawful sovereigns.[67]

The same purely relational defining characteristic was found even in the context of the early Church: what St Paul says on the subject shows that, in the absence of a Christian sovereign legally empowered to declare which opinions must be regarded as heretical, 'an heretic is he that, being a member of the Church, teacheth nevertheless some private opinion which the Church has forbidden'.[68]

The long pleas presented in later works like the *Answer to the Catching of the Leviathan* and the treatises on heresy only add historical and legal arguments to that basic framework, together with an attempted demonstration of the conformity of Hobbes's theological doctrines to Scripture: they do not reinforce by themselves what has been achieved in *Leviathan* (and which no doubt must have aroused the anger and indignation of many of Hobbes's readers), that is, the destruction of all philosophical or theological grounds for legitimizing the notion of heresy. As such, heresy has no connection with truth; it does not even deal necessarily with religion; it has no probable divine sanction; although it has to do with matters of interpretation (theological or otherwise), it exists as the result of an act of authority on the part of the sovereign and, to that extent, it must be inspired by political considerations, that is, by the concern for civil peace, and not for dogmatic purity or adequacy. In fact, one may doubt that, from that standpoint, peace and truth can be separated, as Hobbes intimates in his commentary on the sovereign's right 'to be judge of what opinions and doctrines are averse, and what conducing to peace': 'though in matter of doctrine nothing ought to be regarded but the truth, yet this is not repugnant to regulating of the same by peace. For doctrine repugnant to peace can no more be true than peace and concord can be against the law of nature.'[69]

---

[66] Ibid. XV:9. [67] Ibid. XLII:130. Italics in the original. [68] Ibid. XLII:25.
[69] Ibid. XVIII:9.

When Bramhall objects that, according to such principles, 'if Christian sovereigns, of different communications, do clash one with another, in their interpretation, or misinterpretation of Scripture, as they do daily, then the Word of God is contradictory to itself', Hobbes's reply confirms that the sovereign's decisions on religious issues bear no relation to truth and, consequently, have no saving or damning power:

It does not follow. For the interpretation, though it be made by just authority, must not therefore always be true. If the doctrine in the one sense be necessary to salvation, then they that hold the other must die in their sins, and be damned. But if the doctrine in neither sense be necessary to salvation, then all is well, except perhaps that they will call one another atheists and fight about it.[70]

The historical example repeatedly used by Hobbes of a sovereign deciding a crucial theological dispute (one which bore upon the foundation of the Christian faith), that of Emperor Constantine at Nicaea, serves to illustrate this point. It was not the contents of the Arian controversy which led Constantine to intervene in the dispute (Hobbes always neglects to recall the emperor's own sympathies), but the fact that it was, to quote *An Historical Narration concerning Heresy and the Punishment Thereof*, 'the cause of much bloodshed in and about the city [of Alexandria], and was likely then to spread further, as afterwards it did', and that this situation 'so far concerned the Emperor's civil government, that he thought it necessary to call a general council'. The way in which Constantine's general attitude is evoked and commented on by Hobbes is eloquent:

When they (bishops and divines) were assembled, they presented the Emperor with libels of accusation one against another. When he had received these libels into his hands, he made an oration to the fathers assembled, exhorting them to agree, and to fall in hand with the settlement of the articles of faith, for which cause he had assembled them; saying, whatsoever they should decree therein, he would cause to be observed. This may perhaps seem a greater indifferency, than would in these days be approved of. But so it is in the history; and the articles of faith necessary to salvation, were not thought then to be so many as afterwards they were defined to be by the Church of Rome.[71]

'Indifferency' to doctrine might well appear appropriate to many of Hobbes's readers. It was obviously chosen with care to underline what, in his eyes, were a sovereign's priorities in theological matters of the sort. All that then remained to be demonstrated was that there existed no legal basis for prosecuting Hobbes (or anybody else) as a heretic[72] and that, furthermore, his own religious views conformed with Scripture.

---

[70] *Answer to the Catching of the Leviathan*, 340–1.

[71] *An Historical Narration Concerning Heresy and the Punishment Thereof, Works*, iv. 391–2. See also the appendix to the Latin version of *Leviathan*, II:24.

[72] Hobbes's case, which I can only summarize here, rests on two main arguments. Assuming the Church had ever possessed the right to declare and condemn any one as a heretic, it had lost

Whatever their own merits, however, the texts dealing with those topics did not strike at the root of the case of Hobbes's various adversaries. More telling was his demonstration that the notion of orthodoxy was void of meaning, that it corresponded to transitory and reversible historical situations (Hobbes takes care to recall that a long time elapsed before the decisions reached at Nicaea became effective), and that, consequently, no Church was entitled to the role of defender of the faith. This judgement obviously applied to the Church of Rome, with its pretensions to infallibility in matters of belief and doctrine. It also concerned all the major Churches to which the Reformation had given birth, in so far as they conducted their theological wars in the name of orthodoxy and acted as self-proclaimed heirs to the true original religion. The fact that this notion was understood by reference to the creed formulated by some early ecumenical Councils of the Church (the first four for the Anglicans, as stated in the 1559 Act of Supremacy) did not affect the essence of the problem, as it had to be admitted that any lawful sovereign could modify that situation by choosing other terms of reference. Any constituted ecclesiastical body could proclaim itself orthodox with just as many titles as another, which made a mockery of such contentions.[73] Tradition was disqualified as a way of acceding to truth and as a legitimizing factor. It was only if such rational arguments failed to convince that Hobbes's two other types of approach, based on legal and on scriptural interpretation, were needed.

Hobbes thus estranged himself not only from the Church of England, but from the mainstream of Protestant Churches, which believed, rightly or wrongly, that they could not win the confrontation with Rome and their fratricidal disputes unless they established their credentials as unimpeachably orthodox authorities. He ran the risk of marginalization and aligned himself with radical religious groups which placed their struggle outside the bounds of official Church history. This tendency was reinforced by his advocacy of theological views which were akin to theirs. The assertion that only the souls of the elect were to enjoy immortality[74] and the denial of

---

that right to the civil sovereigns after their conversion to Christianity (history confirming political theory, as it always does with Hobbes). As far as England was concerned, heresy had ceased to be a crime, due to the repeal of all existing legislation on the subject under Elizabeth, and secondly to the abolition of the Court of High Commission and the Star Chamber (which could still claim a competence in that field) during the Revolution. See my introductions to the French translations of *An Answer to the Catching of the Leviathan* and of the various texts on heresy contained in the two volumes entitled *Liberté et nécessité* and *Hérésie et histoire* (*Œuvres*, 11/1 & 12/1, Paris: Vrin, 1993).

[73] As one remembers, this was to be part of Locke's case in favour of religious toleration: orthodoxy being an empty notion, persecution of so-called heretics was deprived of one powerful justification. From that viewpoint, Hobbes did lay an important foundation of toleration theory. See, on that point, Yves Charles Zarka, *Philosophie et politique à l'âge classique* (Paris: Presses Universitaires de France, 1998), 255 f.

[74] See in particular *Leviathan*, XXXVIII:4 and XLIV:15–16.

eternal suffering for the damned[75] were known to be part of the Anabaptist heritage[76] and had been the objects of repeated condemnations: the former, for instance, in the 40th of the 42 Articles adopted by the Church of England in 1553; both in book III, chapter 25 of Calvin's *Institutes* and, in Hobbes's time, in articles 32 and 33 of the 1646 Westminster Confession of Calvinist inspiration.[77] However, the main theological point bound to cause an outcry—as it did—was Hobbes's treatment of the Trinity, which also suggested that he had Socinian leanings. The question has been sufficiently researched not to require a long commentary.[78] It should be enough to stress that what was certainly problematic in Hobbes's position was his evident tendency to reduce Jesus Christ to some purely human dimension on the one hand, and, on the other hand, to identify the persons of the Trinity with three successive historical representatives of God. As duly noted by Bramhall among many others, little seemed to be left by Hobbes of the traditional definition of the Trinity (since the Council of Nicaea) when one read in *Leviathan*:

To conclude, the doctrine of the Trinity, as far as can be gathered directly from Scripture, is in substance this: that God, who is always one and the same, was the person represented by Moses; the person represented by his Son incarnate; and the person represented by the apostles. As represented by the apostles, the Holy Spirit by which they spake is God; as represented by his Son (that was God and

---

[75] Among other passages, see ibid. XLIV:29.

[76] Both tenets were part of the ten fundamental points agreed upon at the Anabaptist synod of Venice in 1550 (see E. M. Wilbur, *A History of Unitarianism. Socinianism and its Antecedents* (Cambridge: Harvard University Press, 1946), 85). They could be found in the writings of the two Sozzini (see the texts published in *Per la storia degli eretici italiani del secolo XVI in Europeo*, ed. D. Cantimori and E. Feist, Rome: Reale Academia d'Italia, 1937) and throughout Socinian literature. The Quakers were adherents of those views. On the specific question of mortalism, see Norman T. Burns, *Christian Mortalism from Tyndale to Milton* (Cambridge: Harvard University Press, 1972). On Hobbes's mortalism, Nathaniel H. Henry, 'Milton and Hobbes: Mortalism and the Intermediate State', *Studies in Philology*, 48 (1951), 234–49; David Johnston, 'Hobbes's Mortalism', *History of Political Thought* 10/4, (1989), 647–63, and my own 'Mortalisme chrétien: l'étrange rencontre entre Hobbes et Milton', *Bulletin de la société d'études anglo-américaines des XVIIe et XVIIIe siècles* 32 (June 1991), 21–33.

[77] On the flood of virulent reactions provoked by Hobbes's defence of those heterodox views in Anglican and Puritan circles, see the so far unreplaced study by S. I. Mintz, *The Hunting of Leviathan: Seventeenth-Century Reactions to the Materialism and Moral Philosophy of Thomas Hobbes* (Cambridge: Cambridge University Press, 1962).

[78] Besides George Wright's 'Hobbes and the Economic Trinity' (see n. 5), see D. H. J. Warner, 'Hobbes's Interpretation of the Doctrine of the Trinity', *The Journal of Religious History* 5/4 (December 1969), 299–313; Alexandre Matheron, 'Hobbes, la Trinité et les caprices de la représentation', in Yves Charles Zarka and Jean Bernhardt (eds.), *Thomas Hobbes. Philosophie première, théorie de la science et politique* (Paris: Presses Universitaires de France, 1990), 381–90; and my own two articles, 'Le vocabulaire de la personne', in Yves Charles Zarka (ed.), *Hobbes et son vocabulaire: études de lexicographie philosophique* (Paris: Vrin, 1992), 155–86; 'Christologie de Hobbes: le soupçon de socinianisme', in Guido Canziani and Yves Charles Zarka (eds.), *L'interpretazione nei secoli XVI e XVII* (Milan: Franco Angeli, 1993), 549–64.

man) the Son is that God; as represented by Moses and the high priests, the Father (that is to say, the Father of our Lord Jesus Christ) is that God. From whence we may gather the reason why those names *Father, Son,* and *Holy Spirit* in the signification of the Godhead, are never used in the Old Testament; for they are persons, that is, they have their names from representing; which could not be, till divers men had represented God's person in ruling or in directing under him.[79]

It did not help Hobbes to dispel the suspicion caused by this statement to grant some years later that it contained 'a fault in the ratiocination' (although 'no impiety') and that he should have written:

God, in his own person, both created the world, and instituted a Church in Israel, using therein the ministry of Moses: the same God, in the person of his Son, God and man, redeemed the same world, and the same Church; the same God, in the person of the Holy Ghost, sanctified the same Church, and all the faithful men in the world.[80]

Although the former persons of the Trinity now became ministers of God, the triune nature of the divinity was still understood in terms of historical representation and, from that viewpoint, Jesus played a role undistinguishable from that of Moses and the apostles, as both an instrument and a stage in the development of God's action in history. Hobbes's revised wording of his interpretation confirmed what his description of the Saviour's office in *Leviathan* had suggested: Jesus, one reads, 'is to be king' in future, but 'no otherwise than as subordinate or vice-gerent of God the Father, as Moses was in the wilderness, and as the high priests were before the reign of Saul, and as the kings were after it'; he also 'resembled Moses in the institution of *sacraments*, both of *admission* into the kingdom of God, and of *commemoration* of his deliverance of his elect from their miserable condition'.[81]

Such views dealt with key points in Christian doctrine, and it did seem that Hobbes had much in common with a very particular offshoot of the Reformation. Yet, one must again beware of hasty assimilations. With Anabaptists of all shades, Hobbes had at least two capital differences. Most of them rejected predestination as injurious to God's benevolent nature, which they argued implied man's free will and his capacity to gain salvation by his own endeavours.[82] In that respect, it was the Arminians' position

---

[79] *Leviathan*, XLII:3. Bramhall commented: 'What is now become of the great adorable mystery of the blessed undivided Trinity? It is shrunk into nothing. Upon his grounds, there was a time when there was no Trinity . . . What is now become of the eternal generation of the Son of God, if this sonship did not begin until about four thousand years after the creation were expired?' (quoted in *Answer to the Catching of the Leviathan*, 315).

[80] *Answer to the Catching of the Leviathan*, 316.

[81] *Leviathan*, XLI:7–8. Needless to say the kingdom of God mentioned here is the 'prophetical' one, founded on a pact with the chosen people which is renewed later with Christ's disciples.

[82] See the Rakow Catechism, which contains the complete Socinian confession of faith, on free will: *Catechesis Ecclesiarum Polonicarum* (Stauropoli, 1684), sect. 6, ch. 10, 'De libero arbitrio'.

which, paradoxically, was similar to that of the Anabaptists. Moreover, the
latter were in favour of a complete separation between the temporal and
the spiritual spheres and preached abstention from civic (and military, for
that matter) activities:[83] on these two points, the distance from Hobbes
could hardly be greater. The author of *Leviathan* was indeed difficult to
situate in the constellation of Protestant creeds.

II. QUESTIONS OF LOGIC

Trying to assemble Hobbes's various religious doctrines into one coherent,
identifiable whole requires finding—if it is possible—the logic behind them,
disengaging the principles which, perhaps, serve as connecting threads
between them. One basis of elucidation which immediately comes to mind
is politics. The primacy of political concerns might explain the peculiar
form of Hobbes's set of doctrines. More precisely, his theory of sovereignty
seems to make it necessary that he favour a national Church, support royal
supremacy in ecclesiastical matters, endorse episcopacy as the most efficient instrument of Church government and as the most pliable to the sovereign's rule. One might, in fact, go further in that direction and observe
that the same logic contributes to the intelligibility of other aspects of
Hobbes's thinking in the field. The refusal to concede any divine right to
bishops is very largely a political matter, in so far as what is at stake is the
possible emergence of two rival forces in the commonwealth. Rejecting as
fatally dangerous the distinction between a spiritual and a temporal power
is not enough to secure the necessary monopoly of authority in the civil
sovereign's hands:[84] the denunciation of the worldly ambitions of all clergies must be completed by the legal demonstration that, as shown by the
example of England, bishops can only hold what prerogatives and rights
are entrusted to them by the ruler and are not in a position to compete
with him as regards the source of their power. Similarly, one could argue
that Hobbes's treatment of heresy can be explained by the determination
to weaken the political influence of Churches. The arguments used to criticize the persecution of heretics are primarily rational, legal, and historical.

---

[83] See H. J. McLachlan, *Socinianism in Seventeenth-Century England* (London: Oxford
University Press, 1951); G. H. Williams, *The Radical Reformation* (London: Weidenfeld and
Nicolson, 1962); T. L. Underwood, *Primitivism, Radicalism and the Lamb's War: The Baptist-
Quaker Conflict in Seventeenth-Century England* (Oxford: Oxford University Press, 1997).

[84] 'Temporal and spiritual government are but two words brought into the world to make men
see double and mistake their lawful sovereigns' (*Leviathan*, XXXIX:5). What makes this specific
distinction especially dangerous is that the representatives of the so-called 'spiritual' or 'ghostly'
power can take advantage of their apparent capacity to facilitate (or prevent) salvation to require
the believers' obedience at the expense of the latter's submission to the sovereign (Ibid. XXIX:15).
See also ibid. XLII:124.

They are aimed at establishing the lack of any solid grounds for justifying such an attitude. They do not show that Hobbes qualifies for the status of orthodox Christian, but that a well-regulated commonwealth excludes any public reference to orthodoxy and heresy. To some extent, even Hobbes's christology has a strong political dimension. The exact nature of Christ's role in the history of men is cast in political language through an identification of Moses, and all Old Testament prophets, with the high priests of Israel and all rightful representatives of God on earth, that is, all civil sovereigns.

Although he was both God and man (in traditional doctrine, as reflected in some Hobbesian statements), Jesus never ruled over any kingdom while he lived in the flesh;[85] it would be absurd to contend that he exercises any authority over the present world, either in a so-called spiritual way or through special representatives;[86] his kingdom, which will begin at the resurrection, will exist on earth,[87] and Christ will reign over it as a man,[88] in the same subordination to his Father as Moses, the high priests, and later kings.[89] He will then complete the fulfilment of his function, which was 'to restore unto God, by a new covenant, the kingdom which, being his by the old covenant, had been cut off by the rebellion of the Israelites in the election of Saul'.[90] It would be relevant to add, in this connection, that the essentially secular picture given of Christ's presence among men is only a reflection of God's mode of ruling over his own particular kingdom, which was made up of the Jewish people at first and was extended later to include all of Christ's disciples: it results from the same process of contractual

[85] 'For as much, therefore, as he that *redeemeth* hath no title to the *thing redeemed*, before the *redemption* and the ransom paid, and this ransom was the death of the Redeemer, it is manifest that our Saviour (as man) was not king of those that he redeemed before he suffered death (that is, during that time he conversed bodily on the earth)' (ibid. XLI:3). One might object that, according to this text, Christ as God has always reigned over men: but the point is precisely that this mode of presence of Christ in the world is explicitly rejected by Hobbes.

[86] 'But spiritual commonwealth there is none in this world. For it is the same thing with the kingdom of Christ, which he himself saith is not of this world, but shall be in the next world, at the resurrection, when they that have lived justly and believed that he was Christ shall (though they died *natural* bodies) rise *spiritual* bodies; and then it is that our Saviour shall judge the world, and conquer his adversaries, and make a spiritual commonwealth. In the meantime, seeing there are no men on earth whose bodies are spiritual, there can be no spiritual commonwealth amongst men that are yet in the flesh' (ibid. XLII:128). Neither pope nor 'presbyters' can claim to be Christ's representatives on earth: see XLIV:5 and XLIV:18. Consequently, 'we are not now under any other kings by pact, but our civil sovereigns' (XLIV:4).

[87] 'For if as in Adam all die (that is, have forfeited paradise and eternal life on earth) even so in Christ all shall be made alive, then all men shall be made to live on earth, for else the comparison were not proper' (ibid. XXXVIII:3).

[88] 'it is evident that our Saviour's kingdom is to be exercised by him in his human nature' (Ibid. XLI:6).

[89] 'Again, he is to be king then, no otherwise than as subordinate or vice-gerent of God the Father, as Moses was in the wilderness, and as the high priests were before the reign of Saul, and as the kings were after it' (ibid. XLI:7).   [90] Ibid. XLI:4.

institution as any other commonwealth;[91] the relation between ruler and ruled by which it is characterized works in the same way; it must be viewed, in short, as a civil kingdom.[92]

The political logic provides a set of notions which at once inform and illuminate Hobbes's religious doctrines. No evidence can be produced that it is reducible to mere imagery: in the world thus interpreted, God *does* hold sovereignty in the full sense of the word; Christ *is* the instrument of a new covenant; the role and place of the Church (of any Church) are properly determined by the conditions in which any commonwealth is built and functions. Another logic then comes into account, which is the historical one. The rationality of politics finds expression in theorems applicable to all nations and communities. What those maxims and dictates of reason teach can also be deduced from history, whose lessons are also of universal value. Although, as 'the register of knowledge of fact' and nothing else, it is below the level of science, whose registers 'contain the demonstrations of consequences of one affirmation to another',[93] history can be profitable in terms of prudence and 'moral learning', which is why it can be good or bad: 'in a good history the judgment must be eminent, because the goodness consisteth in the method, in the truth, and in the choice of the actions that are most profitable to be known'.[94] There is much to guard oneself against in 'the histories and philosophy of the ancient Greeks and Romans', notably on the points of liberty, tyranny, and rebellion.[95] This, however, does not mean that nothing is to be learned positively from a careful and orderly study of the past. As concerns antiquity, reliable sources exist, such as Thucydides. Hobbes himself acted as historian for England by investigating the question of the law on heresy or again by trying to identify the causes of the Civil War, most extensively in *Behemoth*. Scripture supplies irreplaceable records of men's actions.[96] Now, two fundamental lessons can be drawn from those various types of inquiry into apparently very different fields. One is that Churchmen all over the world have always been inspired by the same

---

[91] 'I find the KINGDOM OF GOD to signify, in most places of Scripture, a *kingdom properly so named*, constituted by the votes of the people of Israel in peculiar manner, wherein they chose God for their king by covenant made with him, upon God's promising them the possession of the land of Canaan; and but seldom metaphorically; and then it is taken for *dominion over sin* (and only in the New Testament), because such a dominion as that every subject shall have in the kingdom of God, and without prejudice to the sovereign' (ibid. XXXV:2).

[92] 'In short, the kingdom of God is a civil kingdom, which consisted first in the obligation of the people of Israel to those laws which Moses should bring unto them from Mount Sinai ; . . . , and which kingdom having been cast off in the election of Saul, the prophets foretold should be restored by Christ' (ibid. XXXV:13).   [93] Ibid. IX:3.

[94] Ibid. VIII:5.   [95] See *Leviathan* XXI:8 and XXIX:14.

[96] 'I see not therefore any reason to doubt but that the Old and New Testament, as we have them now, are the true registers of those things which were done and said by the prophets and apostles' (ibid. XXXIII:20). The 'authority' of the Bible, in the sense of what makes it law to Christians, is a completely different issue, which, as is known, much engaged Hobbes's attention and which it would be irrelevant to examine here.

self-interested motives and have always resorted to identical means in order to advance their cause, exploiting men's credulity and superstitious fears, using violence when needed, enlisting the help of philosophers to disguise their aims. Seen from that angle, no real difference exists between the astrologers and charlatans of ancient times and Christian clergies, of whatever denomination: this historical reading sketched out in *Leviathan*[97] is developed to its full length in *Historia Ecclesiastica*.[98]

The anticlericalism perceptible throughout Hobbes's political and historical writings branches off in two directions. It tends to minimize the sympathy expressed for the Reformation, which appears as a necessary development, but one which failed to change substantially clerical behaviour and ambitions. Apart from a few words of appreciation for the destruction of the Pope's supremacy over Europe, *Historia Ecclesiastica*, which surveys Church history down to and including the sixteenth century, hardly flatters the Reformers or their immediate forerunners.[99] Peter Valdo is said to have heralded 'the true faith';[100] Wyclif is only described as 'learned';[101] Luther, although praised for his eloquence,[102] is briefly credited with having denounced the impostures of the Church and refused to let faith remain captive.[103] Calvin is not mentioned at all. Nothing is said about the contents of the Reformers' doctrines. The English Reformation is missing. The little that is suggested by incidental remarks in *Leviathan* reinforces the impression of a superficial and unfinished achievement: universities have continued to spread the politically damaging scholastic doctrines;[104] bishops have retained their claim to divine right;[105] the persecution of so-called heretics has persisted.[106] It may well be that Hobbes alludes to the Church of England in the confession: 'I may attribute all the changes of religion in the world to one and the same cause, and that is, unpleasing priests, and those not only amongst Catholics, but even in that Church that hath presumed most of reformation.'[107] One feels the same impression when reading the concluding remark of chapter XLVI:

But who knows that this spirit of Rome (now gone out and walking by missions through the dry places of China, Japan, and the Indies, that yield him little fruit)

---

[97] See VI:36, XI:26–7, XII:8–21, XXXVII:5, XXXVII:10.

[98] See from line 71 down to line 470 in *Historia Ecclesiastica*. Edition used: original 1688 Latin edition.

[99] In this, Hobbes's treatise does not conform to the pattern of most works illustrating the genre of sacred history. See my 'Hobbes and Sacred History', in G. A. J. Rogers and Tom Sorell (eds.), *Hobbes and History* (London and New York: Routledge, 2000), 147–59.

[100] 'vera fides': l. 2108.   [101] 'doctus': l. 2146.   [102] 'magno ore loquens': l. 1625.

[103] 'servam noluit esse Fidem': l. 2214.

[104] See *Leviathan*, I:5, VIII:27, XXIX:15, XLVI:7:18, Revision and Conclusion 16.

[105] Ibid. XLII:3.

[106] See the whole Appendix to the Latin version of *Leviathan*.

[107] *Leviathan*, XII:32. As noted by Edwin Curley in his edition, Clarendon believed (to his indignation) that the Church of England was the target of Hobbes's allusion (see Edward Hyde,

may not return, or rather an assembly of spirits worse than he, enter and inhabit this clean swept house, and make the end thereof worse than the beginning? For it is not the Roman clergy only that pretends the kingdom of God to be of this world, and thereby to have a power therein distinct from that of the civil State.[108]

The second implication of Hobbes's perception of history is a corollary of the first. It is the underlying preference given to what we may call an anti-theological form of Christianity, reminiscent of the time of the Early Church and based on a minimal creed. A twofold conviction accounts for that inclination. First, the original Christian faith was corrupted by the interferences of Greek philosophers, who, for mercenary reasons, imported into the new religion notions which were foreign to its nature and were bound to provoke endless disputes and to supply the clergy with ideal weapons of control over the believers' minds.[109] Second, the English revolution was directly caused by such controversies.[110]

What comes over from the constant hostility displayed by Hobbes towards theologians *as such*, that is, as professional disputers of abstractions, specially trained in schools and universities and skilfully employed by men of power, is something which looks like a nostalgia for the primitive Church, in which neither apparatus nor speculators paralysed the spontaneous expression of the natural impulse to worship. After the secession from Rome at the time of the Reformation, then the abolition of episcopacy by the Presbyterians during the Great Rebellion, then the overthrow of Presbyterian rule at a later stage in that period, English Christians, Hobbes writes, find themselves in the same state of religious chaos as the Early Church, and this situation could well be preferable to all others, as the most favourable to free individual piety:

And so we are reduced to the independency of the primitive Christians, to follow Paul, or Cephas, or Apollos, every man as he liketh best. Which, if it be without contention, and without measuring the doctrine of Christ by our affection to the person of his minister (the fault which the apostle reprehended in the

---

A Brief View and Survey of the Dangerous and Pernicious Errors to Church and State, in Mr. Hobbes's Book Entitled Leviathan (Oxford, 1676), 25). One could also argue (as Edwin Curley does: see p. 74, n. 20) that the Presbyterians deserved more than the Church of England (especially the Laudian one) Hobbes's pique about 'presuming of reformation'. The point is that, whichever hypothesis is justified, it is English Protestants who seem to be aimed at.

[108] *Leviathan*, XLVI:34.

[109] See again *Leviathan*, XLVI:12–20 for the denunciation of the theory of separated essences, but also the *Historical Narration Concerning Heresy*, 387–403.

[110] Recalling the circumstances of composition of *Leviathan*, Hobbes assumes (not wrongly) that 'it is quite apparent' to readers of the book 'that the author thought the civil war which was being waged then throughout England, Scotland, and Ireland, had no other cause than the disagreement, first between the Roman Church and the Anglican, and then in the Anglican Church between the episcopal pastors and the Presbyterians concerning theological matters' (Appendix to the Latin text, III:1). This historical thesis is argued at length in *Behemoth*.

Corinthians), is perhaps the best. First, because there ought to be no power over the consciences of men but of the Word itself, working faith in every one, not always according to the purpose of them that plant and water, but of God himself, that giveth the increase. And secondly, because it is unreasonable (in them who teach there is such danger in every little error) to require of a man endued with reason of his own, to follow the reason of any other man, or of the most voices of many other men (which is little better than to venture his salvation at cross and pile).[111]

Several essential themes we have already encountered are fused in this almost idyllic picture (whose actualization is yet conditional): the supremacy of Scripture as a rule of faith; the illegitimacy of any human interference with God's guidance of his creatures; the wisdom of letting every man find his own way by himself in spiritual matters. Another, which makes a discreet appearance here, is the doctrine of Christ as the key to salvation. It is logically connected to the anti-theological motif, in so far as it suggests that true Christian faith has nothing to do with philosophical niceties and is reducible to a single message, commented on by Hobbes elsewhere in *Leviathan* and in other works:[112] the *unum necessarium*, the one article on which the whole of the Christian creed rests and salvation depends, in other words, the belief that 'Jesus is the Christ', that is, 'the king which God had before promised, by the prophets of the Old Testament, to send into the world to reign (over the Jews and over such of other nations as should believe in him) under himself eternally and to give them that eternal life which was lost by the sin of Adam'.[113] One might think of other articles of faith as necessary to the same end, such as the belief that God is the omnipotent creator of all things, or that Jesus rose from the dead, but they can all be deduced from the *unum necessarium* (the former being implied in the observation that Jesus was the Son of the God of the Israelites, who believed in divine omnipotence, the latter being a logical prerequisite to the eternal rule of Jesus). Accordingly, one can adhere to that single article of faith and be assured of its benefits without needing any special instruction or talent: 'In sum, he that holdeth this foundation, *Jesus is the Christ*, holdeth expressly all that he seeth rightly deduced from it, and implicitly all that is consequent thereunto, though he have not skill enough to discern the consequence.'[114]

---

[111] *Leviathan*, XLVII:20. As noted by E. Curley (p. 482, n. 4), Clarendon saw in the word 'independency' a clear admission of support for Cromwell and his faction (*A Brief View*, 308–9).

[112] See *Leviathan*, XLIII:10–23; *Answer to the Catching of the Leviathan*, 345.

[113] *Leviathan*, XLIII:11.

[114] Ibid. XLIII:18. The natural capacity of ordinary individuals to grasp, although unclearly, the significance of Christianity's central tenet parallels their ability to understand the basics of politics. Cf. Hobbes's reply to the 'objection from the incapacity of the vulgar' concerning his theory of sovereignty: 'But they say, again, that though the principles be right, yet common people

Hobbes's christocentric view of religion is at the heart of his reading of history.[115] It is also directly related to his politics, because it touches upon the extent of State and Church power. Someone who believes that Jesus is the Christ can be certain he will be saved. Therefore, no ecclesiastical discipline, let alone extreme sanctions like excommunication, can affect his future spiritual destiny.[116] Conversely, it must be evident to the sovereign that, although it is part of his mission to control the doctrines taught in the commonwealth, he has no capacity to confer any saving virtue on a belief other than the *unum necessarium*, just as he has no power to cause the damnation of any of his subjects by imposing a different interpretation of Scripture.[117] It is not enough, however, to observe the decisive importance of that creed in Hobbes's thought. Two further remarks need to be made, which are causes of renewed perplexity. The political and historical logics emphasized so far are, in the context of a Christian commonwealth, inseparable from a third, which pertains to Hobbes's particular theology and forms as it were their background. At the same time, this theology—with its pivotal tenet that Christ *is* the Messiah and Saviour—is based on a text, the so-called Word of God, whose nature is so uncertain as to make the very idea of divine revelation problematic and thus imperil the coherence of the whole theoretical structure.[118]

The phrase 'Word of God' can be understood in two senses: a narrow one, in which it refers to the words spoken by God (as in the Ten Commandments), and a broad one, in which it signifies words spoken *about* God, or the 'Doctrine of Christian Religion'.[119] Only in the second sense

---

are not of capacity enough to be made to understand them. I should be glad that the rich and potent subjects of a kingdom, or those that are accounted the most learned, were no less incapable than they' (Ibid. XXX:6).

[115] Pocock's original interpretation of Hobbesian theology as essentially messianic is based on the acknowledgement of this fact. See J. G. A. Pocock, 'Time, History and Eschatology in the Thought of Thomas Hobbes', in Pocock, *Politics, Language and Time: Essays on Political Thought and History* (London: Methuen, 1972), 148–201.

[116] 'he that believeth Jesus to be the Christ is free from the dangers threatened to persons excommunicate. He that believeth it not is no Christian. Therefore, a true and unfeigned Christian is not liable to excommunication' (ibid. XLII:29). That is one more reason why the Church ought to restrict its teaching to the core message of Christianity and leave the enforcement of discipline, whether in doctrine or in manners, to the state.

[117] 'But suppose that a Christian king should from this foundation, *Jesus is the Christ*, draw some false conclusions, that is to say, make some superstructions of hay or stubble, and command the teaching of the same. Yet seeing St. Paul says he shall be saved, much more shall he be saved that teacheth them by his command; and much more yet, he that teaches not, but only believes his lawful teacher' (Ibid. XLIII:22). The demonstration that there can be no spiritual danger in political obedience for a convinced Christian also confirms that the extent of the sovereign's power in matters of faith is limited and that, consequently, religious persecutions in the name of the true religion are pointless.

[118] As will be seen at once, the problem I wish to address here is not that of biblical hermeneutics.

[119] See *Leviathan*, XXXVI:2–3.

can Scripture be called 'the Word of God', according to Hobbes, which restricts revelation to a very small number of scriptural passages and casts doubts on the notion of a divinely inspired text, since in most of the Bible, God is just spoken about. It is true to say that, in that respect, Hobbes departed from the Protestant doctrine of a self-authenticating text of entirely divine origin.[120] Yet, what we are given here is only part of the issue. Another essential distinction made by Hobbes is that between two Words of God: the natural one, accessible to all men by the use of their reason and embodied in the laws of nature; and the prophetical one, expressed in special revelations to individual men such as Moses.[121] Now there is practically no way to be sure that a man who says he is inspired by God can be trusted, and even supposing he were sincere, he would be unable to convey his experience of God's inspiration to other men in any intelligible language.[122] That is what makes the very notion of revelation a dubious one (in the eyes of Hobbes), rather than the identification of the Word of God with those words spoken by God himself, an interpretation which seems to imply that we may consider them as non-problematic. In fact, even in the case of Moses or Jesus Christ, there is no cogent reason why anyone should regard their reported words as commanding belief by themselves, and not even a lawful sovereign could force anyone to believe that they are God-inspired words or the very words of God. Apart from rational persuasion, our belief on the subject can only be induced by the two obvious 'marks' of a true prophet: the capacity to perform miracles and 'the not teaching any other religion than that which is already established'.[123] The trouble is not that false prophets can also perform miracles, for they can be recognized by their absence of conformity to the established religion, but that no more miracles have been performed since the time of Christ (who both performed miracles and preached submission to the authorities).[124] That is the reason

---

[120] One reads in the Westminster Confession of Faith of 1646: 'The authority of the Holy Scripture, for which it ought to be believed, and obeyed, depends not upon the testimony of any man, or Church; but wholly upon God (who is truth itself) the author thereof: and therefore it is to be received, because it is the Word of God' (§ 4); 'The whole counsel of God concerning all things necessary for His own glory, man's salvation, faith and life, is either expressly set down in Scripture, or by good and necessary consequence may be deduced from Scripture: unto which nothing at any time is to be added, whether by new revelations of the Spirit, or traditions of men' (§ 6). Text from the Internet at the site: http://www.reformed.org/documents/index.html.

[121] See *Leviathan*, XXXI:2–4; XXXII:1–6; XXXVI:5–7.

[122] Ibid. XXXII:5–6. As a consequence, 'though God Almighty can speak to a man by dreams, visions, voice, and inspiration, yet he obliges no man to believe he hath so done to him that pretends it, who (being a man) may err, and (which is worse) may lie' (XXXII:6).

[123] See *Leviathan*, XXXII:7–8.

[124] 'Seeing, therefore miracles now cease, we have no sign left whereby to acknowledge the pretended revelations or inspirations of any private man, nor obligation to give ear to any doctrine farther than is conformable to the Holy Scriptures, which since the time of our Saviour supply the place and sufficiently recompense the want of all other prophecy' (Ibid. XXXII:9).

why, on the one hand, there is no doubting that Christ, as far as he was concerned, was a true prophet,[125] and on the other hand, only sovereigns can be regarded as God's lawful spokesmen, since their power is based on the law of nature, that is to say the incontrovertible natural Word of God.[126] If, however, one is to believe that 'he which heareth his sovereign (his sovereign being a Christian), heareth Christ';[127] and if Scripture and reason combine to demonstrate that 'none but the sovereign in a Christian commonwealth, can take notice what is or what is not the Word of God', and that 'they that have the place of Abraham in a commonwealth are the only interpreters of what God hath spoken',[128] then, it would seem that saving faith owes more to human rule than to God—hardly a proposition in the Protestant spirit—and that the sovereign has a much greater ability to affect his subjects' salvation than Hobbes admits elsewhere. Politics is unintelligible outside a theological horizon, but theology ends inevitably in politics. Whether this circle is the result of a dialectical *tour de force* or reflects an inner contradiction appears impossible to decide.

***

Few certainties emerge from this survey. That Hobbes was bound to reject Catholicism as an acceptable religious option is one, for both theological and political reasons. That he could not, mostly as a consequence of his political postulates, accept any form of religious settlement implying either the separation of Church and State, let alone the supremacy of Church over State, appears as another. Combined with the feeling induced by historical considerations that changes of religion are always dangerous and that, even when they succeed, they bring few improvements, this argument provided a comparatively strong justification for remaining in the bosom of the Church of England. That such a plausible choice could possibly be a source of serene satisfaction for Hobbes is highly improbable.

---

[125] See *Leviathan*, XLI:3–4.

[126] 'For when Christian men take not their Christian sovereign for God's prophet, they must either take their own dreams for the prophecy they mean to be governed by, and the tumor of their own hearts for the Spirit of God, or they must suffer themselves to be led by some strange prince or by some of their fellow-subjects that can bewitch them, by slander of the government, into rebellion' (Ibid. XXXVI:20).

[127] Ibid. XLII:106. One must suppose that this language is to be received in a figurative sense. Otherwise, one would wonder what is become of Christ's absence from this world until his second coming. [128] Ibid. XL:4.

INDEX